D.H. Lawrence and the Marriage Matrix

D.H. Lawrence and the Marriage Matrix:

Intertextual Adventures in Conflict, Renewal, and Transcendence

By

Peter Balbert

Cambridge Scholars Publishing

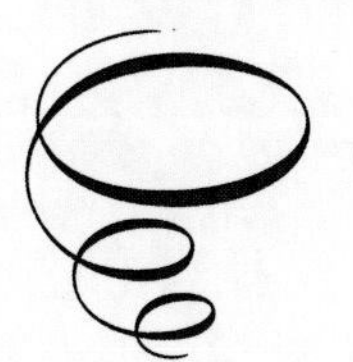

D.H. Lawrence and the Marriage Matrix:
Intertextual Adventures in Conflict, Renewal, and Transcendence

By Peter Balbert

This book first published 2016

Cambridge Scholars Publishing

Lady Stephenson Library, Newcastle upon Tyne, NE6 2PA, UK

British Library Cataloguing in Publication Data
A catalogue record for this book is available from the British Library

ISBN (10): 1-4438-9305-6
ISBN (13): 978-1-4438-9305-3

In blessed memory of Bert Balbert (1911–1978), Marjorie Balbert (1911–2008), William Bollinger (1927–2013), and Tracey Lingo (1960–2013)

To my wife, Lynne, and the growing resonance of our own marriage matrix: daughters Rebecca, Rachel, Reika, Risa, and Renna; sons-in-law Jeffrey, Justin, Dillon, and Joshua; grandchildren Emily, Isaac, and Hannah.

Marriage is the great puzzle of our day. It is our sphinx-riddle. Solve it, or be torn to bits, is the decree.

—D.H. Lawrence, "On Being a Man"

then I shall know that my life is moving still
with the dark earth, and drenched
with the deep oblivion of earth's lapse and renewal.

—D.H. Lawrence, "Shadows"

True criticism recognizes itself as a form of memoir.

—Harold Bloom, *The Daemon Knows*

TABLE OF CONTENTS

List of Illustrations ix

Acknowledgments x

Introduction 1

I. Some Versions of the Matrix: Configurations and Variations

Chapter One 12
The Dark Secret and the Coccygeal Continuum, 1918-1920:
From Oedipus to Debasement to Renewal in *The Lost Girl*

Chapter Two 55
Depression and Renewal at the Border-Line: Balder, Hemingway,
and *The Captain's Doll*

Chapter Three 88
Freud, Frazer, and the Palimpsestic Texture: Dreams and the Heaviness
of Male Destiny in *The Fox*

Chapter Four 121
Thirteen Ways of Looking at *The Ladybird*: D. H. Lawrence,
Lady Cynthia Asquith, and the Incremental Structure of Seduction

Chapter Five 153
From Panophilia to Phallophobia: Sublimation, Projection, and Renewal
in *St. Mawr*

Chapter Six 180
Pan and the Appleyness of Landscape: Dread of the Procreative Body
in "The Princess"

Chapter Seven 206
Impotence, Renewal, and the Honorable Beast: The Aesthetics
of the Fourth Dimension in *The Virgin and the Gipsy*

II. Some Origins from the 1990's: The Early Thematics of Renewal and Transcendence

Chapter Eight 244
From *Lady Chatterley's Lover* to *The Deer Park*: Marriage, Renewal, and the Dialectic of Erotic Risk

Chapter Nine 274
Unarticulated Synergy and Unfashionable Transcendence: Teaching, Research, and the Quest for Something

Chapter Ten 290
From Rejection to "Renuwel" to Renewal: Chairperson, Faculty, and the Research Imperative

Bibliography 308

Index 319

List of Illustrations

1. "North Sea" by D. H. Lawrence (Fig. 4-1) 151
2. "The Lawrence Tree, 1929" by Georgia O'Keeffe (Fig. 5-1) 171
3. "The Kiowa Ranch, New Mexico" by D. H. Lawrence
(Fig. 5-2) .... See centrefold
4. "Two Apples" by D. H. Lawrence (Fig. 6-1) 185
5. "Red Willow Trees" by D. H. Lawrence (Fig.6-2)............................. 196
6. "Villa Mirenda" by D. H. Lawrence (Fig. 6-3)................................... 197
7. "Dance Sketch" by D. H. Lawrence (Fig. 7-1) 232

ACKNOWLEDGMENTS

Grateful acknowledgment is herewith given for permission to reprint early versions of the following chapters where sections of my work were first published: for Chapter One, in *D.H. Lawrence Studies*, v. 23 (2015), 101–39; for Chapter Two, in *Papers on Language and Literature*, v. 42, no. 3, Summer (2006), 227–63. Copyright© 2006 by The Board of Trustees, Southern Illinois University, Edwardsville; for Chapter Three, in *Studies in the Novel*, v. 38, no. 2, Summer (2006), 211–33. Copyright© 2006 by Johns Hopkins University Press and University of North Texas; for Chapter Four, in *Studies in the Humanities*, v. 36 (2009), 13–50. Copyright© 2009 by Indiana University of Pennsylvania; for Chapter Five, in *Papers on Language and Literature*, v. 49, no. 1, Winter (2013), 37–69. Copyright© 2013 by the Board of Trustees, Southern Illinois University, Edwardsville; for Chapter Six, in *Studies in the Novel*, v. 34, no. 3, Fall (2002), 282–302. Copyright© 2002 Johns Hopkins University Press and University of North Texas; for Chapter Seven, in *Papers on Language and Literature*, v. 29, no. 4, Fall (1993), 395–416. Copyright© 1993 The Board of Trustees, Southern Illinois University, Edwardsville; for Chapter Eight, in *Studies in the Novel*, v. 22, no. 1, Spring (1990), 67–81. Copyright© 1990 Johns Hopkins University Press and University of North Texas; for Chapter Ten, with kind permission from Springer Science & Business Media, in *Innovative Higher Education*, v. 16, no. 2, Winter (1991), 139–56. Copyright© 1991 Human Sciences Press, Inc.

Extracts from the *Cambridge Edition of the Letters and Works of D. H. Lawrence*, published by Cambridge University Press, are reproduced by permission of Pollinger Limited on behalf of the Estate of Frieda Lawrence Ravagli.

Illustrations ©1929, 1964 by permission of the Estate of Frieda Lawrence Ravagli. *Paintings of D.H. Lawrence* first published in 1964 by Cory, Adams & Mackay Ltd and The Viking Press, "North Sea", "The Kiowa Ranch, New Mexico", "Dance Sketch", "Red Willow Trees". "Villa Mirenda", and "Two Apples", reproduced by permission of Pollinger Limited and the Estate of Frieda Lawrence Ravagli.

For permission to reproduce the cover painting by Georgia O'Keeffe (American, 1887–1986), "The Lawrence Tree, 1929". Copyright © Georgia O'Keeffe Museum / Artists Rights Society (ARS), New York. Oil on canvas 31x40 in. The Ella Gallup Sumner and Mary Catlin Sumner Collection Fund, 1981.23. Wadsworth Atheneum Museum of Art, Hartford, Connecticut. Photography Credit: Allen Phillips / Wadsworth Atheneum.

My warm appreciation to the Estate of Norman Mailer for a willingness to permit me to quote from his published work and from published and unpublished letters from Mailer to me. In this regard, I am grateful to Michael Lennon, Mailer's biographer and archivist, and to Susan Mailer, for guidance in this permission process. Copyright © Letters of February 1, 1998 and January 17, 1985 by Norman Mailer, currently collected in *Selected Letters*, Copyright © 2014 The Estate of Norman Mailer, used by permission of The Wylie Agency LLC.

The talented secretarial staff in the English Department at Trinity University consistently has offered me energetic and continued support to put together this complex manuscript on the computer; I especially want to express my gratitude here to Sam Jensen for typing the entire book, and to Sarai Santos-Valle for formatting the work for publication. Reliable additional help was provided by Jesse Martinez and the late Caroline Bonilla. A thank you also to the Office Manager, Ruby Contreras. Finally, let me register my abundant appreciation for the meticulous and judicious proof-reading by Peter Simon; I remain grateful for the incisive professionalism he displayed throughout his work on the manuscript. It is also with pleasure that I acknowledge the consistently capable and well-informed staff at Cambridge Scholars for their efficient guidance and implementation through each step in the publication process: Samuel Baker (contractual); (Victoria Carruthers (editorial); Amanda Millar (typesetting); Courtney Blades and Sophie Edminson (design).

It is plainly evident throughout *The Marriage Matrix* how much I relied on the superb biographical research by the late Mark Kinkead-Weekes and David Ellis in Volumes 2 and 3 of the Cambridge University Press three-volume biography of Lawrence (John Worthen's excellent first volume does not fit within the chronological purview of my book). Their probing and scrupulous work is not only persuasive and empathetic in its wealth of detail and intelligent speculation, but it also charts the way for additional exploration of the kind I undertake in *The Marriage Matrix*.

I must also acknowledge a debt to my sprightly and focused students through the years who enrolled in my intense D.H. Lawrence seminar, English-4426. They productively pushed me to clarify and examine my own perspective on his life and art, while they provocatively developed and defended their own exciting and sometimes skeptical "takes" on his genius.

I have also learned much through the years from engaged feedback by colleagues in the D.H. Lawrence Society, as they have responded in helpful ways to early incarnations of my work as it appeared in journals and in presentations by me at International Conferences in the United States, Europe, and Australia.

Finally, a special acknowledgment is herewith given to the late James Gindin of the University of Michigan, who (as Chapter Nine explains) first motivated me (as did the talented poet and teacher, Donald Hall) to study literature, and to the late Harry T. Moore and the late Mark Spilka—both formative influences on my interest in D.H. Lawrence.

INTRODUCTION

This book discusses eight works of fiction by D.H. Lawrence under the rubric of a dominant and consistent motif in his work that I label "the marriage matrix". The use here of "matrix" relies on the encompassing use of the term as "that within which, or within and from which something originates, takes form, or develops" (*Webster's* 835). The gestational resonance of such definition is not surprising on two related levels in any consideration of Lawrence's life and art: first, his fiction and essays repeatedly shed light on the lingering evidence of his own neo-oedipal connection to the powerful matriarchal figure of Lydia Lawrence; second—and even more pervasively—men and women throughout his work conspicuously strive for organic birth, a struggle that is often initiated by their willing entry into marital union, and is often concluded by an achieved maturity and renewal that link them, through their marriage, to what Lawrence variously calls "the unknown" or "the beyond". Marriage thus functions, in effect, as both the obsessive subject and the thematic center of Lawrence's writing, shaping the plots and tensions of his novels and stories as well as reflecting the visionary imperative of the "passionate struggle into conscious being" (Foreword 486) that his characters attempt to achieve. As this volume's subtitle suggests, marriage also serves as the dramatic intersection for issues of conflict, renewal, and transcendence that regularly inform the crises of his fiction, and also preoccupy him—as man, husband, and artist—during his well-documented and strenuous marriage to Frieda.

I use "renewal" here (see Chapter Ten) in its transformative sense of "to make new spiritually", to "restore to freshness" (*Webster's* 990)—a phrase that precisely conveys Lawrence's mandate for personal growth embodied in his fiction. But the mere achievement of marriage in these works in itself offers no solution or equanimity. The various depictions of unstable marital union, of conflicted engagement, and of manipulative courtship often reflect the emotional deficiencies in the respective partner, lover, or suitor; thus, the matrix consistently highlights transitional periods of immaturity, depression, and codependency—patterns that can lead not to renewal and transcendence, but to atrophy and destructive behavior. Indeed, the fundamental issues at odds within this nexus of themes is best stated by Mark Spilka's incisive formulation more than sixty years ago:

"So the chief moral criterion for love in Lawrence's world, or for *any* emotional experience, is this: does it affirm or deny, renew or destroy, the sacred life within us. For it must be made emphatically clear that Lawrence saw all human engagements, sexual or otherwise, in terms of their effect upon the soul's vitality" (22).

Such a rich matrix of sub-topics highlights the strikingly organic feature of Lawrence's work, reflecting an authorial linkage across genres that encompasses the thematics, subjects, and emotional urgencies of his fictional and nonfictional prose. This underlying unity in his poetic intuition and philosophic thought remains an unusual opportunity for critical study; it provides an artistic cohesion with accessible and valuable resources for additional speculation and well-grounded argument. It is in this context that intertextual investigation of Lawrence's voluminous writing supplies interpretive dividends, and especially when the additional material is contemporary with the fiction under discussion. Among the many works by Lawrence I employ to further analyze relevant patterns in selected novels, novellas, and stories are *Psychoanalysis and the Unconscious*, *Fantasia of the Unconscious*, "Introduction to These Paintings", "The Novel", "Pan in America", *Studies in Classic American Literature*, and a wide range of other essays by him, as well as his prolific collection of letters and the invaluable resource material provided by the Cambridge UP biography. These volumes of cathartic correspondence with friends, agents, and editors are justly recognized as among the most insightful and unselfconscious depictions by a major writer of his own intimate feelings and conflicts that we have in literature. They remain crucial in any integrated consideration of his fiction and life.

My basic methodology employs close reading, rhetorical analysis, and historical context, with a distinct emphasis on image clusters and thematic patterns that are both intrinsic to the respective work and corroborate the essential metaphors and doctrines that unify the chapters in this book. I am also recognizably drawn to psychobiographical inference and psychoanalytical theory to extend the reach of my interpretations and their possible bearing on Lawrence's art, friendships, and marriage. Surely such an approach is not uncommon in Lawrence studies, but what may distinguish my perspective is a form of exegesis that has sadly become unfashionable: a straight-line elucidation in each fictional work of Lawrence's superb craft built around his calibrated development of those venerable, essential three elements—plot, character, and theme. One looks in vain today for much criticism that permits the Lawrencian text to demonstrate its surprising ingenuity and its careful artifice, and I attempt to redress some of that imbalance in the following chapters. My primary interest focuses on illuminating the excellence of the fiction, and I stand agreeably guilty of being an advocate, in the Leavisite tradition, for the unparalleled nature of Lawrence's achievement. Let me name my species of criticism as synergistic analysis, an eclectic approach that attempts to productively interface sequential plot development with impinging biography, relevant intertextuality, and authorial doctrine—and all in the interest of demonstrating, in that characteristic Lawrencian phrase, the "livingness" of the respective fiction. It will be evident that my close reading is often very close, occasionally resorting—in the cinematic sense—to a virtual stop-action technique to demonstrate the delicate emotional transitions and/or landscape tableaux that inform Lawrence's creation of a scene. It is important to note that he manifests significant talent as a painter and theoretician of that art, and his unorthodox skill appears as an extension of the kinetic power of scenes in his fiction. Thus several of his paintings reproduced in this volume reflect a sense of harnessed movement suspended between intense moments of live action and in a landscape panorama or a still-life that seems numinously alive with the quality Lawrence calls "appleyness".

In this spirit of full disclosure amid the academy's internecine conflicts over a preferred hermeneutics, I must confess here to the same skepticism articulated by John Ellis on what he calls the "race-gender-class program that criticism should not be concerned primarily with the content of a literary work—its unique stamp, the individual meaning that it makes unlike any other work, the qualities that make readers return to it again and again" (34). In this regard, I hope my speculations on the sexual life of Lawrence and Frieda, on the complex friendships with Cynthia Asquith, J. Middleton Murry, and Katherine Mansfield, on the theoretic research of James Frazer, Sigmund and Anna Freud, James W. Pryse, and Peter Ouspensky, and on the panoply of the marriage matrix—that all this web of relevant reference remains secondary in importance to my commitment to the magic of each Lawrence fiction. This study is primarily focused on a select group of works all completed in Lawrence's last decade during an especially prolific period. The arrangement of chapters follows their chronological order of composition from 1920 to 1928. In my reading of their significance, each work supplies compelling theme and variation within its plot and imagery on seminal aspects of the marriage matrix and related issues of renewal and transcendence, all elements that become more prominent and meaningful through the use of Lawrence's relevant and abundant intertextual material. Although I have augmented chapters since their earlier publication, I have resisted any temptation to radically compromise the original versions of my interpretations with any overly intrusive ligature through all the essays that might make the matrix more prominent than the "unique stamp", in Ellis's cautionary terms, of the individual fiction. In short, the chapters should be able to stand by themselves if excerpted from this volume. In *Out of Sheer Rage*, Geoff Dyer recounts his obsessive and often humorous attempt to write a book about D.H. Lawrence as a "homage to the writer who had made me want to become a writer" (101). Early in the research stages of the project, he expresses his anger at the deadening "hallmark of academic criticism", with its often mechanical focus on arcane literary theory and its related penchant for alleged objectivity and pretentious lack of enthusiasm. Dyer has no doubt read Lawrence on Poe, as he describes the *corpus* of what that "hallmark" entails: "writing like that kills everything it touches… Walk around a university campus and there is an almost palpable smell of death about the place because hundreds of academics are busy killing everything they touch" (101). It is certainly my not intention to commit the same felony in the following pages.

The word "adventure" is used in the subtitle to reflect a central concept that is inherent in Lawrence's notion of marriage and maturity. Once again, the formal dictionary definition proves instructive here, with the word derived from the French "*advenire*, to arrive", and its current usage defined as "an undertaking usually involving danger and unknown risk" (*Webster's* 17). A Lawrencian character who matures sufficiently will "arrive" at the institution of marriage ready to undertake the inevitable arguments, ego battles, and reconciliations that become intrinsic to any couple's risky but transformative venture into the transcendent unknown. Recall that when Ursula Brangwen in *The Rainbow* (part of a cyclical work once titled by Lawrence as *The Wedding Ring*) initially realizes Skrebensky's inadequacy as a marriage partner, her decision is prompted by the realization that "not on any side did he lead into the unknown" (439). But Lawrence's doctrinal beliefs do not limit the versatility of his craft as an imaginative artist who can tell a great story. The variety of courtships and conflicts in these eight works reflects Lawrence's skill at reanimating the marriage matrix by reconfiguring and adjusting the plot-lines and visionary imagery to fit the mood and mandate of the work in question. It is in this context that an unnoted yet impressive aspect of Lawrence's skill resides in the way his obsessional themes—especially the marriage matrix—are absorbed seamlessly into the varied plots and the contrasting circumstances of his characters. Indeed, it may only be in retrospect that the marital motifs became recognized as the consistent and integrative element in so much of his fiction.

The range of such reconfiguration is impressive in itself. In *The Lost Girl,* an unmarried and virginal Midlands woman receives a perverse and life-changing sexual baptism from an uneducated, sensual boy-man whom she marries and then accompanies to his primitive native village in Italy while she struggles to renew herself within this isolated, beautiful, and savage mountain landscape. In *The Captain's Doll*, a retired army officer, is, after the Great War, roused from depression and an unhappy marriage by an intense and embattled affair with a spirited younger woman, as he tries to merge his own personal renewal with the potential marital demands and feisty independence of this mistress after the mysterious and sudden death of his wife. In *The Fox*, an awkwardly callow but persistent young man marries a bisexual older woman after he virtually wills the death of her female partner and then must cope—without confidence or experience—with the sexual expectations and male authority he must fulfill with his wife. In *The Ladybird,* an aristocratic, beautiful, and tepidly married British woman is slowly seduced by an enemy soldier after the war, a grotesquely charismatic officer who perversely renews himself through his gradual seduction of her as he recuperates from his serious wounds while she progressively falls under his spell during her visits to him in hospital. In *St. Mawr*, a middle-aged woman in a fractured marriage leaves her epicene husband in England to undertake a strenuous life in the mountains above Taos, New Mexico—a radical action she takes as her renewal-awareness of the inscrutable "spirit of place" that now connects her directly to the eternal rhythms of the transcendent beyond. In "The Princess", an embittered but infatuated man proposes marriage to a willful but fragile girl-woman whom he brutally rapes when she refuses his proposal and ridicules his manhood after consensual sex with him—a tragic drama of "nonrenewal" that is played out amid a mountain landscape of fierce grandeur. In *The Virgin and the Gipsy*, the over-protected, insightful, and vivacious daughter of a cuckolded and vindictive minister wisely rejects the conventional marriage proposal of a bland local suitor, becomes attracted to an erotic and self-possessed gipsy, ultimately sleeps with his arm around her without sex and awakens as a renewed woman liberated from the constricted life imposed on her by her family and village.

The last three chapters—within the section entitled "Some Origins from the 1990s"—both span and exemplify my three roles during that decade as, respectively, scholar, teacher, and administrator. They provide additional essays that encompass and anticipate the range of themes stipulated in the title of this book, and years before the development of its design: the first, from the perspective of Lawrence's influence on a major contemporary writer; the second, as part of the framing context today of entrenched resistance in the university to notions of transcendence; and the third as a more academic (but presciently relevant) statement on the implications of "renewal" for faculty who must engage the imperative of a consistent record of published research. In retrospect, it seems to me that all three essays—with their roots in the 1990s—suggest in different ways the conceptual origins of this study, and thus I include them as the early incarnations of relevant themes engaged more fully and precisely in the preceding chapters. In a previous book of mine, *D.H. Lawrence and the Phallic Imagination*, that predated early versions of the three "origins" chapters, I discussed the empathy and acumen of Norman Mailer's *The Prisoner of Sex* (1971) concerning the narrative technique of Lawrence's fiction, the existential dimensions of Lawrence's views on love, sex, and marriage, and the relevance of Lawrence's novelistic craft and permeative doctrine both for Lawrence's marriage to Frieda and the formative, intense relationship to his mother. In Chapter Eight I thus take the connection between these two prophetic writers one step further by focusing on a major novel by each of them—Lawrence's *Lady Chatterley's Lover* and Mailer's *The Deer Park*. On the surface, this last novel by Lawrence would seem a natural "fit" within the stipulated themes of this study. In *Lady Chatterley's Lover* an emotionally scarred and silently charismatic woodskeeper initiates an intense sexual relationship with the titled wife of his paralyzed but cold and manipulative employer: as the affair gradually develops into real love, the couple courageously cling to the possibility of their renewal and marriage within the turbulent and uncertain months ahead. But in addition to a pattern of potential rebirth for Connie and Mellors—well-documented by critics through the years—there remains also this compelling issue of general influence and precise comparison involving Lawrence and Mailer and two major works published about a quarter-century apart.

Both novels encountered significant forms of resistance to their publication: the abrogation of Mailer's initial publishing contract because of purported impropriety in a scene in the novel, and the legal prohibition of any commercial publication of Lawrence's novel for several decades because of alleged obscenity. Both novels concern the tensions, commitments, and uncertainties of couples who enact their courtship and passion within plots that emphasize themes evident throughout this volume: infidelity, sexual courage, impotence, and—this above all—a transcendent faith in what Lawrence calls "the unknown" and Mailer describes as the risky arena of "the perilous choice". I conclude the essay by considering the added evidence of Lawrence's impact on Mailer that emerges from some playful but suggestive disinformation published by Mailer to test the alertness of his reading public and, no doubt, to agitate the authority of Lawrence's commentators. He explains this purposeful charade in an intriguing and confessional letter to me, and I quote his revealing remarks to further demonstrate relevant affinities between the two writers and their ideological inclinations. Earlier versions of this chapter have been published in an academic journal, in Harold Bloom's collection of essays on Mailer, and in a yearly journal of Mailer studies. I have revised the essay to make it more relevant to the themes in this book and for the biographical material that has emerged since Mailer's death. Mailer's profound admiration for Lawrence's work also emerges in my chapter on *The Virgin and the Gipsy*: the notion of influence receives added confirmation through an interesting and hitherto unpublished letter to me by Mailer on a relevant theme in that novella that fascinates him.

Chapters Nine and Ten—virtually identical to their initial delivery as presentations in Washington, D.C. and Atlanta, respectively—take on the ambiance of something like a multi-tiered time warp: their preoccupations about the 1990s remain especially relevant today, and in their prescriptive and polemical tone, may suggest, happily or not, future directions within the profession of literary studies. Chapter Nine reproduces without alteration the text of my controversial address in 1996 at the Convention of the Modern Language Association in Washington, D.C. In this presentation, I unapologetically criticized the academy's entrenched aversion to the abstract notion of transcendence in literature and life, and I bemoaned its increasing inhospitability to critical methodologies that employ an empathetic and close textual analysis as a primary mode of interpretation. In the light of the heated responses—both pro and con—that broke out in the audience after my remarks, it was evident that I had touched a raw nerve about several volatile and interrelated topics. I include my comments here because they still conveniently embody—more than twenty years later—a summary explanation of my approach to Lawrence's work, as well as a rumination on the trendy discomfort today with comparable interpretive perspectives. A cathartic letter by Norman Mailer to me about this speech broadens the depressing implications of my concerns. It is noteworthy that both an epigraph to my speech in Washington D.C. and an excerpt from a Lawrence novel in the same presentation, precisely anticipate themes (and even a quoted passage) from this current study before it became my work-in-progress in the following years. Those remarks from the mid-1990s are replete with citations from *Partisan Review* during the last years of its brave and cutting-age tenure as a journal always in the forefront of well-informed and delightfully polemical responses to the bleak terrain of political correctness in the academy. How we miss the inimitable authority of its corrective and cautionary voice today—although aspects of its preoccupations are excellently engaged by the quarterly of the National Association of Scholars, *Academic Questions*.

Finally, Chapter Ten further documents—with a prescient relevance I could not have anticipated—the extent to which notions of growth, change, and renewal, so integral to the essential doctrines of Lawrence and Mailer—find a place within the formative period of my sixteen-year tenure as Chair of the English Department at Trinity University. Initially delivered as a presentation in 1991 at the International Conference of the Society for College and University Planning (SCUP), in Atlanta, Georgia, and later published in *Innovative Higher Education* (1991), the essay attempts to link faculty responsibility for quality publication with the pragmatic working of an academic department; such integrated issues are further related both to archetypal cases of faculty non-productivity and to relevant etymological forms through literary history of the word "renewal". Except for some statistical updating in the footnotes, I include this essay with minimal revision.

John Searle writes incisively about an increasingly elusive imperative of literary study, and about the vanishing mandate of a once bedrock notion in higher education:

> One of the aims of a liberal education is to liberate our students from the contingencies of their backgrounds. We invite the students into the membership of a much larger intellectual community…one might call [it] an invitation to transcendence. The professor asks his or her students to read books that are designed to challenge any complacencies that the students may have brought to the university when they first arrived there (697).

This "invitation" to study D.H. Lawrence in the university carries with it a special "challenge" to teachers who attempt to illuminate his complex art and alien world of visionary metaphor, doctrinal intrusion, polarized emotion, and reiterated belief in the quest for the unknown. Students often, and understandably, remain perplexed today about the mystic *literalness* ("He really means it?" they ask) in Lawrence's assertions about the potential link between marriage and eternity—a connection that operates for him as urgent ideal and echoing obsession in all his writing. Certainly, Lawrence's claims about the transformative aspects of nurturant, non-manipulative sexual intimacy remain out of step with a contemporary culture that promotes hook-up sex and the plastic excitements of cyber encounters and on-line dating. The realization of the transcendent by a select number of Lawrence's characters functions as an integral pattern of perception that reappears with subtle variation on a basic theme: they perceive the Lawrencian unknown through their awareness and appreciation of the inscrutable power that informs a natural landscape, and/or through their sense of the infinite that is part of a committed, preferably marital relationship between a man and a woman who progress beyond delimiting inhibition and willful need for power and control.

The following chapters attempt to demonstrate the elusive nature of that realization in Lawrence's fiction. But early in his career there is a moment that both defines this ideal and anticipates its centrality in all the writing to come. Recall that poignant and poetic scene in *The Rainbow* when a jovial and mildly inebriated Tom Brangwen presides briefly at the reception after the wedding of his daughter, Anna: with an earthy yet sincere simplicity he describes the marital path to transcendence that Lawrence will rephrase frequently in his work but never renounce throughout his nympholetic art and his problematic but enduring relation to Frieda. Here, Tom's colloquial and benedictive words embody the heart and soul of the marriage matrix:

> "There's very little else, on earth, but marriage. You can talk about making money, or saving souls. You can save your own soul seven times over, and you may have a mint of money, but your soul goes gnawin', gnawin', gnawin', and it says there's something it must have. In heaven there is no marriage. But on earth there *is* marriage, else heaven drops out, and there's no bottom to it" (128–9).

"Your soul goes gnawin"—and we are reminded of Tom's abrupt decision years earlier to propose to Lydia after their brief acquaintance, prompted only by his "logic of the soul" (40) as he prepares to leave for her home. For Lawrence, the soul is no sentimental metaphor but the indomitable domain of instinct, and the motivational "something" here is inscrutable and palpable at the same time. Such a ringing confidence by Tom in this soulful version of a heavenly confirmation *on earth* presents unimaginative students and logocentric-phobic critics with the major hurdle of suspending their conditioned disbelief to fully appreciate the dispensations of Lawrence's visionary art.

Allan Bloom provides some further explanation for the inherent skepticism of contemporary students—all inheritors of the freedom and openness granted from the sexual revolution of the 1960s, and all witnesses to the current exponential increase in divorce. Naturally, they remain perplexed about any alleged link between marriage and transcendence:

> Many live together, almost without expectation of marriage. It is just a convenient arrangement...To strangers from another planet, what would be the most striking thing is that sexual passion no longer includes the illusion of eternity (107).

Yet to enter Lawrence's fiction with full receptivity to its underlying assumptions, students must recognize the dimensions of its foreign landscape: for him, the radical nature of his belief involves no "illusion". On this seminal issue of encountering the profound otherness of a writer's work, John Ellis—affirming a wise insistence by George Hunter—argues wisely that it is the basic requirement for critics to reflect "an acute responsiveness to a great variety of texts", and he continues with an essential guideline that should apply not only to critics, but to all enthusiasts of literature: "Receptiveness is indeed the key: in effect, a good critic has to be a good listener...acutely responsive to the particular agenda and emphasis of each one" (Ellis 46, Hunter 83). As this study pursues its synergistic mode of interpretation, I try to follow the essential sense embodied in Ellis's directive. But I am aware that D.H. Lawrence remains famously correct to trust only the tale and to be leery of all such well-intentioned protestations by commentators, including my own.

I.

SOME VERSIONS OF THE MATRIX: CONFIGURATIONS AND VARIATIONS

CHAPTER ONE

THE DARK SECRET AND THE COCCYGEAL CONTINUUM, 1918-1920: FROM OEDIPUS TO DEBASEMENT TO RENEWAL IN *THE LOST GIRL*

A certain amount of this behavior does in fact characterize the love of civilized man.

—Sigmund Freud

All I know is: this is bad, and ought not to be allowed.

—Katherine Mansfield

I loathe the ideal with an ever-increasing volume of detestation—*all* ideal.

—D. H. Lawrence

But Love has pitched his mansion in the place of excrement.

—William Butler Yeats

I

D. H. Lawrence's oft-quoted and nakedly confessional letter to Katherine Mansfield in December 1918 about his continuing susceptibility to the "devouring mother" syndrome must rank among the most self-revealing declarations in literary history by one writer to another (*Letters iii* 302). Yet neither Lawrence's psychological insight nor his risky candor is surprising given the characteristic texture of his work: a consistent and accessible integration of biography and visionary art that remains central to his achievement as man and artist. Those intimate words to a talented and troubled female colleague confirm the critical acumen in Lawrence of a "negative capability" that rivals John Keats and Henry James in its depth of perception and its undisguised revelation of inner demons. The letter, of course, also epitomizes his close and frequently volatile relationship with Mansfield—the neurotic and tubercular wife of his unstable friend-enemy, J. Middleton Murry. Lawrence's comments to her provide a poignant description of his own struggle for sexual satisfaction and manly confidence amid both the strain of his earlier and well-chronicled attachment to his mother, and the current tensions of his marriage to another powerful and often intransigent woman. He recognizes here a form of mournful symmetry that he glibly describes to his correspondent with recently popular Freudian phrases—"a kind of incest" in "this Magna Mater" pattern—and he brazenly includes Mansfield and Murry within the purview of this complex codependency, maintaining that this pathology "seems to me what Jack does to you, and what repels and fascinates you" (*Letters iii* 302).

Despite his significant disagreement with the research of the early psychoanalysts, Lawrence understands that both sexes can suffer from variations of this incestuous pattern; he also insists, in such works during this period as *Psychoanalysis and the Unconscious* and "Democracy", that men and women must retain the innate, organic capacity to emerge from a "mechanical principle" into a fulfilling sexual maturity (*PU* 14). While his optimism stands in stark contrast to the litany of symptomology and pathology he excoriates in the classifications of bedrock Freudian theory, Lawrence acknowledges to Mansfield that there is "much truth" within the arc of his own psychosexual development as a young man in the "mother-incest" idea; he openly indicts Frieda in this same letter as a "devouring mother" figure who persists in denying him the freedom "to take this precedence" in their relationship (*Letters iii* 302). Lawrence then unequivocally states his guiding belief that "men must go ahead absolutely in front of their women, without turning around to ask for permission or approval from their women" (*Letters iii* 302). He unapologetically regards this male primacy as crucial to the essential narrative and ultimate longevity of any marriage. The battle for its achievement—with appropriately as many wins as losses—makes up the livid narrative of so much of his fiction and his embattled life. In this heated context of the gender wars, Lawrence's further comments remain remarkable for his willingness to unselfconsciously define the most personal implications of any rupture in a woman's willingness to "yield some sort of precedence" to a man (*Letters iii* 302). Given the stated complaint about Frieda, his even more intimate accompanying words willingly invite Mansfield to ponder the problematics of his own marital bedroom: "it is awfully hard, once the sex relation has gone this way, to recover. If we don't recover, we die" (*Letters iii* 302). Surely Lawrence must sense—amid such sensitive details about the state of his mind, body, and marriage—that Mansfield's ultimate loyalty will be not to him but to the unreliable and dangerous Murry. Yet in late 1918, Lawrence's own accumulated frustrations, combined with his genuine empathy for Mansfield's physical and emotional plight, have prompted this cathartic and unnuanced letter.

His purposeful and presumptuous use of "we" to her is by no means casual or generic. It suggests Lawrence's awareness that Mansfield's fraught connection to an often choleric and narcissistic husband resembles the anxieties inherent in his own troubled relation to Frieda. In effect, Lawrence exempts none of the four principals in these two embattled marriages from his scorn, for neither has found a way to alter the persistent rhythm of maladjustment so caustically described in the letter. What has precipitated this adamance and self-accusation exactly at the end of the war, as he now vents some bitter private truth while the world breathes again after four years of suffocating death and destruction? Lawrence's frank complaints about his wife and about his own inability "to recover" are understandable in the context of impinging issues earlier in the fall of 1918 relevant to the immediate circumstances of his life and creative work. His repeated conflicts with Frieda over what he regards as her excessive preoccupation with her children and with the postwar condition of her German family—all this discontent reaches a climax with her decision not to accompany him to London, precipitating what Kinkead-Weekes pertinently describes as "their first deliberate separation since she had demanded a London flat in 1915" (482).

While clearly upset over Frieda's lengthy absence, Lawrence surprises himself with an especially productive use of the imposed independence: in an intense several weeks of new projects and major revisions, he completes a radical restructuring of *The Fox*, finishes "John Thomas", and writes several essays on "Education of the People".[1] This lengthy version of the novella is notable for the emotional difficulties it dramatizes that contribute to Henry Grenfel's unwillingness and/or inability to undertake the masculine lead that Lawrence mandated in the letter to Mansfield.

---

1. "Education of the People", completed in the same month (December 1918) that Lawrence writes the revealing letter to Mansfield, functions as a sustained doctrinal assault on many aspects of modern society, focusing on the leveling-down and mechanized quality inherent in the English state school system, family unit, political leadership, and social organization. These integrated polemical pieces also contain hyperbolic expressions of similar sentiments conveyed to Mansfield about the devouring mother: "There should be a league for the prevention of maternal love, as there is a society for the prevention of cruelty to animals" (*EP* 121). With its additional descriptions of the imperatives of male primacy, and its rhapsodic emphasis on instinctual self-awareness as a path to transcendence, this series of essays, in effect, recapitulates in embattled prose several of the themes I examine in *The Lost Girl*.

Although Henry establishes an effective single-mindedness in his successful courtship of March, his initiative and his eagerness are awkwardly compromised by pervasive insecurity about the looming prospect of sexual intercourse with her. He manifests an immature preference for a romantic connection to the older woman that appears more like an adolescent and voyeuristic projection of Lawrence's hated "kind of incest" (*Letters iii* 302) than an adult and phallic passion for a female object of desire. The final conversation between March and Henry indicates that he is perplexed about defining the direction of their marriage, and March seems ambivalent about offering him the Lawrencian "sort of precedence" in their future life together. Like the wounded author who created him, Henry may find it "awfully hard, once the sex relation has gone this way, to recover" from whatever experiences have deprived him of the confidence and energy required for male assertion. In many ways, the uncertain conclusion of *The Fox*, with its fearful and irresolute young man, anticipates—as I will later demonstrate—the final scene in *The Lost Girl*, but with one compelling difference: in the latter novel, an empowered and determined wife tries to invigorate her depressed and frightened husband as he leaves for war.

In that same seminal letter to Mansfield—who increasingly serves in this period as a sounding-board for his turbulent feelings and literary theories—he reveals that his emphasis on the embattled dialectic of his married life is now complemented by nothing less than a reprioritizing of the goals in his writing: he grandiloquently defines his objective as the need to push the boundaries of consciousness across the limits of narrative convention: "If one is to do fiction now, one must cross the threshold of the human psyche" (*Letters iii* 302). From Lawrence's doctrinal perspective, this radical intersection will extend beyond any customary novelistic preoccupation with the dictates of mind and the platitudes of idealized emotion. This new ambition will reflect an attempt to portray in fiction the deeper realms of instinctual desire, and will even further extend the politic boundaries by engaging issues of anal sex and purgative domination. His next major work of fiction after this declarative letter to Mansfield, *The Lost Girl,* illustrates the significance of breaching the psychic threshold in terms that are brazenly psychosexual as well as intimately physiological—comprising, in effect, a significant radicalization of material relevant for the development of the two major characters and for the emotional state of Lawrence through the winter and spring after the war ends in November 1918. Kinkead-Weekes is incisive in his summary of Lawrence as writer and man in this resonant period. He persuasively describes a direct linkage between the difficulties in Lawrence's marriage and the announced objectives of Lawrence's art evident in the patterns of revision that he imposed on earlier versions of his work: "There is no doubt that the dispute with and separation from Frieda refocused very sharply the equilibrium between man and woman which *Women in Love* and *Look!* had celebrated and forced him to rethink the importance of maleness in ways which would also have political implications" (483). Before I engage with some of the thematic and biographical issues revealed in Lawrence's composition of *The Lost Girl* in the first half of 1920, important events in 1919 have a distinct bearing on that novel. Once again, the issues involve Mansfield and Murry.

II

Early in 1919, Lawrence is pleased when Murry suddenly invites him to submit essays to *The Athenaeum*. After this mercurial editor fails to respond to the follow-up query about suggestions of topics to consider for the journal, Lawrence's long-simmering distrust of his friend's character and motivation becomes more heated. Only recently recovered from a near fatal case of the flu, and deeply unhappy with Frieda's impatient and allegedly unsupportive treatment of him during his lengthy illness, the reestablished connection to Mansfield permits Lawrence to complain again to her about his wife. His anger distinctly recalls the emasculated tone and substance of the letter about "a kind of incest" the previous year; however, he now sounds more recognizably not like a lover-husband but as a disconsolate son threatening to run away because of unjustified punishment by his mother. The tone remains immature and unpleasant: "For it is true, I have been bullied by her long enough. I really could leave her now, without a pang, I believe. The time comes, to make an end, one way or another" (*Letters iii* 337). In 1921, Lawrence will experiment in *Aaron's Rod* with the consequences of such abrupt abandonment, and this conclusive action never comes close to fruition in his legal union with Frieda. Yet the bottom-line preoccupation with his rocky marriage and vulnerable malehood is strikingly prominent from 1918 thru 1920. Whether in the letters he writes to Mansfield or in the stated revised emphases undertaken in his fiction, the stakes that involve notions of "the devouring woman" motif are perhaps more urgent to him during these months than when he famously engaged these concerns more directly as a young and healthy man writing *Sons and Lovers* nearly a decade earlier. Lawrence's struggle for confident independence and literary achievement —as Norman Mailer so eloquently speculated in 1971—is linked inexorably to the state of his organic health and his sexual performance, as well as to the well-chronicled hothouse of oedipal complexity that encompassed his formative family life.[2]

His ego and judgment take a major hit when Murry rejects all but one of his essays, and this oddly unanticipated action leads to a period of Lawrence's serious estrangement from him and Mansfield. He then makes an adamant decision (soon to be broken!) to never submit any future work for publication to him. By late June of 1919, the now affable Murry decides to join Lawrence and Frieda near the Hermitage; he mentions nothing to them about the rejected submissions as he dutifully searches in the area for appropriate long-term lodgings for his increasingly ill wife. With notions of male authority a more prominent theme in his art and life, Lawrence then meets the smart, unconventional, and engagingly sensuous Rosalind Thornycroft Baynes, who is separated from her husband and heading toward divorce. Lawrence's developing attraction to her in the months ahead—an infatuation evident in many letters and in periodic encounters with her and her accompanying children—will culminate in a brief, passionate, and (for both of them) memorable affair in the summer of 1920; their romance is reflected obliquely in some of Lawrence's finest poetry, and more directly and more recently in a private account written by Baynes (née Thornycroft) and published by her daughter.[3] But this consummated liaison, perhaps the only persuasively corroborated instance of infidelity on Lawrence's part, remains more than a year ahead. In this intense summer of 1919 Lawrence and Frieda continue the contested patterns of their volatile marriage. Revealingly, Lawrence offers no

2. See Mailer's rumination in *The Prisoner of Sex* (134–160) on Lawrence's fiction and its resonant, often poignant connection both to his marriage to Frieda and to the lingering effects of his intense relation to his mother. I analyze Mailer's treatment of Lawrence more fully in *D. H. Lawrence and the Phallic Imagination.*

3. This fascinating, privately published volume, *Time Which Spaces Us Apart,* provides a well-written and persuasive account of Rosalind's family as it emerges from the relative placidity of the Edwardian era into the fragmented culture of post-war England. More precisely, it captures the zest, disappointments, and independence of Rosalind's life through the cycle of her deteriorating marriage, friendships, affairs, and later years of family and profession. The slowly-developing relationship with Lawrence, and the gentle but frank conversation with him that immediately preceded their initial sexual intimacy, are chronicled in Baynes's notebook with admirable tact and reticence, concluding with that memorably understated line, "And so to bed" (79). Some of Lawrence's finest poetry in *Birds, Beasts and Flowers* offers oblique insight into the erotic context of their affair and its understandably bittersweet effect on each of them when they parted.

objection to Frieda's emphatic desire for a separate room, for "both of them felt they needed independence" (Kinkead-Weekes 517).

In the fall of 1919, Lawrence refuses to accompany Frieda to Germany, and during this separation he again works diligently and effectively, completing small but important final revisions of *Women in Love* as well as composing an illuminating Foreword to that major work. Among the most provocative changes in the work are several images and gestures in the Saracen's Head scene between Ursula and Birkin that clearly connect Lawrence's developing ideas on malehood with his recent reading of J.M. Pryse's theories about the function of a distinct pattern of nerve centers called *chakras* that exist in the human body. Pryse's work popularizes the potential for a stimulative cosmic energy described in ancient Hindu physio-neurology that is called *Kundalini*. He builds on this set of beliefs to develop an even more codified range of neural receptors in this sensory system. The most essential *chakra* is located at the intersection of the buttocks and lower spine—that "darkly independent mystery" of Birkin that Ursula virtually adulates as a living totem of her lover's power and authority: "Unconsciously, with her sensitive finger-tips, she was tracing the back of his thighs, following some mysterious life-flow there… It was here she discovered him one of the Sons of God such as were in the beginning of the world" (*Women in Love* 313).[4]

4. Miles's solid essay gives a clarifying summary of Lawrence's use of Pryse's Hindu doctrines and their relevance to controversial scenes of sexual passion in *Women in Love* and *Lady Chatterley's Lover*. Although he avoids all discussion of *The Lost Girl*, he provides an intelligent guide to a range of responses by critics to problematic issues of sexual arousal and phallic penetration in those two novels. In a more elaborate, wide-ranging, and debate-styled response to perspectives on anal eroticism in Lawrence's fiction by G. Wilson Knight, Frank Kermode, Colin Clark and George Ford, Mark Spilka also does not consider *The Lost Girl* in his illuminating defense of Lawrence's "normative" appropriation of the anal erogenous zone by lovers in several of his major novels. In one provocative departure from a critical consensus, Spilka writes—in opposition to Lawrence's belief and to many of his commentators—that "anal mysteries are not deeper than phallic: they simply originate earlier in infantile development when we first experience bodily shame and self-doubt" (*Renewing the Normative* 106). Spilka's sweeping notion fails to address the liberating aspect of this "mystery" for Alvina and Ciccio at key moments in their affair. Even Daleski's essay on "encoding" *The Lost Girl* is not concerned with the coded indications of the coccygeal nexus; he limits his analysis to a focus on Lawrence's conflicted depiction of female orgasmic power. Such a topic remains relevant in that novel—but its meaning cannot be addressed without consideration of the anal sex that Ciccio initiates. Similarly, while Widmer engages the general issue of sodomy in Lawrence's

The sexually exuberant and uninhibited Frieda no doubt willingly traces the same area on Lawrence's body, but it is doubtful that this woman finds the electric evidence of deity Ursula discovers in her man. Lawrence earlier avows the centrality of this neural region in his 1919 version of the Whitman essay, denoting it as the "cocygeal" [*sic*] *chakra* (*SCAL* 358). The area resonates imagistically as the darkest ganglion in the body, and for him this insistent coloration makes sense on several interrelated levels: it is the receptor region—sometimes called a "plexus" or "ganglion" by Lawrence—most shielded by social propriety and literary convention from the daylight world's public gaze and contemplation; and it is dark with the inimitable imprint of Lawrence's visionary typology, as it resides closest to the bowel—for him always the anatomic nexus of instinctual motivation and existential assertion. The emphasis in this early state of his work on Whitman, as Kinkead-Weekes suggests, is not on anal sex but on profound selfhood and dynamic independence; even the revisions of *Women in Love* in 1919 convey some subtle ambiguity about the precise direction and gymnastics of Birkin and Ursula's sexual exchange. But by the time he starts to write *The Lost Girl* early in 1920—within the heated arena of accelerated conflict with Frieda during the intervening months—this *fundamental* (in its most literal sense) *chakra* will inherit a more explicit sexual significance for Alvina and Ciccio, as part of what I will later describe as the "coccygeal continuum". My use of the phrase is meant to suggest the distinct literal and metaphoric emphasis by Lawrence on this area of the body in *The Lost Girl*, as well as the sequential development of its significance throughout the work. The novel will ultimately also convey the "dark secret" of its erotic significance for one of its angry readers, Katherine Mansfield.

While Frieda stays in Germany, Lawrence goes to Italy in the fall of 1919. He continues to write warm and solicitous letters to Rosalind Baynes that contain helpful advice on her travel itinerary and colorful details about his own experience in several Italian cities. His words to this resourceful and attractive woman sound a distinctly more confident and

---

novels, with special emphasis on *Lady Chatterley's Lover*, he ignores its relevance to *The Lost Girl* as he focuses instead on problems of female orgasm and the effects of Alvina's "psychological submission" (29). See the trenchant comments by Gerald Doherty, who more precisely uses relevant elements of *chakra* methodology to arrive at his conclusions. Althrough his focus is on *Lady Chatterley's Lover*, he provocatively establishes a wider and more skeptical context for Lawrence's use of Pryse's research: "Lawrence is wholly idiosyncratic in his exploitation of chakra psychology as a diagnostic tool in his acerbic and often despairing onslaught on modern civilization and its discontents" (81).

affectionate tone than is present in his numerous correspondence with other female friends during this period, such as Cynthia Asquith, Katherine Mansfield, and Ottoline Morrell. The sense that emerges from his letters to Rosalind is more than simple admiration: he also clearly enjoys the manly feeling of advising and protecting a vibrant young woman who is both more feminine and pleasantly amenable than his strenuous wife, and certainly less neurotic than his other three female friends. This recently separated wife and mother appears willing to gently encourage a flirtatious connection to his beleaguered self, and the timing for her presence in his life is ideal for both of them. Note how Lawrence's nearly paternal concern for her welfare and comfort is combined with a youthful excitement that is almost seductive in its reiterated eagerness for a meeting. He wants to press the issue, and she must hear more than mere courtesy in the pattern of his words:

> November 12, 1919: "If you think of starting very soon, write me tomorrow and I could look after you at Turin or Rome." November 17, 1919: "Italy is nice—very nice indeed—lovely lovely sun and sea. I'll tell you when I have an address." November 28, 1919: "I have your little note—see that you will come early in January…You might possibly arrive here before we leave—fun it would be." December 16, 1919: "I believe you would enjoy it here—but what about the children?…Be careful, when you travel, of *thieves*. Be careful, even in a sleeping car, of your small luggage." March 19, 1920: "We *must* meet in Italy, now we are here. Do you think you could manage to get to Taormina?" May 7, 1920: "Now what are you going to do this summer?…But I do think we ought to effect a meeting somewhere…Why not come here? I can find you a house, and Taormina is simply perfect in the winter" (*Letters iii* 414, 416, 423–24, 432, 488, 520, 542).

Seven letters in six months to Rosalind repeating his desire for her visit: Lawrence distinctly feels the possibility of a self-affirming and passionate entanglement that is free of the anxieties and power-struggles so engrained in his recent relations with Frieda.

In early December 1919 Lawrence writes to Mansfield from Florence what he assumes is a letter of reconciliation as he extols this magnificent city and its people. Probably believing that the split with Murry has healed, he disregards his earlier resolution and submits another essay to him for possible publication—in all likelihood an early version of his speculations on the "incest-motive" that would appear in revised form in 1921 in *Psychoanalysis and the Unconscious*. Frieda joins him that month and they travel together to Capri during the last days of the year. Even in the context of his usual conflicts with his wife, Lawrence then makes an oddly personal and clinical confession to his new friend and fellow writer, Compton Mackenzie, about his own sex life, openly complaining to him that he and Frieda are unable to achieve simultaneous orgasm. Such conversational intimacy with a very recent and notoriously competitive acquaintance is revealing not so much for the clinically personal quality of its revelation: as with Mansfield, Lawrence is often outspoken and unselfconscious about the intimate facts of his illness and sexual capacity. What remains strange is his unperceptive reaction to the understandably disjointed and undependable erotic rhythms of his fraught marriage. As Lawrence will memorably demonstrate almost a decade later in the predictably unfortunate bedroom dynamics between Connie Chatterley and her callous lover, Michaelis, overwrought reactions to issues of the timing of sexual climax reflect a transparent symptomology of deeper disruptions in the relationship, involving elements of ego, control, and gender priority. Thus as a new decade begins for Lawrence, his distress continues about his union with Frieda and his related inability to achieve the "sort of precedence" with her he described in neo-oedipal terms in 1918 to Katherine Mansfield.

III

The first two months of 1920 amount to a propitious time in Lawrence's personal and professional life. He produces major statements in fiction and essays of his literary and visionary doctrines that reflect important elements of the themes and anxieties that have preoccupied him for the last two years. In less than sixty days he now brings to dramatic conclusion several issues that highlight his provocative views on independent selfhood and male responsibility. During this intense period of effective synergy between his not-so-private demons and his writing projects, Lawrence augments and revises *Psychoanalysis and the Unconscious*, a volume that embodies his caustic objections to Freudian psychology; that work also meticulously outlines his adaptation of Pryse's system of *chakras* that Lawrence initially broached in early versions of essays that would later appear in *Studies in Classic American Literature*. The first book about psychoanalysis, and its follow-up study of 1921, *Fantasia of the Unconscious*, essentially deplore what he regards as Freud's abject determinism and pervasive pessimism—a perspective, Lawrence believes, that insists on the ultimately shackled role of consciousness and the limited potential for free will; he also uses the witty attack to insist that the "true unconscious", unlike Freud's rigidly framed catalogue of symptomology, retains the crucial ability "to prompt new movement and new being—the creative progress" (*P&U* 18). In opposition to Freud's formidable and influential *weltanschauung*, Lawrence's organic vision of growth and creativity emphasizes the necessary and innate struggle in each individual to develop and change by attending to the pristine, salutary dictates of instinct. Such a confident mandate includes the correlative emphasis in the essay "Democracy", written in June 1920 just as he completes *The Lost Girl*, for the man to take the lead in marriage and to manifest the courage "to scout ahead" (165) of his wife. The committed and chauvinistic tone here recalls precisely his words to Mansfield in 1918, and that letter remains instructive once again. In the months since its composition Lawrence appears to have resolved that a doctrinal insistence on the intrinsic potential for growth and transformation provides for him both salutary catharsis and effective self-treatment for his own pattern of anxieties; in its valoration of an instinctual progression of awareness that emanates from the lower *chakra*, it even establishes a way to transcend the strait-jacket of the incest syndrome promulgated by Freud.

As I briefly noted earlier, during the same period that he completes *Psychoanalysis and the Unconscious*, he also writes the seminal Foreword to *Women in Love*, a short but crucial piece that directly addresses this notion of organic growth under the rubric of what he famously describes as "the passionate struggle into conscious being" (486). It is an integrative and luminous phrasing, as it refers *both* to his mandate for self-generated change *and* transcendence, and to his belief in the profound responsibility of the novelist to be true to the "frictive" sound and sense of this struggle as it is reflected in real life: "This struggle for verbal consciousness should not be left out in art. It is a very great part of life" (486). That is, the passion must be described with its appropriate verbal texture to chart the stages of an individual's relentless development—with all the relevant patterns of rhythm, repetition, and frictive movement evident in the expression of human emotion.[5] In this framework of necessary stylistic reiterations in narrative fiction, it is noteworthy how often Lawrence's fascination with the coccygeal *chakra* from Pryse's work has influenced the precise imagery and nerve centers outlined in *Psychoanalysis and the Unconscious*. Perhaps more than any other book by Lawrence, this argumentative study is saturated with allusions to darkness, and not merely the usual metaphoric coloration so basic in his symbology. Here, the repetitive imagery directly reflects Lawrence's privileging of the lower plexus receptors, of which the coccygeal is the most prominent. He insists

---

5. See my book, *D.H. Lawrence and the Psychology of Rhythm,* for a more comprehensive concern with how form and doctrine are integrated in Lawrence's fiction by his repetitive use of distinct patterns of rhythmic prose.

on the power of that *chakra* in words that recall an evocative adjective from the letter to Mansfield in 1918, and his accompanying words may imply a physiological antidote to the pernicious oedipal pattern he defined for her: to balance the excessive influence of the devouring mother whose power emerges from the emanations that reside in "the great sympathetic plexus of the breast", he celebrates "the devouring darkness of the lower man, the devouring whirlpool beneath the navel" (*P&U* 29, 32). When Lawrence seizes on a metaphor that fits the patterns of his visionary neurology, he often dares to push the limits of its implications. Here, his pointed criticism of his opponents is informed with a biting wit that refers back to the lower plexus: "The idealists, cannot bear any appeal to their bowels of comprehension" (*P&U* 38). His complaint is direct and unequivocal. From Lawrence's perspective modern science and culture routinely extol the power of the upper centers and invariably fear the darkness that he confidently evokes as the imagistic signature of the coccygeal *chakra.*

Against the emasculating influence of the Magna Mater, Lawrence consistently praises throughout all his work the powerful role of marriage, and especially its potential to accelerate the maturity of the male by often enabling the escape from residual oedipal tension. That he questions the effectiveness of this dynamic in his own marriage does not negate his belief in its formative importance, and he gratefully acknowledges the intermittent periods when the institution has stabilized his very being: "The best thing I have known is the stillness of accomplished marriage" (*Fantasia of the Unconscious* 158). But when he writes the initial book on psychoanalysis, this sense of pervasive calm is lacking; it is interesting that in its first few pages Lawrence returns again to the issues he raised in 1918 to Mansfield, but now he pretends it is not personal in this not-so-hypothetical scenario: "A man finds it impossible to realize himself in marriage. He recognizes that his emotional, even passional, regard for his mother is deeper that it could ever be for a wife. This makes him unhappy, for he knows that passional communion is not complete unless it be also sexual" (*P&U* 13).

Lawrence, of course, retains until his impotence in the final years of his life, a deep sexual connection to Frieda, and in less angry moments he implicitly acknowledges the ebb-and-flow in the tides of any marriage, including his own. To the degree that a marriage is "alive", it is subject to patterns of adjustment and accommodation: "True marriage is a tremendous life-state, a state of being, a state of creative existence" (*SCAL* 412). While he bemoans the unwillingness of Frieda to accede to his notions of male primacy, it is certainly his wife who helped him overcome the most damaging remnants of the oedipal scarring from his mother. For Lawrence the real unconscious is not the static repository of insurmountable repression and neurosis, but a pristine energy source that facilitates movement to maturity in a man that then will be further tested, challenged, and augmented in marriage: "For the whole point about the true unconscious is that it is all the time moving forward, beyond the range of its own fixed laws and habits" (*P&U* 16). In *The Lost Girl,* in 1920, Alvina and Ciccio will, for Lawrence, illustrate aspects of this forward movement through a continuum of coccygeal darkness to the growth and transcendence demanded by their difficult union. It remains a "continuum" because it functions not as a static state of easy compromise; their courtship and marriage initiate a developmental struggle toward instinctual understanding that remains at the center of Lawrencian ideology. This productive forward movement in *The Lost Girl* will finally reside in Alvina and not Ciccio, and such ironic reversal of the male primacy inherent in Lawrence's view of gender roles must stand as graphic evidence of his oft-quoted insistence to trust the tale and not the artist.

In the intermediate version in 1919 of the Whitman essay, the references to the coccygeal area of the body stress its important role in existential self-definition; its instinctual power is consistently contrasted to a modern *zeitgeist* that privileges empirical certainty and Freudian theory. In this destructive idealization of what Lawrence calls "scientific process", the command centers of the human body become dislocated: "The upper or spiritual self gathers the experiences of the lower self, violates, as it were, the lower self, and assumes command" (*SCAL* 362). As Lawrence shortly begins to revise *The Insurrection of Miss Houghton*, it retrospectively becomes apparent that the scenes of anal intercourse several years earlier implied in the sex between Will and Anna Brangwen in *The Rainbow*, and more recently in key moments of passion between Ursula and Birkin in *Women in Love*—such moments begin to function as a counterweight to the incest-motive that Lawrence will engage more directly in *The Lost Girl* as part of the coccygeal continuum. Thus, the darkness of the lower centers already suggests notions of a movement toward risk-taking and embattled independence. In that same Whitman essay of 1919 he already insists that "the cocygeal [sic] center embodies the deepest and most unknowable sensual reality" (*SCAL* 365). Lawrence celebrates its inscrutable power because its "depth" is not accessible to scientific confirmation or empirical proof—in short, its linkage to the domain of the unknown certifies its majesty. More crudely, for this former mother's boy who continues to struggle with the image of a masculine self, the buggery of a woman can doubly serve as an aggressive response to sexual insecurity, doctrinally as an attack stratagem against the lordship of idealized notions of love, and "domestically" as imagined dominance over his often contentious wife. Kinkead-Weekes, in this regard, asserts intelligently that anal sex in Lawrence's fiction functions as a "male reaction to feeling undervalued or held at a distance or defied" (577), an argument by this skilled biographer that still lacks a more precise connection to the immediate tensions in Lawrence's marriage. Here is Lawrence in a more definitive mode about the lower neural receptors two years after completing *The Lost Girl*, as he offers a more explicit statement in the final version of the Whitman essay: "The cocygeal [sic] plexus and ganglion, these are the last, most secret, and most *extreme* dynamic centres of our being. And these also must be conquered" (*SCAL* 412). The novel will also share the dark "secret" of its power and its central role in the struggle for self-definition that creates the organizing ligature of its plot.

IV

Lawrence begins to work on the final revisions of *Psychoanalysis and the Unconscious* on January 21, 1920; two weeks later occurs his most serious estrangement from Murry, who rejects the essay on incest that will be developed more fully in the revised volume. Amid Lawrence's stunned fury at what he regards as Murry's indefensible betrayal and inveterate cowardice, and in the immediate context of his strained relations with Frieda, the long-abandoned and incomplete manuscript of *The Insurrection of Miss Houghton* arrives in the mail on February 12, 1920: he started that lengthy novel in 1913 during the early months of his marriage, and he now begins to radically revise it as *The Lost Girl*—a complete restructuring that is heavily influenced by his marital turmoil in 1920 and by the changing priorities (as enunciated in the Foreword to *Women in Love*) in his literary technique and doctrinal vision. The work creates a male character quite unlike Lawrence in nationality, education, and family life—indeed, sufficiently dissimilar so that the author can easily disguise some salient psychological affinities between Lawrence and the young Italian. Critics have failed to note that Ciccio remains entangled in the web of a devouring mother—a precarious positioning of the psyche that has progressively preoccupied Lawrence in *Sons and Lovers*, in his letter to Mansfield, and in his recent revisions of *Psychoanalysis and the Unconscious*.[6]

6. Certainly, Ruderman's impressive full-length study, a work that meticulously traces the ramifications of that theme throughout the abundant and accessible

From the moment we are introduced to Ciccio and Madame in the novel, Lawrence stresses the actively maternal aspects of the older woman's connection to this attractive but strangely boyish and reticent man. Her loyal bevy of three additional male acolytes and actors all receive some of the same motherly attention, but nothing close to the extent that she smothers Ciccio with advice, attention, and adamant control. She complains that she "shan't be able to see that the boys' rooms are all in order", for Madame insists "they need an overseeing eye, especially Ciccio; especially Ciccio" (125). At twenty-five years of age, Ciccio must be familiar with such nagging comments by Madame, for he reveals no irritation at those condescending words that pose a clear threat to his maturity and manhood. Alvina observes the same lack of independence in him, but for this woman who has experienced many courtships but no sexual passion, his boy-man demeanor and handsome appearance pique her curiosity and erotic interest. In their first trivial and accidental bodily touch, she notes "how light his fingers were in their clasp—almost like a child's touch" (127).

Although lacking any intimate relations with men in her past, Alvina has a lengthy history of many suitors, flirtations, and even one formal engagement—all recounted in the first half of the novel before she meets Ciccio.[7] She has learned to be leery of male pomposity and insecurity, and

intersections of Lawrence's life and art, remains the most trenchant research on the "devouring mother" motif. While her discussion of *The Lost Girl* reveals that novel's preoccupation with "maternal destructiveness" (37), Ruderman only uses her analysis to stress the dangerous relation of Madame to Alvina, *not Ciccio*—all in the context of the critic's interesting summary of Alvina's exposure to three unsuitable mother figures, in Clariss, Miss Frost, and Miss Pinnegar. As my own approach indicates, the greater peril to the achievement of selfhood resides in Madame's influence on Ciccio, and the residue of that relationship lingers in Ciccio's vulnerable psyche throughout the novel. But Ruderman is not alone in ignoring the danger that Madame poses to him. Ross unwisely describes Madame as "a benign den mother" (11), and Franks refers uncritically to her "motherly warnings" to Alvina (30) and makes no mention of Madame's pernicious effect on the immature Ciccio. Moynahan remains the only critic to convey any sense of Madame's true nature, as he describes how Ciccio "acquiesces sullenly in a strange bondage to the matriarchal Madame Rochard" (133).

7. See my essay on *The Lost Girl*, "Ten Men and a Sacred Prostitute", for consideration of the various men in Alvina's life before she meets Ciccio, and how they are precisely differentiated in the ways they variously approach her to cajole, converse, or seduce. My current essay attempts to get beyond this surface patterning to the seminal issue of a doctrine that integrates the Ciccio-Alvina relationship with Lawrence's own psychology and the contemporary circumstances

she asserts to Madame—no doubt recalling a range of unhappy encounters with earlier courtships and with her father's stuffy idiosyncrasies—that "men are such babies", and Madame confirms that they are "children—they are all children" (132, 133). While aspects of this sweeping indictment have some generic validity in the assumptions of developmental psychology, such an angry dismissal of the whole gender can only be uttered by a woman whose various other involvements with the opposite sex stop well short of the intricacies and complexities of real passion. Yet an observant Alvina remains perplexed by the unusual species of passion she senses in Ciccio's intense attachment to Madame. In response to her direct query to him—"Why do you all love Madame so much?"—his answer further confirms the aberrant psychology that informs the relationship: "We like her—we love her—as if she was a mother" (137). When Alvina later asks Ciccio about his family background, and he remarks briefly that his parents are dead and his siblings in America, she innocently accepts the oedipal patterns she already has noticed within the acting troupe: "But you have Madame for a mother" (139). Ciccio's reactions to this passing observation suggest for the first time that he is discontent with his established role as the formidable Madame's adopted and obsequious favorite son: "He made another gesture this time; pressed down the corners of his mouth as if he didn't like it" (139).

Just before Alvina's initial sex with Ciccio, which occurs after she impulsively and fatefully takes the train to Sheffield to join the troupe, Lawrence's refracted narration catches an important and evocatively integrated moment of recognition. Here is Alvina's naïve understanding of Madame's dominant role and busy efficiency; note how she senses that Alvina presents a major threat to her own control of this mercurial man:

> Madame looked up, almost annoyed when she entered.
> "I couldn't keep away from you, Madame," she cried.
> "Evidently," said Madame.
> Madame was darning socks for the young men. She was a wonderful mother for them, sewed for them, cooked for them, looked after them most carefully. Not many minutes was Madame idle.
> "Do you mind?" said Alvina.
> Madame darned for some moments without answering.

---

of his marriage. Thus within my tracing of the coccygeal theme, the following phrasing is meaningful when the doctors flirt with her as she learns to be a maternity nurse: "her back-bone never yielded for an instant" (36). On two essential levels—emotional and anatomic—Alvina will be unable to maintain this stance of coccyx-protection with Ciccio.

> "And how is everything at Woodhouse?" she asked (192).

An interesting vignette—not so much for the further evidence of Madame protecting her turf ("for some moments" is curtly telling!), but because the younger woman does not yet comprehend the stakes that inform Ciccio's attachment to his "wonderful mother". Madame unquestionably "minds" very much. Her consequent warning to Alvina that the possible Houghton inheritance will not satisfy Ciccio misreads his unassuming value system and genuine attachment to Alvina, and it also scarcely disguises her own desire to maintain command over him. She remains a crafty and formidable protector of her own territory, capable of coarseness and innuendo to get her way. As Madame conspicuously violates the socks in front of Alvina as a showcase phallic moment no doubt also enjoyed by Lawrence, she cruelly reveals her own prescient awareness of Alvina's forthcoming deflowering:

> "Men are like cats, my dear, they don't like their bread without butter—Why should they?—Nor do I, nor do I."
>
> "Can't I help with the darning?" said Alvina.
>
> "Hein? I shall give you Ciccio's socks, yes? He pushes holes in the toes—you see?" Madame poked two fingers through the hole in the toe of a red-and-black sock, and smiled a little maliciously at Alvina.
>
> "I don't mind which sock I darn," she said (194).

It is an evocative qualification, for just "a little maliciously" betrays Madame's belief that she retains control. That she also underestimates the enduring power of the sexual dynamic between Alvina and Ciccio reveals Lawrence's brilliant understanding of Madame's limitations. She has long forgotten the sustaining energy of erotic passion and her own sublimated expressions of maternal authority.

Early in *The Lost Girl*, Ciccio is imagistically defined as a Lawrencian creature of the darkness, a silent yet charismatic man often portrayed with "a curl of the lips" (123, 125); in essence, he at first seems reduced to a stereotypical, dark-peasant Italian with predatory inclinations, limited intellectual capacity, and abundant sexual bravado. Lawrence will gradually subvert this characterization by suggesting a range of unusual and contradictory aspects to his personality. But in a more compelling way Ciccio resembles a fantasy synthesis of ideal male equanimity for Lawrence—with his presiding mother figure, significant erotic power, and no pressing issues of money, vocation, marriage, and health. This portrait remains an illusion that scarcely conceals the problematics of Ciccio's undeveloped emotional core. He ultimately fascinates Alvina because he is not only sexy and dangerous, but also vulnerable, defiant, and imprisoned by Madame. While attracted to Alvina's proud and appealing English "otherness", Ciccio recognizes unconsciously that she represents an opportunity to escape from his devouring mother figure. His instant infatuation with this bright and available midlands woman sparks energy and incentive in him—even before the affair starts—for a species of self-assertion that departs from the *literal* script demanded by Madame. In the acting performance, Ciccio suddenly alters his lines to avoid his quick stage-death by the bear: "I am still alive, Madame" (162). His pithy response as to the cause of his improvisation—"I am tired of being dead" (162)—amounts to the first declaration of his emergence from the destructive inertia provided by the protective cocoon of his troupe-family. He is roused to the positive expression of his obstreperous self; the only justification he offers to Madame is that unadorned statement of the priority of his feeling over the expectations of his group. As he awakens from this moribund state, he will turn to Alvina with renewed energy and long-repressed defiance.

V

Raised amid the patriarchal tradition of isolated village life in Italy, Ciccio is prone to experience unmarried and pretty women either as extended family members or as accessible objects of desire. Aware of Alvina's unconcealed interest in him, he arrives at her house to inquire about her father's rapidly declining health. There is legitimate empathy by him here for Mr. Houghton and Alvina, as Ciccio is not merely on the prowl for seduction. Yet there is little doubt that this visible moment of her delicate emotions (the father has just died) presents Ciccio with a propitious opportunity; he has strong sexual desire for Alvina and abundant confidence in his own sensual power. The earliest passionate scene between them involves his initiation of a lengthy and dominating kiss after he tests his hold over her by issuing a simple directive to determine the efficacy of his male primacy: he curtly beckons her to move a few steps toward him, and when she accedes he feels "a dark flicker of ascendancy" (174). Throughout most of their affair—as per Lawrence's letter of frustration to Mansfield—Ciccio will "take the lead" in the sexual connection between them, and he similarly will pursue those desires "without turning around to ask for permission or approval" (*Letters iii* 302) from Alvina. That flickered coloration in Lawrence's description is important even in this early scene. Although the perception of darkness is fleeting, its iteration amounts to the first significant association with the developing relationship between them. The Lawrencian blackness invariably inhibits the "daylight" world of conventional caution and mind-centered willfulness. As the novel proceeds, the depth of that ebony imagery will be reflected in repetitive rhythms and pulsations—versions of the "frictive to and fro" Lawrence announces in the Foreword to *Women in Love*. While the love affairs deepens in the months ahead, both the shaded patterns of imagistic chiaroscuro and the intense auditory reiteration will become more frequent and intrusive, even to the extent that Alvina will feel enveloped and then transformed by a panoply that varies from black to ashy gray to fire-tinged white.

In the scene of that initial kiss, Alvina responds affirmatively to his manipulative question about whether she loves him, as she is without any semblance of artifice or dissimulation. Such guilelessness is recognized easily by Ciccio, and thus her confirming answer lets him know that their sexual liaison can begin. Lawrence's imagery actually looks far ahead in their affair. The current moment resonates as a measure of her immediate plight as well as a premonition of the changes she will undergo. In the following passage she appears on the surface as painful victim and martyr, but note how Lawrence subsumes her virginal victimhood—as Ciccio lifts her up for that first embrace—by suggesting a proximate rebirth of her dark, instinctual self through a hint of Lawrence's most iconic metaphor, the Phoenix: "And smiling he kissed her delicately, with a certain finesse of knowledge. She moaned in spirit in his arms, felt herself dead, dead. And he kissed her with finesse which seemed like coals of fire on her head" (175). What dies here, as later scenes will illustrate more graphically, is a form of self-protection against the darkness: the imagery anticipates the strenuous and difficult rebirth in Alvina that is an integral part of her "passionate struggle into conscious being" (Foreword 486). Trained as an accomplished midwife, the irony remains that she presides at the end of the novel at her *own* birth. This process of parturition begins with that first kiss. Gentle and abrupt in his early physical contact with her, his approach will become more aggressive and even brutal in the days ahead. What will be killed, and how the murder will occur, is for the moment unstated amid her sensual moaning and his knowledgeable smile.

Other than a silly crush on the timid and married Albert Witham, Alvina's litany of experiences with men have failed to arouse her sexual interest during the period before she meets Ciccio. Her impulsive and virginal engagement to the too prim and proper Dr. Graham suggests that the reiterated echo of "love" that she applies to her pre-sexual relation to Ciccio remains an unreliable and unexamined emotion for Alvina. She uses a pent-up erotic desire to validate the often platitudinous word that her conventional upbringing has conditioned her to believe is required as the precondition for intimacy with a man. She now begins to learn that a deep stirring of libido can offer a more reliable entrance into the real world of love than the Victorian prescriptions taught to her by her mother, Miss Frost, and Miss Pinnegar:

> She locked the door and kneeled down on the floor, bowing her head to her knees in a paroxysm on the floor. In a paroxysm—because she loved him. She doubled herself in a paroxysm on her knees on the floor—because she loved him. It was far more like pain, like agony, than like joy. She swayed herself to and fro, in a paroxysm of unbearable sensation, because she loved him (175).

In Lawrence's inimitable "fourth dimensional" prose, the passage describes the peeling away of her veneer of fake emotion and idealized romance. The "doubled" posture is conveyed by a distinct sexual rhythm that uses incremental repetition as it "pulses" and "works up to culmination" in a manner consistent with Lawrence's mandate in the Foreword to *Women in Love*. The waves of sensation simulate also the pains of a slow self-gestation, for her reactions function as the start of her "passionate struggle into conscious being"—a long process that will conclude at the end of the novel with the birth of her powerful demeanor of maturity and confidence. Alvina cannot know her destiny in this early scene, but already she seems willing to follow the dark channels of her instincts, and for Lawrence that is the existential necessity: "The creative spontaneous soul sends forth its promptings of desire and aspiration in us. These promptings are our true fate, which it is our business to fulfill" (Foreword 485).

The depiction of her reaction to his kiss also includes a reference to Alvina's knees, a part of her body that she characteristically clenches tightly when sitting; this tense posture remains unsurprising, for her knees will serve as the focus of Ciccio's seductive advances in the weeks ahead. For now, Lawrence elaborates with a more conscious use of that crucial frictive rhythm to describe Alvina's masturbatory reaction to Ciccio's passionate embrace: "And taking a pillow from the bed, she crushed it against herself and swayed herself unconsciously, in her orgasm of unbearable feeling. Right in her bowels she felt it—the terrible unbearable feeling—How could she bear it"? (175) Her orgasm is an expression of deep emotion and not sexual climax. Despite her intimate appropriation of the pillow against her lower body, Alvina's difficulty in achieving a satisfactory orgasm will function as a significant issue as their affair develops. For now Lawrence notes that Alvina's most intense response resides in her bowels; it is an area of the body in close proximity to the coccygeal *chakra*, the ganglion in Lawrence's visionary neurology connected to the primary stimuli that activate instinctual desire and the impulse for independent selfhood. It is certainly true that Lawrence often refers to "bowels" throughout his fictional and nonfictional prose as an indicator of deep, gut-level emotion—frequently abbreviated by him as the "soul": his quasi-biblical iteration of both terms is meant to stipulate the non-cerebral origin of deep feelings such as love, joy, contentment, and rage. But in this case of Alvina's response, it seems fair to consider the full context of "bowels" in the light of Lawrence's abiding interest in the Yogic *Chakras*. Recall that in the 1921–22 version of the Whitman essay, Lawrence insists that the "cocygeal [sic] plexus and ganglion…must be conquered" (*SCAL* 412). In this regard, Ciccio's constant awareness of Alvina's knees makes perfect sense within the framework of Ciccio's seduction of her and Lawrence's adaptation of Pryse's notions of the *chakra*. When closed tightly the knees literally block the entrance to vaginal sex, but such clenching cannot so easily deter anal penetration. As the effect of this initial and initiatory kiss on Alvina gradually wanes, she is described as "so remote and virginal" that "she felt that nothing, nothing could ever touch her" (176). That pervasive feeling of protective isolation will influence Ciccio's desire—in the disturbing metaphor he will employ—to murder her virginity and anxiety by arousing her in all the remote places.

If Ciccio functions for Alvina as a means for a passionate emergence of her true self, Alvina offers a means of escape for Ciccio from the "incest-motive" represented by Madame's role in his life; even an inexperienced Alvina, who is still obsequious to Madame's commanding presence, begins to recognize the range of residual oedipal tensions that still affects Ciccio. Lawrence now slows the narrative action as she gradually absorbs some relevant insight about him while watching the subtle signals in front of her. It is the novelist's obsessive art at its best—with Ciccio's romantic drama attempting to break through his psychological constraints:

> Ciccio was looking toward the fire. His presence made Alvina tremble. She noticed how the fine black hair of his head showed no parting at all—it just grew like a close-cap, and was pushed aside at the forehead. Sometimes he looked at her, as Madame talked, and again looked at her, and looked away (177).

Alvina correctly senses that Ciccio feels trapped by the presence of Madame, yet he now recognizes more clearly an important path to freedom. To emphasize his need for a break with the troupe and to ratify his commitment to Alvina, he abruptly announces his betrothal to her in front of Madame, who is stunned and displeased at the prospect of losing her adopted son. The betrayal is a small version of Greek drama, with Alvina an innocent intermediary in some complex triangulation of motives and ménage implied by Madame's words to her: "I shall protect you, you don't know him yet" (177). Ciccio correctly realizes that Madame is powerless to stop the marriage: "A smile of triumph went over his face. Madame watched him stonily" (180).

Ciccio has worked uninterruptedly with Madame for three years, and she renders a harsh and jealous verdict to Alvina about the young woman's future with the Italian: "You will go down, with him" (180). Although this definitive warning purports to encompass issues of class, breeding, and money, Lawrence uses her words to establish a basic inversion that bears upon Madame's directional metaphor: it is the downward motion toward purging sex and the coccygeal *chakra* that will ultimately anneal Alvina's connection to her lover and finally lead to the strength and maturity she achieves as she sends Ciccio off to war. Recall the pervasive pattern that Lawrence establishes to legitimize his imagery throughout the novel: years earlier she feels "frightened and fascinated" as she descends into her father's mine by "a sense of dark fluid presences in the thick atmosphere, the dark, fluid, viscous voice of the collier" (47). This precocious affinity for a perversely sensuous environment appears to suggest, well before she meets Ciccio, an intrinsic affinity for an enveloping darkness that blots out the everyday anxieties of her conscious self: "Her lungs felt thick and slow, and her mind dissolved, she felt she could cling like a bat in the long swoon of the crannied, underworld darkness" (47). There is no sentimental affinity projected here by Lawrence for the occupational hazards or risky lifestyle of colliers, but he does convey an anticipatory sense in *The Lost Girl* of the element and the elementality that Alvina later will appropriate as a valuable part of her being. She needs to meet a certain quality of man for that propensity for darkness to further define and unleash her passionate self.

VI

Even with Ciccio's engagement announcement, Madame retains minor aspects of her hold on him and Alvina, and she obligates the younger woman to carry the command about the protocol of the seating arrangement for his departure to the train station: "She wants you to get in with her," says the messenger to her future lover (184). As they depart, in merely five words, Alvina significantly relays to him an open avowal of her desire for him: "You will come, won't you?" (189)—a comment that amounts to her declaration that she expects him to pursue her. When, days later, in the absence of his pursuit, Alvina catches up to the troupe in Sheffield, Ciccio continues his seduction by sensually touching her again in the area that serves as gateway protection of her virginity: her aroused but timid response is to substitute a more mundane bodily offering to him: "Under the table he laid his hand on her knee. Quickly she put forward her hand to protect herself. He took her hand and looked at her along the glass as he drank. She saw his throat move as the wine went down it" (198). Lawrence's bifurcated perspective here—as the reader watches them watch each other—provides excellent insight into the shifting patterns of passion and hesitancy inevitably engrained in courtship. Just before their first sexual encounter, it is Madame who cleverly adheres to the Native American rituals inherent in the creation of descriptive names: she maliciously bestows on Alvina the crass name of Allaye. But it may be Lawrence more than Madame who wittily utters a related line to Ciccio just before the couple goes to Alvina's room; it consists of the French words, "*courage au chemin d'Angleterre*", translated from the French by the Cambridge Edition as "Good luck to the English route" (199, 384). Everyone in the troupe except Alvina knows that she and Ciccio are about to have sex. In British and especially Australian slang, "route" often signifies sexual intercourse, a ribald and vindictive pun that this widely-traveled woman employs with indelicate humor at naïve Alvina's expense. But more pertinently, and I suspect beyond the ken of Madame's experiences or rhetorical intent, is Lawrence's awareness that the coccygeal *chakra* of Pryse is consistently described as the "root chakra".[8] The statement to Ciccio thus anticipates the buggery of the English lady through graphic *entendre* that the novelist could not resist.

---

8. See The "Explanatory notes" section (384) of the Cambridge UP edition for relevant translations of the French language in this scene—used by the troupe members as integral to the humor and irony they embrace at Alvina's naïve expense. The Australian and the English Slang Dictionaries list "sexual intercourse" as the primary definition of "route". As Miles suggests throughout his essay, and as Pryse indicates in his doctrines derived from the categories of *chakras* in Hindu belief (See *The Apocalypse Unsealed* 15–16), the "root chakra" stands as the operative term for that essential point of neural stimulation at the base of the spine and the top of the buttocks; it is the nerve cluster that Lawrence describes in the 1919 version of the Whitman essay as "the cocygeal [sic] ganglion" and the "cocygeal [sic] centre" (362, 365), and that Pryse in his book further denotes as "*muladhara*" and the "sacral ganglion" (16). For the history of Lawrence's use of Pryse see *Apocalyse and the Writings on Revelation*, 3–8.

Although Madame regretfully senses that she will lose Ciccio to Alvina, she at least can enjoy the satisfaction of engineering the circumstances of the younger woman's first sexual experience. By making Ciccio "a secret, imperative gesture" to accompany Alvina, she has, in effect, enabled him to get her alone in the adjacent apartment (201). As he dutifully walks with her before there is any physical contact between them, Alvina understandably lingers under the spell of her own infatuation and the erotic proximity of Ciccio: her sense of his "unknown beauty which almost killed her" (202). That qualifying adverb, which denies her metaphoric death, will be eliminated immediately, as Lawrence insists that the pervasive power of such darkness stimulates in Alvina a transformative daze that is deeply instinctual and *murderous* in its implications. She initially finds herself actually in the darkness by the door, and then—as Ciccio opportunely uses the literal lack of visibility to facilitate her seduction—Alvina realizes that she is under "that black spell of his beauty" (202). In the room she is forced to submit to his desire in a scene that approaches rape because of his aggression and her lack of explicit consent. Now "almost" is removed to starkly convey the effect of Ciccio's action: "he killed her", "assassinated her", and "he carried her away once more" (202). Lawrence stubbornly presents the scene not as a criminal assault but as a willful and justified demolition of Alvina's conventional proprieties, romantic dreams, and over-developed self-consciousness. Kinkead-Weekes captures the precise texture and motivation of the encounter after he quotes a phrase from a relevant letter by Lawrence on *The Lost Girl*, as the critic considers the sex reflective of "the cracking open of ego that [Lawrence] now thought necessary to allow 'the dark half of humanity' to emerge" (575). Lawrence attempts to weaken any allegation of rape when he writes that Alvina "could have fought", but Ciccio's "dark rich handsomeness…numbed her like a venom" (203). This heretical scene also uses a technique, common in Whitman's poetry, to depict the moment as an anti-baptismal cleansing of Alvina within the very element that the sacramental rite seeks to expunge: "So she washed suffocated in his passion" (203).

As several critics have asserted with a varying range of explicitness, there is more to the sex in this scene than two episodes of energetic intercourse. "He carried her away once more" (202), and the reiterations of "killing" and "assassinated", do not merely allude to Ciccio's stamina, as one or both acts of coition appear to involve anal penetration: "He was awful to her, shameless so that she died under his shamelessness, his smiling, progressive shamelessness" (202). The familiar Lawrencian code word of "shameless" recalls relevant scenes between Will and Anna in *The*

Rainbow and Connie and Mellors in *Lady Chatterley's Lover.*[9] Ciccio's essential goal—"to make her his slave" (203)—scarcely conceals a discomforting projection of male sexual primacy in the act of love that Lawrence, by his own angry admission to Mansfield, seems unable to attain amid the frustrations with Frieda. The predatory approach to Alvina clearly amounts to a debasement of her, but for Lawrence the doctrinal legitimacy justifies the assault and the lack of warmth and nurturant sex that he generally affirms. Again, what is murdered here in the novelist's dialectic—"He killed her. He simply took her and assassinated her (202)—is the over-developed dominance of the upper-centers of consciousness that Lawrence associates with convention, conformity, and mentalized emotion.

But the sexual debasement must not be viewed as simply an opportunity for Lawrencian therapy on Alvina. Ciccio's libido also reflects—as a precise echo again of The Foreword—the active assertion of his own "passionate struggle" into the "conscious being" of malehood: he further loosens his ties to a devouring mother by reaching an existential equipoise within a sexual matrix that Freud described in more formal psychosexual terms a few years before Lawrence writes *The Lost Girl.* Freud's seminal essay of 1912, evocatively translated by Peter Gay as "On the Universal Tendency to Debasement in the Sphere of Love", with its controversial emphasis on oedipal issues and incestuous fixations in a young man's sexual development, provides insight into Ciccio's erotic affinities. It also can offer some reasonable entry into psychobiographical speculation on Lawrence's own anxieties and preoccupations. In the strict

---

9. As I have indicated (see note 4), most critics completely ignore the issue of the anal erogenous zone in *The Lost Girl.* Kinkead-Weekes breaks this relative silence by a sustained analysis that concludes with the acknowledgment that "Ciccio may also have buggered her", and he deftly discusses this sexual act in the context of Lawrence's marital sex life, and in the doctrinal framework of Lawrence's adamant belief, in the words of this biographer, that Lawrence's version of the *chakras* insists it is "the lower centres that need to be brought alive…as ways of discovering and awakening the darker part of the psyche…" (576–77). Squires and Talbot, in their generally illuminating biography of Lawrence and Frieda, tend to minimize both Lawrence's ambition and the emotional complexity of the novel in their unprobing reading of the work: "He aimed not to uncover dark layers of the soul but to fuse English sterility with Italian insouciance" (225). Within this concept of imagistic coloring, I commend Moynahan for providing the most incisive definition of the Lawrencian darkness in *The Lost Girl*, describing it as "the stratum of instinct within the self which is ordinarily overlaid by moral, psychological, and social conditioning, and crushed into submission by high-mindedness" (126).

and formulaic terms of Freud, the "profane love" that Ciccio displays early in his intimacy with Alvina demonstrates his need "to avoid the affectionate current" that has been blocked by his more "sacred" relation, even at age twenty-five, to the presiding maternal figure of Madame (Freud 397). Ciccio later will attempt to embody a more mature, generous, and selfless love for Alvina as his primary sexual object, and that attempt will produce the most stable (if sadly transient) stage of their relationship. Freud's words on the etiology of this transitional period remain especially relevant: "As soon as the condition of debasement is fulfilled, sensuality can be freely expressed and a high degree of pleasure can develop" (397).

It will be a long journey for Ciccio to develop this normative capacity and pleasure. Certainly, the once static notions of the normal and pleasurable, and the sacred and profane, have changed considerably since the early years of psychoanalytical theory a century ago. But Ciccio's own history with Madame and his early intimacy with Alvina fit into the parameters of the most basic Freudian notions: for a man "to be really free and happy in love [he] must have surmounted his respect for women and have come to terms with the idea of incest with his mother or sister" (399). For Ciccio, such "coming to terms" will encompass the two-step process of the debasement of Alvina leading to the absolute disengagement from Madame's control. As many critics through the years have demonstrated, and as Lawrence makes evident in his essays, in *Sons and Lovers*, and in letters similar to those he sent to Mansfield, Lawrence has impressively come to *conscious* terms with the personal ramifications of the oedipal issue. But such insight does not mean he has come to an emotional acceptance and stability about this syndrome, and it does not mean that Frieda has acquiesced to his need for primacy—sexual or otherwise. Perhaps the first time in his published work that Lawrence sounds "really free"—within this demanding context of Freud's stipulations—is in his revealing essay of 1924, "The Bad Side of Books". In that poignant and retrospective rumination on his parents, he looks at both his mother and father with a balanced and mature understanding of their formative relation to him. It reads as if a dying and impotent Lawrence has finally achieved the elusive perspective that confidently surmounts the oedipal residue of his upbringing and "comes to terms" with the family drama of his early years.

Freud speaks in the same essay of a period of emergence in a man that requires him to work through the "phantasy situations" which degrade women, and he provocatively acknowledges (as Lawrence never quite does!) that the problem may be universally unsolvable: "There are only a few educated people in whom the two currents of affection and sensuality are properly fused" (397, 399). *The Lost Girl* represents another attempt to resolve these basic issues of sexual maturity through Ciccio's love affair with Alvina, his long-delayed marriage to her, and the depression that ultimately envelops the Italian. That Alvina becomes stronger and Ciccio weaker in the latter stages of their relationship is a testament to Lawrence's commitment to an artistic vision that realizes who usually has the greater strength in the gender wars. The transitions in temperament and perspective in Ciccio and Alvina that are initiated by acts of anal intercourse ultimately result in consequential emotional changes in them that extend beyond the immediate effects of these stark and disruptive sexual experiences. This coccygeal nexus in *The Lost Girl* is part of a continuum that requires a reader to pay close attention to even minor calibrations of adjustment and resistance between the lovers. The relative lack of critical commentary on these key moments as the novel develops amounts to a failure to demonstrate the impressive grasp by Lawrence of central issues of character, structure, and doctrine in the work. The importance of this continuum dictates my own forthcoming attention to the graduated stages in their affair and marriage—which has now reached the period just after Alvina's loss of virginity. The moment offers Lawrence an opportunity to display his wide-ranging awareness of world cultures and totemic practices in order to enrich the implications of Alvina's transformative sexual experience.

VII

Lawrence's reading in the sacred rites of ancient societies permits him to establish an historic framework of symbols and gestures that bear upon Alvina's seduction. After her deflowering by Ciccio, she is gifted the next morning at breakfast by a smiling and titillated Madame, who has surmised the fact of Alvina's loss of virginity but not the pattern of debasement she was forced to endure. Madame has placed violets and carnations by Alvina's plate, recalling the discussion by Frazer in *The Golden Bough*, a work that Lawrence reread only months earlier, of how "ruder races in other parts of the world have consciously employed the intercourse of the sexes as a means to ensure the fruitfulness of the earth". Frazer adds that "the profligacy which attended these ceremonies" is the method by which "the forefathers personified the powers of vegetation as male and female", and that these "charms" of vegetation and flowers served as "an essential part of the rites" (156–57). Lawrence uses this ceremonial context for some provocative counterpoint: the sex that Madame honors between Alvina and Ciccio has more to do with an earthy groping toward existential growth than with any celebration of pastoral germination. Lawrence, in effect, has cleverly enhanced the "essentiality" of the "rites" that Alvina undergoes by including vaginal and anal penetrations within the range of her domination by Ciccio; his notoriously divided attitude toward Frazer's meticulous research emerges here, as Lawrence almost gleefully adds a new dimension to the "profligacy" described by the eminent anthropologist. A dangerous Madame may have set Alvina up to be a defenseless victim of Ciccio's pent-up passion; but she could not have fully anticipated how and why he would use the affair both to escape her control and to rebelliously assert his own manhood and independence. Alvina Houghton continues to justify the state of her connection to Ciccio in terms of an alleged attraction to him caused by the overwhelming beauty of his dark self. Lawrence insists, however, that her inclination to reduce the psychodynamics of her affair to "love" amounts to evidence of the imbalance in the ganglions that he describes in the Whitman essays and in *Psychoanalysis and the Unconscious*.

Ciccio slowly establishes the psychic distance from Madame necessary for breaking the "erroneous connection" cited by Freud (395) and the paralysis mentioned by Lawrence concerning the incest motive. Alvina still retains the "fear of offending Madame", and she is also "only concerned to flatter…the vanity of Madame" (197). The chapter describing the loss of her virginity ends with Alvina still unwilling to accept the "upside" ramifications of *downward* movement into the darkness with Ciccio; even given her strong passion for him, she still thinks of that direction primarily in terms of the class consciousness she learned from her family: "she had really come down in the world", as she sentimentally evokes the images and memories "of her mother and Miss Frost: ladies and noble women both" (209). Yet for all of Alvina's violent entry into the world of passion, and for all the range of such purgative sexual experience she has received from Ciccio, the chapter significantly ends with the casual mention that "her heart burned…with undeniable and unsatisfied love" (209). Perhaps the dissatisfaction results from a lack of orgasmic response; or perhaps it signifies her unconscious recognition that—amid the fury of his desire—she has not fully accepted an erotic episode in which her long-conditioned, mentalized self is virtually extinguished. In that scene Ciccio "numbed her like a venom", as she was "suffocated like a wave", and "she lay inert, as if envenomed" (202). Her experiences, in effect, have provided that "killing" of her mechanical, self-conscious self, but at the cost of no emotional release or cathartic calm for her post-coital soul. Lawrence is under no chauvinistic illusion about the inadequacy of the excitation she has received from Ciccio. Without growth and movement toward the "self-evolving soul", Alvina's sexual experience with him will only amount to a modern version of the "mechanic-material reality" he deplores in *Psychoanalysis and the Unconscious* (38, 41). Yes, the relationship with Ciccio, and the introduction of the coccygeal continuum only *starts* the process of her emergence into Lawrencian womanhood. Lawrence is unequivocal in that study on the issue of growth and maturation through intimate human relations: "It is the circuit of vital flux between itself and another being or beings which brings about the development and evolution of every individual psyche and physique" (4).

Ciccio continues to maintain his dominance over Alvina, and that primacy is evident in one essential area: it is always Ciccio who initiates any form of physical contact between them—and he cannot emerge from the predatory pattern of sexual desire that informed the start of their intense affair. Even the most minor episodes that depict his erotic longing are often integrated by images or body parts that refer to the parameters of the coccygeal continuum. Just before the lovers take the train to Knarborough, "he seemed like some creature that was watching her for his purposes", and his fingers move in the nether direction that stimulates the root *chakra*: "She felt his fingers stroke the nape of her neck and pass in a soft touch right down her back" (211, 212). Feeling more confident as their relationship deepens, Ciccio makes a trivial yet meaningful decision: in defiance of Madame and the other troupe colleagues, he elects to accompany Alvina himself: "I'm going in train with *her*" (212), an assertion of the rebellious self over the expectations of the group that resembles the tone of determination in his decision not to play the role assigned to him in the theatrical vignette. The short train trip itself is a delightful interlude in the novel, a preparation for their more lengthy time together in other trains when they later travel as man and wife through England, France, and Italy.

Through such small gestures of defiance, Ciccio is finding his way as a resourceful suitor and as an independent man; he even rejects the affectionate offer by his friend Geoffrey to accompany him by bicycle to the station. On the train, Alvina confesses her love for him, and for Lawrence that conventional statement has the mechanical sound of its origin in the idealized upper-centers of her consciousness. Ciccio responds with a sensual gesture now familiar to Alvina and to the reader, as he maintains erotic contact by focusing on that same body part that acts as her protector and his gateway: "Beneath the tiny table he took her two knees, and pressed them with a slow, immensely powerful pressure. Helplessly she put her hand across the table to him. He covered it for one moment with his hand, then ignored it. But her knees were still between the powerful living vice [*sic*] of his knees" (215). This scenario repeats the pattern of earlier scenes—not only in his aggressive approach to her knees, but also in her romantic offering of the hand and his quick dismissal of it. "Helplessly" affirms the extent of her instinctual attraction to him and the power of his hold on her. Ciccio must still rely on the exertion of his sexual dominance: for him, that arena remains the most fundamental and effective expression of his developing self-definition as he slowly escapes from Madame's control. Alvina stays in thrall to the darkness he embodies and the darkness he has introduced to her. The inheritor of the staid Midland traditions of Woodhouse, she is now fully committed to the intriguing presence of his profound otherness. The source of his appeal to her is no longer a repressed and dark secret or an unexamined attraction, and Alvina even relishes aspects of its counter-cultural significance: "An outcast! And glad to be an outcast. She clung to Ciccio's dark, despised foreign nature. She loved it, she worshipped it" (215).

But Ciccio remains vulnerable in areas that highlight his ego and sense of a masculine self. Thus both Ciccio's pride in his assumptions of sexual primacy, and the reality of his fragile emotions are reflected in his anger about Alvina's equivocal response to his proposal of marriage. She argues credibly that such a commitment is impossible until the issue of her inheritance reaches some resolution: Alvina believes—partly influenced by Madame's advice—that financial stability is a necessary precondition for her union with Ciccio. He regards such a cautious and practical stance as inconsistent with her expression of deep feeling for him. Ciccio has faith in the sexual bond and believes that their passion *in itself* provides sufficient basis for the marriage. His fury fuels the aggressive sex he initiates against her objections, and the act takes place in the private sanctuary of her late mother's room. It is a location that with its surrounding collection of family mementoes, with its dry and traditional late-Victorian furniture, and with its reminders of the distinctly asexual habits of her prudish and sickly mother—all this ensemble resonates antithetically to the unmodulated passion unleashed by Ciccio on Alvina. The sex is even more intense and willful than their first episode of lovemaking: "recklessly he had his will of her—deliberately, and thoroughly", with that controversial reference to "the broken garments" a clear signature of his frenetic passion (233, 234). This coded language suggests anal intercourse ("taking everything he wanted of her" (233)); as part of the consequence of the coccygeal continuum, the sex function again (for him *and* for her) as a remedial ritual not connected to conventional notions of love, romance, or nurturant sensuality. Lawrence emphasizes in his fiction and non-fiction the innate power of a sexual relationship to liberate, purge, and ultimately transform the respective lovers. The sex in this scene offers an extreme and discomforting example of that transformative potential. Surely the scene remains painful to read. Lawrence's narrative perspective on a virtual rape seems inadequate by any standard today of reasonable consent and shared sexual participation. There is also the implicit sense—so important later in the novel—that Ciccio remains without an additional passion in his life other than Alvina, and for him the coccygeal continuum may provide less of a continuum than a stalled level of erotic expression.

For Alvina, however, the immediate aftermath of the sex provides once again a species of contentment and stability. Lawrence insists on the province of female pleasure illuminated in her exposure to male primacy and purgative coition, as she "snuggled deliciously in the sheets" and is "absurdly happy" (234). But there is still the sense that she understandably stays wary and distant, with the further suggestion that she has held back emotional release and has not achieved satisfactory orgasm: "Why did she still fight so hard against the sense of his dark unseizable beauty" (234)? Although "in love" in deep, dark, and instinctual ways, she cannot fully commit to a life with him. Lawrence is excellent on the circumstantial grounds of her hesitations both in bed and in her doubts about marriage. Humiliated by the formal investigation of the troupe by local authorities, and buffeted by the knowledge from her lawyers that her inheritance amounts to nothing, Alvina cancels the marriage plans and, in effect, ends her relationship with Ciccio. The concluding and strangely understated scene of farewell between them has, oddly, not been noticed by critics. When Alvina reveals to Ciccio her decision to leave him, she informs him of her plans to work as a midwife. After Ciccio expresses surprise that she has such vocational interest and the requisite training, one can only conclude that the lack of verbal exchange and personal discussion throughout their affair must be considered extraordinary. Each knows virtually nothing about the other's background: this significant void will be filled when they later travel as man and wife to Ciccio's native village. While the coccygeal continuum can change these lovers in fundamental ways, its passion cannot as yet bring them beyond the meager quotient of companionability that thus far characterizes their relationship.

VIII

A conspicuous weakness in *The Lost Girl* remains the too casual conclusion of this stage of Ciccio and Alvina's affair. The issue of their union now disappears for nearly fifty pages, with virtually no mention of Ciccio within the lengthy episodes of her vocational experience and her serio-comic engagement to Dr. Mitchell. Ciccio appears to accept her decision to leave him with insufficient objection given the intensity of his passion for her; she also announces her future plans in a manner that belies her strong feelings for Ciccio. The tone here by Lawrence seems not the right key, as if he is planning for their eventual reunion without fully concluding or examining the state of their current connection to each other. The sad and unstated paradox is that Alvina has grown more confident and independent because she has been roused to life by this affair: she now wants to test her acquired freedom and strength in new social and professional settings. Ciccio does not fight for her because he has not fully exorcised his incestuous reliance on Madame and the acting troupe, and he lacks sufficient confidence in his ability to sustain the relationship. When Alvina leaves he slips back to his former life. As much as Alvina has been transformed by Ciccio's unabated passion, she is still defensive and bewildered by her attraction to his inscrutable darkness. The majority of pages immediately after their abrupt breakup is excessively devoted to her peculiar relationship with Dr. Mitchell—an older, insistent, bland, and virginal man who is opposite to Ciccio in every conceivable way. Her return to Ciccio coincides with her evident growth and maturity that she has gleaned through the unhappy interval with Dr. Mitchell and from the formative experiences she absorbs as a midwife. It is the latter capacity that recreates her as a Lawrencian woman ready to return to Ciccio, and Lawrence's handling of her "birth" in the last section of the novel stands as a major accomplishment in its persuasive embodiment of this familiar gestational metaphor.

Lawrence primarily conveys this new maturity in Alvina through "educational" conversations with the affable but distinctly unperceptive Mrs. Tuke; their exchanges prompt Alvina to articulate several essential principles which she frames in emphatically instinctual terms that recall her transformative exposure to the "darkness" of the coccygeal continuum. Note Alvina's pointed responses to Mrs. Tuke, a kindly but unimaginative woman who is perplexed by the power that organic life wields over the willful dictates of the mind. The *uber*-rational Mrs. Tuke cannot fathom how she can get pregnant when "there isn't *one bit* of me wants it" (274). Alvina responds with a pithy and confident assertion of the transcendent power of the unconscious claims of body over mind, as her simple answer, with all its indefinability, is Lawrence's jab at the certainties of science: "Something must want it" (274).[10] Alvina further develops this pattern of

10. At virtually the same time that Lawrence completes *The Lost Girl* (early summer, 1920), Robert Frost publishes the poem "For Once, Then, Something" in *Harper's Magazine.* Thus the American poet initiates the frequent use in his work

belief with two comments to her pregnant patient about the invisible forces that govern mankind: "You should have faith in life," and, "Perhaps life itself is something bigger than intelligence" (282, 283). In *Psychoanalysis and the Unconscious* Lawrence writes of the modern danger that he describes as "the motivizing of the passioned sphere from the ideal", and for him that equals the "final peril of human consciousness" (14). Mrs. Tuke looks for an ideal motivation for her pregnancy, and Alvina functions, in effect, as the guide into the secret, unknowable recesses of the instinctual. Again, Lawrence suggests that Alvina's perspective is directly linked to changes in her catalyzed by her relation to Ciccio and her encounter with his darkness and his sexual energy: "And she submitted to him as if he had extended his dark nature over her. She knew nothing about him. She lived mindlessly within his presence, quivering within his influence, as if his blood beat in her" (290). Her belief in "something". in a force beyond the province of scientific fact and empirical verification, began with the transformation effected by her exposure to the dark and purging power of the coccygeal continuum. Lawrence's insistence here, of course, on female "emergence" stimulated by male sexual passion must remain politically incorrect today, and its dynamic can be reduced, in part, to the projected compensations of Lawrence's unmet needs from Frieda. But for him the insistence is unequivocal: the ultimate maturity that Alvina achieves is initiated by her affair with Ciccio.

Any ambivalence in Alvina about whether to marry Ciccio is eliminated when she responds incisively to the spurious arguments against the marriage given separately by Mrs. Tuke and her husband, Tommy. The

---

of the identical word Lawrence also employs to suggest the inscrutable but distinctly powerful force beyond the self that both writers insist is an individual's responsibility to perceive and embrace. Lawrence and Frost believe that this transcendent connection is sadly increasingly elusive amid modern society's reliance on science and mechanized invention (see Frost's "Mending Wall" and "Take Something Like a Star"—discussed more fully in Chapter Ten of this volume) as the path to progress and contentment. While Lawrence disagrees with aspects of the doctrines and techniques articulated by Frost and other Georgian poets early in the century, he still acknowledges the importance of Edward Marsh's first anthology of their work (see Kinkead-Weekes 130). More significantly, after the war he clearly shares with Frost—evident in Alvina's perspective on the cosmos, and throughout "Education of the People"—the integrated notions of faith in instinctual primacy and in the magical wisdom of nature's eternal cycle. There are moments in the essay that recapitulate the phrasing of Alvina's insight: "To see the pulsation of myriad orbs proudly moving in the endless darkness, insouciant, sunless, taking a stately path we know not whither or how...This is what must happen to us" (EP 136).

latter, a good friend of Ciccio, adamantly opposes the union because of his low opinion of Ciccio's intellect. Mrs. Tuke's objections center around her belief that his lack of money will put Alvina in "a wretched hole" (286)—the metaphor serving for Lawrence as an ironic echo both of Alvina's descent into the mine, and of her affair with Ciccio into the nether domain of the root *chakra*. When Ciccio plaintively moans—with the distinct sound of Lawrence's letters to Rosalind—"come to Italy with me" (286), she still cannot fully agree to his proposal because she cannot totally accept the primal urge that informs his desire for her: "'Why do you want me?' she asks" (287), and he responds by privileging the claims of the unknowable: "I don't know that. You ask me another, eh?" They have sex, and she implicitly accepts his offer of marriage as she yields to the paradox so engrained in his submission to the coccygeal continuum: "Dark and immediate he was; he had no regard for her. How could a man's movements be so soft, and yet so inhumanly regardless?...Somewhere she was content. Somewhere even she was vastly proud of the dark veiled eternal loneliness she felt, under his shadow" (288). That luminous and multi-modified phrase, "dark veiled eternal loneliness", functions both as a summary of the instinctuality and inexplicability of the Lawrencian life-force, and as a prediction of the problems each of them will encounter as they attempt to adjust to marriage, first briefly in England and then in the small and isolated villages of Ciccio's native Italy.

Despite his frustrations with Frieda, Lawrence insists throughout his career that tension is essential for the vitality and growth of the marital union, with the flux of its narrative rhythms an integral component of the partners' individual growth. For Lawrence, the institution of marriage remains especially crucial for a male's ability to feel the transcendent voice of the unknown. The effect of the marriage on Ciccio is noticed quickly by Alvina, and the description sounds much like the emergence of Tom and Will Brangwen after they achieve a level of equanimity in their marriages in *The Rainbow*: "Ciccio really was much handsomer since his marriage. He seemed to emerge…now something unfolded in him, he was a potent, glamorous presence" (289).[11] And while Alvina "lived within his

11. Beyond this emblematic re-iteration of "something" in the description of Ciccio, recall Tom Brangwen's inebriated but strangely profound praise of marriage at Anna's wedding celebration, noted in my Introduction. His encomium to the institution—which has united him to Lydia, and through her opened the path to the Lawrencian "unknown"—relies on Tom's unshakeable belief in that "something" connected to the over-arching force in the cosmos. These crucial lines are worth repeating: "There's very little on earth, but marriage…your soul goes gnawin', gnawin', gnawin', and it says there's something it must have" (128).

aura", and while "she submitted to him as if he had extended his dark nature over her" (290), there are indications of her own discontent. She realizes that "she knew nothing about him", and that "she *knew* she was subjected" (290). These relevant concerns are temporarily mollified when she senses a new form of connection to him that he initiates. It manifests itself, and for the first time, as a nurturant mode of sensuality in Ciccio that finally emerges long after the coccygeal exertions of his more aggressive libido. Indeed, this new aspect of Ciccio's lovemaking provides Alvina with her most satisfying orgasmic response. Her response sounds like the reciprocal and simultaneous sexual climax that Lawrence craves from Frieda: "And he was very good to her. His tenderness made her quiver into a swoon of complete self-forgetfulness, as if the flood-gates of her depths opened. The depth of his warm, mindless, enveloping love was immeasurable" (290). This luminous highpoint of their marriage will not last, as Ciccio brings his wife and his anxieties back to his home amid the Abruzzi mountains.

IX

The chapter, Journey Across, encompassing travel through three countries and by varied forms of transportation, reads as one of the most impressive interludes in all of Lawrence's novels. While the accounts of the lengthy trip cannot follow any strict unity of time, the pace of this relentless travel is slow enough for readers not only to appreciate the transitional landscapes, but also to comprehend the changing moods and priorities of this young man and wife. Lawrence focuses on their volatile feelings as they uninterruptedly pass several days together in this arduous

---

Lawrence, of course, writes these optimistic words in the early passion of his marriage to Frieda, but even in the more problematic period of their relationship as he composes*The Lost Girl*, his affirmation remains evident in his depiction of the commitment between Ciccio and Alvina. In terms of commentary on this issue, Franks is excellent, as her essay on the novel insists that despite the turbulence between Lawrence and Frieda, "he never abandoned his sense that marriage was essential to a worthwhile life" (38). She recognizes that Alvina's link to the beauty of the transcendent "unknown" is tied to the erotic baptism she has received from her lover-husband: "Alvina experiences transports of ecstasy in both her sexual relations and, sometimes, her perception of the spirit of place" (37). Widmer also comments wisely about the significance of Alvina's relation to Lawrence when he describes her transformation as "a sometimes moving fiction of the rebellion and sexual conversion, which was his as well as his heroine's" (30). Ruderman concludes accurately that "Alvina is, in a sense, Lawrence himself" (47).

journey to Ciccio's isolated village. The salient issue during their enforced time together on various trains and ships concerns the contrasting development of emotions in them. The chapter focuses on Alvina's increasing confidence and excitement and on Ciccio's deepening anxiety and depression. He is unable to sustain that sense of calm assurance that he felt immediately after the marriage: he fears that he cannot undertake the responsibilities of a husband given his limited options for finding a reliable vocation and providing a comfortable life for Alvina. His despair is not without a compelling element of poignancy: he finally has his woman as his legal wife, and he can no longer rely on the frenzied dispensations of the dark sensuality that once offered the annealing stimulus and passion for their committed union. Alvina welcomes the challenges of their open-ended future, but an insecure and defensive Ciccio worries whether his wife will tolerate the inevitable privations of rustic life she will encounter. Ciccio feels adrift, and without a tenable vision for their life together. Thus he still tries to use sex as his primary mode of exchange with Alvina, and Lawrence famously believes that such reliance, as *primary* self-definition for a man, must become self-consuming. Less than a year after writing *The Lost Girl*, Lawrence completes *Fantasia of the Unconscious*, a work that expands his attack on Freud and on the "Pisgah" of idealism that pervades modern society. He also develops the earlier notions from *Psychoanalysis and the Unconscious* on the need to achieve a correct balance between the upper and lower *chakra* centers. One passage is painfully appropriate to Ciccio's emotional state as they travel to primitive Pescocalascio and during the months after their arrival: "When a man loses his deep sense of purposive, creative activity, he feels lost, and is lost. When he makes the sexual consummation the supreme consummation, even in his *secret* soul, he falls into the beginnings of despair" (136).

While Ciccio remains withdrawn and anxious during the trip, Alvina continues to mature in the manner most crucial for a Lawrencian character: she is un-intimidated by the vast impersonality of the transcendent "unknown", and she resonates with an appreciative belief in the intrinsic majesty of creation. No sense of programmatic theology or sentimental pantheism here—only the unscientific awe that Lawrence insists is missing from the ever more rationalistic and technologized world. As the train moves through the night on the edge of the Mediterranean, Alvina ponders life in ways that reveal—for all of Lawrence's quarrel with contemporary culture—the essential optimism that frames his visionary doctrines. The refracted narration does not disguise how close her perceptions are to the writer's own perspective:

"She watched spell-bound: spell-bound by the magic of the world itself. And she thought to herself: 'Whatever life may be, and whatever horror men have made of it, the world is a lovely place, a magic place, something to marvel over. The world is an amazing place'" (299). Alvina's mesmerized response simulates the ecstatic state of soul that Lawrence once used to describe her fascination with Ciccio's transformative effect on her through his sexual passion. But now Alvina embodies the next step in the coccygeal continuum, as she illustrates for Lawrence the organic insight that the intimacies of marriage can galvanize in the maturing male and female. Put simply, it frees one to feel the real pulse of the world. She illustrates for Lawrence the organic insight about the resonance of life beyond the confines of self that the erotic intimacies of marriage can galvanize in the maturing male and female. As they near Ciccio's village, she is overwhelmed with her feeling of the transcendent. In a moving and painful scene, Ciccio genuinely attempts to employ warm sensual contact as his primary mode of reaching her. Alvina's insight extends beyond the province of his physical touch, and it also reflects her accurate perception about the gist of his male insecurity. Alvina's estatic perception of the world's magic here resonates profoundly deeper than the simple joy of travel or the innate good nature that is receptive to natural beauty. Her metamorphosis is purgative as well as sensate; in Lawrencian terms it is indirectly related to the emancipating intensity of Alvina's searing experience of sexual passion. The sad irony, of course, is that it also frees her to perceive the self-enclosure of Ciccio's own emotions and awareness. She clearly is not satisfied by the limited framework of her husband's passion, for he seems unable to share the dimensions of her own insight:

> He held her passionately. But she did not feel she needed protection. It was all wonderful and amazing to her. She could not understand why he seemed upset and in a sort of despair. To her there was magnificence in the lustrous stars and the steepnesses, magic, rather terrible and grand (306).

While Ciccio's depressed mood affects the frequency and the intensity of his sexual relations with Alvina, the erotic link between them still exists. But the connection is now also informed by Alvina's increasing maturity and lack of self-consciousness about her emotional needs in their marriage. In their first night at Pancrazio's isolated house, as the cold and darkness descend on her from the surrounding mountains, she feels overwhelmed by the stark and elemental force of the natural landscape. As she anxiously tries to sleep in an uncomfortable bed with inadequate blankets, it is important to note that Alvina—*and for the first time*—takes the initiative concerning sensual desire: she joins Ciccio in the adjacent bed and rouses him to re-establish the link to the darkness that he encouraged earlier in their affair. She is immediately calmed by the powerful contact with him, and the images used by Lawrence intentionally recall key aspects of their initial exposure to the coccygeal continuum. Their passion reflects both the primal effects of the sex, and the male primacy so essential to Lawrence that he currently may lack in his marriage to Frieda: "She felt his power and his warmth invade her and extinguish her. The mad and desperate passion that was in him sent her completely unconscious, again, completely unconscious" (313). But there is that price to be paid in their relationship for the reliance on remedial eros as his primary means of self-definition. Burdened by Ciccio's general passivity, anxiety, and lack of direction, Alvina's feels the weight of Ciccio's depression and limitations: Ciccio "was so silent, there seemed so much dumb magic and anguish in him" (315). The phrase "dumb magic" is evocative here—as if the intrinsic erotic power in him begins to reach her less often amid the increasing prominence of his despair. Alvina experiences not the extinction of the mentalized conditioning that was often exorcised in their sex, but now a claustrophobia caused by his excessive reliance on her, "as if he were forever afraid of himself and the thing he was. He seemed, in his silence, to *concentrate* upon her so terribly. She believed she would not live" (315).

Throughout *The Lost Girl*, Alvina remains resilient and resourceful. She slowly establishes a productive self in Italy apart from Ciccio as she learns a new language and devotes herself to the project of cleaning the house and organizing the chaotic kitchen. Predictably, such compulsive activity only sustains her for several weeks, and soon "even in the sunshine the crude comfortlessness and inferior savagery of the place only repelled her" (319). Ciccio's anxiety increases with his awareness of her discomfort, and that circular pattern of guilt and tension can, notoriously, destroy any marriage. But the dispensations of their initial forays into the realm of the coccygeal continuum still reverberate for Alvina and move her forward to the next stage of their marital intimacy. The essential passion that nurtured their courtship still exists for her—"the same helpless passion for the man" (320). Because it remains a *continuum*, with all the elements of movement and growth, the formative passion is recalled by her in the early stages of her pregnancy. Alvina's enriching perspective on Ciccio is conveyed by Lawrence in a stunning snapshot-in-prose. The writer virtually freezes the action to frame a luminous moment that both recalls this couple's past and evocatively looks to the future. It is

Lawrence at his very best. I quote the passage at length to convey its poetic excellence and its central thematic function in the novel:

> And even as he turned to look for her, she felt a strange thrilling *in her bowels*: a sort of trill strangely within her, yet extraneous to her. She caught her hand to her flank. And Ciccio was looking up for her from the marker beneath, searching with that quick hasty look. He caught sight of her. She seemed to glow with a delicate light for him, there beyond all the women. He came straight towards her, smiling his slow, enigmatic smile. He could not bear it if he lost her. She knew how he loved her—almost inhumanly, elementally, without communication. And she stood with her hand on her side, her face frightened. She hardly noticed him. It seemed to her she was with child. And yet in the whole market-place she was aware of nothing but him (320–21, my emphasis).

This remarkable excerpt moves from their affair's origin to the current state of their marriage—that is, from the deep domain of the root *chakra* in the bowels to the intimations of a baby developing near where her hand resides. The coccygeal origin of their passion exists as mere tremor and ecstatic memory rather than an extant and transformative presence. As Alvina moves to the edge of motherhood, Lawrence includes that valedictory reference to the anal origin of their first sexual encounter as she awaits a baby and he awaits a likely call-up to war. Ciccio is fearful and insecure about his imminent departure, and Alvina is anxious about the prospect of a birth without the presence of her husband. She silently pays the ultimate homage to her man by asking herself two questions that remain central to Lawrence's vision. It is the intimate and inscrutable bond between this man and woman that urges the lovers beyond the enclosure of ego and promises a hint of the transcendent: "What was the terrible man's passion that haunted her like a dark angel? Why was she so much beyond herself" (321)? All of Lawrence's writing engages these questions, and the answers remain the same: the reception of primal darkness leads to the perception of the beyond.[12]

X

In the useful term that Lawrence's friend E.M. Forster employs to describe the authenticity of characters in novels, Lawrence "knows" everything about Ciccio and his masculine but profoundly vulnerable

12. For further relevant discussion on the resonance in Lawrence's fiction of conjoined issues of ego and transcendence, see *The Phallic Imagination,* Chapter Five.

profile. There exists a special empathy between Lawrence and the volatile emotions of Ciccio, and the reason is not hard to fathom: seminal elements of this Italian boy-man's psychology resemble the recurring demons of the older husband from the English midlands who created him. There is little doubt in the last pages of *The Lost Girl* that much of the male primacy that Lawrence desires, and that Ciccio once embodied, is now lost to the Italian and gradually diminishing in the writer within the frustrating dynamics that inform his marriage to Frieda. The resolute female strength and creativity that Alvina has developed throughout the novel has been confirmed and augmented by the timing of her pregnancy—an auspicious event that occurs at the very point in her difficult experiences in Italy when she seemed overwhelmed by isolation and regret. Frieda Lawrence, of course, already has children when she meets Lawrence, and her sense of self at that time remains sufficiently secure (or selfish) to betray her family and aggressively pursue Lawrence, whom she also ultimately will betray. Full of sexual energy and confidence in her easy seduction of him, he happily succumbs to a "devouring mother" at least as willful as Lydia Lawrence. In Italy, it is Alvina who possesses the power, maturity, and the leadership role in all matters, including the issue of Ciccio's likely entrance into the war. As his departure nears, Ciccio has not resolved the damaging effects of his own oedipal connection to Madame; the poignant evidence for this regression resides in his shrunken demeanor and in the apparently decreasing frequency and intensity of his sexual relations with Alvina. Unlike Lawrence's anger and his frequent arguments with Frieda over his need for primacy, Ciccio has retreated into extended silence and a capitulation to his own inner turmoil. Alvina still loves him, but she loses patience with his moodiness and self-imposed isolation. She even notes to herself the split in Ciccio's passional sphere that Freud himself connects to the lingering immaturity in men caused by the incomplete adjustment to their oedipal history. Lawrence's narrative is surely influenced by the Freudian notions he excoriates in *Psychoanalysis and the Unconscious*, as the echo of Ciccio's dialectical pattern of "debasement" and the "sacred and profane" in relation to women, asserts itself once again: "Curious, he was somewhat afraid of her, he half venerated her, and half despised her. When she tried to make him discuss, in the masculine way, he shut obstinately against her, something like a child, and the slow, fine smile of dislike came on his face" (330).

Neither the Lawrence of 1920, nor Ciccio throughout *The Lost Girl*, solves the imposing conundrum of the incest-motive that the novelist highlights in his letter to Mansfield and in his two volumes on the unconscious. Lawrence's angry moods in his prolific correspondence with his closest friends suggest that their ebb and flow are often in direct proportion to the support and/or primacy that Frieda variously gives him or withholds. From the period immediately after the war—encompassing Frieda's major preoccupations over the welfare of her children and her mother—Lawrence is struggling, as he writes *The Lost Girl*, for a manly independence and marital leadership that is (in his mind, if not in fact) under assault from his wife. Yet during this period the novelist makes more progress than Ciccio in achieving a productive stability. Unlike his central character, Lawrence recognizes the dimensions of his problem; he begins to work effectively when Frieda departs during her two extended trips to Germany. Serious illness and impotence remain a few years ahead, and a self-confirming and passionate affair with Rosalind Baynes is only months away. The writing of *The Lost Girl* has no doubt prepared Lawrence to confidently undertake that infidelity in the late summer of 1920. As he nears completion of the novel in May of that year, he writes to Compton Mackenzie in confessional terms that emphasize the work's cathartic and liberating effect on his fractured self. He refers to it as revealing "the crumpled wings of my soul", and adds that it manages "to get me free before I get myself free" (*Letters iii* 522).

Thus, while writing this novel, Lawrence appears to have channeled his discontent with Frieda into a realistic perspective on the greater strength that resides in Alvina and on the prominent weakness evident in Ciccio. By the end of the novel, Alvina has developed into a powerful woman, an empowered wife, and a future mother—in short, an embodiment of Frieda, with the additional quality of unconditional and uncontested support for her husband. But she must deal with a still immature Ciccio, and the necessary life-directives she gives to her worried and pessimistic mate seem more maternal in tone than wifely. Like March in *The Fox*, both women would willingly cede primacy to their mates if only the men would have the courage to take it! So Alvina Houghton firmly recites the mantra of Lawrence's existential faith to a husband who lacks the belief in such organic power: "If you make up your mind to come back, you will come back. We have our fate in our hands" (338). Without essential confidence or an engaged and reliable occupation, Ciccio is roused by his wife to an unpersuasive utterance of "I'll come back", and "be damned to them all" (338). Not one of the principals here—Ciccio, Alvina, and Lawrence—is convinced of Ciccio's chances or his self-belief.

Given the antagonistic state of Lawrence's relationship to Murry and Mansfield as he writes *The Lost Girl*, and in the context of the psychological thematics and graphic sex in the novel, it is not surprising that the reaction of these ex-friends to the novel is vitriolic and uncomprehending. Murry hyperbolically asserts that "Alvina and Ciccio become for us like grotesque beasts" (*Athenaeum* 836), and Mansfield similarly describes the characters as "mindless", and as "animals on the prowl". She further writes, with unintentional insight in her diary, about some "dark secret" (Mansfield *Scrapbook* 156–57) in the work that remains central to her revulsion. The dark secret, of course, that she can sense but not identify, involves the thematic and imagistic nexus of the novel: Lawrence's insistence on the transformative potential in lovers of intense sexual passion, and more precisely, on coition of the coccygeal kind as a purging, emblematically *dark* "root" that accelerates such intrinsic change. There is also, perhaps, an unacknowledged awareness in Mansfield of Lawrence's propensity for provocative touches of *roman à clef* in his fiction. She is cognizant of his use of friends and enemies in his work, and she understands that Lawrence has long maintained that her relationship with Murry lacks any potential for supportive passion, much less transcendence. Lawrence has unequivocally suggested to her that she needs to look for a more manly, reliable, and sexually secure man, and he went so far in his advice (in some remarkably sublimated negative capability) to tell her to stop playing the role of mother to Murry's child.[13]

In 1914, Mansfield writes revealingly in her diary: "I do not trust Jack…I wish I had a lover to [nurse] me, love me, hold me, comfort me, *to stop me thinking*" (*Journal* 61, my emphasis). Recall how such stoppage occurs for Alvina precisely when she is introduced by Ciccio to the darkness of the coccygeal continuum. Mansfield has an affair in 1915 with

13. See Kinkaid-Weekes (470–580) for more detailed discussions of various developments in Lawrence's relationship to Murry, and especially 559–64 for a more focused concern with issues about Murry relevant to my essay. Darroch recently published some provocative research on the connection between Mansfield and the characterization of Alvina, ultimately concluding too definitively that it is Mansfield whom "he portrayed as Alvina Houghton in *The Lost Girl*" (6). She demonstrates several interesting connections, but her conclusion tends to ignore other circumstances, influences, and creative stimuli for Lawrence's memorable character. Worthen refers to a contemporary and distinctly unappreciative review of the novel by Virginia Woolf in which she describes Lawrence as one for whom "'the problems of the body' were 'insistent and important': sex for Lawrence, she wrote 'had a meaning for which it was disquieting to think that we too might have to explore'" (*Times Literary Supplement* 2 December 1920, in Worthen, *Life of an Outsider*, 236). Woolf surely is correct in her understanding of what remains important to Lawrence, and he is no doubt unsurprised at her typically Bloomsbury revulsion at the seminal insistence throughout his work that sexual relations carry special meaning for the human condition.

the French poet, Francisco Carco, but this brief fling does not stop her from returning to Murry and continuing in her role as mother-lover. Murry's well-chronicled inability to adequately integrate love and sex in his neurotic attachment to her offers a graphic example of those issues of the sacred and the profane theorized by Freud, illustrated by Ciccio, and enacted by Lawrence in his complex life with Frieda. But the story of Mansfield's response to Murry and to *The Lost Girl* becomes even more intriguingly entangled. In late 1914 she happens to read in Murry's "little red book" about an instance when "he had told Campbell" that he didn't know whether Mansfield was "more to me than a gratification" (*Journal* 58, 61). So she discovers six years before *The Lost Girl* what Lawrence might consider Murry's dirty little secret of his childish and narcissistic sexuality. But the precise components of the more crucial secret—the dark secret of the coccygeal continuum—neither Mansfield nor Murry can decipher. For Lawrence, Ciccio, and Alvina that *chakra* means more than mere gratification: it is the route to maturity and transcendence—a journey initiated by the Italian, but characteristically completed by his stronger and more confident wife.

CHAPTER TWO

DEPRESSION AND RENEWAL AT THE BORDER-LINE: BALDER, HEMINGWAY, AND *THE CAPTAIN'S DOLL*

To achieve his own soul's wholeness and integrity is the life-work of every man.

—D.H. Lawrence, *Fantasia of the Unconscious*

Things might not be immediately discernible inwhat a man writes and in this sometimes he is fortunate, but eventually they are quite clear.

—Ernest Hemingway, to the Swedish Academy

So exact is the resemblance of the manikin to the man, in other words, of the soul to the body…

—James Frazer, *The Golden Bough*

The loss of a love-object is an excellent opportunity for the ambivalence in love-relationships to make itself effective and come into the open.

—Sigmund Freud, "Mourning and Melancholia"

I

Sustained commentary on D.H. Lawrence's *The Captain's Doll* essentially began more than fifty years ago with F.R. Leavis's extolling and extensive essay on the novella, which he first published amid his innovative series of *Scrutiny* articles on Lawrence, and then reprinted with revisions in his pioneering, full-length study of the writer in 1955.[1] Leavis views the work as a supreme example of Lawrence's genius at demonstrating "a sure rightness of touch in conveying the shifts of poise and tone that

1. Leavis also published a major essay on *The Captain's Doll* in his 1976 book, *Thoughts, Words, And Creativity: Art and Throught in Lawrence*, 92–121.

define an extremely delicate complexity of attitude" (*D.H. Lawrence: Novelist* 197). Such praise for the subtle changes in character development and narrative perspective in this fiction reflect nothing less than "the range of a truly great dramatic poet" (198), and his strong endorsement of *The Captain's Doll* has evolved in the academic community into the consensus judgment—with which I agree—of Lawrence's considerable success in this short novel. While later critics find many reasons for praise of its achievement, they generally convey minimal support for Leavis's confident formulation of its central theme, which he defines as Hannele's "*éducation sentimentale*" during her affair with Captain Hepburn, a process concluding with a "*dénouemont*" that amounts to her "tacit recognition of her own deepest desire or need" (202–03) to finally accept the distinctly partisan terms for marriage proposed by her lover. The subject of marriage is both elusive goal and persistent torment in this work.

In no way does Leavis's discussion ignore or underestimate the impressive wit, energy, and independence manifested by the Countess, even comparing aspects of her strength and feistiness to the intriguingly similar traits in Lawrence's talented and often non-compliant wife.[2] But he still regards Hannele's capitulation as dramatically credible in the context of her recent love-life and as admirably consistent with Lawrence's visionary doctrines in the postwar years. Much of the criticism after Leavis variously questions the persuasiveness of Hannele's acquiescence to Hepburn's demands, disagrees with the implications of Lawrence's sexual politics, or counter-asserts the ultimate primacy of Hannele's corrective

2. Among other critics who have noted compelling aspects of similarity between the Hepburn-Lawrence and Hannele-Frieda relationships, see Spilka, *Renewing the Normative D.H. Lawrence* 248–75 and Kinkead-Weekes 686–89. In a study of the Lawrence courtship and marriage, Squires and Talbot, in writing about *The Captain's Doll*, note "its biographical resonances are richly disguised" (244), as "Lawrence imagines ways of freeing himself from Frieda for a different kind of relationship" (245). Mehl's Introduction to the Cambridge edition of *The Captain's Doll* also provides precise dates and details on the fact that "the second half of the tale evidently grew out of Lawrence's experiences at Thumersbach and in Germany" (xxiv). In his compelling single-volume published biography of Lawrence, John Worthen further confirms that the Lawrences' visit to Austria "provided the setting…for the second part" of *The Captain's Doll* (232). He revealingly describes Lawrence during the period as "setting his house in order" (253), and this summary judgment of the novelist's life and art remains even more pertinent to my approach, as Worthen maintains that this fiction "brilliantly dramatizes both Hepburn's longing for a new kind of relationship and what he is up against, in himself and in Hannele" (254).

influence on the Captain.[3] The latter approach has had strong support in recent years, as it offers a clear if not wholly convincing way to understate

3. Most of the excellent criticism on the novella contributes solid evidence on the energetic role played by Hannele in questioning and engaging Hepburn's real, and his merely rhetorical, demands, and Leavis also recognizes these crucial qualities in her characterization. But in the last two decades there has existed a greater reluctance by critics to unequivocally assert the extent to which Hepburn's developing ideology reflects the largely *unqualified* extent of Lawrence's own masculinist emphasis in the work. Among those critics willing to state the clarity of the male-leadership component of *The Captain's Doll*, Rossman understands that the *dénouemont* reflects "Lawrence's increasingly uncompromising tough mood" (296) in regard to the issue of male and female primacy. Ruderman usefully summarizes the conflict between the characters by noting that Hannele essentially yields to the "new relationship that Hepburn chooses", a union that "demands her honor and obedience and refuses her possessiveness" (89–90). Gilbert is correct in her basic argument that "female creative power is more bitterly described and it is definitively defeated" (151), but she seems less aware of the urgencies and weaknesses of Hepburn's psychological state. Mellown intelligently regards Hepburn as developing into a "dominant male" (228), as he contrasts the development of the Captain from "the somewhat epicene young German lieutenant" (227) in the "The Mortal Coil", an earlier story written before the war that is dramatically revised to create *The Captain's Doll*. Harris's comprehensive and valuable study in 1988 of Lawrence's short fiction initiates a change in emphasis that I define as a relative unwillingness to acknowledge the extent to which Lawrence effectively stacks the doctrinal cards in favor of Hepburn. She may be too equitable in her judgment that "credits both sides" (161) in their headstrong battle during the excursion, and she is not convincing in her belief that the novella is "male supremacist" only "in the most qualified of terms" (284). Similarly, while McDowell correctly notes that the end of the work dramatizes how "the subordination of the women signifies patriarchal domination", he undercuts the clarity of that statement with his unpersuasive assertion that "the need to attain a star-equilibrium, as Birkin propounds it in *Women In Love,* is never quite obliterated in Lawrence's furtherance of patriarchal values" (156). Spilka overstates the ultimate effectiveness of Hannele's entertaining and spirited opposition when he reaches the faulty, too clever conclusion that "it is through Hannele's shrewdly critical eyes that we come to judge the Captain's fallibility" (260)—a problematic assertion given the extent of her capitulation to him in the final scene. Martin is also over-praising of Hannele's effective power when he asserts that "Hannele's criticism is largely responsible for the great change in Hepburn" (19), an argument that underplays the instinctual insight and courage that Hepburn manifests on his own. Doherty, with his reductive categorization of *The Captain's Doll* as an amusing satire, regards Hannele's submission at the end as merely "subversive" (15), as he believes that it reflects how the allegedly parodic implications of the text undercut any invested notion by Lawrence in the doctrine of male supremacy.

the praise for a brilliant novella that presents an uncomfortable problem for many readers today: the work is unapologetically infused with a patriarchal ethic that finally achieves a strong measure of victory in its dramatized battle between the sexes. Many critics search for grounds to praise the novella by somehow denying the fact of its masculinist bias. Among the most extreme versions of invested attempts to diminish the authority of Hepburn and enhance the stature of Hannele, Mark Spilka wonders if the Captain killed his wife to eliminate the major complication of his passionate connection to the impatient Countess.[4]

Related to this growth in revisionist discussions of the work is the increasing tendency to emphasize its comedic aspects, an approach that often highlights a comment made by Lawrence, in a letter written by him as he nears completion of the novella, that *The Captain's Doll* is "a very funny long story" (*Letters IV* 109).[5] Despite interesting attempts to buttress

---

4. On the simple level of important circumstantial evidence, there is little ground to maintain that murder is even a possibility here. Lawrence has supplied a solid rationale that supports the conclusion that it was an accident. Mrs. Hepburn lost her balance near an open window when she unwisely reached beyond the sill for "a certain little camisole" (109) she was drying. The petty and materialistic wife loves her fancy garments, and we later learn of the danger she foolishly risked by ignoring her own phobias: "She could never bear even to look out of a high window. Turned her ill instantly if she saw a space below her. She used to say she couldn't look at the moon; it made her feel as if she would fall down a dreadful height" (110). In addition, there is the interesting evidence of some "coincidence" of preoccupation as Lawrence writes *The Captain's Doll*. An accidental fall from the heights must have been on his mind during the composition of the work; here is the premonition of Mrs. Hepburn's fate in a letter Lawrence writes to Earl Brewster in the days before he completes the novella, describing the mother of his landlord at Fontana Vechia: "She leans on the parapet of our balcony–spaventata [frightened]—terrified of the ghost of her poor dead Beppe" (*Letters IV* 109).

5. Doherty writes—insensitively and wrongly, in my view—of "the comic death of Hepburn's wife" (9), and in his sustained counter-response to Leavis's approach, he expresses surprise that virtually anything in this novella "should be treated by critics at an exclusively serious level" (5). Rossman describes the "charm and humor" (296) in the work, Mellown notes its wealth of "comic assertiveness" (227), Harris describes the excursion as a "comic, holiday jaunt" (160) to the glacier, and Gilbert considers the doll as merely a "playful miniature effigy" (152), harmless in its intent. Each of these critics, when getting beyond the allegations of comic texture or satirical intent in the work, conveys considerable insight about Lawrence's art. But as my own approach to the novella indicates, I regard *The Captain's Doll* as highly serious in its essential tone and doctrinal meaning; its visionary intensity results in part from Lawrence's unflinching view of postwar devastation reflected in the soul of Captain Hepburn and in the culture depicted in

this letter with analyses of allegedly humorous moments in the work, Lawrence's comment must be examined from the perspective of the fiction's more pronounced texture of pained reflection on doctrinal and personal issues of high importance to him. Lawrence's famous admonition to trust the tale and not the novelist must take precedence over his circumstantial musings about intentionality and effect. He uses the wording "very funny" in the same letter in which he announces his struggle to find a satisfactory conclusion for *The Captain's Doll*: as I later note in this essay, a concluding interlude of an awkward and comic argument between characters may provide an agreeable option to facilitate the ending of this fiction, but it should in no way be regarded as stipulative of the primary tone in the work. It is distinctly the sober design of the marriage matrix that is center-stage here—enacted both in the fiction and in Lawrence's turbulent life.

As Leavis's essay, in its meticulous reading of the intonations of dialogue and the resonance of symbols and themes, suggests, Lawrence's novella in many ways recapitulates relevant issue of pain, suffering, and dominance reflected in his volatile marriage to Frieda; similarly, as Mark Kinkead-Weekes so carefully outlines in his biographical research, *The Captain's Doll* also embodies Lawrence's ideological shifts from the 1915–18 period to the "leadership" phase of his career after the war. Both Lawrence and Hepburn search for forms of renewal in their middle age, and each confronts aspects of emotional and "situational" malaise in attempts to revitalize their respective selves. The excessive search for comedic elements also deflects attention from the heavy weight of postwar discomfort that Lawrence documents in the novella with a persistence and poignancy not yet acknowledged in the abundant criticism on the work. While it is true that Hannele establishes an *ur*-feminist counter-voice that is formidable enough to spar effectively with the masculinist doctrines channeled through Hepburn, Leavis's fundamental insistence more than a half-century ago about the persuasive art of Hannele's "*éducation*" may be politically incorrect today, but it remains an accurate reading of this impressive, and not so funny, fiction.

It is not a case, however, of a confident Captain overwhelming his woman with the word-made-flesh. In my reformulation of Leavis's approach, Hepburn must manifest the courage to recover his manly pride so he can convince himself and Hannele of the winning authority of his

---

the work. In this regard, Kinkead-Weekes is characteristically impressive in his detailed description of the "postwar malaise" so crucial to the novella, and in his concern with the adamantly "somber undertone" that informs the conflict between Hepburn and Hannele (687).

message of male-primacy on love and marriage. No critic has sufficiently focused on this crucial process of the reconstruction of Hepburn's ego and energy. [6] It is a transformation best understood first in the light of psychological changes and idiosyncrasies in the major characters, and then in the context of Lawrence's adaptation of a well-known Scandinavian mythology to frame key aspects of the symbology and action in the novella. In *Studies in Classic American Literature*, a work that he is still intermittently revising as he writes *The Captain's Doll*, Lawrence provides, in effect, a concise explanation for his deft integration of theme and technique in the novella: "True myth concerns itself centrally with the onward adventure of the integral soul" (65). Thus it is the careful anatomy of Hepburn's "integral soul" that must precede the evocation of the myth, as Lawrence initiates the depiction of the Captain's "onward adventure" with a *tour de force* of Aristotelian technique to start the novella.

II

The opening scene of *The Captain's Doll* is over ten pages long, and Lawrence choreographs its intersecting movements of exits and entrances by imposing a strict unity of time, place, and action. This lengthy vignette, enacted as a form of witty parlor drama, functions not only to establish the relevant circumstances of Hepburn and Hannele's relationship, but also to suggest the dominant emotions of depression and anger that inform the characterizations, respectively, of the two lovers who are the central actors in the work. Lawrence constructs these initial pages with scrupulous

---

6. There are several notable exceptions to this pattern of insufficient focus on Hepburn's development. Martin is persuasive in commenting on Hepburn's growth from his "flaccidity" (20) at the beginning of the novella. Mellown intriguingly compares aspects of Lawrence's early version of the work, "The Mortal Coil", to *The Captain's Doll*, and he effectively argues that "the change between the 1913 Lieutenant and the 1921 Captain mirrors the development of Lawrence's understanding of male and female identity and the ideal relationship between them", as a "weak man" grows into the dominant male (227). Gurko, in an abbreviated analysis, also describes Hepburn's growth in confidence, independence, and selfhood. In his second book on Lawrence, Leavis correctly maintains that "it is the *Captain* mainly who changes for us" in the course of the novella (95). More recently, Granofsky wisely refers to Hepburn's relation to the mountain excursion as a "process of proving his fitness" (61). But this passing remark is not sufficiently developed to suggest the demanding extent and emotional urgency of this "proof" that Hepburn has put upon himself. Granofsky fails to consider the trek as the courageous commitment I describe, as he notes that "his entire performance on the excursion is childish, not to say infantile" (71).

attention to precise detail and delicate nuance, as even a casual gesture, passing remark, or decorous object in the room conveys valuable signals about the current status of their affair. The novella abruptly begins *in medias res,* as a defiant and preoccupied Hannele does not even bother to lift her head from her adjustments on the completed doll, only "curtly" (75) acknowledging the presence of her friend, Mitchka: Hannele's focus is directed at gleefully dressing the little manikin that she has created as an ingenious form of revenge for Hepburn's pattern of inattention to her awkward status as his mistress and for his persistent lack of formulated plans for their future. Indeed, her delight in such professional handicraft extends to her momentary use of the doll to ridicule, in Mitchka's presence, the proud Captain with whom she is so intensely involved: by ceremoniously holding the doll "head downwards" with its "arms wildly turned out" (75), she reveals Hepburn's body in a conspicuously undignified posture that mockingly reveals his private anatomy to the reader and to her gossipy friend. As this scene later confirms, Mitchka emanates—in a marvelously oxymoronic phrase—"a roguish coyness" (75), amounting to an odd blend of erotic assertiveness combined with a nagging fear about her vulnerable position as a close friend of an outspoken German woman who is the paramour of a Scottish captain in the occupying British army.

Mitchka now questions the propriety of Hannele waiting alone in Hepburn's own attic apartment for his delayed return. She worries that any public display of displeasure by the Captain directed at Hannele could lead to admonishing publicity resulting in the deportation of the two women. Mitchka's timidity is contrasted to Hannele's fierce independence and confidence ("why should I be [afraid]?" 77), and such a defining fearlessness in the Countess remains evident throughout the work. Mitchka's anxieties, however, do not moderate her sexual energy or voyeuristic excitement. She approvingly notices the attractive legs of the doll, and she presumptuously asks her friend if the Captain's limbs are really as sexy as those on the model. It is also an apparently jaded Mitchka who expresses a lack of enthusiasm about her own current lover when she answers Hannele's simple question with the demeaning comment, "only Martin" (76), referring to the entrance of a man who seems more committed to their affair than she, as Martin "much more intimately touched Mitchka's hands with his lips" (76).

As for Mitchka's lover, the awkwardly ignored Martin—an attractive and defeated officer manifesting a firm military demeanor—it is noteworthy that "one could see the war in his face" (77). Thus appears the first explicit reference in the novella to the lingering, destructive effect of the Great War on the men who survived. In this sense, Lawrence's short novel serves as a reminder that "the lost generation" remains as applicable to the winning and losing soldiers stationed in the Rhineland in 1921 as it more famously applies to the expatriates and artists on the Left Bank of Paris so memorably recalled by Hemingway. This novella conveys a wider scope of socio-cultural authority than is generally acknowledged, as it dramatizes the lingering damage to the personal life and the inevitable fracturing of emotional stability occasioned by the First World War. Within this devastated milieu in Europe from 1918–1923—with uninjured, stable, and "eligible" men at a distinct minority—the prospects remain dim for women to find a suitable mate, or even credibly "renew" the vows of marriage disrupted by the war. In many parts of Europe divorce rates rose more than 100% in 1920 (Chester 138). Although the Captain is not injured in the intimate and catastrophic manner of Jake Barnes in *The Sun Also Rises*, his own marriage and love-live are clearly in a shambles.[7]

Mitchka may have an aristocratic title but she has become neurotic in her excessive anxiety over the unpredictable or the unfamiliar: she feels discomforted by what she alleges is Hepburn's strange and indefinable difference from other men, a quality in his temperament that agitates her to the point of unwarranted fear. The aura of mystery in the Captain is even embodied architecturally by the isolate location of his attic apartment and adjoining roof, which "seemed high, remote, in the sky" (78). This quality of his self-imposed distancing and aloofness and its accompanying traces of chronic indecisiveness and perplexity represent for Hannele a major aspect of his sexual allure, an attractive inscrutability that she contemplates several times in the work. In his 1925 essay "Love Was Once A Little Boy", briefly cited by Leavis in his discussion of *The Captain's Doll*, Lawrence asserts a view of human character that might suggest why Hannele's passion for him is based on her accurate perception of his unorthodox demeanor: "If we were men, if we were women, our individualities would be lonely and a bit mysterious" (342). The Countess will be variously enraged and charmed by Hepburn's often inexplicable motivation, peculiar moodiness, and disturbing incapacity for action, but she will never lose her essential infatuation with him.

---

7. McDowell keenly comprehends the general relevance of this event for Lawrence's novella, as he notes that "the psychic and intellectual dislocation engendered by the Great War animated both the nonfiction and the fiction of Lawrence's leadership phase from about 1919 to 1925" (143). He does not examine, however, the evidence of the war's precise effect on Hepburn's body and spirit. Kinkead-Weekes avoids such omission when he insists on the relation of character types in the novella to Lawrence's careful depiction in *The Captain's Doll* of "nihilism in a post-war collapse of values" (687).

Hepburn is unusually late in his return to the apartment, and Hannele is angry about his tardiness as well as the increasingly tense and unresolved nature of their affair. In a superb, two-minute interlude that demonstrates Lawrence's skill in dramatizing the intricacies of emotion by capturing her silent gestures and random movements, Hannele now reveals the intensity of her connection to the Captain even as she provides evidence of her accumulated discontent:

> She went to the table and looked at his letter-clip with letters in it and at the sealing wax and his stamp-box, touching things and moving them a little, just for the sake of contact, not really noticing what she touched. Then she took a pencil, and in stiff Gothic characters began to write her name—Johanna zu Rassentlow—time after time her own name—and then once, bitterly, curiously, with a curious sharpening of her nose: Alexander Hepburn (78).

Note the surfacing of her unselfconscious possessiveness, tinged with cutting vindictiveness—all reflected in her purposeful displacement of the objects she touches. There also exists that reality about her love-life that she cannot deny: Hannele's passionate feelings for Hepburn are emphasized in her compulsive need for physical contact with the items that belong to him. Even the words that she writes reveal her inability to get beyond the ego-defenses of her own anger. Again in "Love Was Once A Little Boy", Lawrence writes admonishingly of humanity's all too common habit of relying on "the dreary individuality of ego" (341), and Hannele documents this inclination as she inscribes *her own name* "time after time," and then (only "once" and "bitterly") the name of the Captain. No romantic digressions for her, no desire amid her displeasure to wistfully combine her first name with Hepburn's last name in playful contemplation of unlikely legal union someday with her lover. With the notable exception of *Women in Love*, in no other fiction of Lawrence is the thematics of the marriage matrix so infused with sudden shifts in tone and "temperament"—a volatility that encompasses elements of the obsessive, poignant, passionate, irate, and comedic. In that same essay by Lawrence —a work that strangely reads as a direct gloss on *The Captain's Doll* four years earlier—Lawrence pertinently describes ego as a "doll-like entity", a "manikin" made into its "ridiculous likeness" to the real individual (345). The interconnections between this totemic doll and the defensive mechanism of ego—as it works in Hannele *and* Hepburn—will function as a major theme in the novella. A version of the omnipresent incubus doll, whether as a manikin, newspaper picture, or painting, will accompany the lovers from the Rhineland, to Munich, and to the Tyrol.

III

While she continues to peruse Hepburn's room, Hannele passes his large telescope and "stood for some minutes with her fingers on the barrel" (78)—an oddly extended interlude ("some minutes" seems grotesquely long!) that in such prolonged intimacy of contact appears admiringly phallic and angrily aggressive at the same time. She shows no inclination to look beyond the limits of self by peering through the telescope to the Lawrencian version of the transcendent unknown: with the sounds of Hepburn's entrance, she relies on her self-protective habits as she quickly "picked up her puppet when she heard him on the stairs" (78). As a thoroughly "modern woman" who embodies some of the mannerisms that Lawrence criticizes in the essay, she uses the doll to vent her anger by making him, for the moment, "cut off like a doll from any mystery" ("Love Was Once" 346). When Hepburn energetically greets her, Hannele glances at him but purposely does not respond. To the degree that such awkward silence from her does not faze the courteous Captain, it seems likely that he has encountered such strategic pouting from her on other occasions. Yet even given her passive-aggressive temperament so memorably charted in this foundational opening scene, Hannele's dependency on the doll for petty vengeance on Hepburn must be considered in the light of the extenuating circumstances of her predicament: she is the committed and monogamous lover of a prominent and married member of a victorious military force that understandably has established certain guidelines for the personal conduct of the citizens of a defeated country. Displaced in her own land, disconnected from the perquisites of her aristocratic lineage, and marginalized in her semi-clandestine affair, Hannele also must be considered a distinct casualty of the war. When Hepburn explains that his lateness was caused by the troubling notification of his wife's discovery of the Captain's ongoing affair with an unnamed woman, he too calmly explains to Hannele that notions of decorum require his attempt to mollify his wife's displeasure by joining her at the hotel for a month. He appears relatively undisturbed by the pretense and hypocrisy that support these convenient plans for expedient restitution with his wife. For legitimate and for self-serving reasons, Hannele is outspoken about the outlandishness of his strategy and the offensive aloofness of his demeanor. Hepburn comes across as a dim and troubled figure here, despite his statement of tentative plans. He remains less bothered by the peculiarity of his marital relationship than by his own chronic and disturbing inability to articulate any confident decision about his future with Mrs. Hepburn or with Hannele; he mumbles a disconcerting series of "I don't know" (82) phrases when Hannele pushes him to develop a sensible blueprint for his life in the months and years ahead.

Such a profound lack of assertiveness and direction from Hepburn—and from a military man, no less, who is trained to command—serves as the earliest symptom in the novella of his considerable fatigue and emotional malaise after the war. He even painfully acknowledges how "tired" he is, a contrast to Hannele and her energetically "bitter" (81) feelings about the state of their affair. The Captain also suffers the indignity of admitting to his mistress that he hasn't made up his mind what to do, a meek and selfish admission not likely to calm an already distraught and embattled Hannele. Although it is evident that he lacks any compelling desire for ongoing connection with his wife and children, he is without the energy and spirit to change the status quo in a more permanent manner. He tellingly refers to his offspring as "her two children" (82)—not an openly antagonistic comment, but one uttered by a palpably wounded and sleepwalking soldier of middle-age who moves "uneasily" and "with a vacant darkness on his brow" (82).

Amid his lethargy and unhappiness, the Captain still retains a full measure of sexual interest in Hannele, and he wants to make love to her that night—a desire not unrelated, of course, to his need to mollify her displeasure over his general passivity. In the following exasperated utterance, he combines erotic desire with the signature of a downcast nihilism that he memorably asserts with a god-like indifference to all that surrounds him: "Nothing in time or space matters to me" (84). It is a line that will resonate throughout *The Captain's Doll* and will take on mythic significance as the fiction develops. Hepburn's hybrid identity of both a wounded man on earth and an oddly vulnerable deity will function as a key thematic element and as an important guide to the condition of his soul. In John Vickery's impressive study of the literary impact of *The Golden Bough*, he writes that Lawrence's "mythopeic vision [is] grounded" in substantial measure in the figurative patterns of Frazer's monumental volume, and that this pattern often reveals itself by way of "a dual level on which the characters are operant: as human beings with roots in Lawrence's own experience and as mythical figures" who are used by him to "define the incarnation of qualities and actions otherwise inexplicable to mankind" (294). Lawrence has not yet revealed in this novella the myth that he will employ to explain the complexities and urgencies of the Captain's emotions and actions. Thus this extraordinary opening scene concludes with a dichotomous Hepburn initiating sex with an annoyed but still responsive Hannele, the woman who receives the advances of a man who seems only partly human: "He kissed her with half-discernible, dim kisses, and touched her throat…it was all like a mystery to her, as if one of the men from Mars were loving her" (84).

The Captain's aggravating qualities of indecision and aloofness are immediately evident when Hannele accosts him on the roof as he examines the moon and stars through the telescope. Here, Hepburn briefly appears to sense a seminal Lawrencian notion he will feel more fully during his later climb in the Tyrolese Mountains: the imperative need to transcend the limitations of self as the only way to break the bonds of his selfish, ego-enclosed solipsism. But Hannele's lack of interest in the transcendent is revealed again when she refuses his offer to briefly glance through the impressive lens. His mood in this meeting with her seems resigned, fatigued, and conspicuously unhappy. Hepburn fully realizes that his pleasure in the relationship with Hannele is now complicated by his wife's interference and threats, by the persistence of Hannele's anger, by the increasing awareness of the authorities concerning his extra-marital affair, and by the heavy burden of his own palpably deepening, postwar depression. His only escape is through the telescope as he surveys the quiet majesty of the firmament, and in his need for this available recourse he anticipates the crux of a highly confessional passage from an essay Lawrence will write in a few years, "The Real Thing". These are the relevant lines from this evocative article, originally published just after Lawrence's death, in *Scribner's Magazine* in June 1930:

> What makes life good to me is the sense that even if I am sick and ill, I am alive to the depth of my soul, and in touch, somewhere in touch with the vivid life of the cosmos. Somehow my life draws strength from the depths of the universe…It is when men lose their contact with this eternal life-flame, and become merely personal, things in themselves, instead of things kindled in the flame, that the fight between men and women begins (310).

Note how the essay also encompasses the "objectification" motif ("things in themselves") that Hannele has introduced by her controversial creation of the doll.

In the ensuing conversation between them about how Hepburn will handle the interference from his wife, he admits—to the consternation of Hannele—that he will rejoin Mrs. Hepburn the next day, The Captain also matter-of-factly grants to Hannele that he now must make love to his wife, describing the duty as a form of connubial obligation that he doesn't mind "if it's only for a short time" (93)—referring, I must presume, to the frequency of the love making rather than the duration of the act. As an understandably stupefied Hannele contemplates both Hepburn's plans for this prostitution of his passion and the idiosyncratic passivity of his reactions, she thinks once more of the odd doubleness of her man, that he is "not to be regarded from a human point of view" (94): it is a notion that seems even more persuasive when he further asserts in his characteristic tone of mournful resignation that "I don't count" and "one matters so very little" (94). His perspective here resonates with the symptoms of clinical depression, and his nihilistic view of the integrity of the self is profoundly antagonistic to Lawrence's normative insistence throughout his career on the sanctity of each human being's life: it is a sanctity Lawrence proudly describes in *Fantasia of the Unconscious,* completed just a few weeks before he writes *The Captain's Doll*, as "the I am I", a being "set utterly apart and distinguished from all that is the rest of the Universe" (80). Hannele finally responds to Hepburn's pathetic self-abnegation with the thought about his paradoxical self that she earlier contemplated: "Was this a man?" (94).

When Mrs. Hepburn meets with Hannele for a second time, the wife's substantial cleverness, as well as her major flaws of character are evident in this exuberant and subtle scene. She deftly uses the strained conversation to manipulate Hannele and the beleaguered Hepburn, the latter performing as an obedient pawn by doing his wife's calculated bidding in the little playlet she has arranged for the benefit of Hannele. In the wife's zeal to bring up the issue of the Captain's infidelity, she latches on to the metaphor of the undependable teapot as a handy expression of the husband's unreliability. But it is Lawrence who conveys the more accurate perspective, as he writes that the deceptive woman "manipulated the tea-pot, and lit the spirit-flame, and blew it out, and peeped into the steam of the teapot" (96). Mrs. Hepburn also develops the trope in her caustic remarks to Hannele: "I don't know what it's made of—it isn't silver, I know that—it is so heavy in itself it's deceived me several times already. And my husband is a greedy man, a greedy man" (96). Her vindictive strategy is to diminish her husband's dignity in front of Hannele, a tactic she accomplishes both by making him look obsequious in the trivial errands she assigns him, and—more important for her real goal!—making him seem ludicrous in the stories she tells Hannele about the outlandishly sentimental statements he allegedly made to her early in their marriage. Mrs. Hepburn foolishly believes that Mitchka is her husband's mistress, and thus she hopes that Mitchka will inform Hannele about the pathos of the Captain's undying dedication to the marriage.

This voluble and insistent wife also employs a transparent rhetoric of extenuation to explain away her husband's current affair. Mrs. Hepburn takes the position that his "little slip" (97) is directly related to the damaging effect of war on the psyche of soldiers—"it's had a terribly deteriorating effect on the men" (97). She thus conveniently rationalizes his submission to temptation in this atmosphere of emotional dislocation—"there's hardly one man left the same as he was before the war" (97)—and the only expedient requirement she demands is never to find out about his infidelity. Lawrence creates a special irony here that has significance for the individual "case" of Hepburn and Hannele as well as for the general culture of the time: Mrs. Hepburn remains absolutely correct about the lingering effect of the war on her husband, but she fails to realize that his affair with Hannele constitutes a potential oasis for him of health and renewal. Her Bloomsbury attitude of modernist tolerance about a promiscuous love-life—a view offensive to Lawrence—provides the further opportunity to brag about her own supposedly unbroken record of fidelity despite many episodes of temptation. She reveals her intrinsic hypocrisy about sex by confusing a dangerous lack of discipline with real passion: Mrs. Hepburn narrates the story of a married soldier who completes a one-night stand with a virtual stranger in the weeks after he returns from the war to his wife, and she foolishly compares such an indulgent encounter with the significant love her husband feels in his serious relationship with the "other" woman.

Despite all her cleverness and careful planning, Mrs. Hepburn demonstrates a profound ignorance about her husband's needs and emotional state: she never acknowledges the committed nature of his affair, and never realizes that his lover is the witty and fearless Hannele and not the dull and frightened Mitchka. She mistakenly identifies the latter as the "other" woman because Mrs. Hepburn trivializes her husband's taste in women as merely a preference for ladies with Spanish features. In addition, the wife maintains an intense and demeaning possessiveness about Hepburn, yearning for him to return from the army (at only age 41) and stay at home. Hannele is wisely perplexed by such a limiting and unimaginative vision for a middle-aged man, and she responds to Mrs. Hepburn's desire for a stay-at-home husband with the more realistic and eminently Lawrencian suggestion, "It is better for a man to be independent" (103)—an advisory statement that anticipates the ideology underlying her own semi-surrender at the end of the novella to Hepburn's mandate about who must supply direction in marriage.

While Hannele remains aware of the Captain's depressed state, an aspect of his allure for her is the inimitable way his sadness seems to enhance that appeal of his inscrutable self: "The curious way he had of turning his head to listen—to listen to what—as if he heard something in the stars. The strange look, like destiny, in his wide-open, almost staring dark eyes. The beautiful line of his brow that seemed always to have a certain cloud on it" (106). In addition to this passage's characteristic imagery of procreative darkness so common in Lawrence's work, the sense of destiny, of communication with the stars, and of the clouded brow suggest a wounded man who also carries the imagery of a troubled god.[8] One of the central motifs in Vickery's research on the impact of *The Golden Bough* on Lawrence is that his "acquaintance with Frazer sharpened his sense of man's participation in the divine", and thus the mythical and archetypal allusions that follow from "the great deities of comparative religion" are used by Lawrence "to define the mental state of a character and so to relate that state to larger cultural issues either drawn from Lawrence's reading or from the world scene as it was at the time of the novel's composition" (294–95). Before addressing the issue of which god Lawrence employs to further enhance his portrait of Captain Hepburn, it is necessary to examine the implications of his wounded soul and the compelling literary anachronism that accompanies such investigation.

IV

It is after the accidental death of his wife that Hepburn's mood takes a significant turn downward: he descends more deeply into the depression initiated by his experience in the war and exacerbated both by the unresolved affair with Hannele and by the lack of passionate feeling for his wife. As noted earlier, recent criticism has too cleverly investigated the possibility that Hepburn murdered his wife, a crime committed, it is argued, to eliminate the major impediment to his life with Hannele. But such an act in no way squares with the direct evidence of Hepburn's own mood after her death, which hardly appears as regret or atonement for any action he has undertaken. Part of his sadness after the accident must be attributed to guilt over the heavy burden of his marital dilemma: he had felt trapped not by a wife he despised, but by a wife he now realizes was equally trapped in their doomed marriage. The poignancy of his confessional explanation to Hannele of that litany of Mrs. Hepburn's needs, peculiarities, and insecurities—offered through theme-and-variation on three caged-bird metaphors—is that he has suffered his own form of imprisonment, locked in a marriage that requires him to cater to a neurotic wife who combines willful pride with irrepressible childishness. There is

8. For more extensive discussion of the meaning of Lawrencian blackness and its relation to issues of transcendence and self-definition, see Chapters One, Two, and Four in my study, *The Phallic Imagination*.

no reason to suspect foul play on his part. His reaction to her death is not the calibrated relief that sends him to Hannele, but a prolonged despair that keeps him secluded and unapproachable for weeks,

In his brief meeting with Hannele before his seclusion, he articulates a pervasive anguish about the lack of sufficient compensations in life for the heartache that is endured: "In a great measure there's nothing" (113). Lawrence then describes the Captain's self-imposed isolation and his wounded emotions as the symptoms of major emotional difficulty:

> The chief thing that the captain knew, at this juncture, was that a hatchet had gone through the ligatures and veins that connected him with the people of his affection, and that he was left with the bleeding ends of all his vital human relationships...The emotional flow between him and all the people he knew and cared for was broken, and for the time being he was conscious only of the cleavage. The cleavage that had occurred between him and his fellow men, the cleft that was now between him and them...what had happened had been preparing for a long time (113–14).

The graphic metaphor of flowing blood and ripped tissue to describe Hepburn's feelings reflects the psychosomatic aspects of his deterioration: that crucial phrase, "for a long time", indicates that the death of Mrs. Hepburn concludes a process of inner turmoil that he has experienced since returning from the war. The Captain now cuts himself off from all people (including Hannele), and soon he lacks the requisite energy and desire even for passing conversation: "He shrank with a feeling almost of disgust from his friends and acquaintances and their expressions of sympathy...He did not want to share emotions or feelings of any sort. He wanted to be by himself, essentially even if he was moving about other people" (114). When solipsism is so unqualified, and when basic emotions are so infiltrated with intense nihilism, Hepburn's feelings affect his organic self: "He could not get over his disgust that people insisted on his sharing their emotions. He could not bear their emotions, neither their activities...But the moment they approached him to spread their feelings over him or to entangle him in their activities a helpless disgust came up in him, and until he could get away, he felt sick, even physically" (114).

The sound and sense of this symptomology must be eerily familiar to readers of modernist literature. The unmistakable accent in the passages above—conveyed by imagery, tone, and psychological urgency—resembles the war-wounded and world-weary characters in Hemingway's fiction in the mid1920s, and especially the beleaguered Krebs in "Soldier's Home" from *In Our Time*, a young man who returns from the battle in Europe with damaged emotions and a need for isolation: "He did not want any consequences ever again. He wanted to live without consequences"

(113). In an interesting coincidence of literary history, Lawrence will review *In Our Time* in 1927, six years after he writes *The Captain's Doll.* In his incisive, brief remarks on what Lawrence presciently describes as the Nick Adams prototype, he selects Krebs and "Soldier's Home" for special mention. His keen perspective on Hemingway's early collection and on Krebs's psyche could easily describe a numb and virtually sleepwalking Hepburn after the war, and especially after the sudden death of his wife:

> Avoid one thing only: getting connected up. Don't get connected up. If you get held by anything, break it. Don't be held. Break it and get away…Mr. Hemingway is really good because he's perfectly straight about it. He is like Krebs, in that devastating Oklahoma sketch, he doesn't love anybody, and it nauseates him to have to pretend he does. He doesn't even *want* to love anybody, he doesn't want to go anywhere, he doesn't want to do anything (*Introductions* 312).

Unlike the younger, unmarried, and inexperienced Krebs, Hepburn is a mature man who eventually will attempt to renew himself through human contact because, at bottom, "Alexander Hepburn was not the man to live alone" (115). This insight remains important in terms of Hepburn's character and within the dispensations of Lawrencian doctrine. For all his dyspeptic pronouncements about the mind-centered world and its pernicious conformists, Lawrence always insists—in his essays, fiction, and engaged life—that there can be no organic renewal in anyone without intense involvement with other people. As he slowly begins to recover, his mind turns back to Hannele: Hepburn realizes that although he may wish to continue their affair, he will not (as with Krebs's aversion) base the relationship on love. Hemingway writes about the Birkin-like skepticism that informs Krebs's position on women: "He did not want to get into the intrigue and the politics. He did not want to have to do any courting. He did not want to tell any more lies" (113). As Hepburn contemplates a return to Hannele, he too wishes to avoid the complexities and platitudes of emotional entanglement: "Love. It means so many things. It meant the feeling he had for his wife. He had loved her. But he shuddered at the thought of having to go through such love again…To him, Hannele did not exactly represent rosy love. Rather a hard destiny. He didn't adore her" (115).

Thus, not long after the death of his wife, he leaves Hannele—uncharacteristically without even his acknowledgement of sexual interest in her—and travels alone to England to see his children. Away from the complexities of his affair and the anxieties experienced in Germany, he begins to emerge from his depression and starts to resolve his ambivalent feelings about *both* his late wife and his current lover. Lawrence implicitly relates Hepburn's gradual, emotional renewal to a narcissistic libido that provides him with necessary ego-support: "And really, the nice young girls of eighteen or twenty attracted him very much: so fresh, so impulsive, and looking up to him as if he were something wonderful" (115). In a provocative essay on depression, "Mourning and Melancholia," that Freud writes only a few years before this novella, he establishes a theoretical framework that can explain aspects of the Captain's psychological state after his wife's death and his departure from Hannele:

> These obsessional states of depression following upon the death of a loved person show us what the conflict due to ambivalence can achieve by itself when there is no regressive drawing in of libido as well. In melancholia, the occasions which give rise to the illness extend for the most part beyond the clear case of a loss by death, and include all those situations of being slighted, neglected, or disappointed, which can import opposed feelings of love and hate into the relationship or reinforce an already existing ambivalence (588).

Hepburn thus finally resolves his "opposed feelings of love and hate" for Mrs. Hepburn and for Hannele, willing to accept the stark resolution that "he was deeply, profoundly thankful that his wife was dead" (115). With this acceptance and the related resurgence of his confident, sexual self, he returns to Germany and attempts to reestablish the intense relationship with Hannele.

When the Captain finally summons the energy to track down Hannele in Munich, he is first entranced rather than angered by the sight of the doll displayed so conspicuously in the shop window. This third appearance of the doll in the novella, following its role in the first scene and later its appearance in the studio, is important because of the tell-tale attitude it engenders in a recently depressed, confused, and unconfident man: Hepburn is gratified to see that the doll is "losing none of its masculinity" (116). In Vickery's provocative discussion of Lawrence's awareness of the role of magic and totemic motivation outlined in Frazer's *The Golden Bough*, he observes that *The Captain's Doll* is one of the stories that "contain characters who exercise and react to spells that are both deliberately imposed and the by-product of the impact of one personality on another" (308). Although Vickery does not elaborate on the specific relevance of this insight for the novella, his remarks suggest the extent to which the doll is central to the action. In a sense, the image of this manikin—as it moves from the Rhineland to Munich and then to the Tyrol—dictates the movement and patterning of the plot: the doll casts a spell over the Captain, thematically because of the creative handiwork of

Hannele, and structurally because of the stages its presence initiates in the development of the relationship between the lovers. In Munich, Hepburn's fascination with the iconic, masculine self he projects onto the doll prompts further consideration by him on changing the texture of any future love affairs: "The temptation this time was, to be adored. One of those fresh young things would have adored him as if he were a god" (116). But he senses that such easy subservience from inexperienced women would not energize him. Thus he follows Hannele to Kaprun to convince her to yield to him the directive role in a marriage that is abstractly "beyond love" but well short of servile adoration. Just before he leaves Munich, his anger at Hannele's creation of the doll is refueled when he discovers the newspaper article that also reproduces the Worpswede still life. The painting contains the image of the manikin, a doll whose masculine energy is satirized by its demeaning placement amid the arrangement of sunflowers and poached eggs on toast.

In the prolonged absence of Hepburn and in need of resources and stability, Hannele has in the interim become engaged to a petty, pompous, and powerful regional bureaucrat in Kaprun, Herr Regierungsrat von Poldi, whose trivial preoccupations and essential lack of passion are exceeded only by his posturing and inflated sense of self-importance. She is on the rebound from the usually non-talkative and indecisive Hepburn, and Hannele is easily seduced by the comforting ease of the Austrian's conversation and by his witty, dead-end sense of how the world works: she cannot see the decadence and mechanization that underlie his grandiloquent and fashionable amorality. Lawrence describes von Poldi in a manner that suggests an early and ambulatory version of Clifford Chatterley, and the metaphors used to describe Hannele's fiancé reveal that like the voluble and crippled owner of the mines, this Austrian's paralysis is also organic, extending through his soul and body: "He seemed almost eternal, sitting there in his chair with knees planted far apart. It was as if he would never rise again, but would remain for ever, and talking. It seemed as if he had no legs, save to sit with. As if to stand on his feet and walk would not be natural to him" (120). Hepburn quickly senses the life-denying sentiments embodied by von Poldi: there is no respect for real love or passion in his servile group of functionaries, who all just dabble in erotic diversions that anticipate the lifestyle of Clifford and the wags at Wragby: "It was extraordinary how many finely built, handsome young people of an age fitted for nothing but love-affairs ran the governmental business of this department. And the Herr Regierungsrat sailed in and out of the big old rooms, his wide coat flying like wings" (121). When Lawrence writes about the motivation behind Hannele's ill-advised engagement, that "the sense of fatalism was part of the attraction" (121), her despair is evident after the breakup of her affair with Hepburn. A determined Captain rows across the lake to meet her at the villa. The lecherous admiration of the many youths who watch her swimming, and her obvious pleasure in their uncensored voyeurism suggest the multiple possibilities for infidelity that await Hannele should she continue in her distinctly unromantic plans to marry the Austrian.

V

The lengthy excursion by Hepburn and Hannele comprises more than one-third of the novella; it encompasses the Captain's attempt to regain sufficient confidence both to discourage Hannele from pursuing a doomed marriage with a pompous and asexual bureaucrat, and to convince her to embrace the life with him that he proposes in the final pages. As they begin their eventful day-trip to the Karlinger Glacier, its huge mass in the distance is described as "coldly grinning in the sky" (125), an early indication, from a human perspective, of its forbidding altitude and icy majesty. The Captain's primary objective in this vigorous trek through the Tyrolean Alps is to progress through the three levels of the journey until attaining the bottom section of the massive glacier. Such an ambitious goal runs counter to his intense dislike of mountains, climbing, and the tourist-congestion he encounters along the way. Hepburn must also work against (as Hemingway and Norman Mailer would put it) his instinctual fear of high elevations and the sobering reality of his lack of proper conditioning for this arduous hike. The tiered slopes in the distance offer a wide-angle view of the miles that must be traversed in the coming hours of this intense mid-summer day. Lawrence's characteristic command of pictorial precision about natural scenery, combined with his emphasis on a relevant range of sense perception are on full display; it includes the painterly touch of a topographic anthropomorphism that he will develop in the novella:

> The glacier, in a recess among the folded mountains, looked cold and angry, but morning was very sweet in the sky, and blowing very sweet with a faint scent of the second hay, from the lowlands at the head of the lake. Beyond stood naked grey rock like a wall of mountains, pure rock, with faint thin slashes of snow (126).

Hepburn's recent history of emotional vulnerability and physical weakness is not helped by the vista of the looming mountains or by the sight of the exuberant and lusty young men early in the morning. Here the formidable climb, the competitive energy of youth, and the specter of death combine to delineate for him the difficult challenge he faces:

> The day was a feast day, a holiday. Already so early three young men from the mountains were bathing near the steps of the Badeanstalt. Handsome, physical fellows, with good limbs rolling and swaying in the early morning water. They seemed to enjoy it too. But to Hepburn it was always as if a dark wing were stretched in the sky, over these mountains, like a doom. And these three young lusty naked men swimming and rolling in the shadow (126).

The "challenging" aspects of the marriage matrix for Hepburn extend, quite literally, to the province of stipulated physical feats. For Hepburn to believe that he can convince Hannele to join him in marriage on his terms, he first must buttress his ego by completing the excursion and, in his own precise way, by conquering the glacier. In this sense there exists between them on this trip a sexual competition and continual tension that is archetypal in its configuration, for it extends beyond his desire to resolve the key issues of primacy in their relationship. Hepburn actually brings along an image of the offending totem—reflected in the Worpswede painting—to document his belief that Hannele betrayed him with her objectifying handiwork. Lawrence engrains the problems in the affair between this man and woman within the generic context of the natural scenery they traverse. The precise topography of the mountainous area implies the stakes of sexual power that will be decided during their multi-level climb. As they begin the ascent and encounter Level One, Lawrence's imagery is explicit on the prominence of the male and female principles that frame the excursion. The landscape vividly announces an alpine brand of gender typology, complete with sexual organs, pubic hair, and the imminence of mythological copulation initiated from the heavens:

> So the two climbed slowly up the steep ledge of a road. The valley was just a mountain cleft, cleft sheer in the hard, living rock, with black trees like hair flourishing in this secret, naked place of the earth. At the bottom of the open wedge forever roared the rampant, insatiable water. The sky above was like a sharp wedge forcing its way into the earth's cleavage, and that eternal ferocious water was like the steel edge of the wedge, the terrible tip biting in into the rocks' intensity (129).

Throughout the vicissitudes of this busy day, the two hikers traverse a landscape that itself appears to move under their feet as they climb. The mountains seem alive with a kinetic process of motion and emotion that often resembles the actions of the two human beings who negotiate the highland trails and ravine bypasses.[9] There is more to this phenomenon for Lawrence than a mere illustration of his justly praised ability to capture "the spirit of place". In *Movements in European History*, a wide-ranging textbook published just a few months before he begins writing *The Captain's Doll*, Lawrence, in effect, offers a possible reason for this livid use of topography, as he insists that "the mysterious and untellable motion within the heads of man is in some way related to motion within the earth" (9). The climbers at times appear to climb in and on their own three-dimensional, spatial world, all within a resistant domain that partakes of magic and unknown power that they can neither master nor understand. In this regard, Vickery is correct in his generalization that

> Lawrence utilizes Frazer's concept of taboo as negative magic and as a dangerous physical power that needs to be insulated. For Lawrence, it is a means of emphasizing both the living quality of the natural world and also the protective nature of space in creating geographical isolation (298).

By claiming such a magical connection between the vagaries of human emotion and the spatial geographies of the earth, and by investing his images of landscape with sexual archetypes and gender conflicts, Lawrence begins to mythologize aspects of Hepburn and Hannele's experience as they climb "the eternal side of that valley" (130). He also stays focused on the personal case of Hepburn's condition: the Captain is depicted as a man so burdened with sadness and so sensitive to the toll taken by his emotional extremity that (like the Nick Adams prototype), his physical state can deteriorate at any moment—as when "people swarming touristy in those horrible mountains, made him feel almost sick" (130). This dichotomous texture to Hepburn's experience—its ability to universalize the journey *and* to individualize Hepburn's own pathology—is craftily integrated by Lawrence through his use of a poignant myth that appropriates much of the relevant imagery and themes of *The Captain's Doll*. It is the legendary tale of Balder that permeates this novella, just as the story of this beloved god functions as the most prominent totemic principle outlined in Frazer's *The Golden Bough*, a favorite work of Lawrence's that is very much in his mind in 1921 as he revises *Fantasia of the Unconscious* and completes final versions of *The Fox* and *The*

9. Doherty remains unconvincing in his belief that Lawrence's anthropomorphized landscape amounts to little more than "elaborate stylistic self-parody" (13).

Captain's Doll.[10] Central to this myth is the theme of betrayal, death, and recovery, embroidered with the imagery of a poison plant (mistletoe) that is used in an arrow to kill the Norse god when he is shot through the chest. The myth pulls together Lawrence's preoccupations with ego, vulnerability, and renewal in *The Captain's Doll*, as he adapts elements of this Scandinavian story to suit the imposing landscape in the novella and the specific urgencies of the lovers. The god Balder is the son of the great Norse god Odin, and as Frazer recounts the story originally told "in the younger or prose *Edda*" (704), Balder is betrayed by his mother, the goddess Frigg, who carelessly reveals to her son's enemies that he is not immune to the poison of mistletoe, a fact that enables the devious Loki to fool the blind and unknowing Hother to shoot Balder with the deadly arrow.

Balder's circumstance of careless betrayal by a beloved and trusted confidant recalls the gratuitous display in the studio by Hannele of the doll as well as her disingenuous confirmation of the model's name to Mrs. Hepburn. Balder was seen as a figure of strength and command until the goddess undermines him through public disclosure of his weakness; his death is commemorated even today by Norwegians who enact a series of rituals and memorial rites described in *The Golden Bough* as integral to the renewal and resurrection aspect of the myth and as fundamental to the concept of Balder as a vulnerable man-god whose spirit has been revived. Frazer prefaces his narration of the myth with a profusion of natural imagery and sexual iconography that sounds startlingly similar to Lawrence's own description quoted earlier of the kinetic and eroticized landscape in the novella. Here is the Frazer passage that, consciously or not, Lawrence has recreated in *The Captain's Doll*: "On one of the bays of the beautiful Sogne Fiord, which penetrates far into the depths of the Norwegian mountains, with their somber pine forests and their lofty cascades dissolving into spray before they reach the dark water of the fiord far below…" (704–5). Two months later Lawrence, in *Fantasia of the Unconscious*, announces his admiration for *The Golden Bough*, the power and sound of water in the deep ravines described in *The Captain's Doll* continue to echo the Norse mythology: "Who would have thought the soft sky of light—and the soft foam of water could thrust and penetrate into the dark strong earth?" (129)

10. Lawrence mentions *The Golden Bough* with admiration in *Fantasia* as a work that offers "hints, suggestions" for his own artistic technique and informing doctrine; it is a Lawrencian vision, he explains, that proceeds "by intuition" (62), not unlike the intuitional beliefs of ancient civilizations anatomized by Frazer.

As the climb continues, they pass a group of non-poisonous relatives of mistletoe—hare-bell, mountain bell, bilberry, and cranberry—plants that will soon be replaced in the scenic foliage, when Hepburn and Hannele gain greater altitude, by deadly members of the actual mistletoe family. Near the end of Level One, the symbology of the Balder myth becomes more prominent and foreboding, as Hepburn discovers that "the high air bit him in his chest, like a viper" (130), a symptom of pulmonary difficulty that the chronically ill Lawrence knows well. In a significant exchange of repartee, Hannele notices Hepburn's distress and asks him, "if you don't like it, why did you come?" His simple and honest response, "I had to try" (130), would surely satisfy Hemingway's developing ethic, as he will shortly write *In Our Time*. Hepburn pushes himself onward without any fuller explanation of why he feels compelled to make this difficult journey. At this point, Lawrence demonstrates his novelistic gift of perfect dramatic timing, as Hepburn and Hannele briefly encounter a young couple descending the trail. The mythological reference is no mere coincidence, nor is the sense of their tense estrangement from each other:

> And the young Tannhäuser, the young Siegfried, this young Balder beautiful strode, climbing down the rocks, marching and swinging with his alpenstock. And immediately after the youth came a maiden with hair on the wind and her shirt—breasts open, striding in corduroy breeches, rumpled worsted stockings, thick boots, a knapsack and alpenstock. She passed without greeting, And our pair stopped in angry silence and watched her dropping down the mountain side (131).

Beyond the explicit mention of Siegfried, Tannhäuser, and Balder—all mythic figures who suffered various betrayals from women—the vignette portrays the image of an energetic and self-contained woman who appears confident and intentionally aloof as she passes by without a word. The young couple, walking at separate paces and distanced from each other, offers a momentary reflection of the unspoken power struggle transpiring between Hepburn and Hannele; the Countess defiantly claims "wonderful, wonderful, to be high up", and the moody Captain, who is irritated by the climb, as well as by Hannele's proud enthusiam for the physical exertion, announces his own difficult adjustment to the ascent: "I want to live near sea level. I am no mountain topper" (131). As the Level One segment ends, Hannele petulantly asks him why he doesn't like the journey: "And if you don't like it, why should you try to spoil it for me?" His response, "I hate it" (130), asserts his feelings but withholds his courageous reason for undertaking the journey.

VI

By the time the lovers emerge from the lowland section of the climb, Lawrence has reiterated two essential facts about Hepburn: the poor condition of his physical and psychological self, and the relevance of his man-god characterization to the myth of Balder. Hannele momentarily gloats over her willing role as teasing betrayer of his manhood: however god-like he may appear to her in his inscrutable eternality, she exultantly notes how he suffers from the day's exertion: "His eyes were black and set, he seemed so motionless, as if he were eternal facing these upper facts. She thrilled with triumph. She felt he was overcome" (132). When they enter Level Two of the trail, Lawrence emphasizes the convergence of the mythological identity of Hepburn with an essential sadness in him that is both personal and infinite, as it echoes through time like the pastoral clanging of the cowbells: "The sound always awoke in him a primeval, almost hopeless melancholy. Always made him feel navré" (132). Like its often existentially related term, "*l'angoise*", the French word "*navré*" connotes a deep and abiding forlornness that in its solipsistic intensity connects through time with the deities and humans who have experienced such deep sadness. As Hepburn moves through a primeval landscape that resonates backward to mythic history, he is reminded of the universality of the sexual struggle in which he is engaged with Hannele. He begins to feel the adrenaline of battle, an early intimation of his renewal as man and lover:

> He was happy in that upper valley, that first rocking cradle of early wonder. He liked to see the great fangs and slashes of ice and snow that thrust down into the rock, as if the ice had bitten into the flesh of the earth. And from the fang-tip, the hoarse water crying its birth-cry, rushing down (133).

But the wounded man-god must remain vigilant if he is to avoid his early death, for nearby exists the profusion of poisonous plants belonging to the precise mistletoe family that killed Balder, all commonly known as "devil herbs". Too high on the mountain for mistletoe to grow, its herbal relatives provide a danger that Lawrence's prose registers with the lyric beauty of a Keatsian ode:

> Many stars of pale-lavender gentian, touched with earth-colour: and then monkshood, yellow primrose monkshood, and sudden places full of dark monkshood. That dark-blue, terrible colour of the strange rich monkshood made Hepburn look and look again. How did the ice come by that lustrous

> blue-purple intense darkness?—and by that royal poison? That laughing-snake gorgeousness of much monkshood (133).

While Hepburn slowly revives and remains pleased with his progress on the second level, he takes out the Worpswede painting and explains to Hannele the source of his discontent: namely that she not only cruelly objectified him through the manikin, but that she further demeaned him by selling the object as a mere commodity on the open market. Hannele, of course, is not without significant defense for her actions, angrily explaining to him that she also felt betrayed, first by his passivity about their future plans, and then by his abrupt abandonment of her when he yielded to the manipulative designs of his wife. Gradually the Captain becomes more hyperbolic and pompous in his protestations in this second argument during the day's excursion. Amid their verbal battle for strategic advantage, Lawrence always maintains the palpable existence of a nurturant and underlying bond between them. It remains for Hannele—distinctly recalling Ursula's role with Birkin—to provide some sensible perspective on Hepburn's pretensions. Here Lawrence employs the forging imagery of fire and darkness from *Women in Love* to remind us of Hepburn's lingering power and his rhetorical excess:

> She looked in wonder on his dark, glowing, ineffectual face. It seemed to her like a dark flame burning in the daylight and in the ice-rain, very ineffectual and unnecessary.
>
> "You must be a little mad," she said superbly, "to talk like that about the mountains. They are so much bigger than you."
>
> "No," he said. "No! They are not."
>
> "What!" she laughed aloud. "The mountains are not bigger than you? But you are extraordinary."
>
> "They are not bigger than me," he cried. "Any more than you are bigger than me if you stand on a ladder. They are not bigger than me. They are less than me."
>
> "Oh! Oh!" she cried in wonder and ridicule. "The mountains are *less* than you!"
>
> "Yes," he cried, "they are less."
>
> He seemed suddenly to go silent and remote as she watched him. The speech had gone out of his face again, he seemed to be standing a long way off from her, beyond some border-line. And in the midst of her indignant amazement she watched him with wonder and a touch of fascination. To what country did he belong then?—to what dark, different atmosphere? (137–38)

Hannele is quite right to wonder about Hepburn's unearthly "difference", that exists "a long way off from her, beyond some border-line". Lawrence himself is preoccupied with a concept of the border-line as he writes *The Captain's Doll* and creates the mythic-human composite who is Captain Hepburn. On October 17, 1921, three weeks before he completes the novella, he writes a revealing letter to Edward Garnett about Emile Lucka's book, *Grenzen de Seele*, and in it, Lawrence reveals his latest thoughts on the issues of male primacy and leadership implicit in Hannele's admiring but skeptical view of her lover:

> I think *Grenzen der Seele* is really very interesting. But you know I'm the last person in the world to judge as to what other people will like, Lucka's study of Grenz-leute—the border-line people—as contrasted with the middle-people seems to me very illuminating and fertile. The Grenzleute are those who are on the verge of human understanding, and who widen the frontiers of human knowledge all the time—and the frontiers of life (*Letters IV* 99).[11]

Lawrence believes firmly in his own genius, and it is obvious that he regards himself as an often betrayed and misunderstood member of the border-line elite who "widen the frontiers" of life and knowledge. But a belief in his own visionary art in no way inhibits Lawrence in his fiction from using his powers of negative-capability so that Hannele can undercut Hepburn's protestations the way that Frieda would question his own assumed authority, and the way Ursula often corrects Birkin's hyperbolic pronouncements. Hannele's fascination with the Captain's odd demeanor and inflated stances during the excursion merges in her mind with her awareness of his inscrutability throughout their affair. Lawrence's reiteration of similar terms, in the following passage, angled from Hannele's perspective, serves to remind the Countess that Hepburn's position in this abstract, border-line category is beyond easy understanding: "He was a puzzle to her: eternally incomprehensible in his feeling and even in his sayings...He had some of the fascination of the incomprehensible...And the strange passion of his, that gave out incomprehensible flashes" (139). Such a mixture of qualities in the Captain comprises the essential aspect of the mytho-realistic quality of the novella, a texture that symmetrically reflects the three levels of the journey to the glacier: on one level Hepburn is a moody, lonely, and vulnerable human being; on another level a pontificating yet vulnerable symbol of a mythic god; and on the third

11. Ruderman also refers to Lawrence's letter on Lucka and to the mention of "border-line" in *The Captain's Doll*. But she does not consider the concept's function in a mythological organization of the novella, or in any speculation on the relation of the border-line elite to Lawrence's own self-image and quest for achievement.

level, a committed and headstrong lover who plans to propose marriage to Hannele during the trip. He remains elusive of easy categorization, and it is relevant to note the words by Frazer of "border-line" demarcation as he begins to discuss the myth of Balder in *The Golden Bough*, describing the Norse man-god as a "deity whose life might in a sense be said to be neither in heaven nor on earth but between the two" (703).[12] The voyage to the high glacier, it might be argued, stands between the heavenly and the earthly, and such positioning by Frazer recalls the words of Hepburn when earlier he irritated Hannele with his glib comment, "nothing in time or space matters to me" (84). Is it not psychologically likely that Lawrence periodically required a confirming sense of his own confident membership amid the border-line elite in order to assert the elements of his visionary art? In fact, as he contemplates additional writing projects while he struggles with the final scenes of the novella, he confides to Mabel Dodge Stern, "Can't write yet, not till I have crossed another border" (*Letters IV* 111).

As they approach the third and final level on the Mooserboden trail—the section that will bring them to the edge of the Karlinger Glacier—an unrelenting Hepburn continues his personal battle with the demon of high elevation, and Hannele feels "a sense of ecstasy" while "it just filled him with terror" (140). Nearing the intimidating and breathtaking mass of ice, Lawrence again stresses its "livingness" as he employs the animate phrasing of "silent living glacier" and "like a grand beast" (141) to emphasize his belief in the kinetic quality of the mountain landscape, a belief that is not unlike the primitive faith of ancient civilizations described throughout *The Golden Bough*. The flow of Hepburn's human emotions during the journey remains super-sensitive to the changing scenery that he encounters. In *Movements In European History*, Lawrence provides what amounts to an anti-theory to explain this process. He asserts that the subtle motions and metamorphoses of the glacial topography, and their essential connection to Hepburn's own feelings, are not amenable to any rational analysis: "Logic cannot hold good beforehand, even in the inorganic world" (9). Lawrence's confidence throughout his life in the primacy of a "blood-knowledge"[13] in each individual explains Hannele's

12. Mellown remains the one early commentator on the work to recognize the integrated aspects of the mythic and the human in Hepburn's characterization, referring to him as "both the earthly and the Divine Lover of his Hannele" (231).

13. See Lawrence's famous 1915 letter to Bertrand Russell on the importance of "blood-consciousness, with its sexual connection" and its oppositional relation to "the ordinary mental consciousness" (*Letters II* 470) associated with mere

own perplexity about Hepburn, that "there seemed to her no logic and no reason in what he felt and said" (139). On Hepburn's similarly unarticulated desire to undertake the trek despite his considerable fear and discomfort, another passage from *Movements in European History* is pertinent. The following lines on the need for *transcendence* recall again Hepburn's telescope as the early indication of his need to get beyond the limits of self: "There is *no reason* why such a passion, such a craving should arise. All that the reason can do, in discovering the logical consequence of such passion and its effect, afterwards is to realize that life *was* so, mysteriously, creatively, and beyond cavil" (9). When pushed by an exultant Hannele who asks if he is glad he came, he convincingly replies (even given his trepidations), "very glad I came" (141). Lawrence then phrases the fact of Hepburn's triumph with the mythic terminology of an internal conflict engaged and surmounted—a conflict contrasted with the superficial thrills of the tourists and the jaded professionalism of the local mountaineers: "His eyes were dilated with excitement that was ordeal or mystic battle rather than the Bergheil ecstasy" (141). Hepburn has demonstrated a courageous willingness to face his fears during a period in his life when he is unsure of his recuperative power and indecisive about the resolution of his affair with Hannele. Lawrence formulates the essentiality of such courage in an unembroidered statement from *Movements in European History* that anticipates Hemingway's most obsessive theme: "Manhood is the same in all men, and the chief part of all men" (255). It is this "chief part" that Hepburn will now put to its greatest test as he confronts one additional challenge on this day of "ordeal or mystic battle".

VII

To complete Level Three and attain the base of the glacier is not sufficient victory for the increasingly confident Captain, who now wishes to climb a section of the ice mass and stand on its treacherous face. In the adamance of this spontaneous decision by Hepburn, he again confirms that next to the guiding imperative of instinctual desire, "logic cannot hold good beforehand" (*Movements* 9). Rational consideration has no role in his decision to construct a "fourth level" objective in the climb. Thus he leaves an understandably worried Hannele waiting below while he slowly ascends the glacier—and without the proper shoes and climbing equipment

---

rationality. In the same letter, he also confirms the importance of his current reading of Frazer.

for this tricky maneuver over a dangerously steep and slippery surface. The only "logic" involved in this daring act recalls Lawrence's luminous, oxymoronic phrase from *The Rainbow*, "logic of the soul" (40).[14] Although he remains "frightened of it", the Captain has "a great desire to stand on the glacier" (143). Certainly, his desire is not unrelated to the spirited war of the sexes that has been enacted by the lovers during the excursion. Who can know for sure how much his avidity for this attainment of the fourth level is related to his awareness of Hannele's terror at his attempt and to her disinclination to join him in this goal.

The other climbers on the glacier, who are capably assisted by nailed boots and alpine poles, speed past Hepburn as he cautiously moves up the surface of "the great monster" that "was sweating all over" (141) from constant violation by the hikers. Even for the more properly equipped climbers, Lawrence is unequivocal about the real danger here, and he phrases the issue in distinctly pre-Hemingway terms: "being human, they all wanted to go beyond their fear" (142). Hannele "down below was crying [to (*sic*)] him to come back", and "as if the ice breathed" (143) in synchrony with the intensity of Hepburn's effort, he reaches the top of the glacier section. He is then faced with the most formidable prospect for any successful ice climb—the inevitable descent, in which gravity is as much an enemy as the frozen surface itself. Hepburn smartly solves this challenge (perhaps drawing on his wartime experience?) when he discovers that "by striking in his heels sideways with sufficient sharpness he could keep his footing no matter how steep the slope" (143). The Captain's reaction to such a significant victory is memorable in terms of the premonitions of literary history: it is conveyed with *precisely* the imagery, rhythm, and restraint to be employed by a young writer from Illinois, who in 1921 is just a few years from his celebrated creation of Nick Adams. For here is Lawrence writing about Hepburn's achievement, affirming it through the benedictive warmth of nature, the stark simplicity of unadorned adjectives, and the emblematic reminder of a wound as the visible badge of triumph: "The sun was shining warmly for a moment, and he felt happy, though his finger ends were bleeding a little from the ice" (144).[15] The ascent completed, adrenaline pumping, the last remnants of

---

14. I discuss the instinctual primacy behind the concept of the "logic of the soul" in Chapter Two of *The Phallic Imagination*, and in my essay on *The Lost Girl* in *Twentieth Century Literature*.

15. Recall Nick Adams in "Big Two-Hearted River" as he temporarily attains some peace for his fragile emotions when he completes the goal of setting up the tent, and he "was happy as he crawled inside the tent…now things were done. It had been a hard trip" (167); or the much younger and frightened Nick of "Indian

depression lifted, Captain Hepburn feels renewed by the pleasure surmounting his fear: he "need never go again" (144).[16]

Immediately building on his feelings of confidence and conquest, Hepburn for the first time initiates a frank and aggressive discussion with Hannele about what is really on his mind. He asks if she intends to marry von Poldi, a question he could only pose after the successful events of the afternoon. But the canny woman hangs fire in order to elicit from him the more compelling question she knows is coming. Sure enough, he responds to her complaint earlier in the day that he never makes suggestions with the carefully understated comment, "I should suggest that you should marry me" (45). Hepburn then uses the developing conversation to convey to her three important admissions: first, that Hannele's creation of the doll, in the light of all the anger and objectification that informed such handiwork, really does him "the greatest possible damage" (147); second, that his reiterated insistence on the lack of "love" in their relationship partly serves his need for a rhetoric of revenge against her; third, that his articulated vision of their affair as necessarily avoiding conventional assertions of love is connected, in part, to the experience of his own tragic and ill-matched marriage. Such a litany of confession by Hepburn is uttered persuasively and honestly, but he also makes it clear that he will not back down from the non-negotiable terms for marriage that he proposes to Hannele. In one final reference by Lawrence to the Balder myth of mistletoe and arrow, Hepburn lets Hannele know that he still regards the existence of the manikin as a form of betrayal that endangers

---

Camp," briefly revived as "the sun was coming up over the hills" (70); or the bleeding hands of Santiago in *The Old Man and the Sea* as he fights off the shark under the blazing yet benedictive sun. The examples are legion in Hemingway's work. For a more detailed examination of the ways in which Lawrence and Hemingway share certain assumptions and beliefs on survival, instinct, and sexual identity, see my article on *A Farewell to Arms* in *The Hemingway Review*. Granofsky's treatment of *The Captain's Doll* encompasses the theme of survival in the post-war years; in its correlative emphases—that he skillfully contextualizes in the novella—on elements of violence and power, and on the lovers' connoisseur-like preoccupation with food and eating metaphors throughout the work, the Hemingway echoes sound unmistakable to me.

16. Vickery aptly describes the stages of any adaptation of the Balder myth as moving "from birth through death to lamentation and anticipation of the future" (114). This four-part pattern perfectly fits the essential movements of the action for Hepburn, as he moves from the birth of the affair before the novella begins, to the death of a wife and the ending of the affair, to a period of intense lamentation and depression, to the doctrinal vision that signals his renewal and his future marriage to Hannele.

him: “The doll just sticks in me like a thorn” (151). Hepburn then slowly asserts his precise conditions for legal union in a manner that echoes the words of Birkin from the “Mino” chapter of *Women in Love*, as he insists that it is Hannele’s “highest fate” (152) to follow his lead in the marriage.[17] It is also, of course, a reiteration of notions of male primacy expressed in his 1918 “devouring mother” letter to Katherine Mansfield. Although Hannele will not initially accept this chauvinistic demand without some effective verbal jousting, it is evident that she passionately loves her man and will eventually submit to the spirit (but not the letter!) of his insistence. As she begins to yield to his proposal and program, she intriguingly stops just short of his stipulated terms, arguing that she will not say “promise to honor and obey you” (152) in the public arena of a wedding service. When a supremely self-confident Captain Hepburn—so different in demeanor from his indecisive and passive self earlier in the novella—responds that such a refusal stops short of his precise conditions, she yields to his pressure. Yet she saves face by insisting on a slight reformulation of his expectation: “But anyway, I won’t say it *before* the marriage service, need I?” (153) It is a minor victory for her, as his silence gives her the final rejoinder on the subject.

But it is not quite that last word in the work. The date is November 6, 1921 when Lawrence completes *The Captain’s Doll* by resolving a problem that he stated in a letter to Earl Brewster four days earlier: “But I have just got it high up in the mountains of the Tyrol, and don’t quite know how to get it down without breaking its neck” (*Letters IV* 109). Such a nervous concern about concluding the novella serves as another way for Lawrence to ask himself how he can resolve tensions between the lovers yet still preserve a delicate and balanced perspective on issues that embrace his life and art; in short, how does he achieve a resolution so Hepburn/Lawrence can retain the essence of his doctrinal position while Hannele/Frieda can retain the spunk and independence so integral to her character? As noted above, Lawrence’s practical, credible solution is to keep the characters sparring until the very end and to include the one pure scene of comedy in the work to enliven their debate: such a scene occurs when an angry Hannele momentarily leaves him behind as she rushes to

---

17. In *Women in Love*, the exact phrasing is as follows, as the more moderate Birkin, with his more equitable “star-equilibrium” concept, eliminates the inflammatory term, “highest”: “He is only insisting to the poor stray that she shall acknowledge him as a sort of fate, her own fate” (149–50). Squires and Talbot, in this regard, describe Hepburn’s mandate to Hannele as “a version of what Birkin finally offers Ursula in *Women in Love*” (245–46).

the bus, precipitating a loud and conflicted exchange of views that is scarcely heard above the din of the motor and wind.

Lawrence is not finished, however, in his goal of finding a conclusion for the work that "gets it down" without breaking the integrity of its structure. This remains a difficult artistic mandate that (as Leavis long ago suggested) must not violate either the complexity of Hannele's character, or the echoes of inimitable obstreporousness in Lawrence's feisty wife. The novelist negotiates the aesthetics and the biographical sensitivities of this problem with remarkable skill. Just after Hannele modifies the Captain's insistence about her obedience in marriage, she offers in response to his silence one more capitulation: it is a gesture that finally satisfies Hepburn's anger about the doll and also provides perfect closure for the Balder myth. She obligingly tells him, "Give me that picture, please, will you? I want to burn it" (153). With this wise decision to destroy the image and substance of the doll, Hannele confirms and addresses her recognition of Hepburn's feelings of betrayal. In a sense, the doll has functioned as Hepburn's mistletoe throughout the novella, an incubus with a beautiful exterior, but with a deadly substance that can poison his life.[18] In destroying this manikin she recalls the words of Frazer in *The Golden Bough* about the Balder story that must have fascinated Lawrence with their potential for fictional development: "When a person's life is conceived as embodied in a particular object, with the existence of which his own existence is bound up", then if the object is allowed to retain its totemic power, it is "perfectly natural that he should be killed by a blow from it" (812). In her gracious willingness to burn the Worpswede painting of the offending doll, she stabilizes the emotional life of her distinctly renewed lover, obliterates the nagging residue of betrayal, and pledges herself to the married life with Hepburn she now formally undertakes.[19]

---

18. Vickery's reading of *The Golden Bough* describes Frazer's view of Balder as "the Scandinavian dying and reviving god" (266), whose symbolic resurrection in the yearly festivals of fire in Norway bear resemblance to relevant rituals and ceremonies that celebrate the rebirth of Christ. While his study of Frazer does not discuss *The Captain's Doll* in any detail, and nor does he relate the fiction to the Balder myth, Vickery writes perceptively of Lawrence's consistent fascination with Frazer's accounts of myth patterns associated with "man-gods" such as Christ and Balder, for Lawrence remains interested in "men who have lost touch with their divine source of strength and power as a background for a quest of recovery" (314). The *renewal* theme remains crucial to Vickery.

19. Lawrence may have absorbed more of the precise narrative of *The Golden Bough* than he is willing or able to acknowledge. Here is Frazer: "And the name of the Balder's bale fires…makes it probable that in former times either a living representative or an effigy of Balder was annually burned in them" (769).

CHAPTER THREE

FREUD, FRAZER, AND THE PALIMPSESTIC TEXTURE: DREAMS AND THE HEAVINESS OF MALE DESTINY IN *THE FOX*

You either believe or you don't.

—D.H. Lawrence, *Fantasia of the Unconscious*

If in the present work I have dwelt at length on trees…

—James Frazer, *The Golden Bough*

There wants a man about the place.

—D.H. Lawrence, *The Fox*

Dreams make an unrestricted use of linguistic symbols.

—Sigmund Freud, *An Outline of Psycho-Analysis*

I

As any cumulative index of articles and citations on Lawrence's work suggests, no short fiction by him has received as much sustained consideration by critics through the years as *The Fox*. This voluminous criticism encompasses a wide variety of subject material and methodology, including a range of opinion concerning such topics as the open-ended conclusion of the novella, the relevance of the purported models for the major characters, and the success of the work as fictional art.[1] Surprisingly

1. For an excellent summary of various perspectives on this novella by a wide range of critics, see the balanced discussion by Harris 163, 284–85. Among the most persuasive and admiring discussions of *The Fox* are Leavis 245–65, Hough 176–177, Moynahan 196–209, and Ruderman, *D.H. Lawrence and the Devouring Mother* 48–70. For the critical opinion that variously regards the work as incoherent, or mean-spirited, or unconvincing, see Gregor 10–21, Harris 163–70,

little attention has centered on the subtle reiteration and development in imagery and motivation that inform the characterizations of March, Banford, and Henry. This relative disregard of thematic pattern and stylistic repetition explains the perplexity and discomfort by many commentators over the uncertain ending of the work, as March and Henry nervously contemplate their decision to leave England and travel across the Atlantic. There exists no in-depth and linear study of *The Fox* that attempts to analyze organized patterns of Lawrence's techniques and doctrines as coherent preludes to the necessarily anticlimactic tone of the final scene.[2] Similarly, there has been little effort to relate the major revisions and radical lengthening of the first version (1918) into the novella (1921) to the changing state of Lawrence's own doctrinal vision within that period—an ideological realignment by him that is connected to the volatile context of Lawrence's marriage to Frieda and to his vulnerable emotions in those "nightmare" years during an especially difficult period in his life. Perhaps the most significant area of neglect involves the lack of relevant biographical and intertextual material on Lawrence's personal and aesthetic preoccupations as he moves from the unambiguous and tightly

---

Ford 101–02, Draper 186–98, Rossi 265–78, Davis 565–71, and Wolkenfeld 345–52. Harris mistakenly argues that Henry's "nature grows more vulpine" (163) as the work develops; her assertions that he is "unswerving in intention and desire" (164), and that "Banford's murder seems unprepared for and unjustified" (163) ignore the key elements of ambivalence and trepidation in him as well as the careful linkage of her death to essential changes that occur in Henry's "soul". Rossi also reduces the crucial complexity of his character by oddly maintaining that he becomes more dangerous and sly at the conclusion of the novella. In similar ways, Simpson (70–73), Davis, and Millett (265) reductively see the work as an unqualified attack against women (e.g. Simpson: a "revenge against independent women" 70; Millett: "not only the taming of the woman, but her extinction" 265), and thus they fail to consider the ways in which Henry's weak and indecisive manhood undercuts the viability of his convictions as the work ends. In addition, while Harris properly acknowledges Gurko (178–82), Moynahan, and Allen (109) as specifically emphasizing mythic dimensions in *The Fox*, the approaches of these critics do not deal with the pervasive influence of Frazer on the work, or with the totemic patterns of primitive believe that inform much of Lawrence's organization of the story. There exists no psychoanalytical treatment of the work except for a short essay by Bergler, and his criticism is exclusively concerned with establishing (too simply, in my view) a formulaic reading of what he regards as a prototypical lesbian relationship between March and Banford.

2. Among the critics who consider the important ambivalence of the ending, see Brayfield 41–51, Fulmer 75–82, and Ruderman ("Lawrence's 'The Fox' and Verga's 'The She Wolf'") 153–65.

resolved tale to the more ambitious novella.[3] This matrix of marital thematics and conflict is configured within a stark and elemental plot involving only three characters; such an uncomplex design, primarily played out in a single geographical location and residence, provides accessible entrance into speculation about the bio-confessional nature of the work's structure, imagery, and doctrine.

When Lawrence begins redrafting *The Fox* in the late fall of 1921, he has just completed final revisions on *Fantasia of the Unconscious*. That often dyspeptic and exhortatory volume on "pollyanalytics" (*Fantasia* 65) offers an elaboration of Lawrence's theories about such topics as sexuality, parenting, education, marriage, and the unconscious; the work is integrated by Lawrence's pervasive interest in the struggle between emotion and intellect that has preoccupied Western culture for centuries. At the center of his argument is a highly charged and cranky attack on Freudian theory. Lawrence asserts, in effect, that Freud dangerously rationalized erotic life and thus seriously underestimated the visionary and religious stimulus in human beings, a primal motivation that Lawrence insists must function irrationally, erotically, and—above all—pre-eminently over the intellect. Philip Rieff eloquently described the oppositional stakes fifty years ago: "Lawrence knew intuitively, if not historically, that reason defends mainly against impulse, and against what he considered the legitimate and undeniable power of love" (Rieff iii). Because of Lawrence's outspoken emphasis on instinct and on the existential primacy of the five senses, it is no surprise that he held Frazer's *The Golden Bough* in high esteem, given that monumental work's unpsychoanalytical inquiry into primitive habits, beliefs, and rituals, all part of a broad and impressive scholarship by Frazer that involved him in a complex and detailed outline of myths, symbols, and taboos enacted in a variety of pre-industrial societies.[4]

---

3. For an intelligent and focused discussion of the "nightmarish" aspects of these years for Lawrence, see Delaney 265–380 on the 1917–18 period, and Squires 173–249 on the years 1917–21. But the most sustained and brilliant achievement in integrating Lawrence's life and work is unquestionably by Kinkead-Weekes in the relevant section (346–673) of his comprehensive volume of biography. Although I take occasional issue in this essay with some of his conclusions, my admiration for his brilliant and thoroughly professional scholarship is unqualified; I trust it is evident in my own analysis of *The Fox* how much I have benefited by the many rich areas for investigation that his research stimulated me to undertake.

4. For a more extensive consideration of Lawrence's views on the instinctual imperative and on his notions of "otherness" and "the unknown," see my essay on Lawrence and Mailer in Chapter Eight, and my essay on "The Princess" in Chapter Six. In terms of Lawrence's awareness of Frazer's importance to his own work, a letter he sends to Bertrand Russell in December 1915 concretely establishes the

Lawrence maintains that "knowledge *must* be symbolical, mythical, dynamic," and that "symbols must be true from top to bottom" (*Fantasia* 113).

He first reads *The Golden Bough* in the fall and winter of 1915–16, and he refers to it in the newly added Foreword to *Fantasia of the Unconscious* (62) as a major influence on his own visionary perspective. As he begins sustained work on revisions of *The Fox*, he had recently read his friend Barbara Low's book on Freudian theory, and her study did little to modify his own contempt for psychoanalytical doctrine. Lawrence's adaptation of elements in Frazer's study of magic, taboo, and superstition often is recognizable in the novella, and I regard it as a serious oversight by critics that Frazer's direct influence on Lawrence's work has not been acknowledged sufficiently in studies of *The Fox*.[5] Yet the undisguised antagonism to Freud evident in *Fantasia of the Unconscious* provides the special dividend of enabling readers of *The Fox* to witness the operative universality of Freud's theories about the unconscious playing itself out against the dogmatically un-Freudian intention of Lawrence: the novelist sounds convinced that the symbologies in his fiction primarily reflect his familiarity with the research of such archetypal primitivists as Frazer, Blavatsky, and Jung. Thus, when salient aspects of Lawrence's life and marriage are engraved on a foundation of Lawrencian doctrine that for *him* is consciously supported by Frazer and unconsciously illuminated by Freud, the result of such a matrix is a kind of palimpsestic fiction, as the various inscriptions of influence on Lawrence compete for priority in this

---

influence and also highlights that primacy of the senses so crucial to the texture of *The Fox*. Here are relevant lines from the valuable letter: "I have been reading Frazer's *Golden Bough* and *Totemism and Exogamy*. Now I am convinced of what I believed when I was about twenty—that there is another seat of consciousness than the brain and the nerve system: there is a blood-consciousness which exists in us independently of the ordinary mental consciousness, which depends on the eye as its source or connector" (*Letters II* 470).

5. Impressive exceptions here are Vickery, in "Myth and Ritual" 79–82, who uses *The Golden Bough* in his recognition of the phallic importance of the corn-fox in March's first dream, and Ruderman, in *D.H. Lawrence and the Devouring Mother*, who understands that the fox is March's "totem animal" (52). In his book-length study of *The Golden Bough*, Vickery wisely indicates that *The Fox* is a work that exemplifies "Lawrence's treatment of the animal or totemic myth whose strangeness has, unfortunately, largely kept it from being taken seriously as an integral part of the tale" (322).

dense and revealing work.[6] The evidence for these strands of influence emerges at different points in the novella, and their visibility is particularly prominent in the two dream sequences experienced by March, when Freud, Frazer, and *Fantasia* complicate and enhance the multi-textured resonance of Lawrence's art.

II

The opening pages of *The Fox* quickly emphasize the unnatural and decreative results of the farming that is so earnestly and awkwardly managed by March and Banford. Through a combination of bad luck, inexperience, and incompetence, the young women encounter a litany of unfortunate events that undermine the fertility of their land and livestock and thereby harm the prospects for their economic survival. The sudden death of the grandfather, the untamable wildness of the heifer, the chickens' obstinate refusal to lay eggs—all seems out of rhythm and recourse even before we learn much about these landowners who attempt an independent life in a difficult and traditionally masculine domain within the severely male-depleted countryside of England at the end of the war. Lawrence stresses this gender inversion and sexual displacement early in the work, as if somehow the women's ill fortune is related to their presumption of unorthodox roles. March is pointedly described as "the man about the place", and Banford "did not look as if she would marry" (7). Yet for all the unconventionality of their household arrangement, Lawrence employs his familiar imagery of procreative blackness to suggest March's potential for the instinctual, creative depths that he praises in *Fantasia of the Unconscious* as the "fathomless blackness" (101) of the eye. He reiteratively mentions that March's "eyes were big and wide and dark" (8), leading to his more direct comment about her unfulfilled passion and repressed needs, that "there was something odd and unexplained about her" (8). For Lawrence, such qualities of inexplicability, strangeness, and unknowability remain the signature of the creative soul: "To know is to lose. When I have a finished mental concept of a beloved, then the love and friendship is dead…To know is to die" (*Fantasia* 108).[7]

---

6. Peter Gay, Freud's eminent biographer, confirms that "the researches of James G. Frazer and W. Robertson Smith into comparative and primitive religion had a very real impact on Freud's speculative writings" (528).

7. On this issue of Lawrence's frequent use of blackness leading to transcendence, and its relation to his style and ideology, see my essay on *The Lost Girl*, and Chapters Two and Five of my book, *The Phallic Imagination*. See also Lawrence's

The farm stands isolated on "the edge of the wood" (9), and from inside the dark and deep border often emerges a fox that is described as a "demon" and "serpent" (9) for the vicious and stealthy manner it attacks the fowl that comprise the working economy of the farm. This picture of the adjoining forest as metaphoric domain, as well as literal sanctuary, reflects the engrained primitivism of the novella that is influenced by Lawrence's reading of Frazer and articulated in *Fantasia of the Unconscious* as his unqualified belief in the "subjective science" that was "taught esoterically in all countries of the globe" and then "remembered as ritual, gesture, and myth story" (62–63). In this context of demonism and magic, Frazer refers in *The Golden Bough* to the Druidical custom in ancient England of burning foxes in seasonal festivals of exorcism, and among the British Celts the burning is an attempt "to break the power of witchcraft" and thus "greater would be the fertility of the land" (761–62). Frazer further explains that the foxes and other wild animals were consigned to the flames because "they were believed to be witches who had taken the shape of animals for their nefarious purposes" (762). March and Banford do not require archetypal justification to seek out the marauding fox, but the mythic implications of serpent and forest alert the reader that rational explanations will not be sufficient to explain the mystical grip of instinct and emotion that informs key moments of the novella. Even the dramatized affection and closeness between the women conveys an obsessive component that seems beyond their control, as the mood swings of one partner create immediate repercussions for the other, and often when the causative issues are trivial or irrelevant. More than joined at the hip, March and Banford stay sealed together in their love, pain, and frustration: it will take a stroke of fate or the imposition of a powerful will to break a bond so entrenched in their daily routine and division of labor: "March had four-fifths of the work to do, and though she did not mind, there seemed no relief, and it made her eyes flash curiously sometimes. Then Banford, feeling more nerve-worn than ever would become despondent and March would speak sharply to her" (9). Although March functions as the heavily burdened and working woman in this shared arrangement, Banford consistently retains the emotional resources to manipulate her partner through her own periodic and well-timed displays of anger, heartbreak, and disappointment.

---

essay, "Morality and the Novel", for his interpretation of the imperative need to convey such a notion of "inexplicability" as part of what he memorably defines as his "fourth-dimensional" style in fiction, in *Study of Thomas Hardy and Other Essays*, 193–98. I elaborate on this style in Chapter Seven of this volume.

While Freud would no doubt have much to say about the neurotic co-dependency of the two women, for Lawrence the issues surrounding them remain visionary and evocative rather than pathological in the clinical terms of modern psychology. This sense of the fox as a devilish and demonic presence in their lives is created by the inexperienced and hysterical perspective of March and Banford, who feel the animal's underworld ambience more than they calmly understand the situational normalcy of its predatory behavior. One of the major themes in the novella will be whether March can distance herself from the range of typological associations related to the fox, and (as a later contingency) whether she can separate Henry from that persistent identification with the fox that informs her preoccupations with this boy-man. It is here that elements of Freudian symbology begin to appear in the multi-layered texture of the fiction, as the unconscious signposts merge with Lawrence's appropriations of regional and totemic primitivism. From the first time that March sees the fox, her awareness is sublimatingly sexual and—more precisely—projectively phallic, with her mesmerized awareness of the white tip of its brush, with her intense concern with its ruddy, snake-like shadow in the deep grass, and with her awkward and mannish use of a long rifle that predictably proves impotent when she uses it in the hunt for the fox.

Lawrence's imaginative use of Frazer's detailed research establishes an additional meaning for the fox that is relevant to March's psychology and emotional development. The fox resembles what Frazer describes throughout *The Golden Bough* as the corn-spirit—that is, the fox as the symbolic incarnation of successful germination and of a bountiful agricultural season. But the fox must die for the harvest to be complete. Frazer describes the urgent need to kill this emblematic intruder to mark the recognition in the community of the necessary and final gesture before the crop can be distributed: "Amongst the many animals whose form the corn-spirit is supposed to take are the wolf, dog, hare, fox, cock, goose, quail, cat, goat, cow (ox, bull), pig, and horse. In one or other of these shapes the corn-spirit is often believed to be present in the corn, and to be caught or killed in the last sheaf" (518). Yet the psychosexual theories of Freud retain viability beyond the documented influence of Lawrencian doctrine and Frazer's primitivism. Here the emphasis on the tail ("brush") of the fox in March's thoughts recalls the totemic terms of Frazer's analysis of a ritual in Bourgogne, while it also illustrates the rites of manhood practiced by an entire village: "The last sheaf [of corn] represented the fox. Beside it a score of ears was left standing to form the tail, and each reaper, going back some paces, threw his sickle at it. He who succeeded in severing it, 'cut off the fox's tail' and a cry of 'you cou cou' was raised in his honor" (518).

As an elusive and natural spirit of procreation that March both respects and reviles, it is difficult to avoid the sexual significance of the presence of the fox in her isolated and frustrated life. When she looks at him, "he was not daunted" (10), for he embodies the Lawrencian "otherness" that as yet March cannot accept, the unknowable passion she cannot engage. She is hypnotically drawn to a part of the fox's body that in its length and bushy prominence seems most male in its full extension: "She saw his brush held smooth like a feather, she saw his white buttocks twinkle" (10). March's attraction to the fox (and soon to Henry) is played off numerous times against the persistent and whining sounds of Banford's voice beckoning her to return: "At last she became aware that Banford was calling her" (10). March is torn constantly between the urgent, choric calls of Banford and the magnetism of the fox or of Henry-as-fox. The desperation in Banford's call will increase proportionally as March becomes more entrenched in the otherness represented first by the animal, then by the man-as-animal, and then by Henry-as-man. This resonant counterpoint, extended throughout the story, between the siren-call of Banford and the temptation of the Lawrencian "unknown" is especially evident in a wonderful passage filled with erotic imagery and the revealing signature of March's isolation and vulnerability under a luminescent moon:

> She took her gun and went to look for the fox. For he had lifted his eyes upon her, and his knowing look seemed to have entered her brain. She did not so much think of him: she was possessed by him. She saw his dark, shrewd unabashed eye looking into her, knowing her. She felt him invisibly master her spirit. She knew the way he lowered his chin as he looked up, she knew his muzzle, the golden brown, the greyish white. And again, she saw him glance over his shoulder, half inviting, half-contemptuous and cunning. So she went, with her great startled eyes glowing, her gun under her arm, along the wood edge. Meanwhile the night fell, and a great moon rose above the pine trees. And again Banford was calling (11).

It is an episode of sexual violation, with March's receptivity reflected in her ability to get beyond conscious thought ("she did not so much think of him") in order to stimulate the feelings, paradoxically, of inviolate "singleness" that for Lawrence (as with Ursula in *The Rainbow*) is always the key to instinctual primacy: "The moon is the pole of our single, terrestrial individuality" (*Fantasia* 188). Just before Henry first appears, March "was content not to talk" (13) as she loses her conscious self in the daily activity of "put[ting] on the wood she had chopped and sawed during the day" (13), a state of soul similar to her earlier experience of watching the fowls "spell-bound without seeing them" (11). In contrast, Banford is mired in the hyperconscious present, with jangled nerves that do not permit her to lapse-out or to feel any hint of the transcendent: "She was afraid to begin to read too early, because her eyes would not bear any strain. So she sat staring at the fire, listening to the distant sounds of cattle lowing, of a dull, heavy, moist wind, of the rattle of the evening train on the little railway not far off" (13). Banford has trouble seeing in the distance; she seems imprisoned in the present and frequently exhibits a compulsive need for habit and orderliness. Her eyes recall Lawrence's discussions in *Fantasia of the Unconscious* of the inadequacy of modern modes of vision: "And we strain ourselves to see, see, see—everything, everything through the eye, in one mode of objective curiosity. There is nothing inside us, we stare endlessly at the outside. So our eyes begin to fail; to retaliate on us. We go short-sighted, almost in self-protection" (102–03).[8]

III

From the moment Henry enters the cloistered world of these women, two integrated factors are reiterated by Lawrence as structural and ideological principles of organization early in the work: Banford insists on seeing Henry as boyish and inconsequential, and March—through a transparent process of displacement and repression—identifies him with the fox. But the Freudian patterns here are no more essential than Frazer's research, for Frazer is precisely relevant about the history of the procreative and phallic potential implicit in the unexpected appearance of Henry, whether he is perceived as fox or corn-spirit. This innovative anthropologist's research into relevant myths and iconography resonates so evocatively today because its offers a viable interpretive design existing apart from the findings of psychoanalytical theory that for many decades after Frazer became the preeminent method for investigations of motivation and metaphor:

> The identification of the corn-spirit with an animal is analogous to the identification of him with a passing stranger. As the sudden appearance of a stranger near the harvest field or threshing floor is, to the primitive mind, enough to identify him as the spirit of the corn escaping from the cut or threshed corn, so the sudden appearance of an animal issuing from the cut

8. It is noteworthy that *The Fox* is saturated with descriptive emphasis on the eyes: no fewer than ninety-two references in this seventy-page novella.

> corn is enough to identify it with the corn-spirit escaping from his ruined home. The two identifications are so analogous that they can hardly be dissociated by any attempt to explain them (537–38).

The Fox reveals Lawrence's palimpsestic effort to fictionalize the process of association and identification described by Frazer, as the novelist embroiders the primitive elements with intentional intrusions of his own doctrine, and with unconscious patterns of motivation and meaning that emerge regardless of his intent. Although Freud is not uninterested in the historic importance of Frazer's expository work, he is understandably more eager to speculate in depth on the psychosexual reasons for the rituals outlined in *The Golden Bough*. Freud's theoretical assertions about the structure and significance of dreams often prove illuminating in the specific case: here they offer a special applicability in terms of an "identification" that March obsessively ponders in her dream-like state: "Wild beasts are as a rule employed by the dream-work to represent passionate impulses of which the dreamer is afraid, whether they are his own or those of other people" (*Interpretation of Dreams* 445). Freud further and famously insists—with open acknowledgement of Frazer's contribution—that such symbolism amounts to "a form of representation recalling totemism. It might be said that the wild beasts are used to represent the libido, a force dreaded by the ego and combated by means of repression" (445).[9] But soon March's repressions will take her from an obsession with the fox to a mesmerized belief in the representation of Henry-as-fox, and this transition also has credible basis in dream theory: "It often happens, too, that the dreamer separates off his neurosis, his 'sick personality,' from himself and depicts it as an independent person" (445).

Despite Henry's social inexperience and sexual immaturity, he impresses his female hosts (and the reader) with his skills at detailed observation. His first extended contemplation of March's demeanor is more curious than erotic, as he ponders quizzically the repressed look she conveys with her tight knot of dark hair, man-like clothes, and receptive eyes—an odd combination of elements capped off with the unwieldy rifle in her hand. March's perspective on him is unequivocal, as she confirms

---

9. Freud and Lawrence are in surprising agreement about the totemic and erotic terror that is often embodied in dreams of wild animals. Lawrence discusses a nightmare about horses in *Fantasia*, and concludes *The Rainbow* with the powerful vignette of Ursula's dream-like experience with horses. He describes a male's relevant dream as evidence that "the great sensual male activity is the greatest menace" (*Fantasia* 183) for the dreamer, and it is reasonable to see March's dream of the fox as a female variant of that pattern.

the syndrome of projection and repression defined by Freud: "But to March he was the fox…The boy was to her the fox, and she could not see him otherwise" (14). His rootlessness and independence are summarized in his military enlistment after he ran away from his grandfather. Such deracination and pluckiness early in his life have provided him with a talent for grasping opportunity and for valuing the virtue of hard work. March perceives little of these qualities during their first encounter. Her immediate sensation that he resembles the fox permits her to relax and to repress the *human* sexual threat and allure he embodies for her. By reductively signifying him as the fox, she avoids (for a time) the full implications of his presence as a man, as Lawrence typically conveys the sensual significance of his appearance for March by means of shadow imagery and of the "lapsing-out" that signals the presence of sexual desire: "There in the shadow of her corner she gave herself up to a warm, relaxed peace, almost like sleep, accepting the spell that was on her…Hidden in the shadow of her corner…she could at last lapse into the odour of the fox" (18). In Freudian terms, March's day-dreams "benefit by a certain degree of relaxation of censorship" permitted by the dreamer in a process of "secondary revision" (*Interp. of D.* 530). Her lapse "into the odour of the fox" illustrates Freud's view that "the wishful purpose that is at work" in the production remains the common but deceptive "phantasy" (529) adapted from childhood memories of passion without interruption or consequence. For March, this phantasy amounts to the bodily rescue and courtship of an adult woman without the undertaking of risk and disruption that real marriage requires. This novella will later elaborate on the relation of Henry and March about issues of conflict inherent in the marriage matrix; but it is apparent even early in their relationship that there exists in both of them a profound immaturity and lack of realism in their perspectives about the complexity and inherent demands of this legal institution. There also exists a more primitive reason for the use of shadows as the metaphor that leads March into intimations of her sexual desire. As Frazer evocatively describes the habits and beliefs of earlier civilizations, he explains how "some people believe a man's soul to be in his shadow," and—as we recall how Henry's view of the fox's shadow will be crucial in his killing the animal—"a warrior's strength waxed and waned with the depth of his shadow" (222). In *The Fox* the crucial and cathartic meetings between March and Henry occur within the shadows produced by encroaching evening. It is during the deeper darkness of March's sleep that Lawrence begins to chart the full implications of her needs and cautions.

IV

March's first dream resonates as a fusion of material from Frazer and Freud, and it also bears the imprint of Lawrence's central notions about the demands of the organic self. In it she responds for once not to the beckoning calls of Banford but to what she believes are the tempting, inscrutable sounds of the fox ("singing outside, which she could not understand" (20)), an animal shaped in the long and lean design of phallic imagery, and with the color and shine of Frazer's famous and totemic subject ("he was very yellow and bright, like corn" (20)). She tries to touch him and he responds with a swipe of the "brush across her face" (20). Lawrence deploys the phoenix-like metaphor of flame that throughout his work indicates the painful but necessary forging *renewal* of the new soul: "And it seemed his brush was on fire, for it seared and burned her mouth with great pain" (20).[10] The dream-work insists on what March's receptive unconscious senses and what Lawrence's vision always mandates: there will be strong consequences from her initial attraction to the fox, consequences that Freud believes are reflected during the dreams of women in which so often "the female genital orifice is [represented] by the mouth," with the tail often functioning as phallic "while the fur stands for the pubic hair" (*Interp. of D.* 394, 118). When March first sees the fox not only does she note "his brush held smooth like a feather", but she also

---

10. See H.M. Daleski's still-unsurpassed study of Lawrence's use of the flame metaphor. I discuss the Lawrencian concept of "forging" in Chapter One of *The Phallic Imagination*, and in Chapter Seven of this volume. In relation to Lawrence's graphic imagery of the elongated brush and its position near the anus, I am not unaware (see Chapter One) of the ample evidence of Lawrence's fascination both with anal eroticism, especially in *The Rainbow*, *Women in Love*, and *The Lost Girl*, and with the resonant symbology of the "signifying" buttocks, memorably employed in his essay, "Adolph", a short work that also emphasizes the prominent brush of an animal. But against the conceivable argument that I have psychoanalyzed March's dream as if she were a real person rather than a fictional character, I call attention to the significant extent to which Lawrence's characteristically prophetic and "intrusive" art militates against such methodological danger: that is, Lawrence's visionary beliefs often graphically intrude on the individuality of his characters, permitting excellent critics of his work (such as Kinkead-Weekes, Ruderman, and Vickery) the galvanizing liberty of the kind of dream analysis I undertake in this chapter. Since an orthodox psychoanalytical approach to images in March's dreams sheds at least as much light on the obsession of the novelist as on the fictional character, such interpretive "doubling" remains a welcome byproduct of any well-integrated psychobiographical speculation on Lawrence's life and art.

"saw his white buttocks twinkle" (10). That the fox's brush is both phallic in shape and positioned on the buttocks of the animal, and that March palpably experiences the fox's assault on her mouth in the dream—such configuration of shape, organ, and sensation is fully explicable in terms of meaningful transpositions and condensation that often occur in dreams:

> One instance of a transposition of this kind is the replacement of the genitals by the face in the symbolism of unconscious thinking. Linguistic usage follows the same line in recognizing the buttocks ['Hinterbacken', literally back-cheeks'] as homologous to the cheeks, and by drawing a parallel between the 'labia' and the lips which frame the aperture of the mouth (*Interp of D. 422*).

Although March "awoke with the pain" of this dream encounter, in the morning "she only remembered it as a distant memory" (20). This lack of retention so soon after a disruptive dream is indicative of the intensity of March's resistance to its repressed significance, and it also reflects Lawrence's defiant and stubbornly anti-Freudian stance that "most dreams are purely insignificant, and it is a sign of a weak and paltry nature to pay any attention to them whatever" (*Fantasia* 178). Much of Lawrence's extensive discussion of dreams in *Fantasia of the Unconscious* relies on a reductive and mechanically "digestive" theory of dream-prompting, as he unpersuasively emphasizes that what the dreamer ate for dinner and how his organs interacted in the body hold major clues to the source and substance of respective dreams. Freud does not dismiss the occasional relevance of physical initiators of the unconscious, but he is famously dogmatic on the issue of interpretability, maintaining without exception that "every dream reveals itself as a psychical structure which has a meaning and can be inserted at an assignable point in the mental activities of waking life" (*Interp. of D.* 35). While Lawrence demonstrates his own resistance to this seminal notion of psychoanalysis, it is likely that some willed disingenuousness on his part explains the adamance of his position. For instance, just a few weeks before Lawrence composes March's dream for the first version of *The Fox* in 1918 (it is virtually unchanged in the 1921 novella), he unreservedly describes his own luminous dream to an important benefactor, Lady Cynthia Asquith:

> I dreamed, also, such a funny dream. When I had been to some big, crowded fair somewhere—where things were to sell, on booths and on the floor—as I was coming back down an open road, I heard such a strange crying overhead, in front, and looking up, I saw, not very high in the air above me, but higher than I could throw, two pale spotted dogs, crouching in the air, and mauling a bird that was crying loudly. I ran fast forwards

> and clapped my hands and the dogs started back. The bird came falling down to earth. It was a young peacock, blue all over like a peacock's neck, very lovely. It still kept crying. But it was not much hurt. A woman came running out of a cottage not far off, and took the bird, saying it would be all right. So I went my way. That dream is in some oblique way or other connected with your aura—but I can't interpret it. (*Letters III* 247–48)

Surely Lawrence protests too much, given the accessible nature of what Freud calls the dream-work, "the process by which the latent dream thoughts were transformed into the manifest dream" (*New Introductory Lectures on Psychoanalysis* 17). The young and sensitive Lawrence, praised and supported extravagantly by his doting mother for his blue eyes and special gifts, here embodied as a proud but vulnerable peacock under assault by the dogs of England, rescued by a mother-substitute who cannot stay with him—the whole vignette, in effect, textured so that Lawrence the artist is both participant (as the peacock) and observer (as the artist). His assertion of ignorance becomes all the more transparent when he sends off the cathartic letter to a titled woman who often has intervened in his life to protect him from the maulings by antagonistic friends, publishers, and government bureaucrats. She is the same woman—as my following chapter on *The Ladybird* indicates—who embodies for Lawrence a compelling combination of beauty, talent, and aristocratic lineage that stimulates his need for her friendship and enhances the repressed evidence of his sexual interest.

March's dream of the fox as an accosting corn-spirit, with its evidence of latent identification of Henry-as-fox, begs the issue of the actual quality of Henry's character and of the relevant skills and vulnerabilities that he possesses. Early in the novella, both women constantly underrate his instinctual intelligence, powerful will, and keen intuition. In the following passage, Henry effortlessly combines his abilities of observation, deduction, and recollection to reach significant conclusions about the condition of the women's farm and the state of their supplies. It is with some developing peril to both women that they fail to fully comprehend the adamance and intricacy of this special talent in him:

> He saw everything, and examined everything. His curiosity was quick and insatiable. He compared the state of things with that which he remembered before, and cast over in his mind the effect of the changes. He watched the fowls and the ducks, to see their condition, he noticed the flight of wood-pigeons overhead: they were very numerous; he saw the few apples high up, which March had not been able to reach; he remarked that they had borrowed a draw-pump, presumably to empty the big soft-water cistern which was on the north side of the house (20).

Henry is as experienced in the ways of animals and farmland as he later will prove uncertain about women and sexuality. He perceives the farm as an "old place", not only because of its age; Henry also recalls his precious residence there with his grandfather, and he still feels at home on this property despite its signs of deterioration. This intrinsic connection between him and the farmland seems mystical and profound throughout the novella. His sensation of what Lawrence memorably calls "the spirit of place" confirms an interesting rumination in *Fantasia of the Unconscious* that also may explain, in part, Henry's later ability to uncannily chop down the tree with such deadly precision. "So there is a definite vibratory rapport between a man and his surroundings, once he definitely gets into contact with these surroundings. Any particular locality, any house which has been lived in, has a vibration, a transferred vitality of its own" (153–54).

Filled with energy and confidence about his role on the farm, Henry uses his insights about the natural landscape and his skill at hunting to shoot a wild duck that the proud male brings to the two women "as a great addition to the empty larder" (21). After this demonstration of his practical value to the ineffective farmers, he brings up his concerns about finding lodging in the village. March appears flexible to Banford's suggestion that he remain with them at the farm, and she accepts the prospect of his residence only by reducing him again to the totem of the fox as she recalls the sensual and "forging" aspects of her dream: "March felt the same sly, taunting, knowing spark leap out of his eyes as he turned his head aside, and fall into her soul, as it had fallen from the dark eyes of the fox. She pursed her mouth as if in pain, as if asleep too" (21). Banford remains acquiescent to this temporary arrangement only by ignoring, through displacement, the sexual threat he presents to her relationship to March. She continues to diminish his manhood by pretending that his presence is inconsequential because the innocence of his youth makes him tolerably gender-neutral: "It's no bother if you like to stay. It's like having my own brother here for a few days. He's a boy like you are…No, of course you're no trouble. I tell you, it's a pleasure to have somebody in the house besides ourselves" (22). Henry now concentrates his attention on March, feeling sexually drawn to her but in the subtle way that his timidity cannot acknowledge as erotic: "Her dark eyes made something rise in his soul, with a curious elate excitement, when he looked into them, an excitement he was afraid to be let seen, it was so keen and secret" (23). It is at this point that he realizes how much he loves the farm, and *then* (sequence is crucial here) he thinks of marrying her as an available practical strategy, of tracking her down in the relentless manner that a capable hunter employs instinct and skill to capture his prey. He clearly shows his age. The prospect of marriage for him is reduced to the proximity of a prize—a reward that functions as the emblem of a competed exploit into imposing terrain. Henry understandably relies on the language of the huntsman to organize the energy of his love-life, but what appears more significant is the relative lack in him of conscious awareness of any sexual dimension in his connection to March. He emanates a calm virginity in his temperament and demeanor even as he functions as a practiced killer with a gun. Such paradoxical qualities of inexperience and power inform the logic and metaphor he uses to justify his initial motivation for marriage: "And it was as a young hunter that he would bring down March as his quarry, to make her his wife" (24). It is a strategy for capture, but with no mature understanding of the consequences of success. Marriage perceived not as renewal but as the way-station for possession—and not even of the sexual kind. The matrix for him is shorn of its essential elements.

V

When Henry asks March to marry him, she responds negatively at first, with precisely the "tomfoolery" phrase he predicted when he contemplated her likely denial of his proposal. When she continues to object to the awkward and precipitous nature of his offer, he touches March for the first time, "with his mouth and chin" on her neck, and she is described as "killed" (26). This moment is crucial for initiating a new movement toward recognition in her that will develop slowly through a series of meetings between March and Henry. What is killed amounts to her unbroken identification of him as the fox, her reliance on a reverse anthropomorphism that has served to camouflage her awareness of the normative sexual presence he can provide in her life. The choric "calling" by Banford then intervenes again, and they both carry logs into the house in obedience to her insistent voice. The unspoken tensions mount while the three characters read quietly, and March begins to lapse-out as she hears the fox singing in the house. Unconsciously aware of the attention Henry directs to her, she represses her consciousness of Henry-as-man by entering further into the instinctual drowse while blurting aloud the identification of Henry-as-fox. March utters the exact words of identity—"'There he *is*!' she cried involuntarily, as if terribly startled" (31), in a virtual dream-state during which she has condensed the salient facts of her dream of the corn-fox with the visual identification of Henry-as-fox—a process exacerbated by the previous touch from him that resembles the touch in the dream. March's dual experience of what Freud denotes as displacement (Henry-as-fox) and condensation (the dream reduced to verbal utterance) is discussed in *The Interpretation of Dreams* in terms that also suggest how the vividness of her "picture" of Henry "under the edge of the lamplight" (30) becomes the immediate stimulus of March's abrupt exclamation. Finally, March can use her dream-thought to state out-loud, concretely, the association that bedevils her. Freud recognizes the pattern that the determinedly un-Freudian Lawrence inevitably confirms in the novella:

> A dream-thought is unusable so long as it is expressed in an abstract form; but when it has been transformed into a pictorial language, contrasts and identifications of the kind which the dream-work requires, and which it creates if they are not already present, can be established more easily than before between the new form of expression and the remainder of the material underlying the dream (375).

During his second meeting with March, Henry insists that she grant him an answer to his marriage proposal. Again, he kisses her neck and cheek, and again "Banford's voice was heard calling" (33). Then Henry, as if he begins to sense the power of Banford to interfere in his plans, enacts the movements and drama in March's dream with eerie correspondence: "He kissed her on the mouth with a quick brushing kiss" (33). The forging process continues as she gives her "yes" to the proposal while the kiss—in the renewing fashion of Lawrence's phoenix metaphor—"seemed to burn through her every fibre" (33). Now Henry makes a tactical misjudgment that reflects his immaturity. He too proudly and abruptly reveals their wedding arrangement to Banford: thus he predictably ends up pouting because of Jill's cutting criticism of their poorly-formulated plans, and because of March's self-conscious silence during this confrontation scene. March herself notices that he lacks the wit and force to respond to Banford's effective ridicule, and March—who still tries to repress her feelings for Henry—too easily sees him as "such a long, red-faced sulky boy" (36). That night Henry overhears the conversation between the two women in which Banford attacks Henry for his alleged lack of ambition and his exploitation of March. But Banford too makes a mistake. She phrases her criticism in volatile class-conscious terms ("A beastly labourer" 37) that offend a young man who is sensitive about his fractured childhood. Banford's intelligent strategy with March, however, is also on display in this manipulative scene, as she just weeps enough to elicit solicitous warmth from March, who now seems under Banford's control again.

Henry recognizes March's wavering as he eavesdrops on the conversation. With his manhood thus assaulted, he takes the long gun, his one reliable and phallic instrument of self-definition, and he stalks out to kill the fox. His intention here is not only to kill the animal: in the act of killing the fox, he realizes that he can obliterate March's persistent identification of him as the fox. This important first recognition by Henry of what needs to be done (the second will be the killing of Banford) is followed by credible evidence of his own increasing maturity caused by March's acquiescence to his marriage proposal. Lawrence asserts Henry's growth in tell-tale phrases of alienation and discontent that sound suspiciously similar to the writer's own perspective in the bitter days during and shortly after the war. The passage also recapitulates some of the images and tone of the dream-letter to Lady Asquith:

> As he stood under the oaks of the wood-edge he heard the dogs from the neighbouring cottage, up the hill, yelling suddenly and startlingly, and the wakened dogs from the farms around barking the answer. And suddenly it seemed to him England was little and tight, he felt the landscape was constricted even in the dark, and that there were too many dogs in the night, making a noise like a fence of sound, like the network of English hedges netting in the view (38–39).

The emphasis on all five of Henry's acutely perceptive senses as he waits for the fox reads as a dramatized translation of Lawrence's discussion in *Fantasia of the Unconscious* of the function of the senses in human beings, described as "activities which are half-psychic, half-functional" (98). Now Henry Grenfel accurately *interprets* ("half-psychic") the subtle signals of sight, sound, smell, taste, and touch in order to *prepare* ("half-functional") for the entrance of the crafty animal:

> He was sitting on a log in a dark corner with the gun across his knees. The pine-trees snapped. Once a chicken fell off its perch in the barn, with a loud crawk and cackle and commotion. That startled him, and he stood up, watching with all his eyes, thinking it might be a rat. But he *felt* it was nothing. So he sat down again with the gun on his knees and his hands tucked in to keep them warm, and his eyes fixed unblinkingly on the pale reach of the open gateway. He felt he could smell the hot, sickly, rich smell of live chickens on the cold air (39).

Henry narrows "his vision into a concentrated spark" in order to watch "the shadow of the fox…creeping on its belly through the gate" (39). Lawrence considers such a sighting by Henry a form of "quick vision which watches, which beholds, which never yields to the object outside: as a cat watches its prey. The dark gloomy look, which knows the *strangeness*, the danger of its object, the need to overcome the object" (*Fantasia* 102). Henry's talent as a hunter should not be underestimated, for he has predicted every move of the fox, an anticipatory precision in him that is part of the irony of his *actual resemblance* to the fox with respect to both his vulpine features and in his sly manner of perception. When he shoots the fox he holds it length-wise by its long brush as he shows the appendage to his fiancée. It is this scene of trophy-display to her (except for a brief moment later when Henry leaves by train) that concludes March's Henry-as-fox correspondence. The fox is dead and so is the imposition by March of a false identity for Henry. Recall Frazer's emphasis of the symbolism of holding up the fox's tail as the community's signature of victory over the animal and the forces it represents, for in that primal gesture "the greater would be the fertility of the land" (762). March and Henry move closer to the consummation of their very human and fertile passion, and the clearest signal of March's progress resides in another graphic dream.

In this morbid second dream, March does not encounter the fox, but she does deal with the death of Banford, who is pictured in her coffin because March comprehends, with a heavy dose of guilt, that the end of the fox-Henry identification also signifies the end of her relationship to Banford. The sequence of the dream-work leads to a relevant interpretation in which Freud's metaphors of the unconscious enhance the evidence of Lawrencian doctrine. March places a fox skin over the body of Banford, with the brush of the fox directly under her head: "And the coffin was the rough wood-box in which the bits of chopped wood were kept in the kitchen, by the fire" (40). Thus March literally presides over a dead Banford and a dead fox.[11] On the symbology of placing a cover on Banford that is surrounded by the remnants of shattered wood, there are Freud's assertions that in dreams an overcoat, of any kind, "can very often be interpreted with certainty as a genital organ, and, moreover as a *man's*," and that "wood seems, from its imagistic connections, to stand in general for female material" (*Interp. of D.* 391).[12] The solemn internment of

---

11. Kinkead-Weekes recognizes that as March "dreams now of interring a dead Banford in the wood box wrapped up in the fox's skin", it amounts to the realization "that *that* part of her too, must die and be put away" (689, K-W.'s emphasis).

12. Note the relevant comments by Freud in *New Introductory Lectures on Psychoanalysis*: "We have not yet finished with symbols. There are some which we believed we recognized but which nevertheless worried us because we could not explain how *this* particular symbol had come to have *that* particular meaning. In such cases confirmation from elsewhere—from philology, folklore, mythology

Banford in March's dream, amid remnants of wood and the coverlet as male organ, becomes a displaced gesture of antagonism that March's conscious self cannot face; that is, the apparent solicitude of honoring a corpse (in the gesture of covering it), scarcely conceals the latent meaning of March's repressed anger about her womanly liaison with Banford, a relationship now in pieces and overwhelmed by the dominant presence of male genitalia, embodied behind Banford by the brush and above her by the covering skin. Unlike the first dream, when "she only remembered it as a distant memory" (20), March is upset when she awakens after her sense of anger and loss experienced in the coffin-dream. Her more intense reactions following this second dream make sense in the context of Freud's view that when a dreamer imagines the death of a beloved "and is at the same time painfully affected...the meaning of such dreams as the content indicates, is a wish that person in question may die" (*Interp. of D.* 282). Even Lawrence finds agreement with Freud on the urgency of dreams that reveal "something [that] *threatens* us from the world of death," for he also acknowledges that "a dream may become so vivid that it arouses the actual soul. And when a dream is so intense that it arouses the soul—then we must attend to it" (*Fantasia* 194). March will now attend to her aroused soul by feeling the fox's body in an intense interlude of Lawrencian communion.

VI

With Henry-as-fox virtually dead to March, and with Banford's influence on her temporarily diminished, March can now touch the fox's brush and feel not Henry but the profound "otherness" of another creature: "White and soft as snow his belly: white and soft as snow. She passed her hand softly down it. And his wonderful black-glinted brush was full and frictional, wonderful. She passed her hand down this also, and quivered" (41).[13] The dramatic extent of her wonder in this scene seems to justify Henry's rumination that "partly she was so shy and virgin" (41–42), and such virginity may suggest—despite the nearly unanimous assumption by

or ritual—were bound to be especially welcome. An instance of this sort is the symbol of an overcoat or cloak [German '*Mantel*']. We have said that in a woman's dreams this stands for a man" (23–24, Freud's emphasis).

13. This passage, of course, offers striking resemblance in its tone, phrasing, and meaning to the awed and intimate awareness of Connie Chatterley of the "otherness" of Mellors and of the frictive beauty of his phallus.

critics of lesbianism—the limits of her relationship with Banford.[14] The mention of "frictional," as well as her sensual excitement over the lingering and soft touch, indicate March's awareness that "the fox was a strange beast to her, incomprehensible, out of her range" (41), and also conveys the possibility of her sexual awakening and impulse for a passionate connection to Henry. But Banford will not be discarded so easily. When she correctly senses that she may be losing March, she purposefully engages him in conversation, with March present, that undercuts his stature by revealing (as Banford suspected) his lack of sufficient preparation for the forthcoming marriage. March slips back into Banford's orbit and Banford confirms March's relapse by asking her to bring up the hot bottle: "'Yes I'll do it,' said March, with the kind of willing unwillingness she often showed towards her beloved but uncertain Jill" (44).

Henry is primed for a counterattack that reveals his own significant growth from Banford's assigned status as "boy". When he watches her trudge up the hill with groceries and with an obsequious March too willing to carry the heavy items, he begins to understand the extent to which Banford remains a problem for the implementation of his wedding plans. As he eavesdrops again on her denigration of his commitment to March, he overhears March, for the first time, respond effectively to Banford's cynicism. He feels the intimacy of his attraction to March, stimulated by the spirited rejoinders she makes to Banford: "And he felt drawn to March again. He felt again irresistibly drawn to her. He felt there was a secret bond, a secret thread between him and her, something very elusive, which shut out everybody else and made him and her possess each other in secret" (47). Thus Henry can take that necessary extra step in his awareness, as he makes the first acknowledgement of his sexual interest in March. His rumination stands as one of the most fetishistic passages of psychosexual revelation in all of Lawrence's fiction:

> He hoped he could touch her soft, creamy cheek, her strange, frightened face. He hoped he could look in to her dilated, frightened dark eyes, quite near. He hoped he might even put his hand on her bosom and feel her soft

---

14. Doris Lessing includes a wise caution about too easily assuming an explicitly lesbian relationship between March and Banford. In the context of her counsel, she provides a pertinent gloss on the working culture in England during the war: "We should not put our assumptions back into such a different time. They share a bed, but women often did then. They were solicitous and careful of each other. Don't forget, it was wartime and men were in short supply. Many a female couple kissed and cuddled because of that great absence. And this kind of speculation is probably precisely what Lawrence wanted to avoid" (Foreword xi).

> breasts under her tunic. His heart beat deep and powerful as he thought of that. He wanted to make sure of her soft woman's breasts under her tunic. She always kept the brown linen coat buttoned so close up to her throat. It seemed to him like some perilous secret, that her soft woman's breasts must be buttoned up in that uniform. It seemed to him moreover that they were so much softer, tenderer, more lovely and lovable, shut up in that tunic, than were the Banford's breasts, under her soft blouse and chiffon dresses. The Banford would have little iron breasts, he said to himself. For all her frailty and fretfulness, she could have tiny iron breasts (47–48).

The superb mimicry of the refracted narration, with its repetitive simplicity and elemental language, captures the exact texture of Henry's uninformed contemplation of sexual proximity. Yes, there is intimate interest in March here, but the tone of desire is more of an adolescent's masturbatory view of a woman's body, almost childlike in its pre-phallic and prurient curiosity, with voyeurism and melodramatic fantasy replacing mature lust and passionate attraction. The rating system Henry uses to compare the bodily assets of March and Banford bespeaks his general unfamiliarity with women's breasts, and the adjectives employed in the comparison might easily apply to the various delectability of food in two competing restaurants. Yet Henry conveys accurate insight about the potential excitement of unleashing March's repressed heterosexuality and about the inherent danger posed by Banford. When a confident Henry enters the room, he senses that March is aligned again with him after her angry disagreement with Banford: both sound like future lovers, as she becomes more feminine and he more appreciative of her allure: "As she crouched on the hearth with her green slip about her, the boy stared more wide-eyed than ever. Through the crape her woman's form seemed soft and womanly. And when she stood and walked he saw her legs move within her moderately short skirt. She had black silk stockings and small, patent shoes with little gold buckles" (49).

In the alternating symmetries and repetition-with-variation of this novella, Henry must perceive March's otherness in the way that she earlier experienced this element of transcendence in the fox: "She was another human being" (49), and with that essential knowledge, so entrenched in Lawrence's doctrine of the "unknown" and Freud's notion of mature love, comes the awesome realization to this boy-man that soon he must make love to March and take charge of the direction of their marriage. The recognition comes with a heavy price: "and strangely, suddenly he felt a man, no longer a youth. He felt a man, with all a man's grave weight of responsibility. A curious quietness and gravity came over his soul. He felt a man, quiet, with a little of the heaviness of male destiny upon him. She was soft and accessible in her dress. The thought went home in him like an everlasting responsibility" (49). The prospect of her accessibility, and of the phallic testing to come, frightens him with its importance and inevitability. But Henry at least feels buoyed by his recognition that he has reached the edge of manhood. When Banford again asks March to do her bidding, Henry confidently asks March to deny the favor. He makes the request to March with "so much tenderness and a proud authority" (51)—in effect, with that elusive combination of sensitivity *and* strength that confirms his developing maturity. As Banford begins to cry, a concerned March wishes to intervene, for she has just "thought of Banford in the wood-box for a coffin" (49). Henry patiently explains to March that it is appropriate to let March cry, a position of directive authority by him that must enhance his masculine sense of self. When he picks up a rug (recall the coverlet in the second dream) and asks March to wrap herself in it, the psychoanalytical implications of March's dream have encompassed Lawrence's artistic intuition: a *man* has offered March the man's symbol of the overcoat, and "she obeyed" (54). Now in the third scene in the cycle, March can feel the otherness not of the fox, not of Henry-as-fox, but of Henry. She recognizes the intrinsic ability in him to help remove her from the choric call of Banford that rings throughout the novella. She can now respond to that different sound from the transcendent unknown: "And then she felt the deep, heavy, powerful stroke of his heart, terrible, like something from beyond. It was like something from beyond, something awful from outside, signaling to her. And the signal paralyzed her. It beat upon her very soul, and made her helpless. She forgot Jill" (52). In the depiction of the fears and hesitancies evident in the naïve responses to the "unknown" in both Henry and March, *The Fox* remains the one novella by Lawrence in which the marriage matrix—and its related themes of renewal and transcendence—are conspicuously connected to issues of maturity and experience.

For all the visionary imperatives of Henry's need for March, he remains a man of caution and qualification about his passionate feelings. Listen to the distinct accent of his youth and inexperience in a charming but simplistically articulated outline of his past, in which it is evident that March represents his first significant relationship with the opposite sex, and likely his first opportunity for sexual intimacy: "Yes, I might easily find another girl. I know I could. But not one I really wanted…Other girls: well, they're just girls, nice enough to go a walk with now and then" (53). His lack of phallic confidence in his expression of desire for her is elaborated further when he anticipates sex with March: "Since he had realized that she was a woman, and vulnerable, accessible, a certain heaviness had possessed his soul. He did not want to make love to her. He shrank from any such performance, almost with fear…It was a kind of darkness he knew he would enter finally, but of which he did not want as yet even to think" (53). The procreative darkness intimidates him, but we must remember that manhood is new to Henry. He rouses himself sufficiently as he "kissed her gently on the mouth," prompting a feeling in a tired and guilt-ridden March not of reciprocal passion, and not of the Lawrencian swoon, but of fatigue: "It made her feel so young, too, and frightened, and wondering; and tired, tired, as if she were going to sleep" (55). It is a fatigue prompted by the history of her strenuous connection to (and current disconnection from) Banford, and March's desire is less for passion and more for the resolution of her situation with Jill: "She felt so strangely safe and peaceful in his presence. If only she could sleep in his shelter, and not with Jill" (56). Henry lacks the sexual force and confidence that can establish a deep and intense erotic connection to Jill—a form of potential renewal for them that might convincingly emancipate March from Banford's domination.

VII

Henry's "saving" presence in her life must end for a while when he joins his regiment. Then occurs a delicate scene that in its kinetic texture would be appropriate for film and the possibility of a stop-action and fade-out portrait. As Henry departs by train he is no longer at March's side to provide the confidence she requires to break Banford's hold on her.[15] She senses her immediate susceptibility to the will of Jill, and as the train moves slowly away and she retains a last glimpse of him, he seems to metamorphose (in her eyes *and* on the page) into the figure of the fox—a relapse in her perspective that later will be confirmed in the rejection letter she sends him. Here is the moment so common in motion pictures, as the gradual distancing leads to a freeze:

15. As I suggested in note 1, Bergler's essay on *The Fox* concentrates so intensely on imposing what he calls "the psychoanalytic theory of lesbianism" on the characters that they are reduced to mechanical illustrations of psychological principles and (in Bergler's reading) pathological patterns. Kinkead-Weekes, like Lessing, is more reluctant to define the work in any way as a judgment on lesbianism: "The nature of the relationship seems what is important to Lawrence, not merely the gender of the participants, though that may help to define the nature" (691). Harris similarly notes that "the love of Banford for March is not represented as repulsive, but it is claustrophobic, deadening" (167).

> So the boy's eyes stared fixedly as the train drew away, and she was left feeling intensely forlorn. Failing his physical presence, she seemed to have nothing of him. And she had nothing of anything. Only his face was fixed in her mind: the full, ruddy, unchanging cheeks, and the straight snout of a nose, and the two eyes staring above (57).

In March's letter she reveals an inability to understand the galvanizing nature of his otherness—not realizing the very terms of her complaint amount to words of praise in Lawrence's visionary lexicon that so privileges the unknowability of the soul: "You are an absolute stranger to me, and it seems to me you will always be one" (57). The rejection of Henry initiates in him the next step in his recognition of Banford's danger: he now knows that not only is she the problem, it is clear that she must be eliminated. Unlike the more indecisive and over-deliberate youth sketched earlier in the work, he goes straight to his officer and impressively wins the approval for a leave. The frenetic bicycle trip that he completes is a major undertaking in the rustic countryside, covering sixty miles in four hours. He is aided in the effort by an adrenalin-rush of anger stimulated by March's demeaning letter and by his awareness that Banford must not prevail.

In *Fantasia of the Unconscious* Lawrence devotes several pages to a metaphor that describes the human body as a bicycle, "and our individual and incomprehensible self as the rider thereof" (97). It is the rider's essential responsibility to listen to the driving force of his soul and move in the direction of "his true dynamic psychic activity," which is "true to the individual himself, to his own peculiar soul-nature" (98). Henry stays true to his soul from the moment he sits on the bicycle, and all through the strenuous trip and the episode of Banford's death. Just before Henry chops down the tree, Lawrence describes him as "perfectly still", for "in his heart he had decided her death. A terrible force seemed in him, and a power that was just his" (64–65). Both this eerie stillness and Henry's emotional resolve are justified by Lawrence in *Fantasia* as he writes of the pregnant pause in the soul before the "whole self speaks", a moment when the soul "collects itself into pure silence and isolation…the mind suspends its knowledge and waits. The psyche becomes strangely still" (155). As Henry chops down the tree with all the power, precision, and will that mandates its felling, he reaches his most impressive stature in the novella, as "his form seemed to flash up enormously tall and fearful" (65). At this point he embodies all his potential attributes of strength and imagination: "the world seemed to stand still" (65) as he emerges from youth into manhood. He becomes for Lawrence, if only in this one scene, the graphic illustration of his doctrine that "only at his maximum does an individual surpass all his derivative elements and become purely himself" (*Fantasia* 76). But as the conclusion of the novella will demonstrate, it is a temporary state of renewal in him.

It is an effective and self-justified hatred that Henry brings to the killing of Banford, and in Lawrence's prescriptive psychology, he is broadly acting on the just dictates of his soul: "The only rule is do what you *really* impulsively wish to do. But always act on your own responsibility, sincerely. And have the courage of your own strong emotion" (*Fantasia* 92). Amid the impulsive fury of his act also exists the poised shrewdness evident when he asks Banford to move away from the area of the tree's possible fall. He knows she will not listen to him, and his futile request protects him from any alleged malicious motive or act of negligence. There is a further irony in the scene that confirms Lawrence's enthusiastic reading of Frazer. In an intriguing passage from *The Golden Bough*, Frazer outlines the ancient belief in the animate life of trees, and such a credo is similar to the vitalism displayed by Lawrence in his entire chapter about the souls of trees in *Fantasia of the Unconscious*, a work Lawrence proudly called his "tree book" (86). Frazer writes: "Trees are endowed with shades or souls, and whoever fells one of them must die on the spot, or at least live an invalid for the rest of his days" (129). Frazer also quotes another scholar who uncovers the old belief that a tree may give a "kind of shriek[es] or groan[es] that may be heard a mile off" when it is felled" (130). In Lawrence's fictionalized appropriation of these taboos, it is the human embodiment of anti-life energy who is killed on the spot rather than the destroyer of the tree; the shriek emerges not from the tree—which was dead before it was felled—but from Banford's beloved March, who "gave a wild shriek that went far, far down the afternoon" (65), as she witnesses a death that resolves her own doubts about commitment with terrifying finality.

Not all her doubts, to be sure. Henry wins and marries her, but "he had not yet got her" (66). As the novella's coda insists, instead of March accepting the principles in *Fantasia of the Unconscious* that "waiting and following" the lead of her man "is inevitable, that it must be so" (199), she has elected to strive for what Lawrence in *The Fox* regards (with unqualified political incorrectness) as the willful dead-end of any relationship: an attempt by the woman to energetically seek "happiness for herself and the whole world" (69). In March striving for this goal—whether with Banford or Henry—she formulates for Lawrence the "blue light" destination that F. Scott Fitzgerald will famously depict four years later as a green light in the final paragraphs of *The Great Gatsby*. Nick Carraway asserts in those lines that the title character believed in a future "that year by year recedes before us", and at bottom Gatsby's "dream must have seemed so close that he could hardly fail to grasp it" (182). The pattern of striving is depicted by both writers as a form of well-meaning but narcissistic and regressive motion, a light that also for March seems to recede the closer she gets to its attainment. "She can see it there at the foot of the rainbow. Or she can see it a little way beyond, in the blue distance. Not far, not far. But the end of the rainbow is a bottomless gulf, and the blue distance is a void pit…So the illusion of attainable happiness" (69). Lawrence's narration, reproducing the perspective of March, claims that a fatigued March "would never strain for love and happiness any more" and that "she would leave her destiny to the boy—But then the boy" (69). The reiterative and dismissive noun of "boy" is the same term Banford uses to diminish his stature. It makes understandable sense that March cannot fully yield to him, that she cannot "give herself without defenses and become submerged in him," for March commits Lawrence's version of the unpardonable sin, and Henry is not man enough to combat it: "She wanted to see, to know, to understand" (69). As Lawrence asserts so essentially in his visionary chauvinism that he earlier stated in his "devouring mother" letter to Mansfield, he wants the wife to follow the husband, who is described as "the pioneer who goes on ahead, beyond her" (*Fantasia* 199). March compromises the simplicity of such a priority with her own more equitable desire "to be alone: with him at her side" (69). After her intense entanglement with Banford, she is tempted to let her own convictions lapse with Henry and thus yield to his notions of precedence ("there was such rest in the boy", (70)). But in the end he remains for her more boy than man. March correctly senses that he lacks the force and maturity that might make her accede to the Lawrencian concept of marriage: "she would have the reins of her own life between her own hands. She *would* be an independent woman to the last" (70).

As Henry and March arrive at this impasse, the narration—clearly channeled now through Lawrence's doctrine rather than Henry's conviction—regretfully adds that "she would not sleep: no never" (70). Henry hopes to solve their stalemate by moving them across the ocean: "He waits to go west. He was aching almost in torment to leave England, to go west, to take March away" (70). Henry momentarily resembles the pioneering male in *Fantasia of the Unconscious* who "wants to break away through the old world into the new" (198). He also sounds a lot like the angry Lawrence of 1921, who carries a similar antagonism about his own country: "He was aching almost in torment to leave England, to go west, to take March away. To leave this shore. He believed that as they crossed the seas, as they left this England which he so hated, because in some way it seemed to have stung him with poison, she would go to sleep. She would close her eyes at last, and give in to him" (70). Here are the relevant lines of the comparable letter he writes to Katharine Mansfield just after the war: "I do so want to *get out*—out of England—really out of Europe…I feel caged somehow—" (*Letters III* 312-13). March may follow him west, but not with confidence in their relocation or pride in her husband's ability to control their fate. Henry has not established what Lawrence requires as the basic requirement for the man in any marriage: "Make her know she's got to believe in you again, and in the deep purpose you stand for. But before you can do that, you've got to *stand* for some deep purpose (*Fantasia* 198). This work concludes so tentatively because its ending directly reflects both the lack of purposeful direction in Henry, and the lingering regrets and guilt felt by March over the death of Banford. Recall that Lawrence finishes the revision of *Fantasia of the Unconscious* just a few days before he revises the 1918 story of "The Fox" into the novella, and the last pages of that non-fictional study focus on the supreme importance of the male's "deep purpose". A lingering question remains: why would Lawrence write a substantial fiction that concludes with such discomforting stasis, with such an inefficacious assertion by Henry of doctrines so central to Lawrence's vision? Any consideration of that issue requires some investigation of Lawrence's life and marriage during the years between 1917 and 1921.

VIII

In October of 1917 the Lawrences suffer a brutal indignity when British authorities, who suspected them of espionage, search their cottage in Cornwall; the next day, on the flimsiest of circumstantial evidence, they are expelled from the region. In the months before this unsettling eviction, an already preoccupied Frieda experiences bouts of anger, depression, and jealousy during interludes of loneliness while Lawrence spends extensive time working in the fields with his close friend, William Henry Hocking, and often visiting with a young American, Esther Andrews. Biographers have speculated about a possible affair during these months between Frieda and Cecil Gray, a music critic and composer as well as a devout admirer of Lawrence's wife; such a liaison seems likely in the light of the vulnerability of Frieda's position in 1917, the ease of opportunity for such intimacy given Lawrence's frequent absence, and the evidence of numerous disagreements between Lawrence and Gray after the alleged intimacy.[16] Frieda is temperamentally unguarded with Lawrence about her extra-marital conquests (e.g. a proud confession about Hobson in 1912), and perhaps Lawrence's later affair with Rosalind Baynes in the summer of 1920 reflects, in part, a declaration by him of the freedom to respond in-kind to his knowledge of Frieda's infidelity.

When the Armistice is signed in 1918, Frieda's concerns about the welfare of her children, mother, and Germany are exacerbated by the public celebrations over her home country's defeat and by the strained relations with Lawrence during the previous eighteen months. To Lawrence's considerable displeasure, Frieda does not accompany him in late November on another trip to London, preferring to remain at the Hermitage. By December 10, Lawrence returns to Mountain Cottage alone, where he finishes the first version of *The Fox*; a later draft of this short tale (compressed even further) would be published in *Huchinson's Story Magazine* in 1920.[17] Kinkead-Weekes persuasively argues that this 1918 short version of *The Fox* is directly influenced by Lawrence's disputes with and separation from Frieda: "That Frieda had openly refused to follow his lead, and may well have decried his manliness again as she often did when tempers rose high, very likely provided an outpouring of imagination and thoughts about maleness and leadership in which the Lawrence of 1918 begins sharply to differentiate himself from the Lawrence of *The Rainbow* and *Women in Love*" (484). Kinkead-Weekes regards this first version of "The Fox", composed by Lawrence amid considerable personal and marital turmoil, as "far less aggressive" than the later novella (484), for neither Banford nor the fox is killed, and Banford even helps to facilitate the planning for the wedding of March and Henry. But Lawrence's capable biographer ignores the most important sense in which this tale *is* more aggressive than the longer 1921 work. In 1918 a betrayed and angrily motivated Lawrence feels no doubt that his character, Henry, can prevail. It is as if Lawrence's accumulated discontent with Frieda combined with his own changing vision about male-female relations, are crystallized in a short fictional work that in its very brevity still contains all the assertive and unequivocal language about Henry's demeanor and decisiveness that are lacking in the more ambitious novella three years later. The strength and confidence evident in the voice of Henry and the narrator stand out in their unambiguous authority in this 1918 version: "March felt the same knowing, domineering spark leap out

---

16. For more in-depth discussion of the possibility of such an affair, see Kinkead-Weekes 404–05 and Meyers 206–07.

17. The best analysis by far of the various versions of the tale is Ruderman's meticulous essay, "Tracking Lawrence's *Fox*".

of his eyes…" (43); "He knew he could *make* her obey his will" (45); "Without knowing, she obeyed him" (47); "But she did what he wanted" (47); "Both women were at his mercy" (47); "The women were at his mercy" (47). Kinkead-Weekes remains correct, however, about the important direction of the tale, in which Lawrence stresses the need of "powerful malehood to make its counterpart fully female…Out of Frieda's refusal to go with Lawrence has become a reversion to an intensification of the Birkin of 'Mino' as against the Birkin of 'Moony' and 'Excurse' …'The Fox' privately rebukes, in imagined assertion of maleness and its value, the woman who breaks orbit" (484–85). The Henry Grenfel of the novella lacks this confidence in his "maleness" that Lawrence assigns to him in 1918.

Three years later, when the Lawrences return to Italy and Fontana Vecchia in the fall of 1921, he is greeted with a litany of bad news. There are changes demanded by publishers for references in *Women in Love* because of Heseltine's continued threat of legal action, rejection notices on Lawrence's manuscript of *Aaron's Road*, excerpts from *Sea and Sardinia* published without his knowledge or permission, and disappointing reviews of *Psychoanalysis and the Unconscious*. By mid-October Lawrence's understandably embattled mood informs his work in terms of his writing's doctrinal emphasis and narrative tone. He finishes revising *Fantasia of the Unconscious*, adding a petulant Foreword that is often witty but pervasively belittling of his readers, and in which the typing of the gender roles of male-leader and female-follower becomes even more emphatic in revision. After he finishes the major changes to *The Fox* during the next few weeks (by November 5h), he favorably receives the invitation from Mabel Dodge to go west and visit Taos, New Mexico. By November 16h he has finished revising the short tale into the novella, but that productive few weeks may have been affected by Lawrence's discovery of still another of Frieda's affairs.

This most recent speculation (dating to 1990) on Frieda's sex life involves rumors about intimacy between her and a young man of twenty-four, Peppino D'Allura, that relevant evidence and circumstance suggest might have taken place between October 21 and December 15—corresponding precisely to the period of Lawrence's creation of the tentatively-concluding novella of *The Fox* immediately *after* the ideologically unequivocal revisions of *Fantasia of the Unconscious*.[18] Might not the uncertainty and fatigue at the end of the novella reflect

---

18. See the excellent discussion of Lawrence's revisions of *Fantasia* and the relation of these changes to his life and art in Kinkead-Weekes, 653–664.

Lawrence's fictionalized expression of persistent failure—now bitterly corroborated by Frieda's latest betrayal—to convince his wife of her need to support him loyally and without any threat to the "passionate purpose" of his work? Might it not also reflect his growing intimations, spurred by his chronic chest congestion and near-fatal 'flu in 1919, of his own inability to satisfy Frieda in bed? There exists compelling evidence that Lawrence's total impotence dates from an illness in Mexico in 1925, but might not a weakened Lawrence have faced periodic intimations of this problem in earlier years?[19] And finally, might not the anger and frustration of his relationship with Frieda in the fall of 1921 inform the portrait of Henry Grenfel's fearful contemplation of sex with robust March?

Or perhaps the intimations are even more dramatic. The tepid passions at the end of *The Fox* might also reveal, in the inevitable manner of the Freudian unconscious, and in the context of his increasing attention after the war to themes of male leadership and *Blutbruderschaft*, over-fond recollections of his friendship with William Henry Hocking enacted not far from the setting of *The Fox*. It is interesting that when Henry is first aware of the sexual configuration of March's body, its appeal to him is phrased in an unfeminine metaphor that recalls expressions of admiration by Lawrence of the youthful demeanor and physicality of Hocking: "her

19. The issue of Lawrence's sexual difficulties is examined more fully throughout the volume, and especially in Chapters One, Five, Six, Seven, and Eight. See also Ellis 163–65, 293–329; Spilka 70–75; Meyers 204–07. There is a compelling fact in Henry's recent history that contributes to his palpable immaturity, and it is ingrained in a pathetic aspect of England's involvement in the war. He mentions that he just came "from Salonika really" (15), and as noted in the admirably meticulous "Explanatory Notes" apparatus of the novella, this Greek port "was the scene of a rather futile Allied expedition in October 1915. Between 1916 and the end of the war, 600,000 men, 200,000 of them British", were interned at Salonika by a Bulgarian army that, other than enforcing this internment, had no other significant participation in the war (239). Henry also mentions that he "hadn't heard for three or four years" anything about his grandfather, a period of time that corresponds to the internment at Salonika (14). The young man's role in the war was static, limited, and conspicuously lacking in combat or travel experience, and thus provided little opportunity to develop any confidence in the masculine authority that is often the byproduct of the varied challenges accumulated as a soldier. It is as if time stood still for him at a critical point in his post-adolescent maturation, and it is then—so in need of renewal and growth—that he encounters March and Banford.

figure, like a graceful young man's, piqued him" (23).[20] Speculation has persisted for years over whether any sexual episode actually occurred between Lawrence and Hocking, and I tend to agree with Kinkead-Weekes's judicious and fair-minded discussion that such a consummated connection was unlikely. But few critics dispute the strong homosexual elements in Lawrence's inclinations, and such an affinity in him returns this essay to where it began: to a concept of dream interpretation that must take precedence over Lawrence's asserted disbelief in such a probing process. The following is a letter by him written to Katharine Mansfield in 1919, after he has completed the first version of "the Fox" but before he begins its revision:

> Frieda said you were cross with me, that I *repulsed* you. I'm sure I didn't. The complication of getting Jack and you and F. and me into a square seems great—especially Jack. But you I am sure of—I was ever since Cornwall, save for Jack—and if you must go his way, and if he will *never* really come our way—well! But things will resolve themselves. I dreamed such a vivid little dream of you last night. I dreamed you came to Cromford, and stayed there. You were not coming on here because you weren't well enough. You were quite clear from the consumption—quite, you told me. But there was still something that made you that you couldn't come up the hill here.
>
> So you went out with me as I was going. It was night, and very starry. We looked at the stars, and they were different. All the constellations were different, and I, who was looking for Orion, to show you, because he is rising now, was very puzzled by these thick, close brilliant new constellations. Then suddenly we saw one planet, so beautiful, a large fearful, strong star, that we were both pierced by it, possessed for a second. Then I said, "That's Jupiter"—but I felt that it wasn't Jupiter—at least not the everyday Jupiter.
>
> Ask Jung or Freud about it? Never! It was a star that blazed for a second on one's soul.
>
> I wish it was spring for us all (*Letters III* 343).

Lawrence's disapproval of psychoanalytic methodology once again remains unconvincing in the light of the accessible clues in the dream. Surely it is his intense and contentious relation to Murry that is visible within Lawrence's pantheistic pleas. What must emerge from the dream is the announcement of his frustrating failure in convincing Katharine and Jack of the viability of the close male friendship that Lawrence depicts in

20. For more detailed accounts, speculative as well as factual, of Lawrence's relationship with William Henry Hocking, see Kinkead-Weekes 379–81, Meyers 213–14, and Delany 309–15.

Women in Love and several other fictions, a theme he will develop more fully in the leadership novels of the 1920s. That "beautiful, large, fearful, strong star" that "pierces" and "possesses" *both* Katharine and Lawrence sounds very much like the coded expression of a sexual fantasy about the third party mentioned in the letter. "As Jung or Freud about it? Never". There is no reason to ask them anything, but not for the reason Lawrence asserts. Like the palimpsestic texture of *The Fox*, the evidence of influence, doctrine, and desire remains inscribed no matter how many erasures, revisions, or protestations Lawrence makes on the rich text of his life and art.

CHAPTER FOUR

THIRTEEN WAYS OF LOOKING AT *THE LADYBIRD*: D. H. LAWRENCE, LADY CYNTHIA ASQUITH, AND THE INCREMENTAL STRUCTURE OF SEDUCTION

I do not know which to prefer, the beauty of inflections or the beauty of innuendoes …

—Wallace Stevens, "Thirteen Ways of Looking at a Blackbird"

I know I am particularly difficult to make love to, and of course outsiders don't know this.

—Lady Cynthia Asquith, *Diaries 1915–1918*

We should find reality in the darkness.

—D. H. Lawrence, in a letter to Cynthia Asquith

The phantasy of seduction has special interest, because only too often it is no phantasy.

—Sigmund Freud, *A General Introduction to Psychoanalysis*

I

There exists surprisingly little consensus on the central aspects of *The Ladybird*. Perhaps no short fiction by Lawrence has provoked so wide a range of evaluative judgments, theoretical approaches, and invested interpretations.[1] This variety of perspectives encompasses strong opinions

1. What distinguishes negative reactions to this work is the unusually strident tone of disapproval that often informs such perspective. Hough, for instance, is unconvinced by Lawrence's confident letter to J. Middleton Murry, in which he memorably describes *The Ladybird* as "the quick of a new thing" (*Letters IV* 447). Hough doubts that "there is anything so very new" (175) and considers it

on its artistic and doctrinal achievement that range from the unequivocally laudatory to the unapologetically demeaning, and they include methodologies that variously focus on such topics as the following: its aesthetic-philosophical inheritances, involving such figures as Nietzsche, Durkheim, Bakhtin, Wagner, and Graves; its authorial influences and relevant echoes of other writers, involving such luminaries as Blake, Shelly, Keats, Yeats, Hawthorne, and Poe; its ethnic and archetypal resonances, involving such innovators as Freud, Frazer, Jung, Darwin, Campbell, and Horney; its intertextual significance and visionary continuities, involving such Lawrence works as "The Thimble", "The Crown", *Study of Thomas Hardy, Studies in Classic American Literature,* and *Fantasia of the Unconscious*; its mythic overtones and classical references, involving such symbolic stalwarts as Dionysus, Apollo, Daphne, Hera, Leda, Osiris, Persephone, and Zeus; and its biographical and topical allusions, involving such friends of Lawrence as Lady Cynthia Asquith and her extended family.[2]

---

unequivocally "a failure" consisting of "pseudo-mystical vapouring" (176). Moynahan regards it as Lawrence's "ugliest story," asserting that it emerges from "an unwholesome region of Lawrence's imagination" (178). Harris sees the novel as markedly unsuccessful, claiming it contains a "stiltedness and a muffling of Lawrence's own clear voice", and she argues that Lawrence is merely "manipulating his heroine according to his idea of the moment" (175, 174). But as I maintain in this chapter, "the quick of a new thing" amounts to Lawrence's use of intimate, highly-charged, and almost "clinical" metaphors to energize the Count's criticism of Daphne and her husband; the "region of Lawrence's imagination" from which this cathartic novella emerges is fraught with repressed desire and multiform anger, and the "clear voice" is embodied in the variable rhetorical strategies and passionate doctrines articulated by Psanek. Harris may not like the Count's technique or message, but Lawrence's clarity here is unassailable.

2. The range of approaches to this work is impressive, and I note below several of the most prominent and useful interpretations. While Daalder offers provocative links to Keats, Shelley, and Wagner in his interesting analysis of relevant influences on Lawrence, he is so thoroughly invested in the complex echoes and associations of the nineteenth century's Romantic metaphors that he *only* treats the novella on the level of myth, insisting that "realistically the narrative is ridiculous" (107). When he does connect the work to aspects of the real world, he oddly insists that "Lawrence is mythologizing the central love triangle in his life, that of Frieda, her husband, and himself" (124). While there is surely some resemblance in pomposity and sexual passivity between Basil Apsley and Ernest Weekley, Frieda is so dramatically different in manner, experience, and erotic intensity from Daphne to render Daalder's speculation here as unpersuasive. Scott provides an intelligent overview of Germanic influence on Lawrence, but he seriously underestimates the complex and incremental stages in the relationship between

The preoccupying importance to Lawrence of Cynthia's friendship from 1915 to 1925 is well documented in their intense letters to each other and in the confirming commentary of their mutual acquaintances and respective family members. Not only an acknowledged beauty of her time and the socially prominent daughter-in-law of the Liberal Prime Minister of England, Cynthia was an accomplished and well-known writer of short stories and a respected anthologist and biographer. Her most enduring work, often deemed her iconoclastic masterpiece, remains her meticulously detailed and often daringly intimate diary of her life during the First World War years, posthumously published in 1968. That work sharply chronicles with insight and sadness an England in profound transition, involving the abrupt death of those pre-war days of abundant leisure, artistic diversion, and political idealism. But it also ingenuously reveals patterns of narcissism and manipulation in her marriage and extra-marital love-life that Lawrence transparently embodies in *The Ladybird* within the character of Daphne Apsley. This novella is situated center-stage for the proliferating themes of the marriage matrix. It is a courageous and intimately transparent fiction that reveals much about Lawrence's secret and passionate desire; it also encompasses his adamant and politically incorrect attitudes about the domain of passion between men and women, and the cultural trends that diminish the belief in sexual transcendence.

Amid this wealth of valuable criticism and biographical material, there exist two interrelated areas that require more in-depth consideration. First, the acknowledged, well-defined resemblances of Lady Cynthia Asquith to Lady Daphne, and of Basil, Lady Beveridge, and the Earl to respective Asquith family members—such a panoply of *roman à clef* has not received the integrated discussion that can illuminate the tone and technique of this fiction as well as the nagging issues in Lawrence's

---

Psanek and Daphne, asserting that the Count only stands "for the principal of decomposition" and that "he can do no more than draw Daphne away from her old life" (122). This reductive reading fails to engage the sustaining value of the eminently Lawrencian "dark knowledge" that Daphne absorbs from her orgasmic episode with Psanek. In his wide-ranging and well-informed discussion of the Appollonian and Dionysian dualities that Lawrence establishes through his depiction of Basil and Psanek, respectively, Cowan describes a variety of myths and philosophical inheritances in the work, and he smartly summarizes the novella's crucial metaphors as "two male figures, the one of light, the other of darkness, compet[ing] for the soul of a woman" (79). Yet Cowan fails to consider the personal, artistic, and doctrinal ways that Lawrence necessarily stacks the argument in Psanek's favor. Thus the primary tension in *The Ladybird* resides less in a "competition" than in an appreciation of the strategies employed in the Count's seduction of Daphne.

turbulent life during the work's composition.[3] Second, Lady Daphne is provocatively stimulated and meticulously seduced by Psanek in a manner that has implications both for the organic structure of this cathartic novella *and* for the lovemaking habits and constrained passion of the Daphne-Cynthia prototype. The Count's prolonged, variable, and clever siege on Daphne's proud and disconsolate womanhood and his related demeaning of Basil's sexual force, engage important Lawrencian notions about sexual intercourse and masturbatory evasion that implicate Cynthia and her husband Herbert (Beb) Asquith; it also includes unusually explicit material on the writer's symbolic and clinical distinctions between vaginal and clitoral orgasm—a preoccupation that circumstances in 1921 in his own marriage and career have made especially urgent and obsessive. Lawrence will never be more caustic and explicit in his fiction about depicting the kind of marriage that he finds contemptuous, as well as the social forces that encourage or at least sanction such relationships.

But a disturbing tone of reticence is recognizable in consideration of this work, and such interpretive omission raises (or conceals) several important questions. Why do critics ultimately remain so timid about discussing the angry thematics and provocatively allusive material of *The Ladybird*? Why have they failed to fully address either the sexual implications of Psanek's insistent rhetoric in this dyspeptic fiction, or the seminal resonance of the "inside out" metaphor he uses so consistently in the work? Commentators have generally contented themselves with the most pallid and least suggestive readings of the relations between—and within—the Lawrence-Psanek and Cynthia-Daphne characterizations, and there is insufficient speculation on the full texture of Lawrence's invested but often frustrating friendship with Lady Cynthia Asquith. A close, linear reading of the text, combined with relevant speculation on Cynthia's intimate life and her relationship to Lawrence, may provide a means to break through the relative silence about the symbolic ramifications and biographical nuances of this novella.[4] Such focused attention to narrative

---

3. F.R. Leavis is among the first critics to acknowledge the relation of characters and circumstances in the novella to Asquith family members, and he praises the novel not only for establishing but also getting beyond, the issue of biographical models. My own approach to this work, however, insists that its idiosyncratic power derives, in part, from its daring and highly personalized provocations centered in Lawrence's connection to Cynthia.

4. In terms of the characterization of Daphne and its resonance for Lawrence's feelings about Lady Cynthia Asquith, Ruderman states the matter incisively as she captures the essence of Lawrence's transparent desire: "In *The Ladybird*, as in many of Lawrence's other works, there is a character who not only speaks for his

development in this novella can contextualize Lawrence's loud cry of defiance against what he regards as the often cynical and permissive attitudes about passion and commitment promulgated by the Bloomsbury and Cambridge group of artists and intellectuals, including many of his close and talented friends.

In addition to these significant gaps in available criticism on *The Ladybird*, there has been virtually no mention of the carefully integrated structure and plot sequence in this intentionally defiant and often perverse novella. The work is a tightly woven narrative of incremental repetition and variation that is organized around a time span of five consecutive seasons and a long sequence of interconnected scenes between Psanek and Daphne. Lawrence's familiar tropes and antinomies of light and dark, cold and hot, out and in, all receive creative and often daring configurations—as if the legitimacy and strength of his dualistic symbology is being tested within the shifting rhetorical strategies that Psanek employs on Daphne.[5]

---

creator but also acts out his creator's wildest fantasies concerning women" (*Devouring Mother* 79). And here Ruderman sounds the most precise of all critics on the fundamental issue that I develop: "*The Ladybird* suggests Lawrence's desire to take lady Asquith as a wife, or at least as a lover" (80). Feinstein also understands this crucial aspect of the novella when she asserts more generally that "characters based on Cynthia usually have husbands who do not offer much physical love, and at the time when Lawrence knew her best, Cynthia showed a stronger interest in admiration than in sexual fulfillment. Indeed she had never had a lover whom Lawrence would have called 'real'" (108). My analysis of the work attempts to demonstrate, in effect, the absolute appropriateness of Feinstein's signature use of "real". More recently, Ellis notes (but does not develop the idea) that *The Ladybird* carries "suggestions of a fantasized sexual relationship between [Cynthia] and the figure closest to the story's author" (277). Jones correctly maintains that "Lawrence is probably being true to his own experience with Cynthia Asquith", as he observes that the novella provides a "way of mythologizing and giving value to a relationship in which, whatever he wished, had to remain limited" (29). But Jones never uses *The Ladybird* as a way of subjecting this key notion of "value" to sustained scrutiny, and his point about Lawrence's real desire in the relationship lacks any concern with the impinging biographical context of the work or its texture of sexual tension. In a more graphic instance of Lawrence's preoccupation with Cynthia, in 1918 he writes to her in great detail about a disturbing dream that continues to perplex him. While he claims to her that he "can't interpret it" (*Letters III* 248), the dream reveals a haunting synthesis of oedipal fixation and lustful desire that suggests Lawrence's repressed longing for Cynthia. See an analysis of this dream in my chapter on *The Fox*.

5. F.R. Leavis comes closest to defining a tone in this novella that relies on reader "acceptance" of an unusual narrative synergy residing in the interplay between Psanek's *mythic* metaphors and his unorthodox *presence* in a real and well-defined

Similarly, critics have too easily dismissed much of the idiosyncratic pronouncements, volatile mood swings, and unorthodox actions by the Count as mean-spirited reflections, or even caricatures of Lawrence's perspective on his own life. But Count Johann Dionys Psanek actually speaks with the precise anger and emphasis on the same topics that preoccupied this talented, depressed, and anxious writer in the turbulent fall of 1921. Lawrence, of course, has supplied Psanek with the tiny body, flamboyant personality, and exotic background that distance him, at least on the surface, from the writer. Indeed, Mark Kinkead-Weekes, in his superb middle volume of the comprehensive Cambridge biography, directly engages this issue of authorial "recognition" when he formulates the conventional attitude on Psanek but then wisely follows it with a lingering and crucial question: "For the Count is also a kind of caricature of Lawrence made into a *little* man, bearded and odd-looking; a sick man and an outsider who says weird if curiously poetic things, a proud and prickly man, who is rather ridiculous really, isn't he? Or is he?" (694) The eerie resonance of this legitimate question lingers throughout the work, and the answer becomes more complex and ambiguous in the light of Psanek's progressive success in his calculating strategy.

It is an angry, frustrated, and scarcely camouflaged Lawrence who writes this novella late in 1921, just after he finishes *The Captain's Doll* and *The Fox* only days earlier, and about a month after completing final revisions on *Fantasia of the Unconscious*. Lawrence remains bitter about critical reception and ignorant dismissal of his writing, by unfair and often brutal treatment by the British government and its authorized censors and arbiters of taste; by tepid reactions and/or passivity by his publishers and by cowardly rejections of his work by editors at major houses; by volatile and often unsympathetic responses to his own needs by his headstrong wife (who may also have had an affair as he completes *The Ladybird*); and

---

world of war and injury. That balance between symbol and actuality, as Leavis realizes, "depends on the maintaining of a grave and noble seriousness, earnestly and prophetically poetic" (*Novelist* 197). Humma remains one of the few critics to praise the novella for its artistic technique and use of metaphor. Yet amid his deft treatment of Lawrence's imagery, in which he recognizes it as a work about "surfaces and subsurfaces" (17), he neglects all concern for the larger issues of narrative structure. Humma's solid knowledge of the inside out trope is not applied to the important issue of Psanek's rhetorical strategy, and he remains silent about its relation to the psychosexual aspects of Daphne and her history of compromised passion.

by irritating disappointments in his valued friendship with Cynthia.[6] Lady Asquith had recently accepted a secretarial position with the unseemly popular J.M. Barrie, a cloying writer for whom Lawrence feels personal and professional disgust. More pertinently, Cynthia had not thanked Lawrence in any of her usually reliable and prolific correspondence for his generous gift of an inscribed copy of *The Lost Girl*, and their letters to each other diminished significantly in the previous year. When he finally breaks a prolonged lack of communication in June of 1921, he chastises her for not acknowledging his gift, but still receives no written thank you during his ongoing months in Italy and Sicily. He does not write again to Cynthia until February 1922, and their friendship—which Lawrence cherishes—gradually wanes and never returns to the intense level it reached during and shortly after the war.

II

The Ladybird is the most angry, patriarchal, and resolute of the three excellent novellas Lawrence composes in his disconsolate but strangely productive fall of 1921. Each of the works is created as a radical and lengthy refashioning of shorter Lawrence stories already published. The development in just six weeks from *The Captain's Doll* to *The Fox* to *The Ladybird* reflects an increasing doctrinal adamance by the time of the third novella that is conspicuously absent within the equivocations of the two earlier fictions: Captain Hepburn cannot quite convince Hannele of the advantages inherent in his masculinist vision of marriage, and boyish Henry Grenfel may have killed Jill, but finally lacks the confidence and maturity to convince March or the reader that his marital notions of male primacy amount to anything but rhetoric and bluster. Yet in those last December days of 1921, almost a month after completing *The Fox*, and perhaps motivated, in part, by a sudden lack of appreciation or even interest from Cynthia, Lawrence creates an angry and unambiguous fictional representation of his most intense fantasy about this aristocratic woman. Psanek-Lawrence takes Daphne-Cynthia to bed while the seductive Count simultaneously demeans her marriage to Basil-Beb and excoriates the habits of their inadequate sex life. Lawrence's affirmation of the grounds of Psanek's verbal demolition of the basis of Daphne's marriage will

---

6. For discussions of the complex dimensions of disappointment and anguish in Lawrence's life during this period, see integrated considerations of his biography and art in Kinkead-Weekes (674–98).

prove to be conspicuously uncensored in its symbology and eminently Lawrencian in its doctrine.

Between the introductory visits of Daphne and her mother, Lady Beveridge, to see the injured Psanek at Hurst Place Hospital in London during the final months of 1917, and the final farewell between Daphne and the Count more than eighteen months later, there are thirteen separate meetings between Lady Daphne and Psanek. These visits comprise nothing less than a *tour de force* of verbal wit, emotional vulnerability, sexual intention, metaphoric exuberance, and doctrinal speculation—and all elements relentlessly geared toward the slow but inevitable seduction of Daphne Apsley. Among the many important analyses of *The Ladybird* is an essay by Sandra Gilbert that alleges that the novella's central theme remains female power personified in Daphne and illuminated through the critic's tightly integrated allusions to such mythic figures as Griselda, Persephone, Ariadne, and Cybele. But all this ingenious, feminist reworking of the novella remains more clever than persuasive, for it emasculates the felt body and spirit of this unabashedly male-chauvinist cry from within the Lawrencian darkness. To quote the Wallace Stevens poem, Gilbert's essay at times makes one think all that "whirled in the autumn winds" at bottom was "a small part of the pantomime" ("Thirteen Ways" 74). She regards *The Ladybird* as a fictional depiction of how "female power creates male energy," and she asserts that Psanek "is continually at [Daphne's] mercy throughout the tale" (143, 146). Surely, Gilbert is correct in her general observation that "Lawrence's self-analyses were always so frank in their confrontation of the psychodynamics that other poets and novelists only more hesitantly explored" (132). But my own understanding of the novella suggests that she reads the novel, in effect, inside out. *The Ladybird* is firmly organized and doctrinally infused to decimate the wisdom and authority of Daphne's pre-Psanek self-definition, and the work makes her a virtual pawn in the rhetorical onslaught by the Count that culminates in her submissive Lawrence posture and in her orgasmic rapture in Psanek's dark bedroom.[7]

Lawrence's Daphne-Cynthia remains his prototypical dreaming and beautiful woman, mired in an unfulfilling and disturbingly "modern" sex life that receives Lawrence's full measure of scorn for its essential lack of

---

7. Granofsky shrewdly senses the inherent weakness in Gilbert's approach, recognizing that she gives Lawrence "more credit than he deserves" in her misplaced assertion of feminist priorities in the novella (*Lawrence and Survival* 83). Ruderman also notes the masculinist bias in the work, observing that "the black-eyed men like Count Dionys…are ready to resume their proper leadership role after pulling woman down from her pedestal" (144).

belief in transcendent passion.[8] Cynthia Asquith's greatest love-affair in her long line of intensely romantic but unconsummated infidelities during her marriage to Beb Asquith was Basil Blackwood, who was killed in the war before—according to Nicola Beauman, Cynthia's biographer—he might have been the one lover who could have provided "the sexual fulfillment she was beginning, tentatively, to reach out for" (184). I am not convinced by Beauman's analysis, for Cynthia's extra-marital escapades (that precluded consummated sex) were long engrained in her relations with her many suitors, part of a compromised pattern of coquettish courtship with men that Lawrence could only regard as indulgent and manipulative. Early in the war Lawrence even writes a letter to Cynthia that contains the exhortation that "the only permanent thing is *consummation* in love or hate" (*Letters II* 376). Given the close friendship of Cynthia and Lawrence during the period of her infatuation with Basil, and in the context of her consistent straying from at least the spirit of marital loyalty that Lawrence knows is the signature pastime of Cynthia and her upper-class friends, there is little doubt that Lawrence is aware of Cynthia's fondness for Basil. Beb Asquith tolerated all of Cynthia's love affairs provided they are reasonably discreet and did not intrude on his own penchant for a serial infidelity that does not stop at what Cynthia describes as—referring to her own dalliances—"gibbets," a form of intense kissing and petting.[9] What a wicked delight for Lawrence to give Daphne's sexually childish husband the name Basil. While there is evidence that Cynthia recognizes (and tolerantly accepts) her portrait in such Lawrence works as "The Lovely Lady", "Glad Ghosts", "The Thimble", and "The Rocking-Horse Winner", the undisguised and sexually-charged theme in *The Ladybird* becomes too stark for her to accept, and in later years she starts to "deny that Daphne is modeled on her, pretending, for example, to the publisher Daniel George that she is based on Enid Bagnold and to the writer George Ford that she is based on Lady Mendl" (Beauman 171).

---

8. See my discussion of sexual transcendence in Lawrence in Chapters Two, Three, and Five of *The Phallic Imagination*, and my essay in *The Hemingway Review*.

9. See her unselfconscious diary notations on April 17 and 18, 1917 ("Did some gibbets with Claud…We did some gibbets") for a sense of the adolescent and repetitive nature of this favorite form of her intimacies (291–92). The term often appears in her diary, and in relation to many "lovers." The implications, it seems to me, encompass the possibilities of both digital and oral stimulation.

III

In the introductory visit to the hospital, in which Lady Beveridge accompanies Daphne, a severely wounded but keenly alert Psanek processes subtle indications from Daphne that reveal to him her vulnerability to seduction. The narrator clarifies that "her eyes told of a wild energy damned up inside her", and the stated comparison of her to "Artemis or Atalanta" cryptically suggests (because Daphne is married) that some fierce form of her womanly chastity is yet to be explained in the novella (161). Thus early in the work, Lawrence uses intrusive narration to reveal his subjective bias that will mandate the unqualified evaluation of character and the metaphoric oppositions that inform *The Ladybird*: this female's undefined "virginity" must be connected in some way to the context of her sexual relations with "an adorable husband" rather than "the daredevil" she deserves (161). The crucial note of antinomy also infuses these opening pages, for "in her *mind* she hated all daredevils" (161)—the first appearance in the novel of the evocative "inside out" metaphor that Lawrence will clarify—with explicit biological ramifications for Daphne—later in the work.

In this stage-setting scene in late fall Daphne arrives at Hurst Place dressed in the most unrevealing, flesh-concealing garment she will wear in any of the forthcoming thirteen visits with Psanek. She wears "a black sealskin coat with a skunk collar pulled up to her ears, and a dull gold cap with wings pulled down on her brow" (164–65). When the injured Count proves unresponsive to her presence in his depressed and sedated state, Daphne typically relies on the allure of her beauty to stir the interest of this saturnine and preoccupied man. Such a pattern of recourse to surface allure was habitual to Lady Cynthia Asquith, a fact that Lawrence often criticized severely to her face and in their correspondence; Psanek soon will assail Daphne's penchant for relying on her beauty as her essential appeal, and his castigation is framed in nearly the exact terms that Lawrence used in his letters to Cynthia.[10] But for now Daphne's habits of self-definition are hard to break: "She felt suddenly stifled in her closed furs, and threw her coat open, showing her thin white throat and plain black slip dress on her flat breast" (165). The flirty gambit fails to rouse Psanek, but he has already duly noted that "she was still a little red round

10. Lawrence is utterly frank and undiplomatic in these admonishing letters. See especially his note to her on July 21, 1915: "It always irritates me, this talk of 'a beautiful woman'. There is something so infinitely more important in you than your beauty. Why do you always ignore the realest thing in you, this hard, stoic, elemental sense of logic and truth?" (*Letters II* 368)

the eyes, with her nervous exhaustion" (165). An emotional and physical casualty of the war, Psanek's melancholia—considerably deeper than Hepburn's depression in *The Captain's Doll*—will be alleviated gradually through the assertions to Daphne of his verbal dexterity and doctrinal power. Thus his "renewal" of a damaged self is linked to the cumulative success of the careful steps in his seduction of her—a perverse pattern of improvement in his body and soul that reflects the versatile dimensions of Lawrence's craft. He can be wicked, as well as wise. When she empathetically tells Psanek that it is his responsibility to survive, he asserts, to the contrary, that he only desires death. Daphne's response to his theatrical pessimism hints at the frustration that also haunts her own life: "Even death we can't have when we want it" (166). She remains puzzled and entranced by the pitch-black look in the Count's eyes, and darkness of any kind will remain for her an enigma and a fear. When she asks him the kind of courteous question that is firmly ingrained in her commitment to volunteerism and social action—"can't I do anything for you?"—Psanek answers with a more directive and radicalized formulation about the lure of "inside" darkness: "No no!…I would not mind if they buried me alive, if it were very deep, and dark, and the earth heavy above" (167). She leaves, fascinated by his otherness, and by the fact that he lies inscrutably in a bed without any need or desire for connection to the social fabric; he appears to her as "a bit of loose, palpitating humanity, shot away from the body of humanity" (167). Psanek has sized up his beautiful and available prey, and in the thirteen meetings that follow he develops a variety of strategies and demeanors to win the soul, spirit, and body of his titled English lady, modeled on the daughter-in-law of a once-besieged and former-Prime Minister Asquith.

In the intervening ten days "she could not forget him" and in her first solitary visit (call it *visit one*) she quickly takes off her furs to reveal that she "wore only her dress and a dark, soft leather cap" (167). Surely, Psanek must observe that with "her face averted" she appears "unwilling to meet his eyes" (167). When the Count states that "the nights are not so long", Lawrence intrudes on her marital privacy by informing us that Daphne knew "what long nights meant" and "he saw the worn look in her face too" (168). In his depressed condition, Psanek refuses her gift of flowers, and he also prescriptively employs the inside out metaphor as a species of compliment that insists her real potential is unfulfilled: he maintains she currently is "like a flower behind a rock, near an icy water" (168). In short, the flower is without the sustenance of warmth and open air, and hence her vaunted beauty amounts to inconsequential, "surface prettiness" lacking the substantive qualities than can enrich its growth. He reiterates that there is nothing she can do for him, as he stresses his own isolation and the compelling fact that there is a species of "devil" in his body that stubbornly keeps him alive (169). But Daphne remains a smart and witty woman who is keenly aware of metaphysical conundrum and rhetorical paradox. In the spirit of gentle debate she asks him if one must "hate a devil that makes one live" (169). She continues her nagging preoccupation with Psanek after this visit, while his talent at breaking into her consciousness appears almost magical, as he "seemed to come into her mind suddenly, as if by sorcery" (169). That last hypothesis of magical interference involves another unexamined dimension of meaning in *The Ladybird*.

Lawrence acknowledges the influence of Frazer's *The Golden Bough* on his notions of myths and symbols as he completes *Fantasia of the Unconscious* before he begins work on the three 1921 novellas.[11] Frazer's most lengthy chapter in that monumental study concerns "Sympathetic Magic", describing how the magician can demonstrate (as "The Law of Similarity") how objects or people that "have once been in contact with each other continue to act on each other at a distance after the physical contact has been severed" (12). Psanek's growing confidence and strength, combined with his increasing assumption of magical insight and mythic domination, connect even more directly to the central tenets of *The Golden Bough* and to its various "accounts of men who have lost touch with their divine source of strength and power as a background for a quest of recovery" (Vickery 314). It is in this sense that Gilbert's essay fails to understand the irony of how Daphne's presence in his life does not really provide her with feminist power as much as it *enables* Psanek to reclaim his uncompromising patriarchal voice. Such reclamation of visionary "authority" remains the key to Psanek's organic renewal. Just as Frazer stresses that "Dionysus was merely a disguised Osiris imported directly from Egypt into Greece" (449), Dionys Psanek, like Osiris, moves from deathly injury to rejuvenated aggressor as the novella progresses through the sequence of thirteen visits. Indeed, as if more cognizant of his growing power over Daphne, in *visit two* the Count becomes more probing and personal in his questions to her, as he inquires about her husband and family. He also surprises her with his awareness that she appears ill, and he is rewarded for this observation by hearing the defensive, insecure note

---

11. His first reading of the *The Golden Bough* occurs in the fall and winter of 1915–16 during the period of his most intense friendship with Cynthia. He later refers to that work in the newly added foreword to *Fantasia of the Unconscious* (62) as a major influence on his own visionary perspective as he begins work in the fall of 1921 on the three novellas.

in her voice when she worries more about her appearance than her illness: "But do I look ill?" (169) She thus reconfirms for the watchful Psanek the shaky basis of her self-esteem. He is always gathering further information about his quarry.

In the short *visit three*, the Count continues to sense the efficacy of his impact on Daphne, for he casually notes, as if conveyed to her merely as a brief rumination, that "I wish the sun would shine on my face" (170). Weeks later *visit four* occurs, in the late winter of February when the first flowers begin to blossom, including crocuses and the scent of mezereon. The exact botanical phrase, Lawrence surely knows, is *daphne mezereum*, a component of the myth of Proserpine, ironically the protectress of marriage.[12] Psanek's first comment when he sees her—as if to ratify the retentive power of his hold on her from the last visit—is "You have come to put me in the sun" (170). So canny Psanek's simple comment about the sun from the earlier *visit three* amounts to a premeditated test of his power over her, as the notion he gently "planted" in Daphne-Persephone (also a goddess of vegetation) has blossomed, by visit four, the way he intended. When the Count now catches her intently staring at him, their first real moment of flirtation begins; it occurs, naturally enough, within the context of Psanek-Lawrence's visionary concept of inside out. The Count mentions that he is a fire worshipper, and that Daphne looks "like a flower that will melt" (171)—a thinly veiled metaphor about the sexual spark *within* her beauty that is as yet unkindled. Such a provocatively sexual comment evokes her first smile at him, one that emerges "with a slow, cautious look of her eyes, as if she feared something" (171). She concludes her response with a relevant metaphor of her own that reads like a coquettish dare in its explicit reference to him and to her own unexplored insides: "I am much more solid than you imagine" (171), a teasing come-on recalling the assertion by Randolph Churchill that Lady Asquith was "the greatest flirt who ever lived" (Beauman 129).

IV

As their witty exchanges continue to heat up in this fourth visit, Psanek takes an abrupt jump in his seduction technique, for it is noteworthy that at this point neither character has physically touched the other in any form, including greetings or good-byes. The Count now announces to Daphne, without the slightest hesitation or prologue that some day he would like to

---

12. See Cowan, Gilbert, and Granofsky for various discussions of mythologies and metaphors relevant to the role of flowers, growth, and germination.

"wrap your hair round my hands like a bandage…You know, it is the hermetic gold—but so much of water in it, of the moon" (171). Here Lawrence alludes to mythic and chaste Diana and Cynthia, who are both also moon goddesses. As Beauman indicates in her fascinating biography of Cynthia Asquith, her first name was intentionally selected by her parents to celebrate the power, poetry, and beauty of the moon in the hope that those qualities would be reflected in their daughter. The presumptuous comments by Psanek about her hair refer to Hermes Trismegestris and the Egyptian God Thoth, the founder of the art of alchemy. The Count's articulation of his sensual desire to embrace the essence of Daphne's hair is directly relevant to that issue of "substance" within her. Further, the emphasis on its healing power recalls *The Golden Bough* and the pages that Frazer devotes to the primitive and totemic use of shorn hair to help crops grow, to ensure a bountiful harvest, and to contribute to the health of human offspring and the longevity of tribal leaders.[13]

Psanek then again changes his tone and technique. With a deceptive shrewdness that complements his overt flattery of Daphne, he now willingly chooses to play the victim. It is a well-timed strategy that allays her fear about the sexual threat he embodies. The Count formulates the kind of appeal he correctly senses that Daphne's empathetic volunteer experience at hospitals during the war will recognize as poignant: he cryptically explains to her that he has lost his manhood for the time being, that he knows he seems childlike, and that he is grateful that she does not "take advantage" of *him* (171). It may well be a sexual wound and impotence to which he refers, but it is more likely his organic soul and psychic confidence that have been damaged by the war. Like the primitive peoples described in *The Golden Bough* who variously idolize, sacrifice, derogate, and appropriate females, the Count has momentarily invested a woman with totemic status, claiming that she is the only one who can get him to talk freely, and thus, only she can return to him the lost essence of his animate soul. Frazer outlines the tribal belief that "when a man is ill, his soul has left his body and is wandering at large" (213). Unlike Sandra Gilbert, who believes in an evocation of female power, initiative, and control throughout *The Ladybird*, I regard Psanek's "victimization" strategy as more rhetorical and manipulative rather than sincere and urgent, for he demonstrably improves in spirit and body very quickly and without the benefit of Daphne Apsley's golden tresses.

In *visit five*, as if encouraged by Daphne's apparent acceptance of the verbal liberties he took in the previous meeting, the Count raises the level

---

13. See Frazer 271–74, 777–90 for fascinating accounts of this custom.

of his presumption considerably. He not only tells her that she is beautiful, but also asks—in a demeaning and aggressive manner—if her husband is a "dear lover" (172). It is an ungracious attempt to demean the sexual force and manhood of her spouse. Certainly, the question crosses the line of appropriate talk with a married woman, but Psanek, like Lawrence, must sense the level of trespass that the flirtatious Daphne Apsley and Cynthia Asquith will tolerate. There is even interesting evidence here of how eerily perceptive Lawrence could be about characters in fiction and in life. He could not have seen Cynthia's diary notations, but consider the following entry by her in March of 1918, coincidentally almost the exact moment in the novella's time-span when the fictional Count asks Daphne about the sexual capability of her husband. In Cynthia's actual life it is Prince Bibesco whom Cynthia (after the death of Basil Blackwood) is encouraging as her latest extramarital flame in a litany of many recreational "lovers" the past year. Note the equanimity of her reaction to the Prince's naughty question as he tries unsuccessfully to get her to bed:

> Lunched tête-à-tête with Bibesco at his earnest request. He obviously wishes to play a large part in my life and took pains to convey the fact that he was cured of Elizabeth…He was *very* personal and ultra foreign, the "Do let's talk about you" technique, with leading questions about erotics: 'Is your husband *follement amoureux* of you?' etc. (*Diaries* 421–22).

When Daphne turns away from the Count's question with only mild displeasure, Lawrence cannot resist developing, almost playfully, the Egyptian mythologies and iconic moments from *The Golden Bough* that periodically intrude into the novella. Psanek momentarily appears to Daphne as the embodiment of the devil, an echo of the earlier repartee with her about the healthy qualities of diabolism. He also here resembles the infamous and powerful crocodile that terrorized the populace in the land of the God Thoth, a creature that Frazer describes as receiving a special and often celebrated respect ("the principle of *lex talionis*" 601) in rites of idolatry and worship. The perspective in the passage is refracted from Daphne's heightened imagination, but as the synthesis of "glass" and "dark" suggests, there is Biblical resonance in how Daphne "sees" the looming visage of crocodile-Psanek: "She could faintly see the flesh through his beard, as water through reeds. His black hair was brushed smooth as glass, his black eyebrows glinted like a curve of black glass on the swarthy opalescence of his brow" (172).

Psanek now further adjusts his rhetoric by integrating prose poetry with primitivistic doctrine, as he eloquently describes to Daphne the poignant gentleness that can exist even in the most predatory of animals.

He constructs a meandering but moving statement about the miraculous rhythms ingrained in life, about the ritualistic magic that inevitably brings potential mates together. As a committed suitor of Daphne gifted with the panache of language, the Count now speaks some of the most rhythmic and stately lines in all of Lawrence's fiction. He mesmerizes Daphne with the suggestion that the "otherness" of creatures also can function as the magnetic element that brings them together as mates. We can only surmise how much the smitten coal-miner's son would love to utter such lines to Cynthia to help him cross the social and class divide that separates her from the Lawrences of Eastwood:

> "Everything finds its mate," he said. "The ermine and the pole-cat and the buzzard. One thinks so often that only the dove and the nightingale and the stag with his antlers have gentle mates. But the pole-cat and the ice-bears of the north have their mates. And a white she-bear lies with her cubs, under a rock as a snake lies hidden, and the male-bear slowly swims back from the sea, like a clot of snow or a shadow of white cloud passing on the speckled sea" (172).

Thus, Psanek will turn on his charm in a variety of ways as he pursues his woman. In his graphic blackness and in the range of his vaunted experience and exotic travels, he sounds like a diminutive Othello who once entranced Desdemona with luminous descriptions of far-away Anthropophigian places, such as where men wear their heads beneath their shoulders:

> "You have been in the north seas?"
>
> "Yes. And with the Eskimo in Siberia, and across the Tundras. And a white sea-hawk makes a nest on a high stone, and sometimes looks out with her white head, over the edge of the rock" (172).

The Count concludes this stage of rhapsodic courtship by noting to her that "Psanek" means outlaw. His words now articulate his real intention, as Psanek moves from casual etymology to the next step in his relentless logic of passionate attraction: "Foxes have their holes. They have even their mates…And an adder finds his female…Outlaws, and brigands, have often the finest woman-mates" (172).

V

It is now the spring of 1918, the end of the war is in sight, and in *visit six* Psanek's spirit and body have improved considerably. Strong enough to get out of his bed and convalescent chair, he is pertinently described as "masculine, perfect in his small stature" (173), more confident than ever. Lawrence again uses his close reading of Frazer's work to emphasize the configuration of Psanek's shadow as the defining space that separates the Count from the nurses, prisoners, and officers: "He seemed to put a shadow between himself and them, and from across this shadow he looked with his dark, beautifully-fringed eyes, as a proud little beast from the shadow of its lair" (173). In *The Golden Bough*, Frazer describes how ancient peoples, especially in the earliest Egyptian cultures, believe that "a man's soul to be in his shadow", and that a man's "strength waxed and waned with the depth of his shadow" (222). Freud will later replace notions of the soul, depth of shadow, and mystic strength with theories about *length* of shadow, unconscious desire, and phallic imagery—but the bottom-line for Psanek remains the same: with his recuperation from injury and with the pleasure of Daphne's visits providing him with added confidence and force, he tries to establish with Daphne the intriguing fact of the crucial and fated continuities in their relationship. He recalls the thimble he gave her when she was only seventeen, and when she acknowledges she still possesses the gift, he insists not only that she sew a shirt for him, but that she also must use the thimble in the process, for it functions as an amulet adorned with the family totem of the ladybird insect and the coiled snake. Once again, Daphne's confirmation about her possession of the thimble provides Psanek with additional awareness of her attraction to him. He does not miss a clue.

The presence of this thimble suggests that more than the Count's desire and rhetorical ability participate in the seduction of Daphne. The transfer of the amulet from Psanek to her years earlier, and its reemergence in their lives, signify a fated inevitability concerning the movement toward passionate consummation between these unlikely lovers. In Frazer's discussion of Sympathetic Magic, what he calls the "Law of Contact or Contagion", he describes how it enables the magician "to infer that whatever he does to a material object will affect equally the person with whom the object was once in contact" (12). Psanek senses that the thimble can function as a powerful form of mystical magnetism between them. Her initial refusal to comply with his outlandish request as the scene ends sounds decidedly unemphatic. In fact, her "I have no reason" reply functions for the Count as additional evidence of Daphne's socially conditional inability to comprehend the imperative of his inside out metaphor (173). That is, her fatigued, purely *rational* explanation of her refusal privileges the dictates of her mind over the primacy of instinct. Yet just two weeks later, and just as Psanek anticipated, her real emotions take precedence over her logical cautions: she arrives in a jaunty, upbeat mood to get measurements for the shirt. Their intimate connection to each other in this short *visit seven* is evident in the warm jocularity of their conversation, as she agrees to his sewing request with the thimble, jokes with him about the absurdity of his "family insect", and humorously wonders how "many spots must it have" (175).

By *visit eight*, in the midst of a refulgent and warm spring day, Psanek's mood is even more energetic. He adopts an approach of unguarded candor with Daphne, even to the point of expressing the intensity and range of his anger at the world. He sounds much like an often cranky and choleric Lawrence in his letters and essays, as he rails against the provincialism of England, the wrongheadedness of humanity, and the pathetic yearnings and ambitions of people for "little red-brick boxes in rows" as their consuming desire (175).[14] As his anger increases and he attacks Daphne's more optimistic reading of the universe, he extravagantly claims that he actually speaks for himself *and* Daphne in his diatribes: when she mildly objects to this egotistical and incorrect definition of her own perspective, he returns more intimately to an echo of his animal-mating metaphors, calling her "a wild-cat with open eyes, half dreaming on a bough, in a lonely place" (177). This strange creaturely and pictorial image of her intrigues Daphne, and she puts aside her previous demurral and responds without equivocation: "I wish I were a wild-cat" (177). As Psanek continues to insist on the priorities of his anger she leaves, unconvincingly "determined never to go and see him again" (177). Surely the Count, Daphne, and the reader must sense that the complexity of their relationship hardly is resolved.

VI

Of course, Lady Daphne Apsley returns, as her acquiescent comment about the wild-cat identity collectively indicates for her his hold on her passion and imagination, the gradual recognition of the unleashed desire *inside* her, and the dissatisfaction with her current state. The crucial *visit nine* in the novella takes place in Voynich Hall after his removal from Hurst Place: with the exception of their sex scene in *visit thirteen*, it remains the most lengthy and complex meeting in *The Ladybird*. By the conclusion of this visit, Daphne's future seduction is virtually assured

---

14. Here is a letter to Cynthia in which the theme and tone is similar: "All these little amorphous houses like an eruption, a disease on the clean earth; and all of them full of such a diseased spirit…all these obscene scaly houses…" (*Letters II* 375).

because of the unspoken understanding he gets her to accept. As the scene starts, "she felt at once the old influence of his silence and his subtle power" (177) when she graciously brings him a second completed shirt. He returns to the issues of her beauty and his anger as he moves to another poetic iteration of animal metaphors and the inexorable mating season: "You remember, dear Lady Daphne, that the adder does not suck his poison all alone, and the pole-cat knows where to find his she-polecat. You remember that each one has his own dear mate…The wild-cat has wonderful green eyes that she closes…like a screen" (179). Psanek significantly includes the wild-cat in his list—the animal that for Daphne has special meaning in the context of her previously expressed desire. When she again accepts the imagery and its implicit meaning for her and their prospective intimacy ("Have you ever heard me snarl?" (179)), something quite intense between them is acknowledged by the narrator: "They were silent. And immediately the strange thrill of secrecy was between them. Something that had gone beyond sadness into another, secret, thrilling communion which she would never admit" (179).

With this intimate bond established between them, Psanek is now energized sufficiently to outline his notion of "true fire" and "the dark sun," tropes that lead to the central credo in Lawrencian doctrine that "we've got the world inside out. The true living world of fire is dark, throbbing, darker than blood. Our luminous world that we go by is only the white lining of this" (180).[15] Lawrence employs the inside out dichotomy just months earlier in his revisions of *Fantasia of the Unconscious*, and in *The Ladybird* he uses the inherent drama and intensity of character-based fiction to make his "pollyanalytical" theories more accessible and immediate. In his insistently dualistic cosmology, the truth is "inside", dark, primitive, and demanding, while the "surface" remains white, titillating, modern, sensate, and ultimately unsubstantial. The Count then connects the inside out metaphor to the essential point about his developing intimacy with Daphne, as he returns to the one animal which Daphne memorably expressed a desire to emulate: "True love is dark, a throbbing together in darkness, like the wild-cat in the night, when the green screen opens and her eyes are on the darkness" (180). As Psanek develops this symbology to merge it with the sexual dichotomies that constitute his real subject in this novella, he speaks of

15. For a more extensive discussion of the meaning of Lawrencian blackness and its relation to self-definition and erotic power, see Chapters Four and Five in *The Phallic Imagination*, and my essay on *The Lost Girl* in *Twentieth Century Literature*. See also Daleski and Humma for extensive analysis of the metaphors of flame and the white-black dualities in Lawrence's fiction.

Daphne's surface beauty as her "whited sepulchre" (180). Such stark imagery, with its ghostly ambience of whiteness and death, will later encompass outspoken criticism of Basil, Daphne, and their manipulative and dispassionate sex life. As the visit concludes, she begins to sense the implications of the different kind of passion described—and soon proposed—by Psanek: "He said her beauty was her whited sepulchre. Even that, she knew what he meant. The fluid invisibility of her, he wanted to love. But ah, her pearl-like beauty was so dear to her, and it was so famous in the world" (181). The precise model here of course, is Lady Cynthia Asquith and her legendary beauty—a woman variously painted, drawn, or photographed by such modern masters as Burne-Jones, Herbert Sargent, Augustus John, and Cecil Beaton.

Daphne anticipates with mixed emotions the "white love" (182) of sex with her husband when he shortly returns from the front, and she contemplates the kind of passion offered by the Count: "it had also made her nerve-worn, her husband's love...What then would the Count's love be like?" (182) Daphne tries to fight against the Count's growing appeal, an excitement about Psanek that penetrates through her praised and domesticated surface allure to her deeper and yet untouched insides. But Lawrence's metaphors in this novella carry a gyno-physiognomic specificity that can only be described as daring and detailed, and it remains peculiar that critics have not addressed this important aspect of the novella. Lawrence transparently uses Psanek's ideology to demean Daphne-Cynthia's alleged habits of clitoral stimulation from her husband, as the angry and infatuated writer also probes the possibility of transcendent sex for her via the vaginal orgasm. Recall in my discussion of *The Lost Girl* how much the issue of orgasm is on Lawrence's mind, as his strangely confessional comments to Compton MacKenzie about Frieda make clear. As Lawrence elaborates on metaphors that attempt to merge the clinical with the metaphysical, the trope of inside out encompasses the protective folds of Daphne's nether flesh. The habits of narcissism collide with the possibility of orgasmic release as a virtual Snow White contemplates a counter-identity:

> She would sit in front of a mirror, looking at her wonderfully cared-for face, that had appeared in so many society magazines. She loved it so, it made her feel so vain. And she looked at her blue-green eyes—the eyes of the wildcat on a bough. Yes, the lovely bluegreen iris, drawn tight like a screen. Supposing it should relax. Supposing it should unfold, and open out the dark depths, the dark, dilated pupil! Supposing it should? (182)

Lawrence's use of "iris" in the passage above deserves comment, for its function goes beyond the standard attributes of this brightly colored and showy flower. The reference here—in the impinging context of the clitoral-vaginal, light-dark, and inside out antinomies in the work—is also to the iris diaphragm, that sensitive, outer part of the camera that determines, by way of its "instinctive" opening and closing, the amount of light it admits to the precious inner lens. Daphne's attempt to repress her growing awareness of the inadequacy of Basil as lover-husband is undercut by the very terms she uses as praise: "She would think of her husband as an adorable, tall, well-bred Englishman, so easy and simple, and with the amused look in his blue eyes" (182). Whether it resonates as Daphne's beauty, Basil's well-bred manners and appearance, or their reliable and unexciting sexual relations, it is all surface and façade in the Apsley marriage. In this regard, Beauman writes how Cynthia's husband consistently "left her unaroused" (184), and when Beb returns for a short leave, Cynthia's diary comment echoes the faint praise by Daphne, as if her husband is a cute and manageable pet: "Beb was at his very darlingest" (458). Similarly, Major Apsley even writes Daphne a fawning letter, in which he self-consciously explains to his wife that his war injury might make him appear ugly when he arrives home on leave: "You will forgive me my appearance, and that alone will make me feel handsome" (183). Basil in the fiction must have learned from Daphne what Beb in 1915 likely has accepted as the attribute that catches Cynthia's roving eyes: "handsome" does matter to the real and fictional wives, and Psanek's ultimate conquest of Daphne also constitutes an assault on her superficial habits of infatuation. Cynthia Asquith can be astonishing in her lack of self-insight about the inherent weakness of her sexual attraction to her husband, as when she rides with him in the car that takes him to the ship returning him to the deadly frontlines of war. Here is the casual diary entry on the day she bids farewell to her spouse, who has a good chance of not returning alive: "Beb was busy most of the afternoon. I sat stupefiedly in the lounge. At about four o'clock I went down to the pier-head in his little motor. His driver is almost the best-looking man I have ever seen" (9).

VII

One year has passed since the first meeting at the hospital. In *visit ten* Psanek unleashes a vitriolic mood that he conveys in his image of the destructive hammer; with his ranting and chaotic outbursts, the Count seems willing to test the endurance and depth of his intimacy with Daphne by forcing her to confront him in the guise of his most frustrated and pessimistic demeanor. As his rhetoric of intemperate anger increases in intensity, the repetitive reference to the hammer becomes phallic as well as nihilistic, with his pontifications taking on the aura of a sexual boast and challenge. With a crass lack of restraint, he now speaks to Daphne about her body and orgasm with metaphors about the clitoris and G-spot that he frames in the mold of unequivocal Lawrencian doctrine: "But I, even I, I know you have a root. You, and your leaning white body, you are dying like a lily in a drawing-room, in a crystal jar. But shall I tell you of your root, away below and invisible? My hammer strikes fire, and your root opens its lily-scales and cries for the sparks of my fire" (188). Psanek's assumptions of Daphne's reliable tolerance of his antics prove correct, as she accepts his notions of visionary machismo with acquiescent silence. As if to confirm the Count's view that her current sex life with her husband is inside out, that her marital relations remain sadly committed to white, surface sensation rather than the deep darkness of transcendence, she breaks the silence with the innocently intimate request that later will bother Oliver Mellors within his own struggles with intimacy and tenderness: "'And you would never want to kiss me?' 'Ah no!' he answered sharply" (189).[16] Psanek only cares about deeper penetrations of Lady Daphne's body, and she appears much like the Lady Cynthia Asquith described by her biographer "as a woman who enjoys seduction only but not the act itself" (188).

But Lawrence intends this work to function even more dramatically as a decimating portrait of the Asquith marriage and as a fantasy of his "therapeutic" seduction of Cynthia. There is a compelling resemblance in appearance between the Basil Blackwood of Cynthia's extramarital infatuation, and the Count Dionys Psanek of *The Ladybird*. Thus the name of Basil is given to the ineffectual husband of the fiction, while the gnome-like Count shares key elements of coloration and stature with Cynthia's

---

16. See Spilka (*Renewing the Normative* 49–69) for an illuminating discussion of the issues of tenderness and kissing in relation to Lawrence and Mellors. In terms of the deeper, phallic penetration of Daphne's body that the Count immodestly describes to her as the necessary substitute for her frustrating habits of mouth-kissing and clitoral stimulation, Lawrence—as I note—appears to anticipate (through the Count's unsubtle metaphors of the hammer and the root) the controversial G-spot that Ernest Grafenberg in 1950 will argue is a legitimate and ideal attainment within the range of female sexual response. The accuracy of these assertions by him of alleged urethral flow and hormonal emission signifying an ultimate dimension of deep orgasmic release remains in dispute even today, with arguments about biological accuracy and sensual receptivity often obscured by the priorities and positionings of different sides of the heated debates inherent in contemporary sexual politics.

doomed and small-bodied lover. Psanek will not settle, however, for the kisses that Basil Blackwood or Beb Asquith were willing to provide as the signature demonstration of their passionate devotion. Here is the relevant description of Blackwood, as quoted in part from a memoir by John Buchan, and it can serve, in effect, as a mini-portrait of the Count: "He was then forty: intelligent, cynical, and entertaining, he was slight in build, with a beautifully shaped head and soft, dark, sleepy eyes, everything about him—voice, manner, frame—was fine and delicate…with his pointed face and neat black moustache…there was always about him a certain foreign grace" (Beauman 185). Beauman further describes how Cynthia "allowed him to kiss her but would not agree to be his mistress"; the biographer pertinently adds an adapted quotation from Emile Delavenay, as she regards Cynthia as an example of a flawed woman in the work of D.H. Lawrence, one "with whom passion exhausts itself at the mouth" (188).

While Daphne awaits the return of her injured husband, Lawrence uses these anticipatory pages to elaborate on the inside out dimensions of her marriage. He constructs a mythic metaphor in *The Ladybird* that he will employ more conspicuously in *The Plumed Serpent* and *Lady Chatterley's Lover* to suggest his antagonism to the penchant of modern lovers to settle for clitoral stimulation rather than vaginal orgasm. The variant phrase is "Aphrodite of the foam", and Lawrence counterpoints the oozing, foaming, surface whiteness to the liquid secretions of black and grey that exist deeper in the body. Here, for instance, is Daphne contemplating her un-Lawrencian excitement as she imagines the familiar tone of the sexual reunion with her husband: "she so purely an English blonde, an Aphrodite of the foam, as Basil had called her in poetry" (190). Cynthia's husband was a mediocre poet and writer, and in a frank letter to her, Lawrence admonishingly describes Beb's work with a put-down that extends beyond mere criticism, calling it "not the great inhalation of desire" (*Letters III* 38). And here is Basil Apsley himself in the novella (or just as easily, maybe Beb Asquith or Basil Blackwood!) using the actual terms of clitoral praise to Daphne while he luxuriates about all the loveliness of her surface beauty: "Here I am, alive and well, and I've got you for a wife.—It's brought you out like a flower.—I say, darling, there is more now than Venus of the foam—grander. But how beautiful you are! But you look like the beauty of all life—as if you were moon-mother of the world—Aphrodite" (191).

Daphne begins to comprehend the stronger appeal of Psanek as he watches her shamelessly idolatrous husband become whiter than white while he articulates the "sacrament of his supreme worship" (193) of her.

When Daphne and Basil finally have sex, the wife tries to make the best of her unconsummated sensations, but Lawrence reminds the reader that Psanek is fated to be her lover: "Nevertheless his homecoming made her begin to be ill again. Afterwards, after his love, she had to bear herself in torment […] It was not her fault she…wanted someone to save her" (195). Her sex with Basil exhausts Daphne because of its mechanical and onanistic qualities, as she continues to capitulate to Basil's tepid desire more as marital duty than any uninhibited expression of real passion. Cynthia Asquith "grew up with the belief that marriage was an economic arrangement set apart from love and sexual excitement" (Beauman 114), and such an understanding is implied in the unfulfilling rhythm of tumescence and detumescence of their characteristic lovemaking: "She could rise to the height for the time…But alas, she could not stay intensified and resplendent in her white, womanly powers, her female mystery. She relaxed, she lost her glory, and became fretful…And then naturally her man became ashy and somewhat acrid, while she ached with nerves, and could not eat" (196).

Her sexual capitulation to the Count really starts amid her preparations for *visit eleven*, a meeting also attended by her husband, who is anxious to meet Psanek. Daphne's selection of clothes to wear for this awkward visit concludes with her decision, in effect, to don those flagship Lawrencian colors already a staple of the Count's wardrobe. The communion of darkness between them begins in this coalescence of two disconnected passages early in the visit:

> Daphne was so beautiful in her dark furs, the black lace of her veil thrown back over her close-fitting, dull-gold-threaded hat, and her face fair like a winter flower in a cranny of darkness (197).
>
> The small smile never left the Count's dark face…the black hair growing low on his brow, and his eyebrows making a thick bow above his dark eyes, which had again long black lashes. So that the upper part of his face seemed very dusky-black (197).

Even Daphne—at best a Lawrencian woman-in-training—senses the essentiality of the oppositional stakes engaged in the issue of chiaroscuro coloration: "she could feel the presence of her tall, gaunt, idealistic husband was hateful to the little swarthy man" (199). As Basil spouts the hypocritical notion of the "higher plane of love" (198), and "dynamic contact between human beings" (200), Daphne is caught between her conditional dislike of Psanek's ideology and the instinctual connection she feels with him against the false appeal of Basil: "It was curious, she disliked his words intensely, but she liked him. On the other hand, she believed absolutely what her husband said, yet her physical sympathy was against him" (201).

VIII

Before *visit twelve* occurs—one that includes the feisty presence of the Earl—Lawrence intrusively remarks that "what followed was entirely Basil's fault" (205). Basil's fascination with Psanek in the previous visit prompts Major Apsley to get permission from the liberal-minded Earl to move the Count from Voynich Hall to the family's estate at Thoresway for two weeks before Psanek is shipped back to Austria. It is at Thoresway where the seduction occurs. The narrator's comment provides a circumstantial reason to indict the husband not only for his inadequacies as a lover-husband, but also for an inveterate blindness to sensual proximity: he cannot imagine the immediate threat to his marriage embodied by the witty and diminutive Count. During the lively dinner, the Earl, Psanek, and Basil verbally spar on a variety of issues, and it is during the conversation that Daphne and Psanek further seal the connection that leads to sexual union. The Count is described as the honored, wounded, and revived Dionys-Osiris of ancient Egypt, and Daphne-Persephone as the devoted goddess who will willingly descend with him into the dark lower world as the ultimate tribute of her love: "From the breast she loved him, and sent out love to him….Only Daphne was making him speak. It was she who was drawing the soul out of him, trying to read the future in him as the augurs read the future in the quivering entrails of the sacrificed beast" (208). This passage is meant to merge with Psanek's later explanation to Daphne that she will follow and obey him after death, consistent with Frazer's description of how the magician-king in life, by dint of his insights about "the order of nature", "became the deified man after his death" (121). Yet it is not surprising that in the days ahead at Thoresway Lady Daphne resembles the disenchanted Lady Chatterley, now a sexually frustrated wife who is revolted by her husband and anguished over the lack of "real contact" with anyone. Daphne Apsley recalls, from the history of her romantic but unconsummated love-life, precisely the type of man Connie Chatterley will encounter later in the decade, a "game keeper she could have loved" (211) but for her fierce and practical consciousness of class difference. Then she further contemplates the Count and her own family history, sounding even more like Connie in that character's consideration both of Mellors and her passionate and unorthodox father. Amid the antinomies so central to *The Ladybird*, and with something close to a justification of indebtedness to James Frazer,

Lawrence describes a Daphne who now unequivocally and finally comprehends the full resonance of the Count's notion of inside out: "Her father had some of the unconscious dark blood-warmth of primitive people. But he was like a man who is damned. And the Count, of course. The Count had something that was hot and invisible, a dark flame of life that might warm the cold white fire of her own blood" (211). *Lady Chatterley's Lover* is more than six years away, but its issues of a woman's sexual frustration in an unhappy marriage, answered by a haunted and appealingly unorthodox male—the issues are already percolating in this novella.

Then when the Count—in the climactic *visit thirteen*—appropriately in a dark room in the darkness of night and amid haunting but undecipherable music—sings his mesmerizing song, Lawrence alludes to Frazer's references to David, Saul, and the Temple of Jerusalem, with the "moving influence of its melodies, being perhaps set down like the effect of wine, to the direct inspiration of a deity" (388). Daphne elects to "cross the border" (213) between surface and substance, outer and inner, as she gives herself to Psanek amid "a darkness answering to darkness" (215).[17] Frazer writes in *The Golden Bough* how the prophets of Jerusalem depended on music "for inducing the ecstatic state" (388) embodied in the consummated sex between Psanek and Daphne.[18] So surface obstruction yields to deeper penetration, as daylight anxiety retreats before nighttime rapture, and "chastity" is finally redefined as the goddess state of achieved transcendence, stillness, and fulfillment:

> She did not care, she did not grieve, she did not fret anymore. All that had left her. She felt she could sleep, sleep, sleep—for ever. Her face too was very still, with a delicate look of virginity that she had never had before. She had always been Aphrodite, the self-conscious one. And her eyes, the green-blue, had been like slow, living jewels, resistant. Now they had unfolded from the hard flower-bud, and had the wonder, and the stillness of a quiet night (217).

---

17. See my chapter *on The Captain's Doll* for more on Lawrence's concept of "the border-line." See also Ruderman (*Devouring Mother* 70–89).

18. Rossman accurately observes about *The Ladybird* that "Lawrence wants the effect of a woman given fuller life through the power of an assertive powerful man" (296). Then he oddly adds: "But the effect he achieves is a woman who loses her 'spiritual consciousness' only to become a sexual zombie, marching mechanically through the night to her lover's bed" (296–97). As I have indicated, there is nothing "mechanical" in the ecstatic *initiative* that Daphne undertakes in coming to Psanek's room, and her awareness of the intricacies of orgasmic release with her new lover does not suggest the walking-dead that Rossman describes.

The thought of sex with Basil now disgusts her, and an increasingly passive and coldly idolatrous husband is only too willing to accede to their new marital arrangement. This understanding means that they dispense with sex except for those urgent moments when his masturbatory needs ("But what if it comes upon me, that other, Daphne?") require such meager satisfaction from a wife who painfully says to him she will grant "what you wish" (219).[19]

Lawrence in *The Ladybird* remains wedded to his primary, dualistic metaphors even to the extent of insisting that the words of his characters further confirm the symbology. For instance, Basil correctly asserts to Daphne that the "sex part" was never a significant component in their marriage, that it "was always a bit whipped up" (219). His milky verb merges with the earlier use of "Aphrodite of the foam", suggesting a surface and bubbly semi-liquidity of the aroused clitoris as a contrast to the flooding cascades of water that Lawrence (and Daphne) associate with the Count's deeper penetration into her vagina and soul: "No, she had found this wonderful thing after she had heard him singing; she had suddenly collapsed away from her old self, into this darkness, this peace, this quiescence that was like a full dark river flowing eternally in her soul. She had gone to sleep from the *nuit blanche* of her days" (219). Note the perfectly nuanced paradox of "*nuit blanche*": it is idiomatically translated as "sleepless night," literally "white night"—so that even in real darkness she can scarcely endure physical proximity to her ashen husband. As Mark Spilka indicated decades ago, it matters not that Lawrence writes about sexual excitation in this (and other) fiction in his adamant and arguably reductive fashion, and decades before Masters and Johnson would employ

---

19. Two critics nicely define the immature dimensions of Basil's sexuality. Granofsky notes that Basil in the end "is satisfied to occupy a regressive state of pre-pubertal love vis-à-vis Daphne" ("Illness and Wellness" 107), and Cowan recognizes Basil's "rapture of courtly love adoration that is really designed to keep her placed on the pedestal of childlike chastity and out of his marriage bed" (81). On this related issue of Daphne's marriage, chastity, and Frazer's influence on Lawrence, Vickery is superb, and his generalized comments about patterns in the fiction can apply to *The Ladybird*: Lawrence "uses what he has learned from *The Golden Bough* about the religious role, the sacrificial character, and the fertility associations of virgins to a twofold end. On the one hand, he endeavors to picture contemporary virgins who possess just these qualities so that the sense of regarding life with reverence, awe, and delight, as he thought Frazer's early civilization did, will be borne in upon his readers. On the other hand, he also sketches pitilessly the virgins of the modern world who lack the divine potency of their predecessors and whose lives are therefore compounded of hesitant timidity and self-centered arrogance" (304–05).

complex and reasonably reliable studies to reach different conclusions about female orgasm. Their research that clitoral orgasm often triggers intense vaginal response would not deter Lawrence, or Mailer, or countless other men from the strong belief that Doris Lessing's Anna summarized so bravely and confidently in *The Golden Notebook*:[20]

> A vaginal orgasm is a dissolving in a vague, dark generalized sensation like being swirled in a warm whirlpool. There are several different kinds of clitoral orgasm…but there is only one real female orgasm and that is when a man, from the whole of his need and desire takes a woman and wants all her response (215–16).

IX

I return to the issue raised earlier in this essay. Why have critics so often assumed the notion that Lawrence accepted with equanimity the asexual status of his relationship to the beautiful Lady Cynthia Asquith? Evidence from his fiction and from his correspondence with her suggests an obsessed and frustrated man who was increasingly agitated by the impossibility of passionate intimacy with Cynthia. *The Ladybird* presents a graphic sexual fantasy that concludes with a seduction of Daphne so

---

20. Although he does not deal with *The Ladybird*, I remain indebted to the late Mark Spilka for his brilliant discussion of orgasm and sexual conflict in several Lawrence fictions, and for his appropriate quotation of the Lessing passage reprinted in *Renewing the Normative Lawrence* (142). See also Chapters II and III in that invaluable volume. Spilka is one of the first Lawrence critics to relevantly discuss the resonance of Lawrence's symbolic and doctrinal distinctions between clitoral and vaginal orgasm, noting the extent of neurotic clitoral aversion evident in the beak-like friction described in the *The Plumed Serpent* and *Lady Chatterley's Lover* (*Renewing the Normative* 171–90). See also Cowan's pertinent contextualizing of Lawrence's use of patriarchal vaginal metaphors in *Lady Chatterley's Lover*, as the critic connects the novelist's perspective to the way Lawrence has been "conditioned by cultural attitudes" of "male dominance and female sexual passivity", a pattern graphically reflected in "his repeated image of the sexually aggressive woman as tearing at the man with beaked vagina, the vagina dentata that Mellors fears" ("The Fall of John Thomas", 281). In another excellent essay by Cowan, but one that strangely omits any discussion of *The Ladybird*, he focuses on the psychological origins of Lawrence's sexual fantasies; it is a pity that Cowan does not engage this novella, for his analysis of Lawrence's animus to masturbation and to all forms of mechanistic or materialistic passion has distinct relevance for the reality of Cynthia's unconsummated liaisons and for the negative depiction of Daphne's compromised connection to her husband (see "Lawrence, Freud, and Masturbation").

effective that the *woman* initiates the bodily touch that leads to her capitulation in *visit thirteen*. The doctrines uttered by Psanek and the abundant evidence of precise resemblances in the novella's character and plot to Asquith family members and circumstances—such transparent patternings indicate Lawrence's willingness in the fall of 1921 to air his anguish and lust in a brilliantly structured work of fiction. Nicola Beauman skeptically quotes Harry T. Moore's prescient comment decades ago that "Lawrence made barmecide love to [Cynthia] in his stories" (Beauman 162, Moore 452), and it is helpful to consider the incisiveness of Moore's precise but forgotten metaphor. "Barmecide" is defined as "any illusory hospitality or abundance", and the term owes its origin to Prince Barmecide from *The Arabian Nights*, who memorably "serves an imaginary feast to a beggar in empty dishes" (*Webster's* 112). The passion of this coal miner's son for the aristocratic and glamorous Cynthia remains an unrealizable illusion that cannot square with the reality of her class-consciousness, practical caution, and unconsummated liaisons. More than any of his several Cynthia-based works, Lawrence permits his creative genius to "go all the way" in *The Ladybird*, and it is impossible to know if such cathartic art brought him some degree of release from the preoccupation with his fantasy lover.

His imagination had been fired with Cynthia's presence for a long time, including images that continued to invade the texture of his unconscious. Here are excerpts from separate letters to Cynthia from the most intense period of their friendship—dating from the last year of the war into the spring of 1919—a period that corresponds, coincidentally enough, to the exact fictional timeline depicted in *The Ladybird*: "I was dreaming of you two nights in succession" (*Letters III* 195); "I dreamed of you so hard a few days ago" (*Letters III* 247); "I dreamed of you two nights ago" (*Letters III* 335). In each case the dream variously depicts Cynthia as a companion, savior, and erotic goddess, and the representations scarcely conceal the repressed love and lust he feels for her. Cynthia Asquith clearly valued Lawrence's lively mind, and energetic emotions, and the public appearance of Lawrence's devotion to her caught the attention of members of her own family. Katharine Asquith, her sister-in-law and close confidante, alleged that Lawrence was in love with her (*Diaries* 57): her good friend Jean Hamilton heard Cynthia say that "D.H. Lawrence was passionately in love with me" (*Diaries* 133); and Cynthia's own mother suspected that Cynthia was a major love-interest for Lawrence (Beauman 160). Even Lawrence himself uses the word in a letter to her, carefully disguising its applicability with a defensive phrasing that is ludicrously disingenuous: "But I will write to you because I feel a sort of love for your hard stoical spirit—not for anything else" (*Letters II* 336). From Cynthia's own perspective, as Beauman notes, the excitement and the boundaries of their relationship remain easily understood: "Cynthia's friendship with Lawrence was no more complicated than her friendship with Whibley, Raleigh, Barrie, Desmond MacCarthy, Lord David Cecil, L.P. Hartley—and so on. She liked writers, and she responded to them—she knew *how* to respond to them" (160).

But friendship is not all that he desired from Cynthia. Near the end of his life, with all connection to Cynthia severed for several years, he completes a painting entitled "North Sea", and there is general acknowledgment of the close resemblance of the woman in the work to Cynthia.[21]

Commentaries on the erotic painting describe a passionate embrace between the two prominent figures—a bearded man behind a striking woman, both of whom are displayed in full frontal nudity. But I see the contortion of the two bodies rather differently, and my perspective merges with the frustrations of Lawrence's desire for Cynthia. The exposed woman in the foreground seems restrained by the man behind; his phallus is openly shown and her pudendum is obscured by shadow and pubic hair. She awkwardly pushes him away with her hand while her arms remain immobilized by the pressure of the man's arms. The background dimly appears as the cold and frothy rock and water of the North Sea—perhaps the appropriately forbidding locale for Lawrence's futile effort to light the fires of erotic interest in his unobtainable fantasy-woman. Shortly after Lawrence first meets Cynthia, he writes a letter to Ottoline Morrell in which he acknowledges his "fondness" for his new friend and also describes her with an incisive estimate of her character that he would never modify. Indeed, the churning, isolate waters of the "North Sea" painting depict those qualities in Cynthia as well as the passion in Lawrence that was more than fond: "She has never been in contact with anyone. It's as if she can't. There is something sea-like about her, cold and with a sort of passion like salt that burns and corrodes" (*Letters* II 339).

Lawrence completes his introduction to Magnus's *Memoirs of the Foreign Legion* during the same days in which he finishes writing *The Ladybird.* Near the end of that brilliant essay, Lawrence writes with evident urgency of the "modern form of vampirism" that predominates in the world (*Introductions* 65).[22] He could easily have transposed the following

21 .See Beauman 171, Ellis 432, and Moore 452.

22. See Ruderman (*Race and Identity*) for more on relevant issues of vampirism and the outcast in Lawrence's fiction, 133–35.

"North Sea" by D.H. Lawrence (Fig. 4-1)

words to the novella, as he insists it is imperative to "reinstate the great old gods of the passionate communion: Astarte, Cybele, Bel, Dionysos. It will never be any better till we admit the sacredness, the profound and *primary* sacredness of the passion of the living blood. Not this white, nerve-thrilled, modern excitement which passes for sensuality" (65). But if this essay's psychobiographical reading of *The Ladybird* remains essentially valid, can Lawrence be exempted from the very "vampirism" that he confidently disparages? No evidence exists that he ever confronted Cynthia directly with any hint of the passion and frustration that he feels in his relationship with her. Lawrence relies instead on powerful and sublimating depictions in his fiction that scarcely disguise the intensity of his eroticized longings. Surely he knows that any confession to Cynthia of his deeper feelings would destroy the privileges he enjoys through his valued friendship with this talented, beautiful, and aristocratic woman; his understandable reticence here confirms Freud's famous definition of sublimation as "a certain kind of modification of the aim and change of the object, in which our social valuation is taken into account" (*New Introductory Lectures* 97). To the extent that Lawrence can only play the artist-as-voyeur as the Count achieves "the passionate communion" with Cynthia that Lawrence craves for himself, is not the writer himself guilty of embracing "this white, nerve-thrilled excitement which passes for sensuality"?

CHAPTER FIVE

FROM PANOPHILIA TO PHALLOPHOBIA: SUBLIMATION, PROJECTION, AND RENEWAL IN *ST. MAWR*

A man who should see Pan by daylight fell dead.
—D. H. Lawrence, "Pan in America"

Here we have one of the origins of artistic activity.
—Sigmund Freud, *Three Essays on the Theory of Sexuality*

Who does not know Turner's Picture of the Golden Bough?
—James Frazer, *The Golden Bough*

But of course the English delight in landscape is a delight in escape.
—D.H. Lawrence, "Introduction to These Paintings"

I

On August 18, 1923, an angry D.H. Lawrence accompanies Frieda to the pier for her departure from New York to England. The married couple had just endured one of their bitterest and most representative quarrels according to their bystander friend, Catherine Carswell: the subject of their argument is not simply Lawrence's adamant refusal to accompany his wife back to Europe.[1] The livid issue between them—as it has persisted for more than a decade—remains Lawrence's resentment over a divided loyalty in her that he insensitively can no longer tolerate: the understandable need in

1. I remain indebted to the comprehensive work of David Ellis in the third volume of the Cambridge biography for his precise sequencing of dates and events discussed in this essay and for his incisive speculations on Lawrence's emotions and preoccupations during the 1923–24 period. Much of my own analysis clearly starts with several conclusions in Ellis's probing work, and his judicious methodology must stand as a model of objectivity and insight concerning Lawrence's life and artistic achievement.

Frieda to see her children stands as the primary reason for her decision to abandon for an undetermined period an emotionally volatile husband as he completes his travel in America and Mexico without her. Lawrence's superb biographer for this period in his life, David Ellis, quotes an unequivocal letter that he writes on August 7 1923, to Middleton Murry: "F. wants to see her children. And you know, wrong or not, I can't stomach the chasing of these Weekley children" (*Letters IV* 480, Ellis *Dying Game* 124) Frieda is just as adamant and scathing: on board the transatlantic liner, she writes to Adele Seltzer of her complete disgust with her husband's mood and vows not to return to him.

While not justifying Lawrence's lack of empathy, Ellis maintains persuasively that Frieda's persistent guilt feelings, maternal anxieties, and distracted preoccupations over her children were "often to be interpreted by Lawrence as a betrayal" of him (126). After she departs, Lawrence initially embraces the belief that "his mission would have to be sustained alone"; perhaps too optimistically at first, he accepts his new status of independence as an "implicit denial of his relationship with Frieda as the centre of his life" (132). As he travels alone in the weeks ahead, he rewrites parts of *The Boy in the Bush* to include an intrusive vindictiveness about the entire institution of marriage by making Jack suddenly consider the virtues of bigamy; it is an odd and unpersuasive revision of the novel that seems to suggest an attempt by a resentful Lawrence "to contemplate a way of life without Frieda" (136). A typically gracious letter by his loyal companion Götzsche in late October describes how intensely Lawrence pines for Frieda and how clearly the rationalized confidence in the husband about the value of the separation has dissipated. Lawrence sails back to England in November 1923 in a depressed and anxious state. It is difficult not to connect his condition to Lawrence's view of the return as a major defeat for his bedrock notions of manly authority and self-reliance, involving an inevitable awareness in him of "that overly dependent temperament" (140) he would trace after 1919 to the contorted relationship with his strong-willed and often smothering mother.

Much has been chronicled and analyzed about the months of emotional pain experienced by Lawrence after his return to England—with special emphasis within such commentary on his suspicions about the conspicuous closeness between Frieda and Murry when they meet him on his arrival, and on his distinct feelings of betrayal by his wife and close friend at the Café Royal dinner several weeks later.[2] His developing perception of Murry as

2. For some of the most provocative considerations of these controversial incidents, I recommend the revealing accounts in Ellis 143–53, Worthen 290–302, Squires 276–85, Meyers 305–08, and Feinstein 196–203.

a sexual rival and narcissistic manipulator, and of Frieda as a potential or actual adulterer, is sublimated effectively in the three "Murry Stories"—"The Last Laugh", "The Borderline", and "Jimmy and the Desperate Woman"—that Lawrence composed during this uncomfortable interlude in Europe before his return to New Mexico with Frieda. The stories remain notable as a collective unit because of their various episodes of magical realism, disturbing violence, ghostly ambiance, and unorthodox sex and passion; whatever erotic consummation does exist appears ambiguous in its unconventional body-positioning and in its compulsive psychological motivation. Indeed, the apparent lack of phallic penetration depicted in the hazy drama of "The Borderline" is presented as an unembroidered and unclarified *given*—that is, without any sense in the narrative of regretful compromise or imposed adjustment by the frenetic participants. The strangely sexual but phallophobic atmosphere is also complemented in this tale by the transparent projection of Lawrence's accelerating lung disease onto the Murry character of Philip. Deftly working with a range of psychobiographical clues in all three stories, Ellis provocatively surmises that at least by the start of 1924, as Lawrence's health deteriorates and his emotional connection to Frieda becomes more fraught with his own anger and suspicion, there "may not be sex in the usual sense" between them any more (164).[3]

There is, of course, a wealth of possibility suggested in Ellis's necessarily imprecise and diplomatic phrase "that usual sense"; whether in Lawrence's case the impinging issue is total impotence, lesser incapacity, or emotional indisposition, he may well have initiated the Murry tales to make an ideological virtue out of a psychosexual necessity by creating a compensatory doctrinal infatuation that now would last for many months: he begins to develop, through those three stories and through several essays written in the winter and early spring of 1923–1924, an idealization and explanation of Pan-energy and its associated mythologies.[4] The thematic nexus is first embodied in "The Last Laugh", in which "Lawrence's return to Europe is conflated with a new liberating atmosphere associated with Pan" (Ellis 157). This atmosphere, for Lawrence, is intense, transformative, and distinctly unsexual. The center of Pan-life for him becomes the espousal of practices, rituals, traditions, and—this above all—landscapes

3. For further discussion of the artistic and psychological consequences of Lawrence's sexual health and libido, see Spilka (70–95) and Chapter One on *The Lost Girl*.

4. See several relevant essays in *Mornings in Mexico and Other Essays*: "Indians and Entertainment" (59–68), "The Dance of the Sprouting Corn" (71–76), "Pan in America" (155–64), and "The Hopi Snake Dance" (79–94).

that animistically unite man and nature, and such bonding is dramatically integrated with the texture of the changing seasons. No sentimental pantheism here, but a deep admiration in him for the challenging and energizing engagement between the human and the numinous residue of Pan primarily embedded in the topography of the south-west United States and Mexico. Lawrence clarifies important aspects of this panophilia in "Pan in America" in the spring of 1924, an essay that has distinct relation to the structure and substance of *St. Mawr* written June to September 1924.

II

Any sense of masculine force or phallic presence is undercut by Lawrence at the very start of *St. Mawr*—and this pattern of diminishment is reiterated throughout the work. The narrative tone on this issue often sounds too intrusive and archly self-satisfied not to be a part of a doctrinal framework that is central to the novella. Not only does Lawrence insist that Rico is easily "mastered" (21) by Lou in their adamantly dispassionate marriage, but the repeated and doggerel phrasing of their premarital "love affair in Capri" (21, 22) reflects Lawrence's mischievous glee in his portrait of devastated manhood and fractured marriage in postwar Europe.[5] Lou suffers a fashionable breakdown after a separation during their neurotic courtship that confines her to a "convent nursing-home in Umbria" (22): her return to stability is evident throughout *St. Mawr*, and it is only compromised by her unwise choice of a pompous and effete husband. When she announces to her cynical and spicy mother that she and Rico are engaged, we get the first glimpse of Mrs. Witt's characteristically withering and defensive attitude toward all men, for she "was at the age when the malevolent male in man, the old Adam, begins to loom above all the social tailoring" (23).

As man and wife, Lou and Rico discover that their initial erotic attraction has mutated to become "a nervous attachment rather than a sexual love" (24): without the energy or motivation to reject their compromised condition, they conveniently become "like brother and sister" (24). While they contentedly adjust to the material comforts of leisurely travel and titled nobility, Mrs. Witt stays nearby in England to

5. F.R. Leavis writes eloquently of "the economy of these opening pages" (226), and his pioneering essay more than fifty years ago helped to establish the reputation of this novella. On that same issue of the tone and effectiveness of the first few pages of *St. Mawr*, Fleishman seems less sensitive to the intricacies and economies of Lawrence's perspective, believing that they "can be faulted for their tinsel and casualness" (171–72).

enjoy the privileges of the social elitism she pretends to deplore. Her fear of the "malevolent male" ultimately reflects the paradox of her expressed need to find "real men" (24) only to fuel her irrepressible penchant to dominate and diminish them. Smart and experienced enough to bemoan the adulteration of traditional gender definition in the traumatized landscape after the war (*"your virility or your life!—Your femininity or your life!"* (26, emphasis in the original)), and defiantly depicted as a dowager who "loved men – real men" (24), it is also evident that at 54 she lacks any significant desire for honest passion from the opposite sex. The lady doth protest too much: "It was difficult to define what she meant by 'real' men. She never met any" (24). Critics tend to overrate the instinctual insight and social acumen of the redoubtable Mrs. Witt, generally failing to note that although she is often smugly correct about people and their respective affectations, she remains brutally class-conscious and makes errant judgments about the eligibility of men as marital partners—as in her absurd considerations of Dean Vyner and Lewis as suitable mates.[6] Beyond her jaunty wit and comic timing, she remains at bottom unimaginative and snobbish, and she will never comprehend the profound change in spirit and ambition that slowly develops in her daughter.

This pervasive atmosphere in *St. Mawr* of emasculated libido and contorted gender-definition is intensified as the narrative moves closer to the horse's stable by way of introducing the epicene Mr. Saintsbury, the owner of the mews, who "flashed his old-maid's smile" (27). But there is nothing androgynous *or even phallic* about this imposing stallion.[7] Our

---

6. Even several of our finest critics on Lawrence tend to be excessively impressed by the remarks of Mrs. Witt. While Cowan does comprehend her destructive side, he puts too much stock in the value to Lou of her mother's caustic barbs and satirical portraits; Ellis does not sufficiently develop the acknowledged element of Lawrence's "authorial satire" (191) of Mrs. Witt herself—a puncturing of her own set of pretenses that tends to diminish the power of her societal critiques. I do like the resonant phrase used by Hough in his description of her essential demeanor—a "hideous virility" (182). Simpson totally misses the edge of Lawrence's disapproval of Mrs. Witt, claiming that Lawrence is correct because "no criticism is offered of the strong-willed sardonic American"; Simpson further oddly asserts that "Lawrence allows her natural superiority to the other characters to shine through unimpeded" (117).

7. Cowan mistakenly sees the horse as "the incarnation of prelapsarian phallic mystery" (91). Wilde considers the function of the ranch as an "anticipation of the reborn society, the phallic millennium" (167–68). Vivas criticizes Lawrence severely for abruptly dropping the horse from virtually all consideration after the novella moves to America (150–64). That decision by Lawrence remains disconcerting but wise, as the powerful landscape of New Mexico must relentlessly

view of him is always defined by Lou's remarkably attentive and intimate perspective. Her first perception of him resonates throughout the work with the depth of Lou's intimate awareness and the heightened sensitivity of this animal. Here the focused incisiveness of Lou's eyes provides details that are as acute and fetishistic as those emanating from an infatuated soul-mate, as the horse responds to Saintsbury's touch with a minute body signal that only Lou Carrington could possibly notice: "Loquacious even with the animals, he went softly forward and laid his hand on the horse's shoulder, soft and quiet as a fly settling. Lou saw the brilliant skin of the horse crinkle a little in apprehensive anticipation" (28). Already described as "half in love" (28) with St. Mawr, it is for Lou his inscrutability, the unfathomability of his profound otherness that entrances her. He stands before her as an elusive compound of embodied strength and anxious sensitivity that seems to emanate from some older and long-displaced world: "He was of such a lovely red-gold colour, and a dark, invisible fire seemed to come out of him…somewhere deep in his animal consciousness lived a dangerous, half-revealed resentment" (28).[8] It is interesting to note that when Lou, buried in a marriage that exudes the tepid sexuality of siblings, is informed shortly that St. Mawr is a stallion, "she became more afraid of him", and she also quickly learns with apparent relief, that although raised for stud purposes, he doesn't "seem to fancy the mares" (29). No carnality or even the hint of erotic passion in this novella of any kind—by human or animal—and oddly enough, no regrets by Lawrence. He has a different direction in mind.

Whether inferred from Lou's reactions or from the bearing of this massive horse, such are the early signals in this work of its phallophobic texture, representing an important realignment in this turbulent period of Lawrence's life of the usual doctrinal priorities of his fiction. When Lou "laid her hand on his side, and gently stroked him," she is "startled to feel the vivid heat of his life come through to her", and in her "weary young

---

replace the panophilic aspects of St. Mawr; the animal now—in a country free from the provincial restrictions of England—not coincidentally develops a fondness for the mares in his new and unfettered environment that Lawrence acknowledges in a mere aside. Indeed, even the meekest "phallic" success in *St. Mawr* reflects Lawrence's profound aversion to such hint of eros. For another and related perceptive response to Vivas's objection, see Humma (45–61).

8. Cowan is excellent in showing how "Lawrence's expanding conception of the horse, the centaur, and Pan coalesce in the dynamic symbol of St. Mawr" (90). Similarly, Sagar supplies an intelligent summary of "how the horse came to focus and embody so many of Lawrence's deepest and most lasting preoccupations" (252).

woman's soul, an ancient understanding seemed to flood in" (30). This looming sense of otherness perceived by Lou is not the usual typology of male-female polarity often depicted in Lawrence's fiction. It is rather an intuitive sense in her—intensified by that resonant phrase of "ancient understanding"—that the horse's inner heat ("as if that mysterious fire of the horse's body had split some rock in her" (30)) suggests the remnant of an understanding between human and animal that exists no more. In this formative context, Lawrence initiates further reading in Frazer's *The Golden Bough* just before he begins writing *St. Mawr*, and the essential influence of that monumental study is evident throughout the novella.[9] Frazer emphasizes that in primitive cultures it was believed that animals possess defined and accessible souls; that Lou can consistently sense so much emotional architecture in the horse merely by observing surface details ("great, glowing, fearsome eyes, arched with a question and containing a white blade of light like a threat" (31)) directly illustrates Frazer's research into the old totemic belief that human and animal "are united by a bond of human sympathy" (792). This ideal unity from the past provides an instance of the Pan-energy Lawrence extols in "Pan in America", for it exemplifies that essay's focus on the "vivid relatedness between the man and the living universe" (160)—a connection at the heart of Lawrence's panophilic preoccupations in 1923–24. Significantly, when Lou presents the horse as a gift to her unmanly husband—with the implied offering of this animal's considerable strength and authority—he typically quips that he would "prefer a car" (32), recalling Lawrence's scathing criticism in the essay of the modern reliance on the increasing "mechanism of the human world" and its accompanying indolence "for the sake of a motor-car" (164).

---

9. See Ellis's persuasive speculations (187, 649) on the strong likelihood of Mabel Luhan offering Lawrence *The Golden Bough* to reread in April, 1924. Vickery's valuable study of Frazer's influence on a wide range of artists and works remains the standard volume on this issue, and he is especially provocative on Lawrence. Although Vickery has little to say about *St. Mawr*, his summary insight about Lawrence's art works perfectly for the novella: "Lawrence's acquaintance with Frazer sharpened his sense of man's participation in the divine" (294). For more on the important influence of Frazer on Lawrence, and the ways he precisely appropriates material from *The Golden Bough* into the thematic structure of other stories and novellas, see my chapters in this volume on "The Princess", *The Lost Girl, The Fox, The Captain's Doll,* and *The Ladybird.*

III

What remains so intriguing in Lawrence's portrait of St. Mawr himself—as it will be for the celebrated pine tree at the Kiowa ranch—is that both images initially appear to reflect Lawrence's standard form of phallicism, but in each case the potential of this symbolic association is unfulfilled because of the distinct phallophobia that informs each description. Here, Lou tries to rouse the horse from its unreceptive drowse, and note the provocative terms of her failure: "And she spoke softly, dreamily stroked the animal's neck. She could feel a response gradually coming from him. But he would not lift up his head" (35). That pivotal qualifier "but" carries the real meaning of the moment. Even the most gentle rousing will not work, for the recipient of the caress is not embodied (or erect) malehood, but the karmic reappearance of the vestigial remnants of Pan.[10] St. Mawr elects not to stand tall in the scene, as Lawrence projects both the reality of his own wounded phallic self *onto* the horse's petulant disinclination and the compensatory doctrine *within* the keen awareness of Lady Carrington. Lawrence further describes the "older, heavily potent world" that St. Mawr recalls, a "prehistoric twilight" inhabited by Pan that he evokes in his repeated image clusters of "the old Greek horses" and "the old Greek horses, even Hippolytus" (35). As the narrative begins to portray the horse as an uncomfortable creature out of his comfort zone in the modern world, he is increasingly depicted as an avatar of fertile energy rather than sexual prowess. Frazer writes that the spirits of germination "are not infrequently represented in the form of horses," and that such an animal "was sometimes originally the god himself", that is, "a deity of vegetation" (552).[11]

There is one character in *St. Mawr* who articulates seminal aspects of the mythologies and superstitions described in *The Golden Bough* and then appropriated by Lawrence within the scope of Pan ideology. The groom Lewis radiates a special sensitivity to the mysterious energy emanating

---

10. Merivale's meticulous study of the literary, artistic, and historic inheritance of the Pan figure is helpful in describing Lawrence's unusual and varied embodiment of the image in several of his works. Although she offers no in-depth treatment of *St. Mawr*, her framing insight about Pan's importance to Lawrence is reflected in the patterned thematics and psychobiography that I attempt to outline in this essay: "The Pan figure can be internalized, and became part of the character himself, in the fashion of D. H. Lawrence" (147).

11. See Merivale's relevant discussion of how the "rites of Attis and Osiris appear as mythpoeic vegetative form in *St. Mawr*" (319), as she anticipates my treatment of pine trees in the novella.

from this horse. When Phoenix asks him why St. Mawr never gets any foals, his answer establishes a kinship with the animal that is directly related to the doctrinal texture permeating the novella: "Doesn't want to, I should think. Same as me" (46). The unintimidating and diminutive Lewis is far from an embodiment of Pan, but his presence as an acolyte becomes crucial when he later outlines in the trip with Mrs. Witt some unusual notions and visionary metaphors that are crucial to the panophilic context of the work. While Lou and Phoenix manifest some flirtatious interest in each other early in *St. Mawr*, such conventional sexual attraction will dissipate for her during their drive to the Kiowa ranch when she contemplates the manipulative chauvinism and inherent laziness in his character. Long before Lou's climactic recognition of the essential significance for her of the ranch, Lawrence provides a glimpse of her ability to "connect" to the landscape even while she remains in England. This apprentice appreciation of the animistic energy in her surroundings anticipates her epiphany in New Mexico. It is the first step in her education, reminiscent of Alvina's sense of renewal in *The Lost Girl* that she first experiences as an intimation of transcendence riding in the train as it moves past the Mediterannean: Alvina "watched spell-bound: spell-bound by the magic of the world itself" (299). Lou "had learned the new joy: to do absolutely nothing, but to lie and let the sunshine filter through the leaves, to see the bunch of red-hot-poker flowers pierce scarlet in the afternoon" (55). Buoyed by the feeling of independence suggested by her awareness of a "new joy", she begins to formulate—for the first time in her life—a growing aversion to the complexities and compromises required by sexual intimacy and by the institution of marriage: "I'm the harem type, mother: only I never want the men inside the lattice" (55). Lou's notion of the transcendent ultimately will eschew all notions of future courtship and marriage, a form of renewal-without-sex that is unusual in Lawrence's work. In contrast, Alvina will attempt to re-energize her marriage to Ciccio by "renewing" the soul of her depressed mate. Might the different perspectives be connected to the changing state of Lawrence's own marriage and sexual health between 1920 and 1924?

Lou's developing vision of life is constantly contrasted with her mother's values and desires. Mrs. Witt remains quite willing—as she will demonstrate in her marriage proposal to Lewis—to let the men enter the lattice, but only if they follow her inflexible directions and precisely fill her sexual needs. She willfully cuts Lewis's hair, not for any cosmetic imperative, but only to enjoy his discomfort over the subjugation of his male sense of self. Indeed, Lewis will later reject her proposal and the monetary security she offers because the groom understands the contempt that underlies her interest in him. Given the considerable material benefits that would accrue to Lewis if he accepts her proposal, his adamant stance suggests the essential dignity of the man and the willful, manipulative use of the institution of marriage by Mrs. Witt. For all the problematics of his union with Frieda, Lawrence never regards their legal state as a wedded couple as anything less than an affirmation not to be undertaken in the casual manner implied in Mrs. Witt's proposal. Frazer spends several pages in *The Golden Bough* on illustrating how the old myths stress the intrinsic relation between a man's effectiveness and his hair. In one section he describes how in a Greek folk-tale, "a man's strength lies in three golden hairs on his head" (777). Mrs. Witt enacts the rituals embedded in some of the most prominent classical themes, as Lawrence integrates the diverse symbologies of the Morai and the Harpy in the predatory approach of Mrs. Witt to the helpless head of Lewis: "She poised a pair of long scissors like one of the fates…holding those terrifying shears with their beak erect" (57–58). While Mrs. Witt, no doubt, has not read the work of James Frazer, she gleefully senses in the proud and isolate Lewis how much his sense of manhood is threatened by her emasculating shears. She complements her approach to him with her un-Lawrencian pontification about the defining qualities of goodness in a man. When she gratuitously expresses admiration for "the animal in man", she makes it plain that her real goal is to relentlessly domesticate that very quality, for "one likes stroking a cat's fur" (59).[12] But, as always in *St. Mawr*, the sound and substance of Lawrence's emotions and vision are filtered through the daughter. Lou responds to her mother's attitudinizing with a statement of her own fatigue over the endless conflict inherent in love relationships: "I don't want intimacy mother—I'm too tired of it all" (60). Recall Lawrence's uncharacteristically exhausted and capitulative response to Mabel Luhan's provocations in the days just preceding his completion of the novella and after weeks of living amid the emotional and sexual tensions that accompany the uncomfortably close presence in his life at

---

12. Frazer notes that the Celts of Gaul indulged in sacrificial rituals in which "the victims most commonly burned in modern bonfires have been cats" (761); as Mrs. Witt progressively emasculates Lewis in this scene, the line between his enforced domestication and his ritual sacrifice becomes very narrow. That unusual phrase, "stroking a cat's fur", sounds more eerie in the light of Frazer's insistence that the sacrifice-festivals were "celebrated by the primitive Aryans in Europe", and "among the British Celts", the celebration involved "principal rites of fire, including the burnt sacrifices of men and animals" (761). It is intriguing to speculate about Lawrence's view of how much in Lewis's abundant childhood mythologies recalled the long-established sacrifice of cats.

Kiowa of the unmanageable triangle of Frieda, Mabel, and Brett: "'Nay, nay, lass', he said in a voice ever so gentle and low. 'I am never really mad any more'" (Ellis 177). It is a denial steeped in the fatigue of a man without the energy or interest in resolving the commotions and competitions that swirl about him.

IV

It is at this point in the novella, with the assertion by Lou of a lack of direction and transcendent meaning in her life—"I want the wonder back again, or I shall die" (62)—that Lawrence introduces an eccentric but crucial character who appears in only one scene in the novella. As a wizened and wise man who looks goatish and emanates the regretful tone of a fallen Pan, Cartwright speaks with experienced insight and admiration for the ancient mythologies that form the doctrinal center of this work.[13] He exists to provide a short but illuminating explanation about the origin and history of the Pan figure, and much in his commentary corresponds to the didactic content of Lawrence's essay, "Pan in America". He confidently describes the authentic Pan not as an embodiment of Wordsworthian sensibility or as an anthropomorphic God. Cartwright insists that Pan is properly seen as a palpable yet inscrutable force—"the hidden mystery—the hidden cause", and he suggests that the human perception of such energy requires, in an eminently Lawrencian metaphor, "your third eye, which is darkness" (65). Lou pertinently asks if such Pan-power might be embodied in St. Mawr, an understandable query because of the unusual experience she has just undergone while observing the horse:

> Lou escaped to look at St. Mawr. He was still moist where the saddle had been. And he seemed a little bit extinguished, as if virtue had gone out of him.

13. See Cowan's incisive comments on the fascinating connections between Cartwright and the image of a fallen Pan. In the brevity and centrality of Cartwright's appearance in the novella, along with his aura of lapsarian imagery and trenchant insight, he has always reminded me of Conrad's use of the French lieutenant in *Lord Jim*. Cartwright articulates important issues of doctrinal substance and symbolic relevance in *St. Mawr*, just as Conrad's "fallen" character outlines the themes of courage and cowardice that are crucial to that novel. The literary life of each character spans about four pages; they never reappear, but their words linger fatefully in the respective works.

> But when he lifted his lovely naked head, like a bunch of flames, to see who it was had entered, she saw he was still himself. Forever sensitive and alert, his head lifted like the summit of a fountain. And within him the clean bones striking to the earth, his hoofs intervening between him and the ground like lesser jewels.
>
> He knew her and did not resent her. But he took no notice of her. He would never "respond." At first she resented it. Now she was glad. He would never be intimate, thank heaven (64).

This powerful vignette—like a slow-motion unfolding of a layered symbol—forces Lou to contemplate briefly the phallic force of the huge stallion reflected in the wet emissions on the saddle. Yet Lou also notes that he ultimately lacks sexual interest in anything, and she is revealingly pleased by a disinclination in him that mirrors her own preference for singlehood. The passage remains impressive as it poetically moves between her awareness of the animal's valuable energy to her contentment about their shared aversion to intimacy. Now erect for the first time in the novella, as Lawrence twice asserts that his head is lifted, his numen is committed to the earth rather than to people.

When St. Mawr finally explodes with anger in his understandably antagonistic response to Rico's willful and incompetent handling, Lou achieves a sudden understanding of the dangerous aspect of Pan that Lawrence carefully outlines in "Pan in America": it is the destructive component that she will comprehend more fully when she undertakes the challenge of confronting the vagaries of landscape and season at the Kiowa ranch. Lawrence insists in the essay on the inherently unpredictable force that is Pan, for "this is Pan, the Pan-mystery, the Pan-power", and "among the creatures of Pan there is an eternal struggle for life" (162). Lawrence, in effect, provides a gloss on *St. Mawr* as he further comments that "Pan keeps on being re-born in all kinds of strange shapes" (156), and Lou's sudden insight about the horse also represents a larger awareness of (quite literally!) the underbelly of Pan:

> It was something horrifying, something you could not escape from. It had come to her as in a vision, when she saw the pale gold belly of the stallion upturned, the hoofs working wildly, the wicked curved hams of the horse, and then the evil straining of that arched, fish-like neck, with the dilated eyes of the head (78).

This virtual philogenetic word painting, describing a serpent-fish-goat-horse creature, presents a composite-image of Pan common in Greek mythology. The Hellenic versions of satyrs frequently combine qualities of man, snake, and hoofed- animals such as horses and goats, and in terms of basic morphology, they all resemble the prevailing perception of Pan as a form of centaur.[14] Lou's brief glimpse of evil extends to her realization about the essential cowardice of humanity, and the related inclination—so evident in the Manby girls and their many suitors—to "undermine" (79). It is appropriate to read the following passage and its angry irony as an implicit recollection by Lawrence of his recent experience at the Café Royal dinner and as a restatement of its dominant theme of betrayal. The fury here projected through Lou's refracted perspective may strike the one false note in the novella, for the precise wording of her judgment is too intrusively Lawrence's:

> *Let us undermine one another. There is nothing to believe in, so let us undermine everything....Never, by any chance, injure your fellow man openly. But always injure him secretly...* inward treachery, in a game of betrayal, betrayal, betrayal. The last of the gods of our era, Judas supreme! (79, emphasis in the original)[15]

Lawrence is more effective when he uses Lewis's discussion with Mrs. Witt during their trip together to suggest the ancient taboos and totemic customs embedded in his version of panophilia. The entire episode with these unlikely fellow travelers constitutes one of the most memorable and unorthodox doctrinal interludes in all of Lawrence's fiction; it conveys the magical aura of mythic beliefs through the cathartic and metaphoric language of an uneducated but sensitive Welshman, who remains proud and undefensive about the rituals and stories that conditioned his approach to life as a young boy. In his unintrusive and detached narrative framework for the scene, Lawrence does not endorse the extra-terrestrial dimensions of Lewis's cosmology, but he wisely permits this impeccably honest groom to articulate the transcendent ideas virtually without interruption. Lawrence lets Lewis articulate his doctrine in a way that inoculates this groom's ideas from criticism: the Welshman's heartfelt depiction of an organic and vitalistic universe emerges as a confident and subjective statement of one man's acute sense perception and inherited set of cultural myths. How does one begin to disagree with such declaimed

14. Merivale is comprehensive on this Hellenic inheritance, and note especially her opening chapter (1-47), and the relevant illustrations provided between 144–45.

15. Although Hough is less positive than I about the achievement of this novella, he reflects an awareness in one of his observations many decades ago that is crucial to my understanding of the generative process at work in *St. Mawr*. He maintains that Lawrence wrote it "out of a need and a mood that are too partial and too close" (181). As I attempt to demonstrate, the "closeness" is not "partial," and the "need" and "mood" become the springboard for great art.

subjectivity? Call it "transcendence-lite-and-literal"—his belief in a magical force that is notable for its lack of doctrinal explanation or empirical support. It is what he believes, what he feels is true. In effect, his gentle language of fantasy carries with it an appealing momentum and legitimacy, and his words finally function as an unlikely and radical antidote to the *uber*-rationalist and cynical world that Lawrence openly deplores in *St. Mawr* and "Pan in America". What Lewis so earnestly portrays to a bemused Mrs. Witt bends the limits of realistic discourse: Lawrence enhances the power of Lewis's visionary dialogue by backgrounding the scene with a bewitching landscape that remains suitable for the improbable content of Lewis's descriptions.

The episode develops like an inset stage-scene or a flash transition in a film—with no preparation for its dramatic appearance within the developing narrative of the cross-country journey to Merriton. It abruptly begins with an invocation that itself is integrated by a beckoning iteration of a full name, a legendary place, and an astral superstition, as the tone of the novella suddenly changes. We are thrust into the world of a child's picture-book by the fabulous tone and metaphors that invite us in. Even Mrs. Witt must be impressed:

> So, in a while she came to the edge of the wood's darkness, and saw the open pale concave of the world beyond…Yet, as Rachel Witt drew rein at the gate emerging from the wood, a very big, soft star fell in heaven, cleaving the hubbub of this human night with a gleam from the greater world (107).

It is Lawrence functioning as the off-stage narrator or cinematic voice-over who introduces the dialogue that meshes with the fairy-tale ambiance created by the above lines. The sudden statement of Mr. Witt's married name suggests the imposition of a pleasing fluidity of time and space just before Lewis begins his talk—a bending of the stabilities of sequence and place that function conventionally in the rest of the novella. This chrono-kinetic effect is complemented by the presence of the shooting star, creating an atmosphere of magical-realism that is perfect for two characters who stand exactly on the demarcation line where all the haunting tales of our childhood begin: on "the edge of the wood's darkness", where once existed, at "the wood's-edge, the darkness of the old Pan" (107).

V

Lewis quickly connects his observation of the star to a talismanic belief in the transcendent "long-distance places in the sky", an area for him comfortably not amenable to rational confirmation or scientific analysis: "I think I hear something, though I wouldn't call it God" (107). That undefinable "something" uttered by Lewis to an incredulous Mrs. Witt is a phrase carefully chosen by Lawrence: recall that it is the same term used by a tipsy Tom Brangwen in the marriage celebration for his daughter, Anna. As Lewis continues his clarifications of personal belief and ritual, he briefly becomes a filter for a hyper-energized depiction of his author's numinous cosmology. He elaborates with relevant detail on the contrasting qualities of various trees, concentrating on their animistic properties and elaborating on the significance of each type of tree for the life rhythms of human beings. One of the distinctive aspects of Lewis's benedictive descriptions is its reverse anthropomorphism—what I regard as a profound and committed *arbomorphism*: the honor he bestows on the Pan-livingness of trees is conveyed by a metaphoric taxonomy in which people are privileged to take on the qualities of trees, as the human being becomes reduced to an organic essence:

> They see people live and they see people perish, and they say, people are only like twigs on a tree, you break them off the tree, and kindle fire with them. You make a fire of them, and they are gone, the fire is gone, everything is gone… people all appearing and disappearing like twigs that come in spring and you cut them in autumn and make a fire of them and they are gone (108).

Lewis also elaborates on the dangerous ramifications for human life when trees are cut down, an issue that Frazer connects to the primitive belief that when there is illness, "the life of the patient depends on the life of the tree" (791).[16]

In this spectral world recalled by Lewis, he conveys a quaint authority by referring to himself in the third person and with his full name, as he continues to dramatize the luminous messages from the trees: *"Is that you passing there, Morgan Lewis?"* (107, emphasis in the original). Thus *St. Mawr* gives fictional expression to Frazer's several chapters defining the

---

16. See Vickery's discussion of pine trees and their relation to ancient vegetative rites outlined by Frazer and appropriated by Lawrence (294–325). I analyze more thoroughly Lawrence's treatment of the visionary and metaphoric aspects of trees and his relevant indebtedness to Frazer in my chapter on *The Fox*. Banford's death is not unrelated to Lawrence's totemic beliefs.

ancient theories of "sympathetic magic" (19), as Lawrence relates the Pan-like force to Lewis's discussion of bushes, trees, and the magical properties of certain foods and plants.[17] Many of the richly detailed harvest myths outlined by Frazer include a range of rites enacted in North Pembrokeshire in Wales, including what he calls the "quaint old customs" (468) involving rituals with blades of corn: these totemic celebrations have lingered into the early-twentieth-century period encompassed by Lewis's childhood. Despite the groom's intense narrative and its striking imagery, he cannot budge the abiding skepticism felt by Mrs. Witt about the fantastic beliefs of his childhood. It is also fair to assume that a similarly "modern" superiority informs the perspective of the eminent scholar James Frazer on the customs and beliefs he meticulously describes in *The Golden Bough*. As I noted, Lawrence remains sufficiently impressed by the depth and breadth of Frazer's monumental scholarship that he returns for a more thorough reading in the spring of 1924. But in the seminal essay, "Pan in America", that he writes during this same period, he cannot resist leveling a broadside at this impeccably sober and talented researcher. Frazer's investigations clearly are valuable to Lawrence, but Frazer also embodies for him the contemporary Western world's lack of faith in the transcendent vibrations of Pan: "What can men who sit at home in their studies and drink hot milk and have lambs-wool slippers on their feet, and write anthropology, what *can* they possibly know about men, the men of Pan?" (162)

In the series of letters that Lou writes to her mother, Lawrence's ear for light social satire and perfectly-pitched mimicry is on full display. He also uses Lou's account of the events to develop amusingly the novella's phallophobia, as Lou describes Rico in those absurd pajamas that extravagantly display a priapus logo. The terrain of masculinity and amorous engagement is meant to be out of joint in this work and in the world, and Lawrence enjoys sending out the signals of such denuded sexuality. In this novella, the usual ramifications of passion from men that resonate from the marriage matrix are reduced to the level of maladjustment and immaturity. There is a husband who is content with a platonic relationship with his wife and adolescent flirtations with shallow lady-friends, a groom who shuns intimacy with any woman, and another groom who fancies a manipulative erotic connection to Lou. On the drive to Kiowa that Lou ill-advisedly takes with the predatory Phoenix, she begins to comprehend his profound limitations as a potential lover.

17. This Frazerian issue of "sympathetic magic" is developed more fully in my chapter on *The Ladybird*—a novella in which the properties of magic play a special role.

Initially attracted to Phoenix's isolate, confident, and mysterious sense of self, Lou is experienced enough to realize that his chauvinistic and uncommitted sense of sexual passion is too confining and unimaginative to sustain her interest: "How could there be any answer in *her* to the phallic male in him?...Only, the aboriginal phallic male in him simply couldn't recognize her as a woman at all" (135). With such depressing recognition that she cannot risk intimacy with Phoenix, we sense again the exhaustion and despair in a D.H. Lawrence who felt he had been betrayed by Frieda and Murry at the Café Royal earlier that year, and is now caught at Kiowa within the competing tensions and rivalries of his wife and two other women. Lou wants what Lawrence desperately wants: "She knew what she wanted. She wanted relief from the nervous tension and irritation of her life, she wanted to escape from the friction which is the whole stimulus in modern social life. She wanted to be still: only that, to be very, very still, and recover her own soul" (137).

Part of this recovery for Lou will entail what amounts to the calibrated imposition by her of a new chastity—a modern equivalent of "the meaning of the Vestal Virgins", who "were symbolic of herself, a woman weary of the embrace of incompetent men" (138).[18] The keen awareness in Lou of the inadequacies of the opposite sex merges into the larger framework of discontent that has relevance for the emotional and physical disposition of Lawrence from late 1923 through the summer of 1924. The essential balancing of male and female polarities—a "singling-out" that during the preceding decade often was a shorthand for that "baptism of fire" in passion that leads to the Lawrencian "unknown"—such a syndrome no longer works for him in his life or fiction. The phallophobia so intrinsic to this novella is a reflection of postwar malaise and of the wounded state of Lawrence's body and soul. In a crucial passage, as she recalls the inanity of her marriage and the immaturity of former lovers, Lou understands the existential mandate to get beyond the self but does not know how to do it: "I want my temple and my loneliness and my Apollo mystery of the inner fire" (139). She quickly realizes—with the authority and poetry of a Joycean epiphany—that where she now stands, above Taos, New Mexico offers itself as a living remnant of Pan-fire, and the flames are etched in the surrounding landscape: "She felt a great peace inside herself as she made this realization. And a thankfulness. Because, after all, it seemed to her that the hidden fire was alive and burning in this sky, over the desert, in the mountains" (139). As Frazer explains, the image of Apollo "was

18. See the related discussion of virginity and the use by Lawrence of the image of the Sacred Prostitute in my 1990 essay on *The Lost Girl*, a work in which the heroine must avoid the advances of several "incompetent men".

thought to impart superhuman strength", and the fire here associated with Apollo suggests the fertility-worship rites in Scotland and France to honor "the ancient Celtic god Grannus, whom the Romans identified with Apollo" (110, 708). Lou's search for the fertile grounds of a new existence will not end with a man but with a ceremony of transcendent recognition, quite simply, of where she wants to live.

VI

Lawrence is acutely aware of the danger, as he archly describes it in "Pan in America", of letting Pan-power reduce itself to an easy and often sentimental pantheism akin to the vision of the British Romantic poets. Lou's commitment to her "spirit of the place" (143) in New Mexico—for Lawrence a term that always amounts to the spirit of Pan—focuses on an isolated and decrepit ranch on the exposed side of a mountain: in reality, the ranch is recognizably Kiowa, the mountain Lobo, and it provides a vantage point overlooking an impressive desert vista and a distant range of towering mountains. The ranch carries a history of energetic but ultimately failed management through the several generations of ownership that vainly sought to manage the savage vicissitudes of the seasons and the encroaching animals and plant-life that gradually undermined its productivity. A key phrase is introduced when Lawrence makes more precise the implications of Apollo fire by referring to Lou's signal contemplation of "the latent fire of the vast landscape" (140). Its most prominent expression resides in "the great pine-tree" (144) that Lawrence celebrates a few months earlier in "Pan in America"—the same tree that his friend, Georgia O'Keeffe, memorialized in her painting, "The Lawrence Tree, 1929".

This huge tree stands as a graphic microcosm of Lawrence's emphasis in *St. Mawr* on the interplay between panophilia and phallophobia. What Lawrence describes, with the unsubtle phrasing of sublimated erotic energy, as "the stimulus" of the ranch, "seemed to enter like a sort of sex passion, intensifying her ego" (144). Is this pattern not a transparent version of the primal ego-support Lawrence once enjoyed with Frieda that was annealed in their sexual appetite for each other? Note the important contrast in emphasis between the description of this same tree in "Pan in America" and in *St. Mawr*. In the earlier description from the essay, there is a focus on aspects of panophilia evident in Lawrence's perception of the tree, variously describing it as a "guardian spirit", with a "powerful will of its own", similar to the eternal vestiges of Pan that have survived into the modern era, it "is always there, alive and changeless, alive and changing",

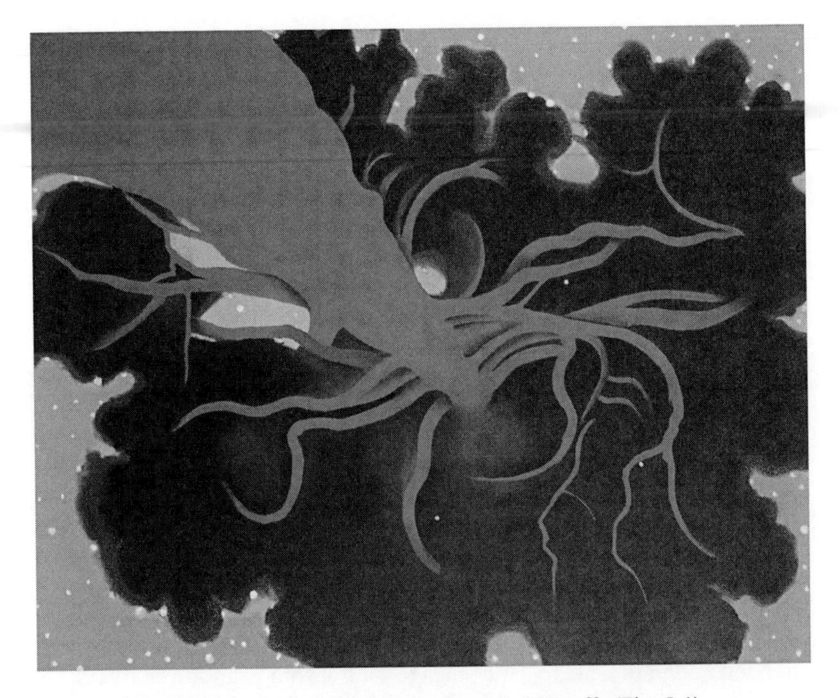

"The Lawrence Tree, 1929", by Georgia O'Keeffe (Fig. 5-1)

with an "aura of life", and "still within the allness of Pan…it is a tree which is still Pan" (157,158). As Lou will discover when she bravely takes ownership of the ranch, her life will be intimately connected to (and ultimately dependent upon) the shifting parameters and intensities of Pan-energy, symbolized for Lawrence by this powerful tree. Lawrence sounds unequivocal and Biblical in tone in "Pan in America" about these permeable and transformative effects:

> And we live beneath it, without noticing. Yet sometimes, when one suddenly looks far up and sees those wild doves there, or when one glances quickly at the inhuman-human hammering of a woodpecker, one realizes that the tree is asserting itself as much as I am. It gives out life, as I give out life. Our two lives meet and cross one another, unknowingly: the tree's life penetrates my life, and my life the tree's. We cannot live near one another, as we do, without affecting one another…It vibrates its presence into my soul, and I am one with Pan (158).

Just a couple of months later, as Lawrence describes the same tree in *St. Mawr*, there are two significant adjustments in his perspective. First is the recognition of the more aggressive and intimidating elements within Pan-energy not evident in the rhapsodic words from "Pan in America" about the tree's "assertive" and "vibrating" qualities absorbed by Lawrence. The novella highlights the tree's "callous indifference", its "grim permanence", and the alarming sound of "the wind hissing in the needles, like a vast nest of serpents" (144). This dualistic panophilia anticipates the range of challenges Lou must encounter with the Kiowa ranch as an integral part of her inheritance of Pan-power. But secondly, the energy embodied in this tree is accompanied with a phallophobia that Lawrence announces in explicit terms. If Lou does feel the stimulus of New Mexico "like a sort of sex passion" that serves to intensify her ego, Lawrence adds a reiterated caveat in relation to the tree's atavistic qualities: "A passionless, *non-phallic column*, rising in the shadows of the *pre-sexual world*, before the hot-blooded ithyphallic column ever erected itself" (144, emphases mine). In case there is any doubt concerning Lawrence's revised attitude about the tree, he repeats again his pointed caution in the description of its pine cones, "lying all over the yard, open in the sun like wooden roses, but hard, sexless, rigid with a blind will" (144).

Lou Witt will now direct her energy and ego into the constant struggle of leading a productive and vitalized life at the Kiowa ranch. Such a strenuous commitment to both engage and absorb Pan-power offers no guarantee of success—only the excitement and profound meaning in undertaking the challenge. Thus she will encounter Lawrencian otherness as her portal to the transcendent, not from a man but from the powerful and distinctly unphallic "spirit of place" that is situated in the enveloping landscape of New Mexico. And what a landscape of inspiring otherness it is, as Lawrence now provides one of the longest and most poetic sentences in all his work: his prose sweeps across the livid tiers of the topography with a wide-angle lens that captures the coloration and—in the evocative French phrase—the *différance* that constitute the source of Lou's renewal. This link between transcendence and the renewed soul starts with the "felt" perception of a magnificent and eternal landscape:[19]

> The desert swept its great fawn-coloured circle around, away beyond and below like a breach, with a long mountain-side of pure blue shadow

---

19. Vickery is trenchant in noting "how extensively Lawrence saw his landscape and natural settings with the eyes of the ancient people who appear in *The Golden Bough*" (319); perhaps also, as I have noted, he saw with the eyes of the celebrated anthropologist who describes the perspective of these ancient peoples. See my chapter on "The Princess" for further discussion of Pan imagery and its relation to Lawrence's doctrines about landscape description and the province of painting.

"The Kiowa Ranch, New Mexico" by D.H. Lawrence (Fig. 5-2)

> closing in the near corner, and strange bluish hummocks of mountains rising like wet rock from a vast strand, away in the middle distance, and beyond, in the farthest distance, pale blue crests of mountains looking over the horizon, from the west, as if peering in from another world altogether (145).

Less than a year after Lawrence finishes final revisions of *St. Mawr*, he paints one of his few landscape paintings, "The Kiowa Ranch, New Mexico" (see colour centerfold).

More accurately, he contributes to the creation of visual art that is a cooperative undertaking (after a period of quarrels) involving himself, Frieda, and Dorothy Brett. Lawrence paints the forefront figures, Frieda the white chickens, and Brett, as the more accomplished artist, is responsible for the looming landscape. Brett's admiration of Lawrencian aesthetics, and her perception of his moods and preferences are well documented by commentators about this complex and often volatile three-person ménage in Taos. What remains intriguing about the painting is how its near-and-far perspective, and its kinetic depiction of the ranch area with its enveloping topography, conform so precisely to the prose description cited above, from *St. Mawr*. Note the arrangement and coloration of the "long mountain-side of pure blue shadow", and the sequential tiers of "strange blue hummocks of mountains" in the middle distance, and "beyond, in the furthest distance, pale crests of mountains looking over the horizon" (145). The recognizable figures that Lawrence places in front of the mountain ranges are not randomly distributed. Perhaps as a mollifying statement to Frieda about ramification of priority and commitment within this often-tense unit of Lawrence and two females, he conspicuously places his wife in the lead position on the horse, followed by himself and then Brett: recall how adamantly Lawrence usually prefers to "lead".

In provocative ways, this 1925 painting also anticipates a fundamental notion from "Introduction to These Paintings", a work he wrote from late 1928 to early 1929. As I will note more fully in Chapter Six, the essay relates the English delight and talent in landscape painting to his conviction that it is a "form of escape for them from the actual human body they so hate and fear" (195). He elaborates with terms that resonantly connect to the thematic context and compositional components of the "Kiowa Ranch" painting, and more exactly, to the purposeful arrangement of those three human figures. Lawrence is not a fan of English landscape art, and he offers an accessible explanation for his animus: "But, for me, landscape is always waiting for something to occupy it. Landscape seems to me *meant* as a background to an intenser vision of life, so to my feeling painted landscape is background with the real subject left out" (194). Yes, on the narrowly situational and internecine level, the "real subject" connects to patterns of conflict and resolution in Lawrence's marriage. But in the larger and more doctrinal frame of reference, involving the recently completed final scenes of *St. Mawr*, the painting insists on confronting other characteristic Lawrencian concerns. Can courageous Lou Carrington, or any human being, manifest the grit and instinctual understanding to not only survive in the beautiful and ultimately dangerous landscape, but also embrace its fundamental message of a link to the transcendent? The human figures are overwhelmed in the painting by the breadth and grandeur of the desert and mountains that surround them. The challenge that a resolute Lou faces is significant.

What Lawrence describes in "Pan in America" as the essential energy that emanates from the "vivid relatedness between the man and the living universe that surrounds him" (160), has become more threateningly in *St. Mawr* a dangerous panoply where "the great circling landscape lived its own life, sumptuous and uncaring. Man did not exist for it" (146). Frazer speculates about the "original character of Attis as a tree spirit", about the central role the pine tree plays in his legend, and about how and why "the Phrygians should have worshipped the pine above other trees" (409). His conclusions define what amounts to a precise integration of the tree's central function for Lawrence as an eternal, unphallic, yet fertile symbol of endurance that conveniently recalls the sweep of Frazer's precise wording on the source and embodiment of the very Pan-power Lawrence describes in the novella. It is fair to wonder if Lawrence has absorbed not only the substance of Frazer's superb scholarship, but also the exact metaphors and perspectives of his prose. The similarities to Lawrence's painting and to the rhythm and detail of Lawrence's prose are fascinating:

> Perhaps the sight of its changeless, though sombre, green cresting the ridges of the high hills above the fading splendour of the autumn woods in the valleys may have seemed to their eyes to mark it out as the seat of diviner life, of something exempt from the sad vicissitudes of the seasons, constant and eternal as the sky which stooped to meet it (409).

VII

For more than a century, highlighted both by Freud's important and informal essay on civilized sexual morality followed in 1909 by his controversial study on Leonardo da Vinci's aesthetics and psychology, it has been understood that the process of sublimation can contribute effectively to the creation of great art.[20] Anna Freud will develop her father's pioneering theories into the more liberalized construct that regards sublimation as an integral part of a person's defense system and asserts that it contributes to normative ego development. Given Lawrence's intense feelings of sexual betrayal, his scarcely repressed anger toward Frieda and Murry, and his volatile emotions and increasing sexual incapacity, his artistic achievement must stand as a graphic example of the basic notion, summarized by the scholar Lore Schacht, that "the pleasure the person gets from sublimation is something more stable, without the ups and downs, with more continuity in it than the pleasure from instinctual satisfaction" (qtd. in Sandler 184). In this context, Anna Freud virtually stipulates the dynamics of Lawrence's conception of the three Murry stories when she describes, in *The Ego and the Mechanisms of Defence*, how "the readiness with which such instinctual processes can be displaced assists the mechanism of sublimation" (192). Yet an inevitable question must arise in any psychobiographical speculation about D.H. Lawrence from the winter of 1923–24 through the late summer of 1924. Can the defense mechanisms anatomized by Freud and his daughter really provide Lawrence with the sufficient confidence and clarity to formulate an integrated set of beliefs such as panophilia, and can such doctrine give him the sense of completion, release, and satisfaction that is so intrinsic to the physiology and psychosomatics of consummated sex? Can an uncharacteristic interval for Lawrence of reiterated phallophobia serve to keep him reasonably effective and fulfilled as man, husband, and artist? Here is Freud's applicable affirmative response in some of his most quoted and influential remarks:

> If this displaceable energy is desexualized libido, it may also be described as sublimated energy; for it would still retain the main purpose of Eros—that of uniting and binding—in so far as it helps toward establishing the unity or tendency to unity, which is particularly characteristic of the ego. If thought-processes in the wider sense are to be included in these displacements, then the activity of thinking is also supplied from the sublimation of erotic motive forces (*The Ego and the Id* 35).

Freud's comments above conveniently encompass both the motivation and implementation of Lawrence's ability to establish "the unity" that is

20. See the Alan Tyson translation of Freud's *Leonardo da Vinci and a Memory of His Childhood*, and note his relevant consideration of Freud's mistake concerning his infamous misinterpretation of a key word in his study. See also Peter Gay's biography of Freud for consideration of sublimation as well as the issue of Freud's translation error (164, 272–73, 292).

"characteristic of the ego" of this artistic "processer" of thought and doctrine. Something more dramatic, however, occurs in *St. Mawr* than the common mechanism of sublimation-through-displacement. Lou Witt's fragmentary yet ultimately unified articulation of panophilia mirrors the tone and substance of Lawrence's own emotions and "thought-processes" at the time of the novella's composition. In *St. Mawr*, Lawrence successfully demonstrates the uncommon instance in fictional art of a cross-gendered authorial *projection*—the process by which one's own traits and emotions are attributed to someone else. He recreates himself in drag-disguise as Lady Carrington to carry forth his visionary message, and the reason for undertaking such a daring and clever literary camouflage across the formal categories of sex and class is not difficult to decipher. Would not a male voice of phallophobia sound too plaintive, too close to the anguish of Lawrence's own problematic libido and marital pain for him to tolerate its public utterance—or even, perhaps, for him to consciously confront for himself the meaning of such projection? He famously told us to trust the tale and not the artist, and I suspect much of the psychological generativity of *St. Mawr* properly resides beyond his awareness.

Aside from the doctrinal and emotional correspondences between Lawrence and Lou, how precisely synchronous is his own sensibility to her projected perspective in the novella? Here is Lou in the latter pages of the work, as the narrative resonates with the remarkable anachronism of a pre-channeled D.H. Lawrence summoning the future voice and rhythm of the man from *The Escaped Cock*: "You know, dear, I ache in every fibre to be left alone, from all that sort of thing. I feel all bruises, like one who has been assassinated. I do so understand why Jesus said: *Noli me tangere*. Touch me not, I am not yet ascended unto the father. Everything had hurt him so much" (120). As an even more eerie example of anticipatory narrative that spans the boundaries of gender and chronology, Lou now formulates the tone and outlook of Oliver Mellors, as Lawrence in a few years will return to the phallic centrality absent in *St. Mawr*. Lou's voice here remains so intimately cathartic *for Lawrence himself* that she becomes—unbeknownst to the artist who created her—the harbinger and herald for a future step in his career development. All she needs is Mellors's dialect. Lou's rumination even employs, in the last word of the passage, the exact term that Lawrence soon will consider as the first title for *Lady Chatterley's Lover*. She points the way to Lawrence's ultimate belief in the path to renewal:

> It seems to me men and women have really hurt one another so much, nowadays, that they had better stay apart till they have learned to be gentle

> with one another again. Not all this forced passion and destructive philandering. Men and women should stay apart, till their hearts grow gentle towards one another again. Now, it's only each one fighting for his own—or her own—underneath the cover of tenderness (122).

VIII

An additional question remains, involving the issue of Lawrence's stylistic presentation of his doctrine in *St. Mawr*. Why is he so insistent, so dogmatic, so reiterative about the essential elements of panophilia and phallophobia that inform the work? On one level, of course, the Foreword to *Women in Love* addresses the issue of repetition and its relation to "the struggle for verbal consciousness" (486) in his art. But something more fundamental is at work in this intimately revealing novella, as the work must recall Lawrence's seminal letter to McLeod more than a decade earlier: "But one sheds one's sickness in books—repeats and presents again one's emotions, to be master of them" (*Letters 11* 90). Lawrence writes *St. Mawr* as explicit confirmation of the viability of that central metaphor in the letter to his friend after the publication of *Sons and Lovers*: he uses this novella to "shed" his emotional tension and weakening libido through an integrated process of sublimation and projection. Then an alarming circumstance intervenes during his composition of this work. About five weeks before Lawrence completes *St. Mawr*, he ominously spits "bright red blood" for the first time, and although Lawrence and Frieda might pretend "nothing wrong, the lungs are strong", I suspect David Ellis is correct in his speculation that from August 1924, "it is legitimate to regard him as tubercular" (195).

On September 13 1924, Lawrence completes *St. Mawr*. Events occur that day that may have coincidental—or even karmic—relevance as he composes the concluding lines of the work. He first writes a letter to Professor Edward McDonald in which he explains that on the previous day he posted to this devoted and scrupulous compiler of Lawrence's publications "the little preface" that he titles "The Bad Side of Books" (*Letters V* 119). This lyrical and endearing essay has much in it about Lawrence's family life and formative beliefs that is memorable, but perhaps its most moving lines involve the reactions of his father as he holds in his hands Lawrence's first book, *The White Peacock,* and responds to his son's proud admission that he received fifty pounds for the work: "'Fifty pounds.' He was dumbfounded, and looked at me with shrewd eyes, as if I were a swindler. 'Fifty pounds! An' tha's niver done a hard day's work in thy life'" (*Introductions and Reviews* 75). Clearly, to this unimaginative miner and hard working, yet undisciplined, man, such payment for the achievement of the mind seems beyond his reductive understanding of the legitimate province of masculine exertion and reward. Arthur Lawrence's comment reflects his inability to understand his talented son as well as the sad fact of the gradual deterioration of the father's aura of respect in a home ruled by the indomitable Lydia Lawrence. A decade later the wound to his married son's pride occasioned by betrayal and illness could be camouflaged and sublimated by the artifice of narrative projection in *St. Mawr*. But the encroachment on his father's sense of male authority primarily through the dominant will and fierce resentment of the mother was beyond the ability of Arthur to repress or to counter with effective strategy.

Later on the same day of the novella's completion, Lawrence is informed by a cablegram from his sister Emily that their father has died, and the next day he writes a short but revealing note to her acknowledging his pain: "It was the last thing I expected. Ada had just written he was as well as ever—it is better to be gone than lingering on half helpless and half alive. But it upset one, nevertheless, makes a strange break" (*Letters V* 124). Lawrence will increasingly revise the negative opinion of his father in the six years remaining in his own life; he comes to more fully realize his unfortunate lack of empathy for Arthur's besieged plight, as well as his overestimate of the salutary role of Lydia in the intensely matriarchal household. There may be even more encoded within Lawrence's mournful and measured response to his father's death, and perhaps it involves the tone imposed on the conclusion of *St. Mawr*, as Lawrence completes, edits, or revises those final lines on September 13 with the haunting echo of the incident with his father—recorded for posterity just days earlier in "The Bad Side of Books"—no doubt lingering in his understandably recollective mind. The clipped and ironic ending of the novella has never felt right to me, with a sense of abruptness and interruption created by the gratuitous and meek concession in Mrs. Witt's concluding comment: "Then I call it cheap, considering all there is to it: even the name!" (155) Given her abiding skepticism about buying the long-embattled Kiowa ranch, it is a witty and unconvincing response to Lou's sincere enthusiasm for what the ranch means to her. It serves also as the for-record statement of the $1200 purchase price—exactly the amount that Mabel reportedly paid for it. In "The Bad Side of Books", Arthur's amazement at the fifty pounds received by his son is followed by Lawrence's unforgiving and hurt response: "I think to this day, he looks upon me as a sort of cleverish swindler, who gets money for nothing" (76). The phrase "to this day" must give Lawrence pause, for now Arthur has no days remaining. Lawrence completes this confessional essay less than two weeks before he mails it the evening before he finishes *St. Mawr* on September 13, a date on which the phrase must have echoed for the son with a poignant guilt. Thus both "The Bad Side of Books" and *St. Mawr*, in the scene with his father and in the conclusion to the novella, respectively, sound a note of victorious achievement against the similar allegations of the naïve father and the cynical Mrs. Witt that Lawrence and Lou are getting something for nothing. So the ending of *St. Mawr* may be right after all—with Lawrence claiming a victory against unbelievers as he appropriates a ranch and landscape for his own. The Lawrence of September 1924 needs victories wherever he can get them. On that same and by now ultra-meaningful September 13, Lawrence writes to his publisher, Martin Secker, about the completion of *St. Mawr*, and implicitly about the energy required of him to sustain the magic of literary projection in the work: "But thank God I don't have to write it again. It took a lot out of me" (*Letters V* 122).

Norman Mailer's summary comment on Lawrence's fundamental desires and embattled marriage suggests the core of his frustrations as artist and lover in 1924. It can also serve as a relevant gloss on the impinging circumstances in Lawrence's life that lead to the compensatory creation of doctrine and disguise in *St. Mawr*:

> And sexual transcendence, some ecstasy where he could lose his ego for a moment, and his sense of self, and his will was life to him—he could not live without sexual transcendence… His lungs were poor, and he lived with the knowledge that he would likely have an early death. Each time he failed to reach a woman, each time he failed particularly to reach his own woman, he was dying a little…He was ill, and his wife was literally killing him each time she failed to worship his most proud and delicate cock" (155–56).[21]

---

21. For more on Mailer's insights into Lawrence's life and art, and on Lawrence's influence on Mailer, see my full-length study, *D.H. Lawrence and the Phallic Imagination*, my essay in *The Hemingway Review*, and Chapters Seven and Eight in this study.

CHAPTER SIX

PAN AND THE APPLEYNESS OF LANDSCAPE: DREAD OF THE PROCREATIVE BODY IN "THE PRINCESS"

So much depends on one's attitude.

—D.H. Lawrence, "Pan in America"

He withdraws and touches the black stone of his inner conscience. And in a new adventure, he dares take thought. He dares take thought for what he has done and what has happened to him.

—D.H. Lawrence, "On Being a Man"

Every dream reveals itself as a psychical structure.

—Sigmund Freud, *The Interpretation of Dreams*

I

Characteristic praise for "The Princess" fails to acknowledge the integrative context of its excellence within the Lawrencian canon. This lengthy tale also remains impressive for the seamless way that it connects Lawrence's developing stylistic notions on writing and painting with his doctrinal beliefs about Pan mythology and marriage during the last six years of his life. Yet for most critics, the versatile achievement of "The Princess" is related variously to the detailed evocation of the New Mexico landscape, to the fluid changes in a narrative tone that moves from satiric to lyric to somber, to the imaginative adaption of a vignette Lawrence originally heard from Catherine Carswell, and to the violent and credible inevitability of the tale's conclusion.[1] While such critical perspectives

---

1. Among the many critics who have written intelligently on this story, there are surprisingly few in-depth examinations, and none that include extended consideration of the issues of Pan and/or painting that I employ in this essay. S. Ronald Weiner offers one of the most sustained looks at irony and symbolism in the tale, with a valuable emphasis on how the tone, imagery, and natural

provide relevant entrances into dimensions of the work's success, the story, in my reading, actually recalls a short essay, "Pan in America", that Lawrence wrote a few months before "The Princess", and it also anticipates, with unusual depth and precision, a major essay, "Introduction to These Paintings", that he wrote nearly five years later, an extensive piece that he frankly described as "one of the best things I've ever done" (*Letters VII* 125). In their emphasis on the desexualized body and the often contested relations between men and women, both essays offer insight about the configuration of the marriage matrix in this often admired but relatively unexamined tale of idiosyncratic courtship and deadly conflict. But it is first to his brilliant and risky polemic on painting, written in January 1929 as an introduction for the Mandrake Press edition of his paintings, that I wish to turn.[2]

In this essay, Lawrence is less interested in the technique or evaluation of his own skill as a painter than he is in outlining a scathing criticism of the quality of English painting through the centuries. He repeatedly insists—with the undiplomatic wit and subjective fervor that are among his signature rhetorical qualities as a critic—that this alleged failure of his country to produce great visual art involves fundamental issues of sexual self-definition and cultural taboo inherited by the English people for nearly

---

descriptions convey subtle tensions and conflicts in the characters. But there is insufficient concern by Weiner on how the landscape's animate qualities participate in the plot as active presences that gradually expose fundamental inadequacies in the emotional states of Dollie and Romero, 221–38. While Cowan provides insight into the relation of monomyths, derived from Joseph Campbell, to the fixated psychology of Dollie's attachment to her father, his use of the "American" setting in "The Princess" also tends to ignore the ominous energy and primitive power that emerges from a distinctly national landscape to affect the characters' journey into the mountains as well as the metaphors of separation, initiation, and return so central to Cowan's argument, 65–70. Robert H. MacDonald similarly looks at the way various symbolic structures reveal psychological patterns in the story; his discussion of the central characters as imagistically antithetical, however, fails to consider the comparable terms of stasis that Dollie and Romero exemplify, and MacDonald's personification of images and archetypes in the landscape too easily reduces the resonance of Lawrence's depiction of the New Mexico scenery to the level of formulaic dualities. For a more balanced and sensitive reading, an accurate summary of the perspectives of several critics, and a clarifying explanation of the adaptation of the Carswell story by Lawrence, see Harris, 165–97, 291–92.

2. For a pertinent discussion of Lawrence's state of mind when he writes this essay, and the impinging circumstances in his own life about his painting, publishing, writing, and conflicts with the British authorities, see Ellis, 463–67.

five hundred years. His eclectic argument attempts to bridge the traditional boundaries among genres of literary art, among different forms of artistic expression, and among categories in his own life of artistic creativity, impinging biography, and encompassing doctrine. Such a sweep of synthesis in "Introduction to These Paintings" is all in the service of some stern conclusions about national character, medical trauma, and conditioned fear. It must be stated that Lawrence's argument involves unsubstantiated judgments that even today are teasingly difficult to confirm or disprove. His general tactic is to rely on the force and conviction of his assertions to quiet the concerns of those historians, art critics, epidemiologists, and psychologists who must notice the scant evidence he provides for his provocative opinions. That he writes with such energetic confidence and poised irony about areas that only specialists venture to investigate—such polemical panache serves to enhance the authority of his sweeping interdisciplinary conclusions.

Lawrence first declares, as his adamant but unsupported premise, that England has produced relatively few great painters. He finds the cause of such under-achievement in a lack of "instinctual, intuitional" consciousness that goes back to the Renaissance, and this insufficiency prevents the English from manifesting what he denotes as a sense of physical, "true awareness" (190) so crucial to painting. As Lawrence often suggests in less embattled ways earlier in his career, he now maintains that the Anglo-Saxons remain the most prominent victims of the historic movement from the physical to the idealized mental initiated by the Greeks and then buttressed through the ages by the sacrificial symbology and flesh-denying didacticism of Christianity. It is in this essay by Lawrence, and for the first time in such sustained form, that he probes more deeply into the precise causes of such inadequacy in the English character. Certainly part of his motivation must be his accumulated anger over the intolerable (and intolerant) treatment of his own work by British authorities, a blindness by those "censor-morons"[3] that shortly would reach another level of conflict with the legalized confiscation of his own paintings.

Lawrence employs the metaphor of an infectious psyche to explain that the origin of such repression and anxiety has much to do with the sudden and epidemic appearance of syphilis in Europe in the sixteenth century, and the consequent unconscious fear of sex and the procreative body that

---

3. For a full discussion of Lawrence's use of this phrase and of the context of his battle with censorship authorities throughout his career, with special emphasis on the last years of his life, see Harry T. Moore's Preface and the Introduction, "D.H. Lawrence and the 'Censor-Morons,'" in *D.H. Lawrence: Sex, Literature, and Censorship*, 7–30.

this scourge engendered: "For an overmastering fear is poison to the human psyche. And this overmastering fear, like some horrible secret tumour, has been poisoning our consciousness ever since the Elizabethans, who first woke up with dread to the entry of the original syphilitic poison into the blood" (188). He further maintains that since the time of Shakespeare and the incursion of syphilis, the English people, in their unconscious need as well as in their painting, have sought an escape from "the *reality* of substantial bodies" (193), and that this escape continued to be evident through the eighteenth and nineteenth centuries, when clothes and decorative elements on canvas became more significant to artists and art connoisseurs than the skin and bodies inside them. Lawrence anticipates an objection to his digressive methodology, and he responds in graphic and comparative terms:

> All this sounds very far from the art of painting. But it is not so far as it sounds. The appearance of syphilis in our midst gave a fearful blow to our sexual life. The real natural innocence of Chaucer was impossible after that. The very sexual act of procreation might bring as one of its consequences a foul disease, and the unborn might be tainted from the moment of conception (189).

He further insists that the lingering shock of this disease in the English and American soul is related to the development of a religion that is uncomfortable with the claims and urgencies of the human body: "The terror-horror element which had entered the imagination with regard to the sexual and procreative act was at least partly responsible for the rise of Puritanism, the beheading of king-father Charles, and the establishment of the New England Colonies" (189). Because this discomfort with the procreative body stays well-entrenched, according to Lawrence, in national temperament, culture, and religion, the English painters gradually compensated by becoming adept at landscape, and especially in the less substantial, less corporeal medium of watercolour. Although Lawrence admits that he has a special fondness for landscape watercolours by Turner, he argues that even these paintings lack a sense of instinctual vitality and energy, giving the impression of a background waiting to be occupied, of an escape "from the actual human body they so hate and fear" (195). Lawrence also considers the French Impressionists as lacking any well-defined inclination for bodily presence in their work, but he approvingly singles out Cezanne as crucial in galvanizing an attempted return "to the understanding that matter *actually* exists" (201). What he essentially admires in Cezanne's work is the palpable search—particularly evident in his memorable still lifes—for the special, luminous quality in existence reflected in a radical technique that offers more than realistic, literal embodiment: "But I am convinced that what Cezanne himself wanted *was* representation. He *wanted* true-to-life representation. Only he wanted it *more* true-to-life" (211). In this context, Lawrence ruminates on the recent innovations of photography and the resultant danger that versions of this "machine" might establish an artificial art-form and will overwhelm the ambition (and effectiveness) of painters who need to follow the mandate of Lawrence's aesthetic credo: "And once you have got photography, it is a very, very difficult thing to get representation *more* true-to-life: which it has to be" (211).

As he describes the best of Cezanne's still lifes, Lawrence derives a wonderful phrase adapted from the most famous object in Cezanne's painting, praising his art for its "appleyness"—that is, for an ability to let the object "exist in its own separate entity", as the painter intuitively "let[s] it live of itself" (201). He associates this elusive appleyness with Cezanne's double-sided talent, defined by Lawrence in terms that echo the writer's own notions of "fourth dimensional" prose.[4] Here, Cezanne manages to capture the integrity of the object in present time and space *and* to relate such individuality to the pervasive life-force that Lawrence, throughout his fiction, typically denotes as the "unknown" or the "beyond": "When he makes Madame Cézanne most still, most appley, he starts making the universe slip uneasily about her. It was part of his desire: to make the human form, the *life* form, come to rest. Not static—on the contrary. Mobile but come to rest" (213). Lawrence suggests that this paradoxical element in Cezanne's work is caused by the painter's intuitive understanding—as the writer confers upon him a species of Lawrencian insight—"that nothing is really *statically* at rest" (213). Note the significant influence of Cezanne's art on Lawrence even as early as 1910, during his brief tenure as a teacher at the Davidson Road School in Croydon. His own painting, "Two Apples", which precedes the "Introduction" essay by almost two decades, seems to reflect early intimations of his theory of applyness:

---

4. On the issue of Lawrence's use of this term and its relation to his relevant fiction and essays, see my discussion in this volume of *The Virgin and the Gipsy*, and Chapters One and Five of my study, *D.H. Lawrence and the Phallic Imagination: Essays on Sexual Identity and Feminist Misreading.* See also Lawrence's essay, "Morality and the Novel," for his interpretation of fourth-dimensionality in fiction, 193–98.

"Two Apples" by D.H. Lawrence (Fig. 6-1)

While the painting is a still life, it appears luminously in motion, or just *after* the cessation of motion as the eye moves across the appearance of circles within circles; the resting plate, the scars on the fruit, the patches of light, the shadows, and the apples themselves commingle to establish not only the concrete existence of the objects but a kinetic, transcendent energy that Lawrence captures as a version of applyeness. In effect, the apples are not so much connecting to the plate as declaring their active "being", It is here that Lawrence's notion of appleyness in still lifes connects with his insistence on "the awareness of touch" (211) in successful *landscape* painting. He notices that in the best of Cezanne's late landscapes, our eyes encounter a vision on canvas that displaces "mental-visual" clichés with the "great revolution" of "intuitive consciousness" (211). As Lawrence will clarify throughout "Introduction to These Paintings", it is precisely this sense of animate vitality, of procreative livingness, that was so diminished by the onset of syphilis in the Renaissance period.

II

In the same essay, Lawrence elaborates on the effects of this disease, offering an apocalyptic but unsupported synthesis of investigative pathology and genetic speculation. He emphasizes that by the late-sixteenth century, syphilis was well established in the royal families of England and Scotland. Lawrence then outlines a depressing roll call of illness theory in a tone that reveals bitterness toward England:

> Edward VI and Elizabeth born with the inherited consequences of the disease. Edward VI died of it, while still a boy. Mary died childless and in utter depression. Elizabeth had no eyebrows, her teeth went rotten, she must have felt herself, somewhere, utterly unfit for marriage, poor thing... And so the Tudors died out: and another syphilitic-born unfortunate came to the throne, in the person of James I. Mary Queen of Scots had no more luck than the Tudors, apparently. Apparently Darnley was reeking with the pox, though probably at first she did not know it. But when the Archbishop of St. Andrews was christening her baby James, afterwards James I of England, the old clergyman was so dripping with pox that she was terrified lest he should give it to the infant. And she need not have troubled, for the wretched infant had brought it into the world with him, from that fool Darnley. So James I of England slobbered and shambled, and was the wisest fool in Christendom, and the Stuarts likewise died out, the stock enfeebled by the disease (189).

In such a hyperbolic and undifferentiating summary, Lawrence takes considerable historical license. Most conspicuously, he employs questionable diagnoses to place all the symptomologies of the royal line under the single pathological causation of syphilis, when a variety of other illnesses (e.g., scrofula, smallpox, leprosy, congenital defects, etc.) may also be relevant in individual cases.[5] Whatever the exact causes were of such

---

5. The most recent medical research today, complied in an essay by Verano and Ubelaker in a collection edited by Viola and Margolis, tends to support Lawrence's central notion of the outbreak of especially virulent forms of syphilis in Europe beginning around 1500, for "medical historians have repeatedly noted the absence of any unequivocal descriptions of syphilis in the medieval literature of Europe...before AD 1500" (217). But an opposed theory undercuts Lawrence's view of a sixteenth-century origin of the disease in England, as it argues that "syphilis was present in Europe long before Columbus's voyage—it was simply misdiagnosed or confused with other diseases such as leprosy" (218). See Verano and Ubelaker, "Health and Disease in the Pre-Columbian World," 217–21. See also Verano and Ubelaker's own collection of relevant essays, *Disease and Demography in the Americas*, for a more in-depth analysis of issues of symptomology, pathology, and forensic investigation that bear upon the works I discuss in this essay. Lawrence, of course, could not draw upon this recent and highly technical research, but the essays in this volume tend to support many of Lawrence's speculations in "Introduction to These Paintings": on the key issues of leprosy resembling syphilis in certain stages of its infection, and of the syphilis

disturbing physical symptoms from the Tudors through the Stuarts, Lawrence at the very least properly emphasizes a recognizable pattern of physical and emotional disease that corresponds with the outbreak of the syphilis epidemic in England. He understandably insists that syphilis is the primary problem because he wishes to dramatize the prominence and pervasiveness of this originating dread of the procreative body. As he moves from the physical to the organic-metaphoric, he further maintains that after syphilis "had entered the blood, it entered the consciousness, and it hit the vital imagination" (187).

Such a compromised vitality of imagination, in Lawrence's inflated reading, reverberates through the centuries in emotional repression, unsensual national character, and compromised artistic expression. In this regard it is interesting to note that early in "The Princess", Lawrence conjoins (and anticipates) key aspects of his argument five years later in the essay on painting:

> Colin Urquhart was just a bit mad. He was of an old Scottish family, and he claimed royal blood. The blood of Scottish kings flowed in his veins. On this point, his American relatives said, he was just a bit "off". They could not bear any more to be told *which* royal of Scotland blued in his veins (159) .

Neither unstable Colin nor his frail wife is drawn to passion or spontaneity: the matrix of their marriage provides no renewal, for it is created out of a dread of the procreative body, as it develops from a union between a man whose skin "was not all there" (159) and a New England virgin conditioned to the aversions of her engrained Puritanism. Living with "a fascinating spectre", Hannah suspects "he was a little bit mad" (160) the night her baby was born. It is tempting to see Colin's lack of embodied physicality as an extreme, ghostly reminder of the trauma of syphilis that Lawrence describes in "Introduction to These Paintings": he "was like a living echo" and "his very flesh, when you touched it, did not

---

epidemic in Europe in the sixteenth century. See also Ortner's essay in *Disease and Demography*, edited by Bogdan and Weaver, "Pre-Columbian Treponematosis in Coastal North Carolina," 155–63; even more crucial, perhaps, for the "trauma" theory advanced by Lawrence about the cumulative effect of syphilis on the collective psyche of a country, culture, and community, Ubelaker and Verano in the same collection emphasize that "disease epidemics led not only to population decline but also to major changes in social structure," in "Conclusion", in *Disease and Demography*, 281.

seem quite the flesh of a real man" (160).[6] Hannah died early in this ethereal marriage, and the daughter, Dollie, grows up in an insulated world, over-protected and spoiled by an idiosyncratic father-guru who grooms her to be his acquiescent pet, travelling companion, and professional virgin. Her sexual immaturity and superficial prettiness appear to reflect—in a potentially volatile combination for men—the eternal pre-pubescence of Peter Pan and the photographic but desexualized beauty of Rapunzel: "She was a quick, dainty little thing with dark gold hair that went soft brown, and wide, slightly prominent blue eyes that were at once so candid and knowing. She was grown-up: she never really grew up. Always strangely wise, and always childish" (160).

When Colin makes his memorable and deranged speech to Dollie in which he stresses the glory of their allegedly noble blood and the cautious way their pedigree must affect relations with others, he concludes the advice with a tactile metaphor that eerily invokes memories of disease in Shakespearean England:

> And so darling, you must treat all people very politely, because *noblesse oblige*. But you must never forget, that you alone are the last of the princesses, and that all others are less than you are: less noble, more vulgar. Treat them politely and gently and kindly, darling. But you are the Princess, and they are commoners. Never try to think of them as if they were like you. They are not. You will find, always, that they are lacking, lacking in *the royal touch*, which only you have—" (161).

Lawrence makes Colin look back to an unusual custom of the past, and Lawrence may have been led to the memory by some relevant reading. Just a few months before he begins work on "The Princess", it is quite likely that Lawrence reread Frazer's *The Golden Bough*, a probability further enhanced by a fascinating passage in Frazer's capacious study that directly bears upon Colin's speech and his Stuart ancestry:

---

6. It is interesting to contemplate the possibility that Colin's gradual descent into madness and the peculiar touch of his skin suggest the slowly developing symptoms of syphilitic illness, for Lawrence ambiguously notes early in the tale that "many women had been fascinated" with Colin before his wife, "but Urquhart, by his very vagueness, had avoided any decisive connection" (159). If this "decisive connection" is deemed to be marriage and not a sexual liaison, the syphilis hypothesis becomes more intriguing, with multiple ironies possible given Colin's consequent isolation from the touch of living humanity after the birth of Dollie and the death of Hannah. See Ortner for insights on the existence of "congenital syphilis" (10) that may buttress the radical hypothesis that Colin and his wife passed on the virus to his suspiciously diminutive daughter at birth.

> In the Middle Ages, when Waldemar I, King of Denmark, travelled in Germany, mothers brought their infants and husbandmen their seed for him to lay his hands on, thinking that children would both thrive the better for *the royal touch*…Perhaps the last relic of such superstitions which lingered about our English kings was the notion that they could heal scrofula by their *touch*. The disease was accordingly known as the King's Evil. Queen Elizabeth often exercised this miraculous gift of healing. On Mid-summer Day 1633, Charles the First cured a hundred patients at one swoop in the Chapel Royal at Holyrood. But it was under his son Charles the Second that the practice seemed to have attained its highest vogue. It is said that in the course of his reign Charles the Second *touched* near a hundred thousand persons for scrofula[7] (103–04, my emphases).

The difference between the eras compared in Frazer's comments sounds familiar. Recall Lawrence's assertion that in the pre-Renaissance generations, before the syphilis scourge hit England, the "natural innocence of Chaucer", with its frank celebration of "the very sexual act of procreation" (189) was the adamant and passionate temperature of the time. Chaucer embodied this exuberance without the fear that venereal diseases would begin to foment in the next century. But significant questions remain about the reliability of the information provided by Frazer and Lawrence. Does Frazer possibly misconstrue cases of syphilis and/or smallpox for scrofula, and/or does Lawrence overestimate the omnipresence of syphilis? In any case, it is intriguing that Frazer's perspective insists that the significance of "the royal touch" moves form a literal celebration of procreative seed in

---

7. For a comprehensive analysis of the range of applicability of Frazer's research to patterns of art and doctrine in Lawrence's fiction, see Vickery, 294–325. While Vickery does little more than mention "The Princess", he helpfully notes that the story is one of several Lawrence works in which "the relevant myth is that of the Sacred Marriage, while the rites of initiation, taboo or prohibition, and fecundation present a definition of the central character's reaction toward the myth itself" (323). Such an insight supports my own analysis of the dread of fecundity at the heart of Dollie's emotions, and of the vitalistic aspects of a landscape in "The Princess" that functions to expose the inadequacy of this "central character's reaction" to the complexity of primitive life she observes on the journey through the mountains. The evidence for the strong likelihood that Lawrence reread Frazer in the spring of 1924 is provided in Ellis's meticulous volume of the Cambridge biography, *Dying Game*, 187. I also am indebted to a passing observation in Weiner's essay, for it prompted me to investigate further the implications of the metaphor of touch in the tale and the issue of disease in Renaissance England. Weiner comments on "the delicate suggestion of disease in reference to an English king's supposed ability to cure scrofula by his 'royal touch'" (225). As I have noted in this essay, more than scrofula may be involved here.

the Middle Ages to a totemic belief in its curative properties by the late sixteenth century—a transition that precisely corresponds to the metaphors, dateline, and substance of Lawrence's argument in "Introduction to These Paintings". Also, whatever the actual diseases engaged through his benedictive touching by the Kings and Queens of England were, might not the huge crowds stated by Frazer, along with the closeness of so many potentially contaminating bodies, suggest a contagion of disease affecting the Royal lineage, with the tragic effect that such undiscriminating touching possibly exacerbated the prevalence of the very illness that it proposed to cure?

III

That Lawrence writes "Pan in America" while he rereads Frazer in April, 1924 deserves further comment in relation to Lawrence's preoccupations in this period, shortly before he writes "The Princess" in September. The essay is a short, despairing, and admonishing piece about Lawrence's evaluation of a gradual change in civilization from unselfconscious expressions of natural energy and intuitive belief to an easy dependency on modern machines and materialist sentiment. It offers a nostalgic lament over the adulteration of "Pan-power", that for Lawrence means the diminishment of instinctual primacy in our culture, along with the gradual loss of the awareness of sensuous relationship among all things—including the animate and the inanimate. He further insists that the remnants of Pan in the world only reside in an individual's engaged and changing relation to the livingness of natural landscapes. Such a limited context of Pan-survival is a long way from what Lawrence describes as the original demonic force associated with the mythological Pan, for he believes that such force has been domesticated through the centuries by Christianity's Manichean imagery and by the rampant pantheism of the nineteenth century American Romantics.

The gradual loss of Pan-energy in the twentieth century amounts to the metaphoric equivalent of the move away from the procreative body that Lawrence ties to the outbreak of syphilis. In "Pan in America", he deplores the way that the growth of mechanical inventions and materialistic narcissism has separated most people from an active apprehensions of their physical environment. Just as Lawrence the artist values the appleyness of a fully revealed object or landscape in a painting, he writes admiringly in "Pan in America"—virtually offering it as an *exemplum*—of how the American Indian respects the anima of a tree even when he has cut it down to provide him with heat: "And what does life consist in, save a vivid relatedness between the man and the living universe that surrounds him? Yet man insulates himself more and more into mechanism, and repudiates everything but the machine and the contrivance of which he himself is master, God in the machine" (160).[8] As an Englishman transplanted in America's south-west, Lawrence claims that "here, on this little ranch under the Rocky Mountains" (157) the power of Pan is alive and well in the primitive landscape of new Mexico, amid its pine trees, catkins, wolves, chipmunks, valleys, and mountains. The central image for Lawrence of living-Pan is the tree, with its firm, nourishing, and resistant grounding within the earth, *and* its proud, naked and assertive prominence in the air. This duality of resistance and assertion—the dialectic at the heart of the static-mobility paradox of appleyness—is what painters generally cannot reflect in their landscape art, and it comprises the elusive element that Lawrence seeks to portray in "The Princess". As noted in the previous chapter on *St. Mawr* and on O'Keeffe's painting of "The Lawrence Tree, 1929", it is her genius as an artist to capture this combination of kinesis and stasis by establishing a perspective of someone lying on their back and looking straight up near the trunk of the tree; the result is the perception of the branches that reach upwards toward the transcendent sky in an active movement that seems beseeching and doomed at the same time.

In "Introduction to These Paintings", Lawrence offers precise examples of the way that the mechanization of modern culture has served to further diminish the waning Pan-power he describes in "Pan in America". He emphasizes that the development of photography has brought us images, however exact they may be, that lack the life-resonance, the appleyness of real perception that a Cezanne still-life (or a later landscape) can capture. Lawrence explains in another relevant essay, "Art and Morality", written a year after "The Princess", that people have unfortunately been trained in "the slowly formed habit of seeing just as the photographic camera sees", and consequently man "does not, even now, see for himself. He sees what the kodak has taught him to see. And man, try as he may, is not a kodak" (164). In the same essay, Lawrence further contemplates this lazy habit of contenting oneself with the "outer image": "The identifying of ourselves with the visual image of ourselves has become an instinct; the habit is

8. For a well-researched and valuable analysis of the history of the Pan motif in literature, see Merivale, and especially her lengthy chapter on D.H. Lawrence, 194–219. Merivale does not discuss "The Princess," but she is excellent on "Pan in America," realizing that Lawrence uses Pan to emphasize (as I attempt to do in my reading of "The Princess") a return to the fount of universal energy, from which the evolution of self-consciousness has separated us" (114).

already old. The picture of me, the me that is *seen*, is me" (165). But it is fair to say that certain characters, whether in fiction or the real world, may convey as their determining "aura of life" ("Pan" 158) a mechanical finality, an unappley absoluteness, so that the camera can reproduce their inherent stasis with confident accuracy. It is significant that from the moment Dollie Urquhart is introduced in "The Princess", she "looked as if she had stepped out of a picture" (162). Thus Lawrence implies a relation between her invested virginity and the fact that she seems so supremely unvarying as to be not merely photogenic but, quite literally, *picture-like*, with a plastic lack of corporeality that effortlessly fits into a pre-measured frame. Such an absence of changeability is directly opposed to the kinetic power Lawrence connects with appleyness, and Dollie's organic stasis informs her view of the world as well as her contemporaries' view of her. When she rides alone with Romero amid the shimmering landscape, "She felt quite in the picture" (179)—as she presumptuously even reduces the animate scenery to the reductive terms of her own bearing in life.

Lawrence underlines the unchanging qualities of Dollie as she ages: "So the years passed, imperceptibly. And so she had that quality of the sexless fairies, she did not change. At thirty-three she looked twenty-three" (164). When her father died, after he descended into a madness of which he showed symptoms earlier in his life, she remained "quite unchanged. She was still tiny, and like a dignified, scentless flower", with her face described as "apple-blossom" (165) rather than appley; she stays just as unvital as the beautiful but dormant still lifes that Lawrence criticizes in "Introduction to These Paintings", with Dollie "modelled with an arched nose like a proud old Florentine portrait" (165), the kind of art, that provokes only "cerebral excitation" ("Introduction" 190). It is a version of the tactile metaphor that recalls the use of "the royal touch" in "The Princess", and in the essay the image of untouchability further suggests bodies that are dead to intuitive awareness. This "finished" quality in Dollie—in both the organic and artistic meanings—is related to the absence of any unrehearsed connection to other people, for she regards them as either serving her needs or irrelevant. After the death of Dollie's father, Miss Cummins joins her in this willed isolation from the normal rhythms of humanity, and this companion also caters to Dollie's demands and supervises the idiosyncrasies of the Princess's often willful desires. Lawrence makes it clear that the consideration of other men and the possibility of marriage is unattractive to Dollie not simply because it reflects a conventional concept of comfort and material well-being; marriage is unappealing to her because of the distinct reality of its sexual component. In no other fiction by Lawrence is the notion of the marriage matrix so disconnected in one character's perception from its passionate roots in physical intimacy. As a calculating Dollie calmly contemplates the easy practicality of marriage, she intrinsically rejects, without irony, the inevitable sensual closeness that for Lawrence must remain basic to any legalized union. She thinks of such a union in terms that highlight both her dread of the procreative body and her irrepressible fondness for the convenient distancing from the sensual and the concrete afforded by ideas. Lawrence's italicized reiterations are meant to stress the fundamentality of her misperception: "She was still neither interested nor attracted toward men vitally. But *marriage*, that peculiar abstraction, had imposed a sort of spell on her. She thought that *marriage*, in the blank abstract, was the thing she ought to *do*" (166). Dollie's version of marriage remains profoundly divorced from Lawrence's formative notions of renewal and transcendence.

Dollie's attraction to Romero initially is motivated by their shared inheritance of alienation from the masses. The last of a Spanish family that years earlier included major landowners, he is now no more than a Mexican peasant, an angry, dark, silent, and handsome young man, with a face described as "static…Waiting either to die, or to be roused into passion and hope" (168). Lawrence then defines the agonized quality of Romero and his fellow peasants in a passage that integrates the character's state of being with the New Mexico environment. The words hold ominous significance for the developing plot in the tale, for they outline what amounts to a Lawrencian unpardonable sin: "Unable to wrest a *positive* significance for themselves from the vast, beautiful, but vindictive landscape they were born into, they turned on their own selves, and worshipped death through self-torture" (168). In his non-communicative and smoldering discontent, his "spark in the midst of the blackness of static despair" (168), and his experienced insight into the New Mexico topography, Romero embodies the recognizable and meager remnants of the Pan-power that are discussed in "Pan in America". Lawrence insists on the necessity of resistance and assertion as crucial to the energy of Pan, an energy now only present, in its pure form, in the primitive landscapes relatively untouched by machine. Until the tragic conclusion of the tale, Romero lacks any effective strategy of resistance *or* assertions, as he drifts in the victimized stasis that prefigures his end.

Yet that touch of an inscrutable Pan remains in his isolate bearing; it is also often reflected in his insightful comments about animals, mountains, and the habits of hunters, all part of an expertise that nearly echoes the intuitive awareness Lawrence praises in "Pan in America". More pertinently, Romero's conspicuous disinclination to *talk* about anything ("he wasn't chatty and cosy" (168)), including the very landscape through which he guides the tourists, echoes Lawrence's approving description in the essay of the man who "is careful never to utter one word of the mystery. Speech is the death of Pan" (160). When Romero instinctively shows Dollie how to reposition herself near the stream to successfully land a fish, she immediately gets a catch. Given the silence and ease of his manner as he demonstrates to Dollie such a technique, Romero reveals the Pan characteristic from the essay of an affinity for prey emerging from "a primitive hunter's consciousness", which he further specifies as "a psychic attraction, a sort of telepathy" (169). In the hyper-intuitive world of the original Pan, "the contact between all things is keen and wary" (163). Such caution informs "The Princess" when Romero rejoins Dollie at the end of her surprisingly unwary meeting with two opportunistic Indians who unsuccessfully attempt to conceal their recent illegal hunting in restricted areas by hiding a dead deer under one of their saddles. Romero realizes (although characteristically he never articulates his knowledge) that given Dollie's previous distance from him on the trail, given her chaste beauty that intrinsically provokes antagonism in other men, and given her unwise, accommodating offer of food to the Indians that too easily permits them to belabor the interlude with her, Dollie was fortunate to escape unharmed. The moment they leave the men's vicinity, Romero's stare reveals the admonition of a *Pan manqué* to a willful, child-like woman who can scarcely glimpse the turbulence at the edge of the previous encounter: "When they were alone, Romero turned and looked at her curiously, in a way she could not understand, with such a hard glint in his eyes. And for the first time, she wondered if she was rash" (180). Those lawlessly self-reliant, "soiled", "untidy" (179) Indians may be closer than Romero to incarnations of primitive Pan that Lawrence defines at the start of "Pan in America", but the writer is under no illusion that these unkempt poachers offer much of an alternative to the materialism infecting modern life: "And still, in America, among the Indians, the oldest Pan is alive. But here, also dying fast. It is useless to glorify the savage. For he will kill Pan with his own hands, for the sake of a motor-car" (164).

IV

Between the bored savagery of the Indians and the morbid stasis of Romero, Pan-power, for Lawrence, can only reside in the very land that he appreciatively inhabits. The Pan essay artfully combines autobiography with doctrine, as it focuses on a singular natural object I discuss more fully in Chapter Five: "Here, on this little ranch under the Rocky Mountains", where "a big pine tree rises like a guardian spirit in front of the cabin where we live" (157). And it is in precisely this landscape, depicted by Lawrence through the breathtaking journey to the shack undertaken by Dollie and Romero, that the notion of appleyness derived in "Introduction to These Paintings" provides relevant insights to Lawrence's stylistic achievement in the tale. True appleyness in painting for Lawrence is to be distinguished from photography by its oxymoronic ability to convey an active stasis—that is, a scene which is "mobile but come to rest" (213). As he praises this elusive quality of Cezanne's best work in "Introduction to These Paintings", he elaborates with a crucial passage that comes close to summarizing the same requirements for fictional narrative that Lawrence has mandated in other essays for his own, self-styled "fourth dimensional" prose. Lawrence's comments are concerned with the potential geometries of the eye's perspective in evaluating paintings, but their wonderful applicability for all forms of art seems beyond question:[9]

> The appleyness, which carries with it also the feeling of knowing the other side as well, the side you don't see, the hidden side of the moon. For the intuitive apperception of the apple is so *tangibly* aware of the apple that it is aware of it *all around,* not only just of the front. The eye sees only fronts; and the mind, on the whole, is satisfied with fronts. But intuition needs all-aroundness, and instinct needs insideness. The true imagination is forever curving round to the other side, to the back of presented appearance (212).

Lawrence's emphasis on the intuitive, sensate perception intrinsic to appleyness is evident on his canvas as well as in his related aesthetic theory. In two paintings that he completed only months before "Introduction to These Paintings"—"Red Willow Trees" and "Villa Mirenda"—the six people (three in each work) face to "the other side", or reside in the rear, or emerge from a background. Thus the artist's skill (embodying "true imagination") is to lead the viewer's eyes in "Red Willow Trees", curving back to the image of the stream, itself curling away to infinity; in "Villa Mirenda", the subtle focus is on a hazy being down a road who is acknowledged only by two men in the foreground, who simultaneously know of his approach from the rear but scarcely affirm his presence:

9. See Young's discussion of Lawrence's conceptualizing of the fourth dimension in prose, 30–44, and my development of related issues of time and space in chapter seven.

"Red Willow Trees" by D.H. Lawrence (Fig. 6-2)

"The Princess" also reveals the consistency of the connection between Lawrence's doctrines about painting and his fiction. Near the end of their arduous trek through the mountains, Lawrence's prose provides a superb glimpse of this "hidden side of the moon" as he freeze-frames a fast-moving, living object to capture a rare view of "the other side" that normally evades a human sight and conventional prose: "She was dazed and a little sick, at that height, and she could not *see* any more. Only she saw an eagle turning in the air beyond, and the light from the west showed the pattern on him underneath" (182). When Lawrence focuses more intensely on the effectiveness of Cezanne's landscape paintings, the notion of appleyness comes closer to the texture of prose encountered in "The Princess":

> In the best landscapes we are fascinated by the mysterious *shiftiness* of the scene under our eyes: it shifts about as we watch it. And we realize, with a sort of transport, how intuitively *true* this is of landscape. It is *not* still. It has its own weird anima, and to our wide-eyed perception it changes like a living animal under our gaze. This is a quality that Cezanne sometimes got marvelously (214).

"Villa Mirenda" by D.H. Lawrence (Fig. 6-3)

Lawrence creates the prose equivalent of this vibrancy of scene throughout the depiction of the changing landscape they move across in this fiction. One paragraph of poetic incantation can illustrate the elements of "weird anima" so central in Lawrence's doctrine:

> It was a little valley or shell from which the stream was gently poured into the lower rocks and trees of the canyon. Around her was a fairy-like gentleness, the delicate sere grass, the groves of delicate-stemmed aspens dropping their flakes like petals. Almost like flowers the aspen trees stood in thickets, shedding their petals of bright yellow. And the delicate, quick little stream threading through the wild-sere grass (178–79).

It is a beautiful passage informed by lyrical repetitions of sound and compelling urgencies of movement. Rhythmic reiterations of such phrases as "stream", "sere grass", "delicate", and "petals" are employed to establish a hypnotic back-and-forth motion that is then spurred to a forward momentum by the graphic and active verbs of "poured", "dripping", "shedding", and "threading". It is a profoundly appley landscape that conforms to Lawrence's seminal stipulation of mobility within stasis.

In "Art and Morality" he supplies further justification for the same intense and intermingling activity in landscapes that he later will designate as an essential component of appleyness: "What art has got to do, and will go on doing, is to reveal things in their different relationships" (166), and the reason for this imperative on fluidity—even amidst the inanimate—concerns the endless adjustments that *everything* in existence constantly undergoes. In a sense, it is Lawrence's vitalistic answer to the depressing notion of entropy: "All moves. And nothing is true, or good, or right, except in its own living relatedness to its own circumambient universe" (167). In the mid-1920s, Lawrence has not yet derived the concept of appleyness to define the way an artist can embody this energy. The narration of "The Princess" offers an intriguing example of the living "design" Lawrence creates within landscape description, as he integrates the disparate elements of stream, flower, petal, canyon and tree, and all in the terms specified in "Art and Morality": "Design, in art, is the recognition of various elements in the creative flux. You can't invent a design. You recognize it, in the fourth dimension. That is, with your blood and your bones" (167). In Lawrence's prescriptive doctrine, a major aspect of the inadequacy of Romero and Dollie is that they lack the ability to change; whether it is Romero's morbidity and defeatism, or Dollie's immaturity and narcissism, there is no *creative flux* in them, a failure that is underlined in the tale by reiterations of the Princess's eternally young appearance and Romero's uninterrupted solipsism.

Dollie's dread of the procreative body, nurtured in her since birth by an equally static father, is characteristically reflected during the journey by her need to look into the core of the mountain canyons from a safe distance that will not disrupt her with a perception of the "various elements" in the flux of life. It is only as a species of voyeurism that she wants to witness this naked natural force and to perceive the spectacle as a titillating photo opportunity: "And she just had a fixed desire to go over the brim of the mountains, to look into the inner chaos of the Rockies" (178). Later, when she nearly completes her trip with Romero, she regards the experience as a complete and successful look at the secret insides of the mountains; in this lack of resonance in her perspective, Dollie conveys no sense at all, in Janice Harris's poised description, that she must recognize "the god of darkness and light," and must see "that real virginity or newness of being comes only through accepting the same qualities of light and dark, of delicacy and oppressiveness, that mark the forest" (197). It is as if the vision of the mountains teaches her nothing, with one more item checked off her self-involved list of to do's, and one more stop completed on the rich girl's grand tour: "And yet now one of her desires was fulfilled. She had seen it, the massive, gruesome, repellant core of the Rockies…She had looked into the intestinal knot of these mountains. She was frightened" (181). The Princess's fear of experiencing disruptive truths from her view of the mountains' procreative depths offers a telling index of the willful stasis in her character. Her apprehension of existence is so pre-rehearsed and inflexible that she fails to grasp the primary sexual element of Romero's interest in her from the moment they meet. She too conveniently categorizes his attentions as mere "male kindliness" (169), never acknowledging a shred of insight about his repressed passion. She neither recognizes the deep pathology in her parents' marriage or comprehends the nurturant and renewing potential of real marriage. Certainly, the radical disjunctions of her own upbringing have much contributed to her warped perspective. Recall that she grew up without a mother and with the fastidious over-attentiveness of a neurotic father whom she willing accepts as a desexualized partner in a perverse domestic arrangement: "But Papa and I are such a crotchety old couple, living in a world of our own" (162).

V

When Dollie attempts to sleep that first night in the hut, predictably cold from the night air and disoriented from the assaults on her equilibrium during the journey, the sex with Romero is a secondary aspect of her request for him to supply the warmth she requires. He is merely the handy instrument of soothing for her own fears, frigidities, and confusions, and it is clear that an unLawrencian impetus leads her to the lovemaking: "She had *willed* that it should happen to her. And according to her will, she lay and let it happen. But she never wanted it" (188). After the mechanical and cold act of sex, her dread of the procreative body, spurred by her own willful intensity, is even more pronounced, and she looks for petty opportunities to tell him that nothing has changed and she is back in command as the Princess. Notice the pattern of four aggressive comments that she uses—or *orders* that she gives—to produce the crisis caused by her open disavowal of Romero:

> "I want a fire," she said.
> He opened his brown eyes wide, and smiled with a curious tender luxuriousness.
> "I want you to make a fire," she said.
> He glanced at the chinks of light. His brown face hardened to the day.
> "All right," he said. "I'll make it."
> She hid her face while he dressed. She could not bear to look at him. He was so suffused with pride and luxury. She hid her face almost in despair. But feeling the cold blast of air as he opened the door, she wriggled down into the warm place where he had been. How soon the warmth ebbed, when he had gone.
> He made a fire and went out, returning after a while with water.
> "You stay in bed till the sun comes," he said. "It's very cold."
> "Hand me my cloak."
> She wrapped the cloak fast around her and sat up among the blankets. The warmth was already spreading from the fire.
> "I suppose we will start back as soon as we've had breakfast?" (189)

Lawrence knows his woman here very well, and she is all of a piece. The passage underlines how she wills her desire for "the warm place" he occupied merely as her need for direct heat. She still resists any possibility of sexual resonance, of creative flux, from her own procreative body. With the warmth from the fire then replacing the residual warmth of the blanket, she can ask that final, rhetorical question as the *coup de grace*. The fallen-Pan made the dinner the night before, and now he cooks the breakfast like the obedient servant she wishes him to be. How different this scenario is from the primitive (and obviously outdated) sex roles that Lawrence too-nostalgically describes in "Pan in America", as he refers to that bygone time in the woods of Pan, before "The idea and the engine came between men and all things, like a death" (162). Here is the pre-industrial tableau that Lawrence includes more as idealized metaphor than as reactionary barbarism: "At evening when the deer is killed, he went home to the tents, and threw down the deer-meat on the swept place before the tent of his women. And the women came out to greet him softly, with a sort of reverence, as he stood before the meat, the life-stuff" (163). When Romero is not sullen, he is domesticated and a willing caretaker *until* the moment that Dollie crosses the line of his remaining pride and indicts the only trace of Pan left in him: the force of his sexual self-definition with women. In "The Novel and the Feelings", Lawrence may shed light on the relative ease and completeness with which Romero has abrogated so much of his spirit and resistance during the previous years: "Man has pretty well tamed himself, and he calls his tameness civilisation. True civilisation would be something very different. But man is now tame. Tameness means the loss of the peculiar power of command" (203).

Dollie's unchanging sense of self, her ice-solid ego structure, depends on a mastery of that limited and unprocreative role she has defined for herself; within this definition exist her dependency on the ministrations of Miss Cummins, her emphasis on the need for expensive and coordinated clothing ensembles, and her reliance on the easy amusement of constant travel. It is not surprising that the unmediated force of the natural landscape that she encounters in the journey through the mountains begins to overwhelm her narrow and enclosed conception of life. Similarly, it is little wonder that the dream Dollie experiences in the hut before she calls for Romero offers a perfectly appropriate example of the envelopment of the ego by the assertions of nature's power. The poetic wording Lawrence employs to describe the dream provocatively resembles the phrases and rhythmic participles that Joyce employs as he conveys the refracted perspective of Gabriel Conroy at the end of "The Dead": "She dreamed it was snowing, and the snow was falling on her through the roof, softly, softly, helplessly, and she was going to be buried alive. She was growing colder and colder, the snow was weighing down on her. The snow was going to absorb her" (187). Unlike Conroy, no swooning epiphany here about the pretenses of ego and no knowledge that this self-encroaching snow falls not just over her but—as in Joyce's story—"falling faintly through the universe" (224). In Dollie's unempathetic soul, even nature begins and ends with her.

Thus Lawrence supplies an appropriate dream-work here for Dollie, with the further irony that its psychical relevance for the fiction might even please the founder of psychoanalytic theory and practice—a man, of course, often the target of this novelist's attack concerning the meaning of the unconscious. Freud's well-known assertion about the impressive "extent of condensation in dreams" (490) is confirmed by the resonance of symbolic patternings Dollie experiences in her sleep during that fateful night. Her entrenched frigidity is itself projected onto the snowy onslaught of a natural causation beyond her control. The coldness from *outside* is now perceived by her as the instigator of the emptiness *within*. When she awakens in darkness to call for Romero to provide warmth, she is acting-out (and insisting on) the interference of a presence other than the self to alleviate her suffering. She lacks any awareness that the heat she receives from him cannot be merely and conveniently absorbed by her without some recompense; she remains ignorant in the morning about the understanding that is implicit in her yielding to him. At bottom Dollie is too much of the neurotic narcissist, too much of the selfish survivalist, to comprehend the real-world meaning of the sexual exchange between them.

Romero has noticed not only her fondness for impeccable clothes but also her frequent vulnerability to cold temperatures when she traverses the high trails and when she calls to him in her pajamas during the night. Dollie takes fastidious care in what she wears and exudes a special pride in her choice of outfits; on the journey she "wore a fleecy sweater of pale, sere buff, like the grass, and riding breeches of a pure orange-tawny colour. She felt quite in the picture" (179). Romero, on one level, is prompted by understandable anger when he throws her clothes into the pond, yet there is also an intuitive sense in him that this act of submerging her clothes might submerge her *being*—in short, her sense of self built on dread of the procreative body and a desire (in an unappley manner) to fit "in the picture". Lawrence includes another significant comment in "Art and Morality" on this hyper-conscious habit of basing one's self-conception on what the person assumes the world sees on the outside. It sounds very much as if Lawrence is thinking here of the Dollie he recently created and of the landscape surrounding her: "There is your sweetheart, complete in herself, enjoying a sort of absolute objective reality: complete, perfect, all her surroundings contributing to her, incontestable. She is really a 'picture'" (165). Once again in *The Golden Bough*, Frazer describes the folk superstition that Lawrence would reread in the spring of 1924:

> If you cannot catch a thief, the next best thing you can do is to get hold of a garment which he may have shed in his flight, for if you beat it soundly, the thief will fall sick. This belief is firmly rooted in the popular mind…Again magic may be wrought on a man sympathetically, not only through his clothes and severed parts of himself, but also through the impressions left by his body in sand or earth (50).

All that Dollie retains after Romero takes her clothes are the pajamas she wore when Romero has sex with her and the cloak she demands from him to keep her warm after she abandons that impression *left by his body* when she "wriggled down into the warm place where he had been" (189). Lawrence remains astute enough in his psychologizing of Dollie's acquisitive and willful emotions that he even anticipates, just before Romero sleeps with her, Freud's famous question about women: "What did she want? Oh, what did she want?" (188).[10]

VI

While Dollie suffers the agony of vindictive rape by Romero, he kills himself, in effect, because he is victimized by the intense will and fierce determination of an emasculating woman who takes away the last vestiges of Pan in a man Lawrence earlier describes as "Waiting either to die, or to be aroused into passion and hope" (168). While not a miner himself, Romero's one piece of property stands as the isolated mining shack that he occupies alone as he hunts in the mountains with distinct traces, apparently, of the "intuitive cunning" ("Pan" 162) that Lawrence considers part of the Pan-mystery. "The Princess" concludes with a defeated and suicidal Romero, briefly aroused into passion and now courting death, killed in an encounter that he clearly provokes to end his misery; his body is laid out evocatively with "his hands clutching the earth" (195) from which he has long ceased to wrest significance or sustenance during his family's decline as landowners. In "Pan in America" Lawrence describes the blaze on the tree near his own cabin, and he emphasizes the vitality he receives from the trees and "the shivers of energy that cross my living plasm" (25). When a bored and tired Romero casually points out the blazes to Dollie, there is no sense from him of "Pan-theistic" interest in the trees, but merely a passing notice of their directional relevance for the journey. "The Princess", in effect, is as much about the death of the human residue of Pan as it is about Dollie's dread of the procreative body. This double-drama in the tale emerges in the tragic intermingling of the two characters and the powerful appleyness of the New Mexico landscape.

---

10. The question, "what does woman want?" refers to an undated remark by Freud to Marie Bonaparte quoted in Ernest Jones, *The Life and Work of Sigmund Freud*, 421. Also in regard to Dollie's remaining clothes, Weiner forgets the pajamas she retains when he incorrectly asserts that the cloak "is the only article of her clothing which Romero does not throw into the pond", (238). In this context of Dollie's emotions, Ruderman wisely points to the "the story's earlier emphasis on the princess's condescension toward the lower orders, which she considers 'coarse monsters' (163 "Princess"), as well as her own exploitation of the servant Romero" (Ruderman 113). Jenkins broadens the theme of oppression to consider the ways in which Lawrence depicts Romero as "himself the victim of U.S.-American imperialism, and he abuses Dollie in order to reassert his lost *derecho de pernada* or right of possession to the land" (98).

John Worthen, the major biographer of Lawrence's early years and his formative relation to his parents, describes in some detail the changing perspective on his mother and father that Lawrence began to evolve in the 1920's. Lawrence is ever more sympathetic to the father in this revised retrospect, a miner who Lawrence increasingly feels had been defeated by an unforgiving and willful wife; when he writes "The Princess," Lawrence is only a few months from formulating his changing attitude in the first of several short essays.[11] As Worthen trenchantly summarizes these pieces, Lawrence had come to believe that his parents' household confirmed his belief that "womanhood has been allowed to triumph, in its declaration of material loyalties; real manhood and human warmth has been denied, together with real sexuality; men are now 'tame'" (502). Romero would not finally accept the taming of his last "spark in midst of the blackness of static despair" (168), and he futilely strikes back at the materialist hater of the sexualized male body. But Dollie will collect her money through a marriage that also permits her to continue the subjugation of the sensual, all this while her emotional equilibrium is the casualty of Romero's violence: "She was slightly crazy…Later, she married an elderly man and seemed pleased" (196). Thus Dollie craftily reconfigures the marriage matrix to conveniently complement her well-established narcissism and to camouflage the scars of her tragic encounter with Romero.

Lawrence is notified on September 13, 1924 of his father's death three days earlier, and "The Princess" becomes the first work that he initiates after this notification, directly following his completion of *St. Mawr*. He begins it only a few days later and finishes it by October 8.[12] The tale reflects an anger at Dollie's will *and* at the surrender by Romero of a Pan-power Lawrence believes is increasingly under attack in the modern world. Does not "The Princess" also perhaps reveal—in early, as yet unformulated hints—Lawrence's developing awareness of the sacrifice of his father's vitality on the altar of his mother's relentless, class-conscious ambitions? At a key moment in the story, as a raped Dollie observes Romero seconds before he is killed, Lawrence's narration catches Dollie's perspective through her profoundly inopportune and aesthetic (not sexual) judgement: "He had a beautiful alert figure" (194). No appleyness in this admiration, no trace of "the gleam of the warm procreative body"

11. See Worthen's convenient listing of the essays that begin to reflect this revisionism in the mid-1920s, in "D.H. Lawrence's Autobiographies," in Volume One of the Cambridge Biography, 500–03.

12. The crucial chronology that I enumerate here is based on the solid research in Ellis's biography, *Dying Game* (173–203) and in the dates provided by Preston's work, *A D.H. Lawrence Chronology*, 113–14.

("Introduction" 194) in the woman whose heart "could not melt" or the man who will presently reveal "a little pool of blood where Romero's breast had been" (194, 195).

Chapter Seven

Impotence, Renewal, and the Honorable Beast: The Aesthetics of the Fourth Dimension in *The Virgin and the Gipsy*

Whichever flame flames in your manhood, that is you, for the time being.
—D.H. Lawrence, "The Novel"

The realization of impotence, of one's own inability to love, in consequence of mental or physical disorder, has an exceedingly lowering effect upon self-regard.
—Sigmund Freud, "On Narcissism: An Introduction"

L. is asleep—the worst was the emotional depression and the *nerves*, it drove one to despair—it was as if he couldn't or wouldn't live on.
—Frieda Lawrence

And only in the novel are *all* things given full play.
—D.H. Lawrence, "Why the Novel Matters"

I

Since its posthumous publication in 1930, it has remained the long-established and oddly qualified opinion that *The Virgin and the Gipsy* is one of Lawrence's most successful, albeit minor, works of fiction. Admiration for the novella's achievement often is tinged with a grudging note of reservation, as if the assigned status as distinctly unmajor must somehow temper the praise for its impressive artistic integrity. Representative praise of the work ranges from the early enthusiasm of F.R. Leavis, who deems it "one of Lawrence's finest things", to the more balanced and generally approving considerations of Carol Siegel and John Turner, and finally to the recent foray into ethnicity and cultural studies by Judith

Ruderman.[1] The various approaches of these critics all emphasize, in quite different ways, the work's anticipatory evocation of several coordinate patterns and preoccupations in *Lady Chatterley's Lover*. Certainly, the conspicuous continuities between these works deserve ample consideration: yet it remains unfortunate that the notable sexual explicitness of the later novel, with its well-chronicled history of legalistic problems and scandalous publicity, has in many ways dwarfed the more innovative treatment of comparable themes in *The Virgin and the Gipsy*.

This shorter fiction portrays a temperamentally cautious, silently charismatic, but distinctly isolated male, a frustrated and vulnerable female, as well as an instinctual connection between them that crosses the boundaries of class and culture; in such crucial correspondence there is much to ponder in the consistent development of Lawrence's doctrine and technique during the last years of his life. With a similar inclination to link the novella to the more celebrated novel, Julian Moynahan—in one of the earliest and lengthiest treatments of the work—explains how *The Virgin and the Gipsy* reflects Lawrence's view of the "aetiology of the diseased condition of life" (215). In a more recent close reading of the metaphoric design in the fiction, John Humma further elaborates on the relevant themes of social pathology and existential malaise by isolating the trope of "inside and outside" (78) in the work—a metaphoric counterpoint used by Lawrence to chart an integrated syndrome of maladjustment, repression, and failure that inhabits the claustrophobic Saywell home *and* the more sprawling anterooms of the decorous Chatterley estate.[2]

But even in this context of abundant affirmative criticism, the tone of hesitancy persists through the decades about the novella's purportedly minor status—that is, about its relative lack of complexity, bulk, and interest next to the major novels in Lawrence's career, and about that

1. Cushman's essay remains the most comprehensive discussion of the continuities and contrasts between the two works. But as my comments below (see note 11) indicate, his demeaning dismissal of key aspects of Lawrence's technique and vision in the novella does not do justice to Lawrence's significant achievement. While Leavis, Moynahan, Humma, Siegel, and Turner all state relevant issues of comparison as Lawrence moves from *The Virgin and the Gipsy* to *Lady Chatterley's Lover*, these critics also establish a distinct appreciation for the excellence of this novella, and thus they avoid the reductive nature of Cushman's evaluation.

2. In his incisive remarks (147) about the "spurious hygiene of life" at the rectory, and the pervasive antinomy of cleanliness and dirt, Turner describes a compelling pattern of counterpoint in the novella that anticipates aspects of Humma's focus on dichotomies in the text. Siegel also writes intelligently about the essential contrast between "openness and enclosure" that Lawrence uses to structure the work (177).

alleged function as mere prelude to issues explored more comprehensively in *Lady Chatterley's Lover*. During the height of Lawrence's reputation from the 1950s through the 1980s, the work failed to attract much critical praise or sustained discussion. Indeed, during that early, formative period, Harry T. Moore, a pioneering Lawrence biographer and critic, set an unfortunate tone by rating it as "among the lowest of Lawrence's fictional achievements", as a distinctly unimportant work that merely recalls "The Horse Dealer's Daughter" and provides "another variation on the Sleeping Beauty motif" that is prelude to *Lady Chatterley's Lover* (*Priest of Love* 333, 416). Similarly, another influential and early Lawrence scholar, Graham Hough, dismisses the work entirely with the condescending evaluation that often appears in later decades: while he briefly compliments the novella for its focus and consistency, he finally rates it as "no more than a preliminary working over of Lady Chatterley material" (188). Even in the most sustained and admiring of three of the first book-length commentaries on Lawrence—by Mark Spilka, Frank Kermode, and H.M. Daleski—the pattern of disregard and underrating continues. Spilka and Kermode strangely do not even mention the work in the text or notes, and Daleski adds in a short paragraph that the gipsy simply functions as "the prototype of Mellors" (280). In the wide range of studies on Lawrence today, there remains minimal concern by most critics with in-depth consideration of the work, and sustained and sequential examination of the development of its plot, symbolism, and doctrine are virtually nonexistent. Text-centered analysis of *The Virgin and the* Gipsy seem constrained by the lingering effect of that early and perpetuated judgment about the novel's uncomplex resonance—what Siegel calls its "reassuring simplicity" (175).

It is certainly true that *The Virgin and the Gipsy*, viewed as either a short novel or long tale, must lack the scope and ambition of Lawrence's more substantial novels. It is also clear that this "limited" literary terrain provides a more unembroidered and less intense treatment of several themes and metaphors that have central importance throughout Lawrence's career. But the work's significance requires more focused attention, more responsive close reading; it is precisely such unusual transparency of artistic technique and reiterative simplicity of structure that contribute to its crucial role in the writer's canon. In essence, the revelatory nature of this important fiction needs more attention. This novella's qualities of an accessible, intrusive doctrine melded to an elemental narrative design offer provocative clues from 1925 about Lawrence's physical and spiritual condition, sexual health, and creative confidence as he begins the last five years of his life. My argument is less about the legitimate excellence of the novella than it is about the innovative resonance and *effective* simplicity of the artifice and vision in the work. There is no other extended fiction by Lawrence (and I include the more poetic and mythic *The Escaped Cock*) in which the prose is so bare, the plot ambitions so uncomplex, and the supporting doctrine and symbology so recognizably reflective of typologies and perspectives long associated with this writer. While critics, as noted, often admire the work, they are disinclined to discuss its unusual contribution to Lawrence's growth as an artist. They prefer to argue that is derivative, anticipatory, and self-explanatory. To be sure, the work reflects those aspects, but it also remains special in the inimitable way that those very qualities operate synchronistically to enhance the novel's meaning, intention, and timing in Lawrence's career. This notion of *timing* involves more than mere biographical relevance. Lawrence uses the patterned structure and intrusive narration to undermine the conventional movement of time in fiction. Before examining this temporal element in the novella's design and ideology, some discussion is necessary on its intriguing positioning in the turbulent life and art of the writer. Considerations of the marriage matrix preoccupation in this work must also begin with a summary of his health and outlook as he begins *The Virgin and the Gipsy*.

II

In June of 1925, D.H. Lawrence continues his slow recovery in New Mexico from his near fatal and recent attack in Mexico of a pernicious amalgam of influenza, malaria, and tuberculosis. He also begins to write the first of eleven essays that he will compose through November; five of those essays justly rank among his most important statements on the art and philosophy of the genre of the novel: "Art and Morality", "Morality and the Novel", "The Novel" (all written in June), and "Why the Novel Matters" and "The Novel and the Feelings" (both written in November).[3] This six-month spurt of non-fictional prose—which includes "Reflections on the Death of a Porcupine"—represents Lawrence's most sustained writing accomplishment since the onset of his dangerous illness at the end of January. After he completes several of these essays in New Mexico, he travels in late summer and early fall first to New York and then to England; in the process he finishes some necessary busy work and

3. I must acknowledge here my indebtedness for the relevant dates to the meticulous chronological account provided by Bruce Steele in *Study of Thomas Hardy and Other Essays*.

derivative writing projects, including proof corrections, drafts of short stories, manuscript revisions, and book reviews. It is important to emphasize that aside from the essays and short fiction in this period, the only new writing from January to November 1925 consists of a few reviews and the play *David*. Thus it is a period of nearly a year from the onset of his illness to his arrival in Spotorno—and Lawrence composes no new major fiction. Despite the fact that his esteemed genre of the novel is unequivocally the central topic of the 1925 essays, and despite Lawrence's consistent assertion that extended fiction is the most important form of artistic expression, he comes to *The Virgin and the Gipsy* after the longest creative drought of his career.

Amid his many pronouncements in earlier years about the value and priority he assigns to the novel, it is evident throughout his voluminous letters and cathartic travel pieces during the relatively healthier years of his life (1910–1920) that the writing of any lengthy work of fiction exerts the greatest demand on his resources of body, mind, and spirit. I have already indicated in previous chapters his acknowledgement of the emotional price exacted from him during the composition of *The Lost Girl* and *St. Mawr*. Lawrence becomes ill in 1925 in Mexico almost to the day he completes *The Plumed Serpent*, a major project for him that he insistently regards as his "most important novel, so far", and one that, as an especially strenuous work, he feels is related organically to the onset of his illness: "I daren't even look at the outside of the MS. It cost one so much…I got my novel 'Quetzalcoatl' done in Mexico at tremendous cost to myself" (*Letters V* 230, 245). What the cost involves we can only surmise. That Lawrence emerges from this encounter with death as a changed man is, however, hard to dispute on logical grounds and on the direct evidence of statements by him, Frieda, and his acquaintances. Above all, Lawrence is painfully aware of his diminished condition in early 1925, and of the alarming prognosis for his future health given the inevitable decline from his tuberculosis. The residual emotional and physical uneasiness in him in the spring understandably detracts from his self-confidence as a man and an artist. He cannot shake loose from the ravages of his experience in Mexico. He seems haunted even months later, still repressing the dire and definitive diagnosis of tuberculosis supplied by Dr. Uhlfelder: On May 21, "Thank goodness I am much better—but don't forget my shakiness"; on June 20, "I was so ill down in Mexico in Oaxaca—with malaria, flu, and tropical fever—I thought I'd never see daylight. So everything slipped" (*Letters V* 254, 269). He omits mention in this letter, of course, of the disease that will kill him.

Thus, by the beginning of July, although Lawrence increases his writing output to include more introductions, essays, reviews, and revisions, there remains no sustained engagement in longer fiction, and no indication (quite rare for him!) that he contemplates such a project in the months ahead. As the weeks go by and Lawrence recuperates sufficiently to spend long writing hours on anything but a novel, it is hard to avoid the conclusion that he is mired in a post-traumatic writer's block that cruelly separates him from his cherished ability to produce major fiction. This condition is a not-unfamiliar psychosomatic syndrome, and it is one of the two most common manifestations of incapacity after a prolonged illness. The other, of course, concerns Lawrence's sex life and dim prospects for his future quality of existence. Frieda claims that, during his sickness in Mexico, Dr. Uhlfelder told Lawrence directly and without qualification of the tuberculosis that the doctor regarded as terminal. James Boulton and Lindeth Vasey summarize the drama of the meeting in moving detail, including the following account of Frieda's precise words from *Not I, But the Wind*: "Lawrence looked at me with such unforgettable eyes". Frieda further recalls the doctor's judgment that Lawrence would be dead in a year or two, and she includes her own alarming prediction: "After the great strain of his illness, something broke in me. He will never be quite well again, he is ill, he is doomed. All my love, all my strength, will never make him whole again" (Letters *V* 78, Frieda Lawrence 166–67).[4]

---

4. In this provocative context of the intersection of art and biography, Turner quotes an alleged remark from Lawrence to Jessie Chambers about George Borrow, in which Lawrence approvingly describes him as a writer who "so skillfully blended autobiography and fiction that no one could tell where one left off and the other began" (Turner 142, from Moore, *Miscellany* 81). It is not surprising that such a comment intrigues me. Much of this current volume is invested in illuminating within Lawrence's works the revealing strands of psychobiography that he candidly extols as intrinsic and effective in Borrow's writing. Indeed, the echoes of such a bio-literary form of synergy exist for Lawrence in many forms—some of them speculative and haunting. For instance, in terms of Frieda's lamentation (already quoted) about the dire prognosis offered by Dr. Uhlfelder, the sad tone of her concern sounds eerily similar to the urgent and maternal emotions Gertrude expresses in *Sons and Lovers* when Paul falls deathly ill with pneumonia—which, of course must resemble the words of Lydia Lawrence about her son's actual illness, which further suggests the elements of control and command so central in Lydia's own personality that are also prominent in Lawrence's wife. This notorious and interweaving triad of maternal-oedipal-and marital becomes endless in its speculative possibilities in the work of many writers, but the open book of Lawrence's life and artistic obsessions inevitably invites considerable attention.

But Frieda, as all Lawrence scholars know, never breaks easily, and her poignant desire to "make him whole again" sadly suggests a broken or missing part. This declaration of her own futile hope sounds like a thinly-camouflaged despair over the lack of any sexual consummation with Lawrence. It is certainly the persuasive consensus of well-informed critics and biographers as early as the 1950s that Lawrence's impotence—whether partial or total—"dated from his terrible illness in Mexico in 1925 from which he never recovered" (Spilka 71).[5] Ellis's careful investigation of Frieda's own sex life suggests that her affair with Ravagli likely begins in April 1926, not many months after Lawrence's illness, and only several weeks after Lawrence's failed attempt (whatever the cause) to have sex with Dorothy Brett in Ravella in March. A compelling story thus develops from the organic consideration of Lawrence's life and art in 1925. As he moves immediately from the completion of his most ideologically uncompromising and aggressively phallic novel, *The Plumed Serpent*, into a sickness that nearly kills him, Lawrence discovers that he cannot make love and will not write lengthy fiction: deprived of these accustomed and cherished relations with his wife and profession, his survivalist instincts tell him what he must do. In effect, his physical and emotional state confirm the pertinent and gloomy forecast by Freud written in the previous decade that also is precisely relevant to Lawrence's physical and emotional condition after the trauma of his near-death illness. During and after the war, Freud's statistical prediction would prove even more accurate in the wake of countless soldiers who recovered from disease or injury but remained unwilling or unable to make love: "I shall put forward the view that psychical impotence is much more widespread than is supposed" ("Universal Tendency" 398).[6] How does Lawrence respond?

---

5. See Ellis 164, 294, and other chapters in this volume for more on issues of Lawrence's sexual capacity. For a skeptical response to allegations of his impotence during this period, see Worthen 338, 482.

6. The subject of Lawrence's possible impotence in the mid-1920s has a long history of commentary by biographers and critics even before the appearance of the Cambridge biographies. Among the friends and colleagues of Harry T. Moore in the 1940s and 1950s is E.W. Tedlock, the Lawrence scholar who establishes a close personal relationship with Frieda Lawrence Ravagli, who generously assists Tedlock in the preparation in 1948 of one of the earliest annotated bibliographies of Lawrence manuscripts. I cite these connections to introduce some additional support for Spilka's confidence in Moore's story about Lawrence's alleged impotence. Here is the relevant—and perhaps *coded*—passage by the notoriously discrete Tedlock: his comments concern Lawrence's stay in Italy just after he wrote *The Virgin and the Gipsy*. Tedlock's metaphors of season and weather perhaps offer a diplomatic and indirect way for this critic to share intimate

He first counters this aetiology by returning to a theoretical and optimistic reassertion of the supreme value of his art. His *instincts*, in effect, tell him that such confirmation can start the process of his organic *renewal*.

III

The short, reiterative, and trenchant essays that Lawrence begins to write in June 1925 become for him confirming, even *renewing* statements about the value and urgency of his aesthetic calling, and—in the always impinging practical arena—they also serve as new work for his agent to sell to journals and then to publishing houses. The essays remain quotable for their wealth of snappy aphorisms, accessible metaphors, and adamant statements; more importantly, they do not break new ground in Lawrencian doctrine as much as they prune and reaffirm the visionary spirit of Lawrence's work a decade earlier. In these prose pieces on fiction, morality, and art—which bring him both more money and satisfaction that he anticipated—he recalls and refines many of the images and preoccupations of the more complex and extensive writings, "The Crown" and *Study of Thomas Hardy*. This series of essays seems created by a reminiscent version of Lawrence in his celebrated pre-leadership phase of 1913–1918, and they function as rallying catalysts for a return to the province of a novella in 1926. In a revealing letter to Edward McDonald on "The Novel", Lawrence writes about his fondness for that essay in terms of its cathartic function in his life: "But it's what I genuinely feel, and *how* I feel, so what's the odds?" (*Letters V* 272)

Such a committed stance by Lawrence about his own genre priority in 1925, and, implicitly, about his own impinging frustration and urgent priorities, becomes more meaningful in the light of the unusual short novel that he writes in 1926, *The Virgin and the Gipsy*. There exists a close correspondence in the abundant metaphors, committed doctrines, and

---

information—no doubt received through his lengthy and scrupulously private association with Frieda—about the frustrations of her sex life with Lawrence:
Ironically, in the Italy of his sun-symbol of vital renewal, the season was often rainy. Once, out of its denial of his need, he dreamed of a flood back in New Mexico in which his horse was drowned and he was able to find only a "bunch of rather weird, rather horrible pintos". *He had never known a spring so impotent as that of 1926*, when after five days of sun, the weather reverted to gray and wet. February was the bad month for him to get through to the resurrection of spring. For a man who had lived intimately with his disintegration and death from childhood, and had felt at times a desire to lapse into them, what was now going on was a newly crucial contest for life (Tedlock 95, my emphasis).

accessible tone of the essays, with the comparable elements of theme and technique in a novella that stands as his first major fiction in many months. When Lawrence is sufficiently energized by the rousing principles enunciated in the essays, he applies himself to this fiction as a preliminary means to re-engage with his "bright book of life" ("Why the Novel Matters" 195)—the genre of the novel. It is also noteworthy that Lawrence first comes to his project of interrelated essays through his growing interest in painting and art criticism. His talents as a painter and art critic offer him welcome distraction in 1925 through his long convalescence that eases the pain of his impotence as husband and writer.

In July, after he writes several of the essays on fiction and contemplates a few more, he reveals an interesting indebtedness to his painting avocation through a declared preference for absolute simplicity in doctrine and style. In the following letter, he writes from the integrated perspective of philosopher, novelist, and critic. The edge of confidence evident in his tone also suggests that he is charting himself back to relative health and writerly productivity by celebrating a simplicity of style and a doctrinal "essentiality" that inform his essays and (just a few weeks away) *The Virgin and the Gipsy*. He knows how to accelerate his recovery:

> I have thought may times it would be good to review a novel from the standpoint of what I call morality: what I feel to be essentially moral. Now and then review a book plainly…To pave the way—and have some stones to pull up and throw at the reader's head—I did two little articles: "Art and Morality" and "Morality and the Novel"…The point was easier to see in painting, to start with. But it wouldn't be so very out of the way, in a literary paper (*Letters V* 275).

And distinctly not so "out of the way" in a novella that will undermine conventional "morality" as it depicts the Lawrencian vision in his most "plain" major fiction. He has "paved the way" in 1925 for a significant breakthrough in 1926 in fictional innovation. The essays contain the "stones" that will disturb readerly expectations of narrative technique in *The Virgin and the Gipsy*. Above all, it will be "good" for his soul.

Lawrence slowly recovers from his winter illness with a vision of moral life and sexual transcendence that is shorn of those obsessive notions of political leadership and submission so engrained in *The Plumed Serpent*. A few weeks after the above letter, he is confident enough in late August about his physical condition and emotional outlook to offer some similarly "plain" advice on the interconnected processes of writing fiction and perceiving the world: "When we get inside ourselves and away from the vanity of the ego—Alice and smart clothes—then things are symbols" (*Letters V* 294). Lawrence still has three important novels to write in the last four years of his life – *The Virgin and the Gipsy*, *The Escaped Cock*, and *Lady Chatterley's Lover*. They are fictions that strikingly conform to his injunction about simple symbology and ego vanities—a significant contrast to the work that immediately precedes his death scare in Mexico. What these symbols announce in *The Virgin and the Gipsy*, and how they artfully reveal that elusive "inside of self", are best addressed through an integrated approach to the novella and to those important essays on the genre of the novel.

IV

In his essay, "The Novel and the Feelings", written as he completes *The Virgin and The Gipsy*, Lawrence insists almost allegorically on the necessity of listening to "the innermost honourable beasts that call in the dark paths of our body, from the God in the heart" (205). This mixed-metaphor phrasing amounts to a roll-call of the standard Lawrencian images on instinctual primacy. More precisely, by 1925 he has used versions of this bestial trope for more than a decade to convey his foundational belief in the dark gods of blood consciousness. The significance of "beasts" in this seminal essay is crucial for any informed entrance to the novella and for any related understanding of Lawrence's emphasis in the fiction after his illness in Mexico on symbolic structure and the "innermost" self. In its uncomplex plot design and fable-like drama, *The Virgin and the Gipsy* includes a virtual animalia of zoological metaphors, with characters analogized to varieties of birds, beasts, and flowers, including similes of the toad, wolf, lion, worm, nettle, snow-flower, weasel, duck, fish, bear, tiger, nut tree, and oyster. Perhaps his penchant to "review a book plainly", and from a perspective that remains "essentially moral", produces from him a fiction in which the *essentiality* of the morality is projected through elemental images that *plainly* stress human kinship with other animals on earth. Never has Lawrence's work submitted itself to so many images of predatory animals and troublesome plants, as if the tale must unleash its "dishonourable beasts" of ego before Lawrence's "God in the heart" can reign supreme.

The pathetic Aunt Cissie, for example, is "gnawed by an inward worm" (6) that is created by her officious subservience to Granny's willful demands, and this spinster will be rewarded by a cancer that her pent-up frustration and engorgement of candy no doubt accelerates. As the empowered Mater, Granny is consistently described with Dickensian caricature as an old, hideous, and ravenous toad. Lawrence supplements his menagerie with relevant animal attributes for Lucille, Yvette's several suitors, Arthur Saywell, and Uncle Fred. It is through the absent but now legendary straying wife, Cynthia, that Lawrence begins to merge the symbolic landscape with his characteristic flame imagery—that is, with the fiery "forging" of the steel of ego that leads to the soul's "singling-out" and to its consequent connection to the transcendent "unknown" or—as I later describe—the realm of the fourth dimension.[7] That Lawrence does not depict in any detail the infamous "she-who-was-Cynthia" is important for her resonance in the rarefied plot, and for her participation, even in her absence, in the framing context and texture of Lawrence's metaphors: she seems to shimmer within Yvette's memory across some undefined dimension of time and space. This abandoned and perplexed daughter understandably has mixed feelings about her mother.

Yvette's most prominent recollection of Cynthia is infused with the image of molten liquidity that will function more crucially later in the novella as an important concept and image to describe her special connection to the gipsy. Here is the significant echo of the mother that lingers in Yvette's mind: "a great glow, a flow of life, like a swift and dangerous sun in the home" (7). In the visionary terms stipulated by Lawrence, Cynthia both emits sufficient heat in her instinctual desires, and legitimate energy in her quest for freedom to spurn her passionless connection to Arthur and depart with her lover. Yvette is not unaware of the elements of selfishness in her mother that also inform Cynthia's precipitous abandonment of family. Yet as Lawrence suggests through the iconic cosmic imagery that intrudes on the domestic scene, and as he intimates through the years about his own elopement with Frieda, such a form of selfishness may provide the only means for Cynthia to save herself. For her to bring the sun into the home is to undermine the clock-entered and ego-enclosed habits of this neurotic and hypocritical family. The Saywells and their friends remain so content in frozen time that they try to relegate Cynthia's name and infidelity to an unreachable past, and in the process they become modern beasts who are cold, grasping, and mean-spirited.

Early in *The Virgin and the Gipsy*, Yvette asserts that all those adoring fellows make her "feel beastly" (10). Lawrence employs this metaphor to highlight the propensity of the young men to bore her with their inanimate deadness as they "hang on like lead" (9). This imagery insists, in the comparison to an ugly species of soft metal, that the men remain difficult to forge into a warm and flowing quickness. Yes, they are easily molded to

---

7. I elaborate in considerably more detail on the significance of this forging metaphor and its variant representations in Lawrence's work, in Chapters One, Two and Five in *The Phallic Imagination*.

suit the whims of Yvette, but they lack the real heat that would burn down their mass of ego to a sexual essence, a sexual otherness. Yvette sounds like the Brangwen sisters in the first pages of *Women in Love*, or like Addie Bundren in Faulkner's *As I Lay Dying*: she resents the inability of these boy-men to scorch her ego, to intrude into her own limited and conventionally defined self-identity. Put simply, she yearns for someone to cut through her repressed and claustrophobic existence at the Saywell home and village rectory.

In "Why the Novel Matters", also written during his work on the novella, Lawrence writes the following description of a form of masquerade that Yvette witnesses every day: "It is useless to talk about my ego. That only means that I have made up an idea of myself, and that I am trying to cut myself out to pattern" (197). As for Mater, the pattern and pretense serve her own presiding interests, and she rules with "the static inertia of her unsavoury power" over a "family [that] was her own extended ego" (8). Yvette is described as a frustrated creature nurturing a pearl-like recognition not unrelated to the pain of her repressed instincts: "deep inside her worked an intolerable irritation which she thought she *ought* not to feel" (11). Thus she is still inclined to hamper the birth of that honourable beast in her by letting the conditioned mind dictate the propriety of the feeling. As the novella will anatomize in several scenes across the boundaries of time and space, Yvette will lose that irritation and self-consciousness through her brief but transformative relation to the gipsy. Before any consideration of her change in "being", some discussion of Lawrence's reading during this period will prove useful.

V

As the critic Richard Young indicates in a provocative essay, Lawrence does not categorically affirm his own concept of the fourth dimension until 1925, shortly after his serious illness in Mexico and "somewhat more than a year after he read and expansively annotated a book-length treatment of fourth-dimension metaphysics, Peter D. Ouspensky's *Tertium Organum: A Key to the Enigmas of the World*" (30). Young traces the beginning of this dialectic of time, change, and eternity in Lawrence through dramatic moments in his early fiction, and particularly in such highly-charged scenes of transfiguration and transcendence as Gertrude Morel's moonlight episode before Paul's birth, and Ursula Brangwen's "mystic experience with the herd of horses which run against her and 'against the walls of time'" (33). Lawrence refines these notions in "The Crown" when he attempts to merge his fascination with the "flux of time and eternity" with his criticism of civilization's valorization of the strait-jacket of ego, which "takes for certain that itself has filled the whole of space and the whole of time" (33). Young's methodology, however, reads more as a compressed summary than an in-depth analysis; he remains content merely to trace brief moments of allegedly fourth-dimensional prose and poetry through a variety of relatively obvious scenes and metaphors in Lawrence's work. It is unfortunate that although the years 1925–1926 constitute the vital, cumulative year of Lawrence's temporary reprieve from the timeless dimension of death, of his affirmation of several key notions of Ouspensky, and of his preoccupation with ego and time in the essays composed in the summer and fall, and despite the compelling nature of such artistic, biographical, and doctrinal evidence—Young offers no consideration or even mention of *The Virgin and the Gipsy*.

There are fascinating connections to ponder between the concept of the fourth dimension and Lawrence's still underrated and often under-examined novella. Young does offer an intelligent gloss of the crux of Ouspensky's theory as it is generally adapted by Lawrence:

> According to writers like Ouspensky, we three-dimensional beings usually perceive momentarily only a minute section of the fourth dimension, that which to us is the ever-flowing present; but in moments of illumination, we are able to see beyond the flux and to perceive the vast and timeless space which, above all else, characterizes that larger world. The past is alive there with the future, and both are free to move in a new direction (33).

It is an apt description that summarizes Lawrence's emphasis both on an entrance to transcendent experience, and on the memorable instances of instinctual primacy in his characters that often precede such communion-like awareness.[8] In the relevant essays, Lawrence writes during the six months leading to his composition of *The Virgin and the Gipsy*, and in the novella itself, there is a distinct pattern of concern with a definition of time and space that Lawrence conveys via an innovative narrative technique that he variously describes throughout his essays. I will later enumerate the aesthetics of this pattern, but for now it is enough to note that Lawrence's

---

8. Even more than sixty years after its publication, Spilka's discussion in *The Love Ethic of D.H. Lawrence* of the techniques and doctrinal centrality of "communion" scenes in Lawrence's work remains unparalleled in its clarity and uncommon understanding of the writer's vision (8–31). See also aspects of Spilka's notion of a "fourth dimension" in *The Rainbow* that can apply to my own reading of *The Virgin and the Gipsy*: "he is dealing with a vague and nourishing force or flow which occurs *in time*" (18, Spilka's emphasis).

brand of metaphysics is consistently related to his conceptual metaphors of forging flame, molten ego, and creative transcendence. In first scene, for example, of Yvette with the gipsy, the fortune-teller, and the impatient Leo, the gipsy woman presciently informs Yvette that "other people are treading on your heart. They will tread on your heart till you think it is dead. But the dark man will blow the one spark up into fire again, good fire, you will see what good fire" (30). Recall also Yvette's "honourable" mistake with the rectory funds, which prompts a crazed Aunt Cissie to hiss "you selfish beast, you greedy little beast" (29) into her niece's room. During this formative period Yvette is secretly—even to herself—gestating into her own form of honourable beast. As the unconscious forging proceeds "inside" her, she ponders how the gipsy's eyes "made her lie prone and powerless in the bed, as if a drug had cast her in a new molten mould" (30).

And as if the tortured eyes of this struggling writer, husband, and lover might recapture the ability to wield such heat and power over Frieda. The gipsy's role is more stimulative that merely initiating the dissolution of Yvette's ego defenses as she gropes toward the fourth dimension. This inscrutable, reticent, and charismatic character functions also as the catalyst of increased confidence in Yvette and in *Lawrence himself*, as the novelist experiences his recent (and perhaps definitive) lack of consummated sex with his robust wife. He is the key to Yvette and Lawrence's renewal of body, spirit, and belief. In that same year of 1926 Frieda will begin her long affair with Angelo Ravagli that will culminate in their marriage in 1950.[9] In the novella Lawrence deftly disguises—as he did in *St. Mawr*—the intimate nature of his sexual failure by projecting the incapacity onto a woman through clever cross-gender metaphors that effectively distance the impotence from him even as the symbology confirms his own understandable preoccupation. Note the intriguing lines from *The Virgin and the Gipsy*, his first fiction since the bad news from Dr. Uhlfelder: "The thought of the gipsy had released the life of her limbs, and crystallized in her heart the hate of the rectory: so that now she felt potent, instead of impotent" (30). For Yvette to "think" of the gipsy in that organic, doctrinal sense that must resonate (for her *and* Lawrence) as more instinctual feeling than analytical thought, is thus to encounter a special mix of psychobiographical concealment and visionary candor. It remains, of course, for the liberating heat to take Yvette beyond the crystallized hardness in her heart, or to bring Lawrence to that state of mind and soul

9. For more on the relevant chronology and context of the start of Frieda's affair with Ravagli, see Ellis 290–296, and Squires and Talbot 312–14, 329, 339, 347–48.

during the last years of his life that David Ellis, using Lawrence's own phrase, will describe as "dying game".[10] In "Morality and the Novel", Lawrence writes definitively of the auspicious meeting of timelessness and flame, a conjunction that makes that myth of the fiery phoenix a perfect icon for him: "By life we mean something that gleams, that has the fourth-dimensional quality" (173).

VI

The earlier pattern of Yvette's flirtation with fourth-dimensional experience continues in her next sight of the gipsy, when from her window she observes him drive his cart. She senses in the gipsy's very posture his entrenched preferences for a natural, unselfconscious connection to the flux and movement of life; the more she exists within or contemplates the orbit of his life, the more she dreamily begins to absorb some inkling of the timeless beyond. Is there any writer more adept than Lawrence in conveying the inward truth of a character by perfectly capturing the delicate nuances of his demeanor, the subtle rhythms of his movement? "The man swayed loosely in the swing of the cart, as the horse stepped down-hill in the silent somberness of the afternoon…The driver sat as if in a kind of dream, swinging along. It was like something seen in a sleep" (36).[11] When the gipsy then leaves Yvette, she remains touched by his

---

10. Ellis's title for the third volume of the Cambridge biography is derived from resonant phrasing used by Lawrence in a letter to Gertie Cooper on January 23, 1927 (*Letters V* 632).

11. Cushman maintains that "the portrayal of the spell the gipsy casts over Yvette is highly unconvincing, not to say laughable", and he reduces the characterization of the gipsy merely to the status of "an unadulterated embodiment of machismo" (165,164). But such "machismo" is certainly "adulterated" by evidence of the gipsy's caution, sensitivity, insight, and troubled past. Cushman's harsh assertion is only justified if the relationship between Yvette and the gipsy is subject to the conventional strictures of a narrative realism that the critic otherwise suggests in his essay is not the essential tenor or intent of the work. Cushman also correctly notes that "when Yvette sees him, she melts" (164), but he does nothing with that wording's seminal relation to the "forging" trope and the fourth-dimensional theme so crucial to the novella's narrative technique. Carol Siegel, however, wisely does not find the attraction between them as unconvincing even in the real world of flirtation and desire. She stresses an important intuitive kinship—in my mind a species of "secret sharer"—that infuses the relationship: Yvette "sees in his defiant, outcast posturing, and even in the free sway of his hips, her own kind of strength and understanding" (178). Such an observation provides a persuasive link

presence again; she repeats to herself the key word that in 1925–26 constitutes a major concern for Lawrence:

> Nevertheless, hiding this time at the landing window, she stood to watch the man go. What she wanted to know, was whether he really had any power over her…'No, he hasn't any power over me,' she said to herself; rather disappointed really, because she wanted somebody, or something, to have power over her (38).

Lawrence wishes to reclaim aspects of that power for himself, and its provenance is not without sexual implications. Thus once again emerges the contorted but artful projections of gender roles in Lawrence's fractured marital and creative life. The intrigue and the achievement are that Lawrence stays artist enough to make Yvette's equivocal desires and his own sublimations appropriate material for the novella. Only a few weeks before he begins to write *The Virgin and the Gipsy*, Lawrence asserts in "Blessed are the Powerful":

> For power is the first and greatest of all mysteries. It is the mystery that is behind all our being, even behind all our existence. Even the Phallic erection is a first blind movement of power. Love is said to call the power into motion: but it is probably the reverse: that the slumbering *power* calls love into being (327).

The speculations about the possible relation between Lawrence's life and art during these years are provocative in the context of his theorizing about power, love, and sexual assertion. Does his consideration of such "reverse" probability offer him a canny way, at the beginning of his last five years of life, to strategically demand acquiescence from Frieda even as he pleads his undying love over an unmoving and detumescent phallus?

Young's discussion of Lawrence's reading of Ouspensky wisely stresses both the affinity of the fourth dimension for initiating a liberating timelessness, and its visionary quality of producing an infinity of perceived space to enclose this endless span of time. In terms of narrative texture in fiction, this dimension will embrace the coordinate and demarcation issues of where and when. Such a tableau of ambiguity is reflected in Yvette's oddly comfortable and accepting disorientation in time and space as she continues to feel the effect, in her soul, of the gipsy: "There was something strange and mazy, like having cobwebs over one's face, about Yvette's vague blitheness…It was like walking in one of those

---

to the mutuality of an attraction between them grounded in an intuitional alertness that even feels persuasive in the realm of psychological realism.

autumn mists when gossamer strands blow over your face. You don't quite know where you are" (57). After a virtual sleep-walking cup of coffee with him near an appropriately blazing fire at the campsite, she is distracted from thoughts of the gipsy for several days by her infatuation with the mildly rebellious, pleasantly romantic, and ultimately superficial couple, Major Eastwood and Mrs. Fawcett. The passage of time she spends is leisurely, but ultimately (like this couple) without much substance. Yvette's diversions with them will develop later in the novella as part of the thematics of her increasing awareness about instinctual primacy, and this couple's presence will serve to highlight their own deficiencies and the special attributes of the gipsy.

Close to the conclusion of the novella, Lawrence formulates an aphoristic description of time that conveniently merges his own emphasis on the dark gods of instinct with his recent reading of Ouspensky's fourth dimension metaphysics:

> She did not forget the gipsy entirely. But she had no time for him. She, who was bored almost to agony, and who had nothing at all to do, she had not time, to think, even seriously, of anything. Time being, after all, the current of the soul in its flow (64).

"No time to think", of course, suggests in Lawrencian terms the productive state that is undistracted by mentalized conditioning. I have written at length elsewhere about the considerable influence of Lawrence on the sexual aesthetics of Norman Mailer.[12] More pertinently, in the next chapter of this volume I discuss how the doctrines of "erotic risk" and existential time that inform Mailer's 1955 novel, *The Deer Park*, reveal an indebtedness to relevant notions of "quicktime" and instinctual courage in *Lady Chatterley's Lover*. But such influence on Mailer extends to *The Virgin and the Gipsy* in strikingly precise terms. In this regard, and with Lawrence's words in mind from the passage above on time, current, and flow, I quote Mailer's pithy sentences from the last page of *The Deer Park*, reflecting his metaphysically ambitious statement about time and its potential relation to sexual self-definition and the infinite. His words refer to the education in passion and transcendence absorbed by the narrator in that novel, and it reads just as distinctly as the signature of Lawrence's connection to Mailer. Put simply, Yvette Saywell will learn that she does have *time* for the gipsy; she will also learn that time is "after all, only the current of the soul in its flow". In Lawrence's doctrinal and metaphoric

12. See especially Chapter Five in *The Phallic Imagination* for more on the many aspects of such influence.

terms, how and if that "scorched ego" of the soul melts down will affect the molted liquidity, the fourth-dimensional flow toward essential sexual otherness that is the hallmark of Lawrencian transcendence. Here are those key words from *The Deer Park*: "But God, who is the oldest of the philosophers, answers in his weary, cryptic way: 'Rather think of sex as time, and time as the connection of new circuits'" (375). It is exactly such awareness about the relation between her attraction to the gipsy and the perception about the expansion of time and space that Lawrence will develop throughout the work. In this context of issues about time-flow, Mailer writes a letter to me on Aug. 3, 1994 concerning my discussion of Lawrence's novella in a considerably shorter version of this chapter first delivered as a presentation at an International D.H. Lawrence Conference in Ottawa, Canada, and then published in a journal. In the letter, Mailer writes candidly about Lawrence's pervasive influence on his own work and developing doctrines; more precisely, he considers my perception of the issue of time in *The Virgin and the Gipsy*. Note Mailer's concluding remarks about the precocious sense of Lawrence's eclectic awareness, as well as his own intriguing prediction about the scientific basis of Lawrence's visionary insight:

> I have to tell you that egocentrically, as I was reading [your essay] and came across Lawrence's remark, "Time being, after all, only the current of the soul in its flow," I was struck with how close that was to the end of *The Deer Park* and the remark, "Rather think of sex as time…" Now, mind you, Peter, I had never read *The Virgin and the Gipsy*. In college I was prodigiously influenced by *Lady Chatterley*, which I read in the Treasure Room at Widener—the only way to read it back in the early 40s!—and *Sons and Lovers* and *The Rainbow*. But that was all of Lawrence I read in college and never his short stories till years later and never *The Virgin and the Gipsy* at all. So when a paragraph or two later you chose the same quote from *The Deer Park*, I was truly struck with that, how much the spirit of Lawrence influenced me. Indeed, if I had more of a lyrical gift, I could have written that line: "…the currents of the soul in its flow." You know I suspect he's scientifically correct and a hundred years from now…scientists will even begin to think that way; there are so many signs of it already.

The narrative techniques that Lawrence employs to configure the fourth dimension begin on the novella's first page and proceed in an integrated sequence in the novella. Attention to such a sequence must be preceded by some examination of relevant Lawrencian doctrine.

VII

Time is literally of the essence in *The Virgin and the Gipsy*. Such urgency applies not in the cautionary sense of the bromide, but in the substantive context of Lawrence's reiterated emphasis in "Art and Morality" and "Morality and the Novel" on the essentiality of his fourth-dimensional prose. This stylistic innovation embodies, at its core, an instinctual belief in the sensate texture and rhythm of life—as well as the framing realization of the organic synchrony among its disparate elements, both animate and inanimate. Lawrence thus depicts a kinetic and jigsaw pattern of primal energies that underlie existence and invariably suggests the proximate apprehension of the "unknown". In effect, Lawrence creates a narrative style that can slow this "flux" sufficiently to reveal intense moment of "relation" among "various things." He articulates this fusion in that single passage in "Art and Morality" about his artistic mandate and visionary credo:

> Design, in art, is a recognition of the relation between various things, various elements in the creative flux. You can't *invent* a design. You recognize it, in the fourth dimension. That is, with your blood and bones, even more than with your eyes (167).

His commitment is unequivocal, and it is also implicitly critical of his fellow novelists: he insists in the same essay that is only when the writer finds a way to embody this "perfected relation between man and his circumambient universe" that one can convey "life itself" (171).

Such a Lawrencian guideline for the craft of fiction must engage the elusive concepts of time and space, and his abstract theorizing at first seems adrift in contradiction: "It has the fourth-dimensional quality of eternity and perfection. Yet it is momentaneous" (171). Thus his challenge, within those vague notions of a narrational physics, is to somehow reveal stasis in the midst of motion and motion in the midst of stasis. Lawrence intends to give palpable form and meaning *to the reader* of a synthesis of kinesis and picture that is integral to his depiction of the fourth dimension. In *The Virgin and the Gipsy*, composed late in his life and with the benefit of his accumulated experience as man, writer, and painter, Lawrence creates in a single fiction a poetic and provocative solution to the aesthetic conundrum of merging the static-transitory with the infinite-reverbative. By employing a technique in 1926 that anticipates the century's later developments in film theory and practice, he elongates the *momentaneous* within a repetitive and slow motion narration. In this process of literary collagics he creates that elusive sensation of an immersive present-time—a linguistic "black-hole," if you will—to dramatize that mode of reflected awareness in his fiction that he describes as fourth-dimensional. The distracting confusion is that he uses the term interchangeably to refer to his narrative technique, to the character's perception, and to the reader's narrative experience.

What does remain certain is that *The Virgin and the Gipsy* consistently depicts the inadequacy of the accustomed calculations of clock-time, for any traditional chronology or temporal measurement cannot convey the movement of this transcendent dimension. The Saywell home is a dreary domestic fortress, deeply involved in deadlines, routines, and socio-religious commitment, lacking all sense of spontaneity and exuberant emotion. In the fairy-tale and uncomplex structure of the novella, Lawrence creates—to adopt his words from "Art and Morality"—a plot pattern that establishes a version of the "circumambient-universe." This little world functions as a microcosmic version of "life itself" when it isolates the eternality of time within several scenes between Yvette and the gipsy. Those essays of 1925 clearly anticipate the novella's form and thematics, as the goal for Lawrence in his fiction—to repeat that crucial definition—is to demonstrate that fundamental assertion in "Art and Morality": "by life we mean something that gleams, that has the fourth-dimensional quality" (173).

The opening lines of the novella quickly create a sense of flat time, stalled progress, and obsessive preoccupation with the mother's elopement with her lover. It is the stranglehold of the past that lingers supreme, obliterating the potential of the live-present:

> When the vicar's wife went off with a young and penniless man, the scandal knew no bounds. His two little girls were only seven and nine years old respectively. And the vicar was such a good husband. True, his hair was grey. But his moustache was dark, he was handsome, and still full of furtive passion for his unrestrained and beautiful wife (5).

The litany of delicious sarcasm by Lawrence—is there a greater failing to him than a man with a "furtive passion"?—should not obscure that interesting function of this first paragraph. Its rhythm and tone take us back to the sound of bedtime readings by parents to children: "His hair was grey", "his moustache was dark", "he was handsome"—a setting surely within the fictive arena of stylized portraiture and light fantasy. It amounts to a denuded, softly Manichean, yet comfortably complete mini-world, of aging father, good husband, beautiful wife, adulterous intruder, and bereft little girls. But such a standard cast of characters and trite scenario scarcely tell the tale, and the child-like resonance continues with a purposeful touch of stale melodrama: "Out in the evil world, at the same time, there wandered a disreputable woman who had betrayed the rector and the children" (6). The ironic phrasing here, so ripe with Lawrence's contempt for both the aggrieved husband and the community's narrow perspective on the infidelity, clearly conveys the pernicious nature of the inflexible and bourgeois notions of morality that infect the mood and priorities of Yvette's family.

The hackneyed lilt of those introductory lines in the novella, with their melodramatic echoes of evil, betrayal, and a roving witch-woman, further undercuts the tyranny of conventional notions of morality that Lawrence and Frieda experienced when their relationship became public. Only two characters in the work, Yvette and the gipsy, are depicted within the context of a fourth-dimensional prose that informs their encounters with each other and gradually establishes the instinctual *zeitgeist* that operates against the dominance of both easy moral judgment and mechanical time. After the departure of Cynthia, the rhythm of the home remains mired in obligations and routines that move beyond inertia to the more alarming state of virtual entropy: "a complete stability in which one could perish safely" (7). The lingering effect of the past for this family is invoked in that first sentence: the vernacular and gossipy phrasing of the wife who "went off with a young and penniless man" and caused a scandal – as the terms emphasize the dominating extent to which social stigma and disruptive events obsessively over-determine the present demeanor and perspective of the Saywells. The raging flood at the end of the work will decimate all the relics of the past in the house, including the grandmother – as the waters supply a surging, even angry act of nature that frees Yvette to establish a more productive and life-enhancing future.

VIII

Amid the straight-line movement of time in the plot, the novella interrupts and broadens the standard narrative development at several key points within the five meetings between Yvette and the gipsy. The effect in three of the encounters is to establish an elongation of durational time as well as a deepening of the connection between the two characters. The focus remains consistently on Yvette, who has been mired in despair and longing before she meets him The meetings will provide her with a new dimension of instinctual primacy that Lawrence conveys through his innovative prose with its ability to reflect a "fourth-dimensional quality of eternity and perfection" ("Morality and the Novel" 171). The long-stifled emotional life of Yvette is also thematically linked to an array of her unsatisfactory marriages, liaisons, and boyfriends in this work, as Lawrence's treatment of the marriage matrix takes on a decidedly negative cast. Each of the couples in *The Virgin and the Gipsy*, other than the unfulfilled intimacies between the title characters, is mired in inadequate and/or unserious relationships with the respective partners. Each couple also exemplifies an inadequate model for lasting marriage. Even the fragmentary but powerful connection between the gipsy and Yvette is obviously exempt from the possibility of any lasting or formal commitment. There is no other successful example of legal union, or even the prospect of one. Cynthia has cuckolded her pathetic husband before the novella begins, and Lawrence maintains a discrete silence about her "status" since the elopement. Fawcett and Eastwood remain entertaining, but they are profoundly unserious and indulgent about life, and they lack the ability Lawrence describes in "Why the Novel Matters" to avoid having "made up an *idea* of" themselves that takes priority over the "whole man alive" (197). Similarly, Yvette's callow young suitors dramatize in several vignettes their lack of maturity and imagination. It is a fictional landscape that offers little escape from people who "cut [themselves] out to pattern" and who ignore Lawrence's idealized mandate on a linkage between marriage and the infinite (197).

Surrounded by the stasis and willfulness so endemic to the Saywell household, it is no surprise that the daughters casually contemplate the *idea* of marriage as the most practical and convenient form of liberation from their claustrophobic home. In the initial dialogue exchange between the sisters, Yvette asserts to Lucille that she wants to get married and would "like to fall *violently* in love" (10). The scene also recalls the substance and rhythm of the memorable conversation I earlier noted between Ursula and Gudrun that begins *Women in Love*, but with a major distinction. The two sisters in the earlier novel have more firmly established themselves in the real world—as teacher and artist, respectively—and thus their witty talk about marriage and experience comes with the real prospect of a range of suitable male candidates for wedlock in their larger community. Yvette and Lucille are less mature and experienced, with limited options for careers and paltry pickings for marriage. In their light banter, there emerges, beyond the youthful and repressed touch of eros, no real understanding of the transcendent dimensions and contingencies of love, passion, and marriage. It is in this context that Lawrence begins to integrate the marriage matrix theme with his emphasis on instinctual primacy. He appears fond of both sisters in the work; he uses Lucille as a contrast to the zesty and unpredictable Yvette when Lucille offers the un-Lawrencian words of conventional restraint and caution about the usual protocol for action: "We've got to settle down a bit before we know what we want" (10).

Such sisterly advice may work for most people, but neither Lawrence nor Yvette agrees with Lucille's sober directive. The novella consistently rebuts such a tempered and premeditated approach to life, as the work insists—in prototypical terms for Lawrence—that what Yvette *feels* is what she properly desires. The confidence in instinctual motivation amounts to Lawrence's gold standard for engagement with life and growth into maturity. Throughout the work Yvette eschews compromise and deliberation, as in her unwise and impulsive theft of the Church funds, an act that is less a planned crime than a purgative and foolish act of defiance that Lucille cannot comprehend: "But you never will think beforehand where your actions are going to lead you" (28). Lucille again is correct in her accusation but wrong in the judgment that fuels her indictment.

Yvette remains totally in character when she does not soften the edge of her annoyance over Leo's presumptuous marriage proposal: "I think this sort of thing is awfully silly" (43). Leo's words are inane to her because Yvette realizes that they lack any sense of "penetrating into some deep secret place, and shooting her there" (43). Lawrence's phallic word play functions here as more than easy *entendre* about her lack of sexual experience. His comments suggest both the extent of her deep-seated, *organic* virginity, and her instinctual need to find the right man to violate that innocence. But Yvette remains consistent in yielding to her feelings—whether they are deep-seated or temperamental. Recall how her exasperated attempt to keep open the window in the stuffy family room reflects her existential desire to satisfy the demands of her sense perception. Throughout *The Virgin and the Gipsy* Yvette progressively adheres to the "flow" (a key term in the novella) of her instincts, of her soul. Her actions often conflict with the routinized, clock-centered conformity in the Saywell home, a place presided over by that monument to conventional time, Granny, who "kept her power, as years rolled on, from seventy to eighty and from eighty, on the new lap, towards ninety" (8). Time does not flow in this house; it merely elapses by mechanical fits and starts, entrenched within the stultifying diversions of word games, silly gossip, tasteless food, and dull volunteerism. Yvette's car outing with her friends, punctuated by a literal embodiment of fits and starts, provides an opportunity to examine the aesthetics of fourth-dimensionality early in the work.

IX

As the trip begins, Leo wonders if the group might stop to observe the scenery at the Head, but perhaps only "stay a moment" (19). As with his later marriage proposal to Yvette, he is characteristically in a hurry, not inclined to linger over the scenery when his main goal this day is to find some private time with Yvette. When they reach the vista, the planned stop appears useless: the landscape is visibly blighted by the recent intrusions of industrial machinery and ugly excavation. There is no untouched pastoral here, no natural link to transcendent sky, no sweep through the fertile land and rough hills to the Lawrencian "unknown" extolled on the first page of *The Rainbow*. It is the early twentieth century, and the air and earth are infected with the cacophonous sounds of technology and the scars of unchecked mining. In an excellent passage, Lawrence integrates all the elements of this modern predation—the ravenous earthmovers, the diabolical misuse of land, and the distorted physical body:

> The hills were like the knuckles of a hand, the dales were below, between the fingers, narrow, steep, and dark. In the deeps a train was slowly pulling north: a small thing of the underworld. The noise of the engine re-echoed curiously upwards. Then came the dull, familiar sound of blasting in a quarry (19).[13]

Leo's impatience increases at the stopover, and he is stubbornly unwilling to lose *time* so early in their trip: "'Shall we be going?' he asks"—his anxious plea for a quick departure so he can get to "Amberdale for tea" (19) and enjoy the likelihood of *time* alone with Yvette. The car shortly is blocked by the gipsy's cart, and Yvette, in this initial and fateful

13. While Cushman understands that the natural environment in the novella is far from pastoral, he fails to connect that insight to the entrenched sense of industrial blight that pervades the car-trip scene. Turner's essay, however, illuminates the major critique of "industrial civilization" (141) that resonates throughout the work, and he effectively relates that important theme to relevant metaphors of cleanliness, disease, and dirt described above (see note 2). Ruderman also is excellent on how Lawrence expresses his anger at the ravages of modern industry primarily through the proud independence and fearless otherness presented in the character of the gipsy, who is depicted as a "possible source of personal and societal renewal" (*Race and Identity* 125). The real value of Ruderman's eclectic and comprehensive book resides in the penetrating way she interweaves culture, history, and metaphor throughout Lawrence's art: her remarks on *The Virgin and the Gipsy* are especially notable in her understanding of the racial and social stereotypes that Lawrence both affirms and revises in his layered presentations of Mrs. Fawcett, Major Eastwood, and the gipsy.

encounter with the gipsy, sees his dark eyes "for a second" (20). But on this occasion the tiny second resonates very differently from the passing "moment" earlier suggested by Leo. As Lawrence now unveils his narrative version of fourth-dimensionality, time begins to slow, even melt, through imagery that reflects a heated *forging* of the soul; it is the metaphoric expression of the Lawrencian immersion into the state of total instinctual primacy. These two integral and synergistic elements—the forging heat and the elastic, almost liquid sense of time—will be embroidered and reiterated with subtle variations throughout the novella: "something took fire in her breast" (20), as the singling-out process begins. Her instinctual, immersive response contrasts with the immediate paucity of Leo's following question, by now less of a query than a means for Lawrence to stress Leo's petty obedience to the urgencies of the clock: "What about the time?" Leo asks, as he now worries about time wasted by the group as they contemplate the gipsy's offer to tell their fortune. Leo is neurotically wedded to the calibrations of the clock.

Lawrence is both artful and consistent in his development of the temporal theme. To contemplate one's fortune through the ministration of a seer is, in essence, to permit someone else to predict the future flow of time. Such an extra-dimensional talent requires a deep inquiry or interjection into the present by stopping the immediate movement of time much as an x-ray captures the spatial moment in order to render a prognosis. Thus in relevant response to the sound of Leo's increasing impatience about elapsed time, Lucille speaks for Lawrence when she boldly states the crux of Lawrence's doctrinal complaint about the pace of modern life: "Oh bother the old time. Somebody's always dragging time in by the forelock" (20).[14] The metaphor and the complaint function effectively. Lawrence believes that the trivial business of daily commitments provides a convenient excuse for not opening up the self to the potential magic of the deeper moment. For him the obsession with elapsing time obliterates the opportunities for a slow and enriching transcendence. Fortune-tellers may embody a form of scam, but their impulse remains genuine within the liminal sphere of Lawrence's cosmography.

---

14. The Explanatory Notes section of the Cambridge edition of the novella relevantly adds that Lawrence's use of the "forelock" phrasing builds on its proverbial association to mean "bringing literal time as an excuse to frustrate an initiative" (262). Such an interpretation might also add, "to frustrate the instinctual primacy embedded in Lawrence's concept of the fourth dimension". The image additionally suggests the idea of tugging one's forelock as a gesture of subservience: tugging time *by* the forelock shows it who's boss!

As Yvette's friends get their fortunes told, the gipsy's silent and prolonged gaze at her operates to drastically slow the temporal action recounted in the narration; it effectively retards the forward movement of time outside the caravan as the friends inside become more invested in their prospects for the future. The silent connection between Yvette and the gipsy seems increasingly beyond or outside time, held within some choreography of movement that Lawrence conveys with a lyrical reiteration and fragmentary pause to depict her instinctual swoon. The metaphors of dance and film are appropriate for the essential patterning of the scene, which employs alternating moments of stasis and movement, gesture and freeze-frame, as if the gipsy and Yvette enact an inset-drama with little more than pregnant silence and reiterative phrasing as the only means to formulate the dance between their souls. Yet there is an interesting pre-history here of Lawrence stretching the boundaries of time and space in his art. About two years before he writes *The Virgin and the Gipsy*, he completes a painting in Bandol titled "Dance Sketch" that is relevant to the current consideration of the novella.

Although biographer David Ellis does not connect the painting to either the novella or to Lawrence's developing notion of fourth-dimensional prose, he wisely notes the relation of time, movement, and stasis to the painting's distorted figures: "The naked man and woman are deliberately thin and elongated (the man's left leg tapering into infinity) in order to suggest vivacious movement" (459). I would add several points. The woman's left leg also disappears into the hazy swirls of time, with the swirl of movement and its *stalled* component indicated by the melting liquidity of both legs—an oddity that approximates aspects of Lawrence's image of the forging flow. The specter of that Pan-goat lurking in the background is perhaps suggestive of the woman's instinctual thrall; she resembles Cynthia Asquith (see Chapter Four), and the man reminds us of D.H. Lawrence in body type and facial elements.[15]

15. In the interest of full disclosure, I used "Dance Sketch" as the cover illustration of *The Phallic Imagination*, but this essay provides an opportunity to discuss elements of its relevance to Lawrence's visionary and aesthetic imagination.

"Dance Sketch" by D.H. Lawrence (Fig. 7-1)

X

In that formative scene of fortune telling, Lawrence employs a narrative style that precisely reproduces the fourth-dimensional effect of the "Dance Sketch" painting. The gipsy's gaze forges the soul in her body and melts that hardness that shields her virgin state: "Something hard inside her met his stare. But the surface of her body seemed to turn to water" (24). Then begins that hypnotic emphasis on pause and duration that comprises the central principle of choreographic integration in the scene. As she follows the gipsy woman up the steps of the caravan, Yvette remains "naïve" (Lawrence's pointed term) about a temporal state that is not obedient to conventional clock-time, as she ingenuously predicts to her friends that she won't "be long" (24). While her fortune is being told, "it was a long time to wait, the others felt" (24); her friends interpret the passage of time in consecutive, elapsed moments that do not account for the insertion of Yvette in the *depths* of time. As she emerges from her uncanny experience, she is described as having "witch-like slim legs" (25), a verbal snapshot that again recalls the radically tapered leg in the painting: she seems dazed as she addresses the group through a phrasing that by now serves as a choric echo, "Did it seem long?" (25) Such a question signifies her gradual emergence from the dream-trance initiated by the gipsy and then augmented and deepened through her interlude in the caravan.

This insistent pattern of Yvette's "soft, vague waywardness" (25) in the scene prepares us for the reappearance of similar phrases and metaphors in several additional meetings with the gipsy. Their second meeting occurs when he stops by the Saywell home to peddle his wares. He is described in terms that recall Yvette's demeanor in the earlier scene, for he appears "as if in a kind of dream, swinging alone. It was like something seen in a sleep" (36). There is no refracted perspective here, no attempt to project Yvette's perception of his movements or his emotional state. The novella insists that this view of the gipsy encapsulates his characteristic state of being, his "into-oneself" existential posture. Indeed, he exists perpetually in the confident drowse of instinctual primacy; as more symbol than person, it is not surprising that he lacks a name until the last words of the work. Within the stipulations of Lawrence's doctrine, he can invoke power over vulnerable but secretly receptive women like Yvette. His effect on her is not a summoning of erotic response but a transformation, as in a fairy tale, in which "her tender face seemed to go into a sleep" (37).

After the gipsy departs, the propensity in Yvette for this dream-sleep is more explicitly connected to her moments of a dementalized state of being; that is, her primary consciousness as a "Lawrencian" woman is not rooted in easy obedience to the socially conditioned and conventional materiality in the world; she emanates, in contrast, a fundamental receptivity to sensate experience that can attain the swoon of transcendence. She is "lost" in the very manner that for Lawrence means finding oneself. Recall again those evocative lines that denote the extent of Yvette's lack of standard indications of location and feeling: "There was something strange and mazy, like having cobwebs over one's face, about Yvette's vague blitheness…It was like walking in one of those autumn mists, when gossamer strands blow over your face. You don't know where you are" (38). Gradually Yvette begins to comprehend—"in [her] blood and [her] bones" ("Art and Morality" 167)—the special qualities of the gipsy, as well his effect on her. No more a victim of the petty morality of her family, or the politically correct assumptions of her community, but now alert to the penetrating gaze from the gipsy that gives her a "feeling that she had been looked upon, not from the outside, but from her secret female self," and aware that the gipsy had "seen none of her pretty face and her pretty ways, but just the dark, tremulous, potent secret of her virginity" (39). "Virginity" as "potent" sounds oxymoronic, and such a synthesis of innocence and power will function as a major theme in the work. It also offers further suggestions about Lawrence's own preoccupation with his impotence and his creative energy.

In their third meeting Yvette goes on her own to the gipsy encampment —a visit she undertakes alone as an aggressive attempt to encounter him again. The most important scene in the novella, it functions as a *tour de force* of Lawrence's narrative technique. It carefully establishes the innovative verbal realm of the fourth dimension by manipulating, or *bending*, the usual parameters of time and space in fiction. Lawrence employs an integrated pattern of repetition and the frictive to-and-fro rhythm he described several years earlier in the Foreword to *Women in Love*. The breakthrough here for this writer is to wed stylistic repetition to the theme of time in order to establish the hazy texture of a live dream. The words evocatively blur the distinction between slow-time and defined temporal duration; Lawrence employs dialogue that is staccato and restorative, and within narrative lines that are both metaphorically precise but indefinably abstract:

> Yvette went to the fire to warm her hands…
> Yvette crouched in silence, warming her hands…
> "You said you'd be here on Fridays," she said, "so I came this way as it was so fine."
> "Very fine day!" said the gipsy…
> "My hands!" she said, clasping them nervously.
> "You didn't wear gloves?"
> "I did, but they weren't much good."
> "Cold comes through," he said…
> "You want to come up and wash your hands?" he said…
> Vaguely, as in a dream, she received from him the cup of coffee…On her face was that tender lack of sleep, which a nodding flower has, when it is full out…the waking sleep of its brief blossoming. The waking sleep of her full-opened virginity…
> "You want to go in my caravan now, and wash your hands?" (44, 45, 46, 47, my ellipses)

The lulling repetition of phrases creates the texture of "the waking sleep" described in the passage. The seductive and reiterative question to

Yvette—she senses what "washing hands" really portends—and the image of her flower-like readiness may briefly titillate readers about a forthcoming sexual initiation.[16] But Lawrence, *in this one novella*, is not concerned with the erotic potential of such an encounter. While the gipsy remains aware of Yvette's sensual appeal, he is no crafty and relentless seducer. Note that relevant touch of humane awareness in him that seeks to protect Yvette from even the appearance of impropriety: as they are about to enter the caravan, he tells her that "you want to put your hat on" (47)—an acknowledgement that he hears a car approaching the encampment. The warning breaks that spell of her live-dream, and she returns home with a hint of the deeper realms of her consciousness. Her brief foray into the realm of the fourth dimension has not been in vain.[17]

---

16. The 1970 film version of *The Virgin and the Gipsy*, directed by Christopher Miles, grasps the significance of Lawrence's fourth-dimensional treatment of time and instinct in this caravan scene. Miles portrays the couple in a necessarily hazy and fragmented scene of reiteration and recall: the interrupted present-time and repetitive dialogue work together to appropriately stop and *deepen* temporal sequences to establish the delicate mixture of caution and desire that informs their attraction to each other. The scene wisely blurs the line between dream and reality in focusing on the simmering emotions of Yvette. Miles's understanding of the integrated elements of passion, fear, and opportunity in the scene suggests an appreciation of the visionary and artistic subtleties in the novella. Similarly, Turner's essay intelligently documents aspects of Lawrence's departure in the novella from nineteenth century and Victorian notions of narrative realism. But he never quite connects Lawrence's technique and assumptions to his radical redefinition of fictional *time* in the construction and thematics of the work. Turner, for instance, asks rhetorically—in reference to the various "enclosures" that entrap the Saywell sisters—"What are the thresholds to be crossed?" (150) While Turner incisively discusses how they "feel themselves locked up in their lives" (150), the larger issue, encompassed but not addressed by his question, must engage how Lawrence defiantly "crosses" the customary "threshold" of three dimensions to provide a salutary direction for Yvette's existential awakening and, ultimately, her escape.

17. The illustrious critic, the late M.H. Abrams, in a superb recent book about the significance and definition of "the fourth dimension" for a poem, describes that dimension as an awareness of "the physical aspect of language" (2). In the scene of the gipsy and Yvette exchanging dialogue before they almost enter the caravan—with all the stops, reiterations, pauses, and ellipses in the prose—Lawrence, in effect, is implementing Abrams's view of the fourth dimension as "enunciating the great variety of speech sounds" (2) that are intrinsic to the work in question. Abrams's emphasis is on how the fourth dimension both reflects and affects the sounds of reading aloud a *poem*; but the applicability of his insight to Lawrence's narrative prose is evident when Abrams adds that fiction, like "all art forms, has a physical medium, a material body, which conveys its nonmaterial meanings" (2).

XI

As Yvette becomes more attracted to the superficial charisma of Eastwood and Fawcett, she not surprisingly overrates their apparent freedom and exuberant energy. Compared to the anger and stringencies she endures at home, this agreeable couple represent to her an unforeseen species of rebellion and romance. The dream-effect of the gipsy soon begins to fade in his absence, a diminishment of his power over her that Lawrence presciently qualifies by asserting that he still lingers in "some hidden part of herself which she denied: that part which mysteriously and unconfessedly responded to him" (54). The essence of Lawrence's criticism of Fawcett and Eastwood consists of their inability to seriously engage the incarnate spirit of life: that is, they seem unable to believe in any notion of transcendence, for they are blithely involved in the earth-bound dimensions of Eastwood's love of leisure and Fawcett's fondness for material objects. They remain so eminently "modern", and so contentedly disconnected to the usual obligations of family and vocation. Lawrence displays the rare gift in a writer that can make a couple somehow appear charming but also boring and inconsequential. The attractive and intelligent Major can sense the special character of the gipsy but remains ignorant of the stagnant nature of his own existence: he embodies a profoundly un-Lawrencian and mechanical view of life with a too-confident query that directly connects to the theme of time in the novella: "Why shouldn't my future be continuous days and tomorrows?" (56)[18] He thus lacks the ability to get beyond his coddled ego and his accustomed habits of self-satisfaction. He also carries with him a trendy edge of irritation about the world that camouflages his spiritual emptiness, and Lawrence cannot resist the opportunity for an intrusive putdown within the context of a major metaphor in the novella: "His anger was of the soft snowy sort, which comfortably muffles the soul" (56).

Eastwood's contentment with the diurnal progress of time contrasts with Yvette's instinctual insight about the gipsy's rescue of the Major in the war. Eastwood believes the incident was occasioned "by accident", and

---

Thus, as a reader silently reads the respective scene in *The Virgin and the Gipsy*, the repetitive and fragmented sounds of the conversation echo in the mind to create the dream-ambience of the *material* scene that is crucial to the transformational significance of this auspicious meeting between the two characters.

18. In this regard, Turner has the Major just right: "He cannot turn his anger to creative account" (164). Ruderman is equally incisive on Mrs. Fawcett, seeing her as "a woman whose positive flouting of convention is countervailed by her cosmopolitanism and materialism (60–1).

Yvette disagrees, remarking that "it might be destiny" (58). In her affirmation of the provenance of a fated future—in Lawrencian terms, her belief in fourth-dimensional time and in Mailer's terms the faith in the "connection of new circuits" (375)—she has allied herself with the writer's emphatic vision that extolls the renewing power of temporal states to interrupt and defy normative chronology. Lawrence insists that it is unfortunately integral to modern life that time speeds forward through its repetitive patterns of events and experience. He conveys his indictment in *The Virgin and the Gipsy* in a manner that is integrated within the plot, metaphors, and doctrine of the work. When Yvette returns to her old life and the instinctual flow seems blocked again, she remains cut off from the gipsy except for that carefully worded and brief reminder of him quoted earlier. In the context of Lawrence's influence on Mailer, it is worth quoting once more, for it embodies the central concept of this work: "She did not forget the gipsy entirely. But she had no time for him…Time being only the current of the soul in its flow" (64). Thus, time here is configured as a "heated" and instinctual awareness perceived in and represented by the soul. When the soul remains isolate, hard, or cold (i.e., not in-flow, not "melting"), it is measured by the mechanical passage of hours that preclude the transcendent connection that Lawrence extols.

Yvette sees him briefly from the window when he comes again to the house "with things to sell" (64). Although they do not meet during this visit, their intense connection still exists, for "he knew she saw him" (64). She begins to ponder his appeal in more probing terms, and she realizes that "she liked that mysterious endurance in him, which endures in opposition, without any idea of victory" (64). His is the stance of a silent and inner confidence, of reliable intuition—an "opposition" that contrasts dramatically with the moral hypocrisy of her family and the self-congratulatory life of Eastwood and Fawcett. She also ponders the immature and capitulative view of marriage articulated by Lucille, as her sister argues that she is "not sure one shouldn't have one's fling till one is twenty-six, and then give in, and marry" (65). Yvette feels that in her life "the fling meant, at the moment, the gipsy" (65). On this possibility she cannot take the initiative, and he remains cautious about her vulnerable emotions and community standing. He will not seek her out.

The next time they meet is by accident (or destiny!) as she rides her bicycle and not-so-randomly encounters him with his cart. This brief encounter begins with some of the most quietly sensual lines Lawrence ever writes. Her observation is framed in slow-time to capture the details she enumerates:

> As she saw him, she loved him with curious tenderness the slim lines of his body, in the green jersey, the turn of his silent face. She felt she knew him better than she knew anybody on earth, even Lucille, and she belonged to him, in some way, for ever (65).

In two years, it could be Lady Chatterley watching Mellors—except Connie is no virgin and well knows the sexual capacities of men. But in this livid moment of Yvette's instinctual "knowing", the erotic elements are implied but still unknown to the inexperienced woman. Even for the gipsy, "the desire was still there, still curious and naked, in his eyes. But it was more remote, the boldness was diminished" (65). So, the novella again takes us to the proximity of sexual consummation, but it will always back off. As a form of fairy-tale, explicitness is not part of the genre. It waits for destiny to bring them together again.

The gipsy explains the woman's dream to Yvette, with its advice for her to trust the impulses of her heart and body, and to listen for "the voice of water" (66). As they part and he asks her if she will be "coming up to the Head" any more; her wistful and reiterated answer links directly to the time-bending element inherent in fortune-telling and to the realm of the fourth dimension in the novella: "'Perhaps I will', she said, 'some time. Some time.'" (66) The "time" is as appropriately unspecified as the lack of precise context for the gipsy woman's prediction about water. The image of Yvette just before the flood places her partly in the world of instinct and dream time, and partly in league with the world of the quasi-glamorous couple. The dichotomy functions as persuasive psychological realism that prepares for the more definitive and earth-shaking event to come: "She stayed in the garden by the river, half dreamy, expecting something…Her soul had the half painful, half easing knack of leaving her…Some days she was *all the time* in spirit with the Eastwoods" (67, 68 my emphasis).

It will take a natural calamity to let the flow run freely, and Lawrence organizes the conclusion of this work so that the "unleashing" of her soul will correspond with the breaking of the dam. It is important that in the moment before the flood, her divided soul has resolved itself as it more distinctly flows toward the gipsy: "For this afternoon, she felt intensely that *that* was home for her; the gipsy camp, the fire, the stool, the man with the hammer, the old crone" (68). Recall the disparate lists of objects and people subsumed within the stipulated parameters of Lawrence's description of the fourth dimension. Yvette is now primed for immersion into that dimension beyond conventional time; her instincts have already created a design that works for her, one that reveals "a recognition of the relation between various things, various elements in the creative flux" ("Art and Morality" 167). Yvette's awareness of the interrelationship now comes naturally to her—neither rehearsed or over-calculated. Lawrence's coordination of Yvette's insight, relevant doctrine, and plot development is impressive: "You can't *invent* a design. You recognize it, in the fourth dimension. That is, with your blood and your bones" ("Art and Morality" 167). She has established a species of renewal for herself, even before the climactic meeting with the gipsy, within the context of the Lawrencian ideology that organizes the novella.

XII

As the gipsy drags her to escape the tidal flow of water, the irony is that Yvette's soul now moves in synchrony with the flood: she "was barely conscious: as if the flood was in her soul" (69). Her desperate struggles up and down in the water recall "The Horse Dealer's Daughter", but in this novella the emphasis is less on Yvette's transformation than on a condition beyond the delineation of time: "With a ghastly sickness, like a dream, she struggled...Blind, unconscious of everything...in a state of un-consciousness...in blind unconscious frenzy" (71–72). Lawrence remains admirably consistent in his texturing of *The Virgin and the Gipsy* when he draws that diplomatic curtain between their attic nakedness and the voyeuristic urge to examine their intimate hours together. But there is no sex between them—it would be neither appropriate to their mood nor desired by them within the exigencies of warmth, rest, and survival. The fourth-dimensional sleep that they enter, as the flux of life literally swirls between them, is sufficient testament to the unity of Lawrence's vision and to the legitimacy of their nuanced attachment to each other.

Lawrence also wisely does not offer much "visualized" time about the hours in the attic, or any precise sense of the duration of the scene. Those elapsed and undefined hours of refuge have less to do with the clock-world of ego than with inchoate experience of infinite time and space described by Ouspensky. The discussion by Lawrence in "Morality and the Novel" of his attempt to capture personal vision in a painting is useful for understanding the lack of comment about the lovers' grateful sleep: "The vision on campus exists only in the much-debated fourth dimension. In dimensional space it has no existence" (171). The restrained and cadenced description of their passage into the uncharted arena of the fourth dimension further makes sense in Ouspensky's view that the dimension involves "a new concept of time...Flashes of cosmic consciousness. The idea and sometimes the sensation of a living universe. A striving for the wondrous sensation of infinity (Ouspensky 192–198, quoted in Young 35). Such a sensation, Lawrence knows, requires a special kind of prose to reproduce its properties. Here the endless coiling of clauses in a single remarkable sentence finally slows the frantic rhythm of their escape with intertwining metaphors leading to a shorter sentence and producing a total calm, ushering them into the timeless state that is the aesthetic heart and soul of the novella:

> And although his body, wrapped around her strange and lithe and powerful, like tentacles, rippled with shuddering as an electric current, still the rigid tension of the muscles that held her clenched steadied them both, and gradually the sickening violence of the shuddering caused by shock, abated in his body first, then in hers, and the warmth revived between them. And as it roused, their tortured, semi-conscious minds became unconscious, they passed away into sleep (74).

Until the last line of the novella the gipsy is properly nameless, less of a developed character than an emblematic force, an inscrutable violator of Yvette's routinized life and untouched soul. Whatever personalized element exists in *The Virgin and the Gipsy* is primarily restricted to those eccentric family members at the Saywell residence. As a strong but anonymous provider of the flame that forges a new consciousness in her, the gipsy's symbolic function is anticipated in Lawrence's essay, "The Novel":

> These wearisome sickening little personal novels. After all, they aren't novels at all. In every great novel who is the hero all the time? Not any of the characters, but some unnamed flame between them all…In the great novel, the felt but unknown flame stands behind all the characters, and in their word and gestures there is a flicker of the presence. If you are *too personal*, *too human*, the flicker fades out, leaving you with something awfully lifelike, and as lifeless as most people are (182).

The Mater, Lawrence's most graphically detailed character in the work lacks even a flicker of flame. The grotesque image of the drowned woman, "bob[bing] up, like a strange float, her face purple, her blind blue eyes bolting, spume hissing from her mouth" (71), first appears, in more generic form, also in "The Novel". With karmic precision that essay prepares for the lyrical arrangement in the novella of moving stream, bloated morbidity, and living connection. Perhaps Lawrence writes the fiction to dramatize the essential components of the doctrine—the resemblance is that close: "For the relatedness and interrelatedness of all things flows and changes and trembles like a stream, and like a fish in the stream the characters in the novel swim and drift and float and turn belly-up when they're dead" (185). Granny dies, in effect, inflated by ego, bluster, and water; she is "related" to no thing or person except through the beastly grasp of her petty power: "one old purple hand cleaved at a bannister rail" (71). Now the raging stream carries her away—a woman inert, discolored, and self-contained as a balloon.

A final word on the novella, on the contemporaneous essays, and their relevance to Lawrence's life. What of that presumed lack of sex between the willing virgin and the experienced gipsy in that private attic haven? Even accepting the imperative for survival that prevails over the temptation of eros, and even granting the elemental symbolic function of the gipsy's persona, it is difficult to be convinced about the self-discipline of their chaste interlude between deluge and daylight. Such intimate proximity, such confirmed desire, such passionate potential! Might Lawrence, in the interest of his readers' need for verisimilitude and amorous conclusion, offer them a more torrid performance? For the impotent writer in 1926, a man returning to the craft of fiction but unready to write his magnum-phallic-opus, *Lady Chatterley's Lover*, a man past the *cul de sac* of *The Plumed Serpent* but not yet convinced of a new visionary direction—for this recuperating and committed man, compromised lover, and embattled artist, is it not understandable for him to insist that a sensual and intimate closeness can rival the penetrating heat of lust?

> Sex is flame, too, the novel announces. Flame burning against every absolute, even against the phallic. For sex is so much more than phallic and so much deeper than functional desire. The flame of sex singes your absolute and cruelly scorches your ego ("The Novel" 181).

In "The Novel and the Feelings", a *renewed* Lawrence urges a yielding to the innermost "honourable beasts that call in the dark paths of the veins of our body" (205). Joe Boswell and his creator are mature enough to understand that sex is so much more than phallic. In letting Yvette sleep they have set her free to grow. The beast here is truly honourable, and Yvette Saywell has been scorched.[19]

---

19. Critics are all over the place on the question of the success and significance of the final scene. Widmer oddly asserts that the novella "got surprisingly vague with the tabooed bedding-down scene" (197)—but any explicit passion would have been the real surprise given the development of the work. Siegel argues that we are left with Yvette as a woman who "cannot survive without her admirer" (11), as the critic insufficiently recognizes the strength and independence Yvette has achieved. Turner is excellent in his recognition that "the great climax to *The Virgin and the Gipsy* is not the physical but the spiritual embrace of that which had been taboo" (156). Ruderman hedges her bets: "Whether the rescue by the Gypsy marks a permanent change in Yvette's life is an open question" (132), and Cushman dismisses its credibility entirely, calling it "a fairy-tale ending" (167).

II.

Some Origins from the 1990's: The Early Thematics of Renewal and Transcendence

CHAPTER EIGHT

FROM *LADY CHATTERLEY'S LOVER* TO *THE DEER PARK*: MARRIAGE, RENEWAL, AND THE DIALECTIC OF EROTIC RISK

A man has to fend and fettle for the best, and then trust in something beyond himself.

—D.H. Lawrence, *Lady Chatterley's Lover*

Poor memory is so indispensable to passionate lovers.

—Norman Mailer, *The Deer Park*

I shall put forward the view that psychical impotence is much more widespread than supposed.

—Sigmund Freud,
"On the Universal Tendency to Debasement in the Sphere of Love"

I

The acumen of Norman Mailer's spirited defense in *The Prisoner of Sex* of D.H. Lawrence's life, art, and vision should come as no surprise to those who follow the open book and embattled advocacies of Mailer's personal and intellectual history. The initial publication of that polemical work appeared as the sole content of *Harper's* in May 1971, and the ensuing controversy over its explicit language and masculinist perspectives ultimately led to the cowardly dismissal of the journal's talented and innovative editor, Willie Morris, and soon to the resignation, in impressive support of Morris and the mandates of artistic expression, of several equally talented writers and senior staff members. Mailer's empathetic and admiring preoccupation with Lawrence long precedes his capstone discussion of him in *The Prisoner of Sex*. In several interviews, essays, and letters prior to that embattled volume of catharsis, prophecy, and criticism, he generously acknowledges the seminal influence of Lawrence on both himself and the socio-cultural climate of the twentieth century.

Mailer's intensely Manichean novels—through their familiar litany of concern with ego, sex, inhibitive society, and modern conformity—appear like a karmic reformulation of Lawrence's most prominent doctrines. As he observes in *The Prisoner of Sex*, and as his prolific career variously insists until his passing in 2007, it is a vastly transformed world since Lawrence's death in 1930, "technologized and technologized twice again" (151). Such radical transformation of society is reflected in the conjoined visions, yet dissimilar tapestries and textures of art in the two writers. The sprawling urban environments and political agendas of much of Mailer's fiction and his "new journalism" contrast (and also coalesce) with that integration of biblical intensity and pastoral landscape so predominant in Lawrence's work. Mailer's modern hell, teeming with cancer, plastic, and cowardice, and Lawrence's lost utopia, rife with personal betrayal, entrenched repression, and the destructive "censor-moron" (*Letters VI* 613), also suggest the disparity between Mailer's metafictional coverage of a contemporary event and Lawrence's angry indictment of mankind's misguided goals and mechanized habits of living.

It is the genre of the novel that they both outspokenly regard as most conducive to the sexual aesthetics, conflicted marriages, and rampant infidelities that infiltrate the subject matter of their writing—and ultimately the substance of their lives. Mailer's praise of the intrinsic power of fiction insists, in recognizably Lawrencian terms, on an intimate relation between the metaphysics of a novel and the novelist's obligation to emphasize that philosophy within the respective work, and even at the risk of awkward narrative intrusion. In this regard, he argues that "the novel at its best is the most moral of the art forms, because it's the most immediate, the most overbearing, if you will" (*Advertisements* 384). Such a superlative declaration manages to integrate notions of an ethical imperative ("most moral"), uncensored honesty ("most overbearing"), and instinctual judgment ("most immediate"). This sweeping affirmation precisely recapitulates the tone and imagery of Lawrence's more celebrated statement of genre preference in "Why the Novel Matters", and in chapter nine of *Lady Chatterley's Lover*. In the essay, Lawrence employs a series of organic metaphors to assert that the novel's special quality "can make the whole man tremble" as it depicts "the whole hog" of "man alive" (195); in *Lady Chatterley's Lover* he further highlights the intimate and revelatory potential within any extended work of fiction: "Therefore the novel, properly handled, can reveal the most secret places of life" (101).[1] That daring prehensile image, in effect, connects to the focus on physical touch between Connie and Mellors, and it also emphasizes the special irony and urgency implicit in Lawrence's abiding preoccupation with his markedly different version of "propriety": the eminently proper goal to eliminate what he describes in "Pornography and Obscenity" as the "dirty little secret" of sex (243)—that is, to openly oppose the extremes both of Victorian prudery and postwar decadence.

Mailer further privileges the intrinsic power of the novel with analogous Lawrencian terminology. He describes the subject of sex as "the last remaining frontier of the novel which has not been exhausted by the nineteenth and early twentieth century novelists" (*Advertisements* 270). His praise of that genre and his belief in the doctrinal responsibility of art cohere in an assertion that also remains at the livid center of Lawrence's own vision: "The final purpose of art is to intensify, even, if necessary, to exacerbate, the moral consciousness of people" (*Advertisements* 384). Such definitive phrasing by Mailer echoes the amplitude and conviction of Lawrence's well-known assertions that "even art is utterly dependent on philosophy" (*Fantasia* 65) and "every work of art adheres to some system of morality" (*Study of Hardy* 89). His direct influence on Mailer even extends beyond such notions about the special status of the novel. From early in his career he admits to a more precise debt than the tone of moral fervor or the imperative for prophetic insight emanating from Lawrence's works. Mailer's prominent sexual aesthetic—that active dialectic of risk, openendedness, and growth dramatized most graphically in such fiction as *The Deer Park*, "The Time of Her Time", *An American Dream*, and *The Castle in the Forest*—reflects his essential recognition that Lawrence's insistence on instinctual primacy remains the bedrock faith from which all discussion of the novelist from the Midlands must begin. Mailer further maintains that Lawrence's visionary insistence to get beyond the self in the act of love paradoxically includes the demand to stay in close, sensuous touch with the very self that is to be transcended. In this counterintuitive synthesis of the existential and transcendent (virtually a sexually energized form of Thoreauvian and Emersonian ethics), Mailer absorbs Lawrence's dictum that the true test of personal courage is the willingness to abandon the accustomed props of self-definition in favor of a Truth that resides beyond the protected confines of the Freudian ego.[2] In

1. See Chapter Five of my book, *D.H. Lawrence and the Phallic Imagination*, for a more in-depth discussion of the relevance of this seminal quotation to issues of form and meaning in this novel.

2. The considerable skill of Emerson and Thoreau at lyrically "reading" the promptings of the inner self remains integral to both their transcendental doctrines

the simple terms of a characterological equation, both writers affirm an essential belief that resonates as an uncompromising mandate: reliance on unfettered instinct can lead to displays of courage, further leading to personal growth and change—and such a pattern of *renewal* can lead to *transcendence*.

Amid the waves of cynicism and disillusion that permeate culture after the devastation of The Great War, Lawrence is prominent among those artists who adhere to a vision of the transformative power of the self; for him this intrinsic potential exists through the guidance of emotional and sexual impulses that he defines in "Introduction to These Paintings" as the realm of "instinctive-intuitive" awareness (186). Lawrence firmly believes that our modernist reliance on mentalized rather than instinctual prompting offers merely a culturally conditioned, and often unhealthy, blueprint for

---

and the uncompromising conduct of their lives. In this regard, Mailer's meticulous and comprehensive biographer, J. Michael Lennon, quotes from a journal that Mailer kept during and after the writing of *The Deer Park* in the mid-1950s. The entry reveals the novelist's guiding awareness of the importance for him of a synergistic interrelation among instinctual primacy, negative capability, and accumulated experience in the world-at-large. Here are the pertinent comments by Lennon followed by the Mailer passage from the journal: "Toward the end of the journal, Mailer reflects on several of his salient mental faculties, which, as they developed, resembled Emerson's":

My capacity to do something exceptional comes from the peculiar combination of powerful instincts face to face with my exceptional detachment. I am one of the few people I know who can feel a genuinely powerful emotion and yet be able to observe it…Instead of poring (pouring) over all the relevant books, and there are five hundred I "ought" to start studying tomorrow, I do better to "waste" time and discover things for myself (Lennon 190–1).

The passage contains a distinct echo of Emerson's "books are for the scholars' idle times" ("American Scholar" 68), as well as Thoreau's rhetorical fire: "What is a course of history, or philosophy, or poetry, no matter how well selected, or the best society, or the most admirable routine of life, compared with the discipline of looking always at what is to be seen?" (*Walden* 101) Lawrence, of course, writes brilliantly about the great nineteenth century American writers in his innovative study, *Studies in Classic American Literature*. It is not widely known that his original outline for that volume included a long section on Emerson's essays (see *Letters III* 66). While Lawrence apparently never drafted that chapter, he surely would empathize with the adamance of the perspective enunciated early in "The American Scholar," with its missionary denigration of the limits of book knowledge and its celebration of an immanence that is recognizably Lawrencian: "The first in time, and the first in importance of the influences upon the mind is that of nature. Every day, the sun; and, after sunset, night and her stars…The scholar is he of all men whom this spectacle most engages" (65).

action and/or restraint, for throughout one's life and—here is the crux of his credo—"the thought-adventure starts in the blood, not in the mind" ("On Being a Man" 214). His focus on blood-consciousness, on the inner truths conveyed by spontaneous reactions, along with his penchant for the uncircumscribed implication of the term "adventure"—all this will prove useful in my later consideration of the correlative notions of risk and growth. But for now it is important to note that Mailer begins to derive his own brand of existentialism, inherited in part from various elements in the work of Lawrence and Hemingway, in his novel *The Deer Park* (1955) and—in more volatile and theoretic fashion—in his controversial essay, "The White Negro" (1957). While the latter work notoriously expands on concepts of violence that Lawrence would not admire, the direction of Mailer's remarks clearly is derived from Lawrence's doctrines about instinctual motivation and repressive society. In the preliminary pages of that essay Mailer asserts, in what he approvingly describes as Hemingway's guiding dictum "that what made him feel good became therefore The Good", a list of formative influences on his own developing philosophy: "the intellectual antecedents of this generation can be traced to such separate influences as D.H. Lawrence, Henry Miller, and Wilhelm Reich" (*Advertisements* 340). In the years following "The White Negro", Mailer increasingly clarifies Lawrence's legacy to him, as he expands on issues of risk and courage that intersect, in different ways, with relevant preoccupations in the work of Ernest Hemingway.[3]

II

In D.H. Lawrence's short but trenchant review of Hemingway's first major book, *In Our Time* (1925), he praises the young and relatively unknown writer for his precocious talent in persuasively depicting an elusive quality in fiction: "It is really honest. And it explains a great deal of sentimentality. When a thing has gone to hell inside you, your sentimentalism tries to pretend it hasn't. But Mr. Hemingway is through with the sentimentalism" (*Introductions* 312). Just a year after that auspicious collection of short stories, Hemingway publishes *The Sun Also Rises*, a novel in which the narrator, Jake Barnes, attempts to cope with his war-trauma of impotence through a stringently unsentimental view of the world; a few years later, in a cathartic story entitled "Fathers and Sons",

---

3. I analyze more fully a range of interweaving issues about doctrine and influence concerning these three writers in my essay on *A Farewell to Arms* and in Chapter Five of *The Phallic Imagination.*

Hemingway uses the (by then) transparently bio-fictive Adams family to openly indict his own father for hiding from the realities of life by cowardly displaying the same flaw in character that the writer-son cannot forgive. The sentimentalist's profoundly warped view of life leaves him open to poisonous regret and inevitable mistreatment by others: "he was sentimental, and, like most sentimental people, he was both cruel and abused. All sentimental people are betrayed so many times" (*Complete Short Stories* 370). It is not surprising that Lawrence remains sensitive to this adamant strain about the ravages of self-induced frustration in Hemingway's credo. He displays an emphasis throughout his work on many of the same issues that Mailer absorbs from Hemingway and that Mailer further acknowledges as a major component of Lawrencian ideology in the *Prisoner of Sex*: the integrated themes of personal courage in modern society and an individual's willingness to embrace change and undertake risk in order to avoid the peril of stasis in erotic relations. In this sense, the "sentimental" failure of people to adhere to forms of instinctual primacy, amounting to an aversion at all costs not to endanger their social and/or professional standing—such themes motivate Lawrence's writing as he takes a valedictory look at the embattled courage and accumulated wounds of his own life and begins to write *Lady Chatterley's Lover*. Lines from his essay, "Apropos of *Lady Chatterley's Lover*", declare his own kinship, in effect, with the thrust of Hemingway's early fiction, as Lawrence defends the urgency of his own most controversial novel by reiterating an important epithet: "Never was an age more sentimental, more devoid of real feeling, more exaggerated in false feeling, than our own. Sentimentality and counterfeit feeling have become a sort of game, everybody trying to outdo his neighbor" (*Lady Chatterley's Lover* 312).

In *Cannibals and Christians* (1966), Mailer reprints a 1963 interview that more precisely connects his developing dialectic to a psychosexual attitude that requires the special kind of honesty he gratefully absorbs from the British novelist: "I learned from Lawrence that the way to write about sex was not to strike poses, but be true to the logic of each moment. There's a subtle logic to love" (197). His emphasis on "logic" conveys an interesting clue to the paradoxical insight about erotic passion that he derives from Lawrence. It embodies a powerful motivation that is emotional rather than rational, for it relies on the guidance of instinct and the related messages relayed by the five senses. Such a fiercely existential basis for love—or for *any* intensely committed action—is further confirmed and augmented by the accumulated life-experience of the individual.[4] This tripartite nexus of instinct-sense perception-experience provides Lawrence, Hemingway, and Mailer with a more confident Truth than is supplied by formal education or popular societal trend. Thus the "logic to love" cannot be rehearsed or preformulated and it often will supply revelations in subtle, even inscrutable ways, as if absorbed from the recesses of one's soul. The direction of depicted passion in the work of the two writers is characteristically spontaneous and unpredictable; the tenor of a scene depends on the transitions of mood in characters that result in moments of sexual exchange that are searing and unorthodox. The drama emerges without a blueprint.

Even a minor scene of seduction in Mailer's *The Deer Park* illustrates the dialectic of erotic risk, and with a serio-comic touch that enhances the sense of unrehearsed libido unleashed by the lovers. It occurs in the torrid yet awkward vignette that plays out amid the frustrating twists and turns in the car seats during the initial sexual encounter between the voluptuous and available movie star, Lulu Meyers, and the occasionally impotent and—in Mailer's coded term—"adventuring" Korean War veteran, Sergius O'Shaugnhessy. Lulu's neurotic fears and coquettish restraint at first foil his adolescent aggressiveness and priapic urgency; given his recent history of sexual problems, his understandable anxiety about erectile function makes any delay in his desire a possible inhibitor of his performance. But the scene provides an unanticipated conclusion, with its own persuasive rationale only after the chances for success diminish with the greater likelihood of Sergius's anguished failure. When he finally feels exhausted and resigned by the coy adamance of her refusals, she suddenly and gently caters to his needs as she rouses Sergius and helps them make love. The transitions in this intense encounter are unpredictable and intense, and they all make perfect sense in the context of Mailer's notion of erotic risk: in an ad-libbed strategy that combines instinct and guile, Lulu must reconnoiter the tenor of foreplay and devise her own scenario of control and encouragement before she will yield. As a much-pursued siren in Hollywood, she well knows the terrain of falsity and manipulation that often precedes courtship and submission. In this scene, her inimitably charming and ingenious "logic" is to discover, fresh for herself, that "feel good" temperature and posture for sex. To Lulu's generous praise that he is a "wonderful lover", he correctly answers that he's "just an amateur"

---

4. In an interview in France in 1999, during which Mailer ruminates on aspects of his doctrinal perspectives during the 1950s and 1960s, he sounds much like a committed advocate of Lawrence's notions about the wisdom of blood-consciousness: "Let's get back to the instinctive life. Let's get back to where we can feel what's going on in ourselves" (Lennon 274).

(95)—his acknowledgement, no doubt, of the lesson in patient passion he has learned from her in the sedan's front seat. It is the resonant texture of creative surprise that defines it as a Mailer sex scene, sprightly influenced by Lawrencian notions of spontaneity and the "subtle logic to love".[5]

The developing dialectic of erotic risk in the above encounter—as the exchange transitions through moments of lust, fear, courage, and resolution—recalls an anecdote Mailer relates about Marilyn Monroe (surely an iconic version of Lulu Meyers) and the existential element in any sexual episode. It concerns an incident that Lawrence would understand in the light of his emphasis on the self-defining and inchoate territory intrinsic to the act of love: "Once after going to bed with Marlon Brando, she said next morning to Milton Green, 'I don't know if I do it the right way', but then which of us does know?...Sooner or later we all reveal our innocence about sex in a candid remark" (*Marilyn* 75). Thus Mailer's phrase, the "subtle logic to love", comprises an appropriate oxymoron in which the heart, not the mind, creates and directs the sexual impulse. That terminology provides a provocative echo of Lawrence's comparable formulation, the "logic of the soul", a term that he uses decades earlier in *The Rainbow* (1915); it occurs as Lawrence poignantly describes the aura of otherness of Lydia Lensky, who entrances Tom Brangwen from the moment of their first meeting. Tom's need to formally propose marriage to this inscrutable woman functions as an example of erotic risk that embodies a species of courage in this young and relatively isolated man. His earlier intimate experiences with women were limited to unsatisfactory episodes that disillusioned him and frustrated his "innate desire to find in a woman the embodiment of all his inarticulate, powerful religious impulses" (21). In the scene in which the phrase "logic of the soul" appears, Tom abandons—as a graphic instance of that transcendent faith in the "unknown"—the rational and incremental steps of an ordered courtship. He has scarcely met this older, divorced, foreign, and reticent mother, a woman who—by dint of that precise litany of qualities—formidably radiates an "otherness" to Tom on multiple and profound levels. He feels this compelling need for her in his blood, and he abruptly

5. Lennon's impressive research discovers that Lois Mayfield Wilson, "a blond graduate student whom [Mailer] met at a party", was the likely model, not for Lulu, but for the bodily gyrations in the car: "She recalled that she left the party with him, and they had an erotic wrestling match in the car, which became the basis for Sergius O'Shaugnessy's tussle with Lulu Meyers in *The Deer Park*" (Lennon 118). Another example, it would seem, of Mailer using primary experience—in which he "discovers things for [him]self"—as the material for a zany and sensual episode in his fiction.

leaves his farm on the strength of that feeling: "It's got to be done, so why baulk it?" (41). As he resolves to propose to her, Lawrence is superb at establishing a line of motivation in him that remains concrete and abstract at the same time—the synthesis that creates the fourth-dimensional prose he initiates at this stage in his career: "There was an inner reality, a logic of the soul, which connected her with him" (40).[6]

Lawrence's visionary doctrines include a correlative notion that integrates his transcendental doctrines with a bedrock conservatism concerning an essential tradition of modern society: his belief that a man's instinctual need for the unknown, embodied in that otherness of a woman, must receive its apotheosis in the "risky" undertaking of the volatile state of marriage. Such a heterodox integration of instinctual primacy with the most basic social contract anticipates Mailer's blended designation of his own ideology in *The Armies of the Night* as "Left Conservative" (124); that hybrid term suggests his view of gender relations, which seeks to combine an existential eroticism with the drive to engage and maintain the institution of marriage.[7] Mailer's prolific output lacks the range and frequency of primal urgencies that dominate Lawrence's works. For

6. Occasionally Mailer's attraction to dominant Lawrencian notions about love, sex, and marriage is evident in surprising, almost karmic ways. Before he marries Norris, who would become his sixth and final wife, Lennon recounts that during the passionate months of their developing relationship, "Mailer recommended that Norris...read D.H. Lawrence's *The Rainbow* with its frank examination of sexual relationships. His vision of the love he hoped to achieve with her owed something to the dynamics of Lawrence's" (Lennon 480).

7. Although Lennon surely is correct (see note 6) about the controversial "frankness" he confirms in *The Rainbow* (copies would be confiscated and destroyed by way of the draconian and obscure Obscene Publication Act of 1857), Lawrence frames the erotic content of that novel with an undisguised celebration of the transcendent power and value of marriage. Indeed, it is that intimate depiction in the novel of varieties of sexual passion *within* the context of marital life that appears to have most upset the censors. See Chapter Two of *The Phallic Imagination* for more on the thematic and stylistic treatment of this prothalamic doctrine in *The Rainbow*. Note also Mailer's acknowledgement, in an interview in *The Paris Review* shortly before his death, of the centrality *and* the challenge represented in marriage: "Every wife is a culture, and you enter deep into another culture, one that's not your own, and you learn an awful lot from it. And given the fact that marriage is not always a comfortable institution, you chafe in that culture" (75). Mailer also distinguishes between mere cohabitation and the special aura of marriage. It is a distinction by him that meshes with Lawrence's insistence on the visionary texture of legalized union: "First there's living together, it's often thought equal to marriage. Not by half. You can live with a woman and never begin to comprehend her at all, not until you get married to her" (Lennon 595).

example, Tom Brangwen's yielding to the logic of his soul reflects the same intense command of blood-consciousness that urges Ursula to annihilate Skrebensky under the moon ("not on any side did he lead into the unknown" 439), or which spurs her mother, Anna, to dance naked before Will as an annulment of her defaulting husband (she "danced before the unknown" 169).[8] Often, the urge does not directly encompass the unknown, or even the integrating theme of marriage; instead, the spontaneous mandate involves entanglements with the opposite sex that are risky, open-ended, and even exclude any notion of committed love. While Mailer's intention is to courageously "encounter" the state of marriage in his fiction and life, his six wives suggest that he reserves the freedom to leave when he so chooses.

The shape and texture of instinctual responses in Lawrence's fiction remain as varied as the idiosyncratic emotions of the characters themselves. His creative imagination conjures up scenarios that demonstrate the powerful force of mandates from the soul. In the following examples—all gleaned from works discussed in greater depth in earlier chapters from this volume—there is no equivocation about the need for the specified action. It is the existential imperative that rules here—Mailer's version of "if it feels good it is good"—and it is irrelevant if the end-result proves not good at all for the respective individual. Characters seem captured by forces both within and beyond them; the pattern is conveyed as part of the inimitable texture of Lawrence's fourth-dimensional prose, as it probes "really a stratum deeper" (*Letters i* 526) into the uncharted domain of blood-motivation. The dominant instigation is never defined—but it is strongly felt: the Princess feels that she *must* continue the trip into the mountains with Romero, and that she *must* invite him into her bed to warm her frightened body and soul; Yvette *must* meet the gipsy at the door when he peddles his wares, and she *must* visit him at his camp; Daphne *must* visit the Count at the hospital, and she *must* come to his darkened room at the house; Captain Hepburn *must* climb up to the Karlinger Glacier, and he *must* attempt to negotiate the dangerous ice face; Ciccio *must* depart from

8. Mailer even shares Lawrence's numinous obsessions about moon power. In *Of a Fire on the Moon*, he writes about his fourth wife, whom he "had met on a night when the moon was full". Mailer continues: "She was extraordinarily sensitive to its effect; she was at best uneasy and at worst unreachable when the moon was full. Through the years of their marriage Aquarius had felt the fullness of the moon in his own dread, his intimations of what full criminality he might possess, had felt the moon in the cowardice not to go out on certain nights, felt the moon when it was high and full and he was occasionally on the side of the brave" (Lennon 420–1, *Of A Fire* 436–7).

his scripted role in the playlet, and he *must* take Alvina back to his native village; Lou Carrington *must* rescue the stallion, and she *must* commit herself to a solitary and strenuous life in the cabin above Taos. Henry Grenfel *must* shoot the fox and *must* capture March as his wife. In effect, all these sequences of urgencies provide no possibilities of alternative action or response. The reader feels their inevitability as intensely as the characters enact their fate.

While the force of blood-consciousness remains both immediate and relentless in the above cases, it is not instinct alone that influences the "logic of the soul". Recall the challenge so intrinsic to Lawrencian doctrine: a character's faith in the "beyond" must be sufficiently strong to transcend the security and strength that the ego generally provides. In Lawrence's fictional world, such transcendence—often carrying a religious tone of ritualistic communion—can be initiated by a powerful natural object, force, or landscape, such as moon, mountain, sun, tree, flame, and animal. Mailer also is especially sympathetic to the commanding presence of irrational inclinations and irresistible objects and desires. Throughout his novels, characters enact their passion with a perverse abandon their head and nerves cannot comprehend or ratify, but which their heart and courage insist is the only recourse. One thinks most graphically here of the obsessed walk on the parapet that Rojack takes in *An American Dream*, and—two decades later—the analogous climb up the needle that Madden must endure in *Tough Guys Don't Dance*, and—also two decades later—the compulsive need for perilous rock climbing mandated at the start of *Harlot's Ghost*. Such scenes of enrapture and taboo-violation are different in degree but not in kind from the frenetic sex in the rain between Connie and Mellors, or their ritualized benediction of genital decoration with flowers. Their actions emanate from the guiding logic of their souls. They intensely feel what is right for them.

III

For a comparative portrayal in Lawrence's writings of ego-dominated "poses" that Mailer insists comprise a crucial influence on his own depiction of sexual tensions, the examples are numerous and graphic: the evasive gamesmanship of Michaelis in his affair with Connie; Birkin's decadent diversions with Hermione and her willful demands on him; Skrebensky's pompous affectations with Ursula and her belabored devastation of his inadequate being; Paul's increasingly bored sex with Clara, and his prolonged tolerance of Miriam's stifling nullity; Rico's effete prancing on the stallion in London, and his immature flirtations with the Mamby girls; Phoenix's macho posturing with Lou, and the childish assumptions about his suitability for marriage to Yvette by her local suitor; Daphne's obscene infatuation with the seductive count. What Mailer, in effect, absorbs from Lawrence's fiction is how a novelist can portray, with variety and insight, society's entrenched habits of cheap sex, manipulative passion, and aggressive posturing. *The Deer Park* reveals, through the wide-angle lens that frames a movie community, how poses become *de rigueur* in this artificial environment because of their easy utility and wide acceptance in personal and community relations. No one talks about the game-playing because everyone takes part in the charade. The litany of poses creates liaisons at the lowest level of erotic risk, offering narcissistic sex that superficially enhances career confidence in its tawdry catering to self-image and silly notions of romantic conquest. Thus characters in Mailer's work often desire what Lawrence in *Lady Chatterley's Lover* (and in his related essays) calls mere sensation. Lawrence angrily insists—with the Bloomsbury circle of promiscuous egotists no doubt on his mind—that most sexual affairs amount to masturbatory gymnastics, and he primarily blames men for the prevalence of this narcissism: "It is the hardest thing in life to get one's soul and body satisfied from a woman, so that one is free from oneself" (*Letters II* 115). Without the ability to achieve this freedom-through-transcendence, men are incapable of taking that crucial step within the dialectic of erotic risk: "Today men don't risk their blood and bone. They go forth, panoplied in their own idea of themselves" ("On Being a Man" 217). Lawrence directly describes his insistence on a necessary linkage in men between sexual energy and the encompassing cycles of time and nature. He defines the "real sex in a man" as one that "has the rhythm of the seasons and the years" (*Apropos* 318).

Mailer's discussion of Lawrence in *The Prisoner of Sex*, and his forays into psychosexual speculations about the volatile marriage to Frieda, center on a precise and unadorned formulation of the essential credo evident throughout the earlier novelist's life and work. Forty years after Lawrence's death, a single sentence by Mailer captures the basic theme with an inimitable mixture of the lyrical and the vernacular: "He believed nothing human had such significance as the tender majesties of a man and a woman fucking with love" (*Prisoner* 134–5). That lingering qualifier, "with love", correctly suggests the one element that infiltrates all the phrases of Lawrence's career, from *The Wintry Peacock* through *Lady Chatterley's Lover*. But it is only by the time of his last novel that he has abandoned the earlier stages of belief in utopia and leadership to formulate the doctrine that Mailer recognizes as the touchstone of Lawrence's existence as man and artist. Here are Oliver Mellors' unequivocal and unadorned words, refracted courageously from the humane and experienced perspective of the impotent and dying writer who created him: "Yes, I do believe in something. I believe in being warm-hearted. I believe especially in being warm-hearted in love, in fucking with a warm heart. I believe if men could fuck with warm hearts, and the women take it warm-heartedly, everything would come all right. It's all this cold-hearted fucking that is death and idiocy" (206). Although Lawrence considers men, with their characteristic tendency for ego-driven sex, as primarily responsible for such lack of warmth, he does not exempt women from his censure. At one point Connie consciously tries to suppress her passion for Mellors, as the scars from her experiences with Michaelis and Clifford prevent her from yielding: "She resisted it as far as she could, for it was the loss of herself to herself" (135).

Mailer's memorable rumination on both the urgency and authenticity of sex in Lawrence's fiction—replete with Hemingwayesque metaphors of military engagement, risk-taking, and mortal stakes—functions as the most trenchant explanation of why sex-with-love remains the ultimate and elusive goal in the work of Lawrence and Mailer.

> Lawrence's point, which he refines over and over, is that the deepest messages of sex cannot be heard by taking a stance on the side of the bank, announcing one is in love, and then proceeding to fish in the waters of love with a breadbasket full of ego. No, he is saying again and again, people can win at love only when they are ready to lose everything they bring to it of ego, position, or identity—love is more stern than war—and men and women can survive only if they reach the depth of their own sex down within themselves. They have to deliver themselves "over to the unknown". No more existential statement of love exists, for it is a way of saying we do not know how the love will turn out. (*The Prisoner of Sex* 147–8)

Such an existential reading of Lawrence's sexual ethics, which Mailer, in effect, defines (as above) as an organic synthesis of central notions variously configured in Hemingway and Thoreau, must be viewed through the perspective of Mailer's own advocacy of risk and open-endedness in the conduct of one's life. His brief discussion in *The Prisoner of Sex* of the spirited conflict between Ursula and Birkin about marriage and love, properly stresses how and why Birkin's proposal to her avoids a neo-platonic relationship that inevitably would be tied to the cloying habits of vanity and narcissism. While both writers extol the institution of marriage and acknowledge the challenges it presents, they also remain leery of any extended erotic affair that is built on sex-without-love. But an obvious problem remains engrained in this very perspective: How does such a conservative impulse that celebrates marriage reconcile with the abundant evidence of Mailer's serial adultery, with Mailer's litany of marriages, with Lawrence's intimacy with Rosalind Baynes and Dorothy Brett, and with Lawrence's tolerance of Frieda's infidelities? There are possible answers to all such understandable queries, however inadequate they may be to fully explain the gaps between doctrine and behavior. An excellent and recent biography of Mailer by Michael Lennon anatomizes the "double life" of the late writer, and the work describes with abundant detail how Mailer attempts to compartmentalize (in the European manner) his hectic sex life in and out of marriage.[9] As for the essentially monogamous Lawrence, he understands—from the start of his connection to Frieda—the perils of attachment to this headstrong and sexually liberated woman; there remains little doubt that he supremely valued her and their embattled marriage despite her pattern of cheating.[10] In addition, Lawrence's one-night affair with Rosalind occurs during a period of great frustration with his wife, and the warmth and understanding he received

---

9. Lennon's analysis of Mailer's motivations smartly combines several explanations for his pattern of adultery, and he may understate the powerful effect of a paternal example during Mailer's formative years: "A few months before his death, he told his biographer, 'When in doubt about my motivation, *cherchez la femme*'. Barney's double life gave Mailer a model and even sanction for his own. His infidelities were numerous, but they were not motivated solely, or even mainly, by his desire for sex, although it was always strong. His thrust for new experience was the final cause of his duplicities. If risk was involved, so much the better; it added sauce" (Lennon 124).

10. See David Ellis's poignant discussion of Lawrence's alleged comment to Frieda in 1925 in Oaxaca when he was deathly ill: "'If I die, [Frieda] reports Lawrence as saying, 'nothing has mattered but you, nothing at all'" (*Death and the Author* 34–5). Ellis persuasively suggests that Frieda's recollection of the comment sounds credible. Certainly Lawrence, by the end of his life in 1930, knew about (or suspected) Frieda's intimacies *at least* with Hobson, Murry, and Ravagli, and perhaps with Gray and D'Allura; his assertion in 1925 to Frieda (and perhaps a comparable one on his deathbed) of the absolute primacy of his wife in his own journey through life indicates the extent of his need for her and his commitment to their rocky but enduring marriage. Although he ponders leaving Frieda several times, his sense of the marriage's importance to him is acutely related to his *felt* perception of the animate universe that he evokes (and celebrates) in his fiction. To end their union would, for him, signal a retreat from his belief in the connection of their marriage to the unknown infinitudes that define and nourish him as a man: "Marriage is the clue to human life, but there is no marriage apart from the wheeling sun and the nodding earth, from the straying of the planets and the magnificence of the fixed stars" (*Apropos* 323).

from this younger woman briefly satisfied needs in him that Frieda could not—or would not—meet at the time.[11]

It is true that sex-without-love often is depicted as passionate and satisfying in the work of both writers, but they share a measured "caution" about such affairs: unless the lust develops into the complexity and challenge of committed love, these prophetic artists invariably document the corrosive nature of the respective relationship. They disapprove not for puritanical reasons, of course, but because of the greater tendency of liaisons outside of marriage failing to transcend over to "the unknown", as they often remain mired in petty competitions for power and prominence. Surely the same flaws and pitfalls exist in marriage, but in Mailer's demanding dialectic the existential states of failure and success are energized by the formal authority of the union. Put simply, there is more to lose, more guilt to assume in failure, and thus more "edginess" and self-definition to appropriate when the marriage succeeds. Perhaps Mailer best describes the stakes implicit in this appropriation in an oft-quoted passage from *The Armies of the Night*: "For guilt was the existential edge of sex. Without guilt, sex was meaningless. One advanced into sex against one's sense of guilt, and each time guilt was successfully defied, one had learned a little more about the contractual relation of one's own existence to the unheard thunders of the deep" (24). Now add on to this self-defining dimension of committed obligation the legal contract of marriage, and Mailer's thunder roars even louder as he defiantly moves from wife to wife.

In the context of unmarried lovers failing to achieve the link to the unknown, recall Skrebensky and Ursula in *The Rainbow*, as she virtually bypasses her inadequate lover to commune with the stars. She reaches for the transcendent by reducing him to the level of convenient gigolo: "He served her. She took him, she clasped him, clenched him close, but her eyes were open looking at the stars, it was as if the stars were lying with her and entering the unfathomable darkness of her womb, fathoming her at last. It was not him" (430–1). Denise and Sergius commit themselves to a similar form of masturbatory passion in Mailer's "The Time of Her Time", when his superficial victory as a sexual athlete is undercut by a neurotic lover who punctures his bravado with a witty and unanswerable final riposte. In a published letter, Mailer articulates the issues inherent in the

11. There is no illusion in Lawrence that the centrality of his conception of marriage assumes a pleasant voyage into the sunset. He never loses sight of the impinging reality of life on earth: "The sense of the eternality of marriage is perhaps necessary for the inward peace both of man and woman. Even if it carry a sense of doom, it is necessary" (*Apropos* 317).

conjoined and the separate incarnations of sex and love, and he also provides some pertinent ruminations about authorial influence on his own perspective. His remarks are especially notable for the cathartic nature of their revelations, and also for the transformative power he ascribes to one novel in particular:

> Lawrence's main influence for me was *Lady Chatterley's Lover*. I had the privilege of reading it back in 1941 in the unexpurgated edition. That was in the Treasure Room of the Widener Library…It changed my sex life, or rather, accelerated it into a direction it had been proceeding on nicely by itself. I accepted Lawrence's thesis about untrammeled rights and liberties of sexual love and the tension between the two. I don't think anyone ever before, whether in literature or personal life, had stated it so forcefully for me, that one could not have sex-without-love, or love without sex, period. I know from the other side of 40-plus years, that this is an extraordinary thesis, and can be half right, or all-wrong, as well as absolutely so. For this reason Lawrence's hypothesis has lived with me as my own, with all the excitement of an ongoing hypothesis that you can never quite confirm or deny (hypotheses are so much more life-giving than obsessions!). At any rate, such is my essential debt to Lawrence. His other works I admire, and I think he was a great writer, but *Lady Chatterley* changed my life (*Selected Letters*, Jan. 17, 1985, 592).

Thus Mailer recognizes that *Lady Chatterley's Lover* is profoundly persuasive in its depiction of a relationship that begins in opportune lust and terminates with open-ended prospects of love and marriage. In 1955, Mailer publishes *The Deer Park*, a novel that engages the same dichotomies of love and sex in a narrative framework not unlike *Women in Love*: two couples who move through various stages of love and sex within a developing plot-line that provides occasional intersections among four characters. Both affairs in Mailer's work scarcely progress beyond the level of sex-without-love; each dramatizes the lack of *growth* in the relationship—the crucial quality that Mailer and Lawrence regard as fundamental for any affair or marriage. But it is *Lady Chatterley's Lover* that Mailer emphatically cites in the letter. I want to build on his assertions about the seminal importance of the novel by considering its provocative connection to Mailer's first extended fiction on the dialectic of erotic risk, *The Deer Park*.

IV

What Mailer calls his "essential debt" to Lawrence is evident when *Lady Chatterley's Lover*, the book that "changed [his] life", is compared to

The Deer Park in terms of setting, character, and thematic emphasis. The similarities are striking and they suggest the full extent of Mailer's generous acknowledgement of how Lawrence's "hypothesis" has "lived" with him since his student days in Widener Library. The 1920s setting of the English Midlands bears distinct resemblance to the early 1950's environment of Desert D'Or. Mellors's post-World War One disillusion and anger are not unlike the depression and lack of direction that afflict Sergius O'Shaugnessy, a traumatized veteran of the Korean War. Similarly, the decadent indolence and repeated posturing of the wags at Wraghy, presided over by Clifford Chatterley, anticipate the hypocritical and amoral court of the movie mogul, Herman Teppis. Two analogous communities in which everyone knows his place, as coal miner and starlet, housekeeper and film director, colliery superintendent and publicity executive, chief butty and hair stylist—all are subjected to the mandates of sociosexual conformity and public righteousness. Whether is it through the autocratic control imposed on the colliers or through the hierarchical subjugation of Hollywood movie stars and ambitious hopefuls, both Clifford and Teppis demonstrate how a lust for power and sexual perversity can be satisfied through subtle hypocrisies and useful poses. Even the choric framework of the two novels drums an echoing beat: the cacophonous sounds of relentless bins of coal and clanging tools in *Lady Chatterley's Lover* are replaced in *The Deer Park* by the repetitive clicking of celluloid reels in projectors and by the curt shouts of anxious movie directors.

Both cultures remain indistinguishable in their obsession with the "bitch-goddess" of money and success (*Lady Chatterley's Lover* 62). When such versions of mechanization and officious control reign supreme, inevitably the qualities of humane nurturance and genuine passion are under assault. Demeaning notions of sex as mere commodity and as overrated diversion animate the cynical discussions at Wragby estate, as competing versions of evasion and nihilism emanate from Strangeways, Dukes, Michaelis, and Clifford. In the incestuous film network of *The Deer Park*, Munshin, O'Faye, Teppis and other fawning hangers-on enthusiastically exchange their lovers, pimps, business partners, and friends in that casual promiscuity so fantasized by the futurist talkers at Clifford's country mansion. The Herman Teppis-Clifford Chatterley comparison extends to crucial parallels between the novels, as both characters, who each controls his own dominion, bear primary responsibility for the crass instrumentalizing of the theory and practice of love and sex. Teppis's pathetic demand—not unfamiliar in the flippant land of filmdom—that Lulu Meyers marry the leading man and homosexual actor, Teddy Pope, is similar to Clifford's calculating suggestion that Connie get impregnated by another man in order to ensure an heir for the estate. Both the studio head and the owner of the mines feel eminently comfortable with an utter contempt for the distractions and obligations of real fatherhood, genuine marriage, and sexual fidelity. An entrenched and cowardly mendacity underlies their warped perspective on prostitutions of the body: paintings in Teppis's office loudly glorify for his gullible public the beauty of innocence and marriage, while Clifford is eager for his deluded village to believe that Connie's anticipated baby is his own.

When the various couples in the two novels are not engaged in the dehumanizing and manipulative sex that exists between Connie and Michaelis, or between Connie and her former lovers on the continent, or between Munshin and Elena, or between Marion and Elena, the men often face the fact or fear of impotence. Mark Spilka suggested nearly sixty years ago the profoundly humane "love ethic" that is embodied in Lawrence's final novel. Spilka persuasively argues that Clifford's literal paralysis and sexual incapacity are not meant as gratuitous or cruel symbols, but as a resonant metaphor that reflects the organic depth of his inadequacy as a man. His literal crippling thus documents what a reader must feel about his diminished stature: he has "no moral feet to stand on" (*Love Ethic* 183). Lawrence himself comments on this aspect of *Lady Chatterley's Lover* and on the symptomatic evasions of his generation when he remarks that "when people act in sex, nowadays, they are half the time acting up. They do it because they think it is expected of them" (*Apropos* 308). Mellors initially worries about his sexual energy and performance with Connie. Although not impotent, in recent years he has chosen chastity and isolation after his beleaguered history of intimacy with his wife. In his spontaneous and unanticipated rebirth of love and passion with Connie, he defiantly risks the return of painful memories as well as the social and legal turmoil that he will encounter because of this unorthodox and illicit affair. One aspect of the poignant poetry of this novel is the structural symmetry and irony that frame the accounts of Mellors's history with women: before his experience with Connie, the choice of chastity clearly reflects his depressed and embittered soul; by the novel's conclusion the same choice embodies his confident strategy and optimistic hopes, as Mellors now loves the period of chastity "as snowdrops love the snow" (301).

That Mellors trusts his instincts about Connie and remains willing to initiate the reengagement with sex—such faith indicates the quality of courage that informs Lawrence's dialectic of erotic risk. Some speculation about Lawrence's life at this time seems inevitable. Shortly after he completes *The Virgin and the Gipsy* in 1926, and only months before he begins a version of *Lady Chatterley's Lover*, he meets in Capri his friend and admirer, Dorothy Brett, during a period of deepening illness, increasingly strained relations with Frieda, and the final months of any sexual potency in his weakened body. Brett's written description of her alleged and aborted sexual encounter with him has received its share of speculative commentary through the years as to what actually transpired between them—and it would appear, at least, that nothing in bed was consummated. I am inclined to believe her account of his last minute spurning of her body for the simple reason that it would be illogical for anyone to recount such a deflating account if it did not occur.[12] But I am less interested in the causes or conclusion of this minor event than in the response of the participants in the following days. Lawrence's essential humanity resonates in his understanding that their failed attempt at sexual connection had deeply affected Brett's self-image. She had always idolized Lawrence, and he writes her a generous letter in the hopes of lifting her spirits. One sentence artfully combines notions directly relevant to this essay: "The greatest virtue in life is real courage, that knows how to face facts and live beyond them" (*Letters V* 408). Lawrence knows how to spark the process of renewal for her.

This humane response to Brett amounts to a Hemingwayesque acknowledgement of the power of dynamic self-definition, an unequivocal homage to the courageous resources of the spontaneous self and to the primacy of instinctual motivation. In addition, that use of "beyond" in the letter points to the urgency of transcendence for Lawrence, the mandate for the "lapsing-out" that is as much an act of faith for him as it is the goal of a secure existential self. Thus at this final stage in his life, Lawrence's letter revives his benchmark beliefs via some pertinent advice to a forlorn friend. Perhaps he writes it as much to himself as to Brett. He will start on early versions of *Lady Chatterley's Lover* within months of the letter. It is notable that Mellors is tempted intermittently to use the scars from his experience in the war and with his wife as an excuse to back off from intimate connection to a woman who is also devastated by the war and by her marriage, a woman who amazingly wishes to enter the passionate arc of his fractured life: "Especially he did not want to come into contact with a woman again. He feared it: and he had a big wound from old contacts" (88). Mellors initiates the healing process within the risky crucible of his

---

12. See David Ellis for a balanced consideration of the relationship between Brett and Lawrence (*Dying Game* 205).

affair with Connie, and he begins to display the quality of erotic risk-taking that an astute Connie recognizes as an uncommon and organic trait in his character. It is an instinctual courage that in its genuine passion erases class differences and—through Mellors's vernacular directness—plays havoc with the words and assumptions of political correctness. Even Lady Chatterley's downright speech—absorbed no doubt from her lover—summarizes those sociosexual aspects as the titled woman enunciates it with a naked appreciation that is close to poetry:

> "Shall I tell you?" she said, looking into his face. "Shall I tell you what you have that other men don't have, and that will make the future. Shall I tell you?"
>
> "Tell me then," he replied.
>
> "It's the courage of your own tenderness, that's what it is: like when you put your hand on my tail and say I've got a pretty tail."
>
> The grin came flickering on his face.
>
> "That!" he said. Then he sat thinking.
>
> "Ay!" he said. "You're right. It's that really. It's that all the way through" (277).

V

In "On Being a Man", an essay written in 1925 that anticipates several procrustean doctrines in Mailer's *The Prisoner of Sex*, Lawrence writes that "when a man and woman actually meet, there is always terrible risk to both of them," and he continues with prescriptive terms that inform aspects of this volume's subtitle: "Take the risk. Make the adventure" (217). In Lawrence's fiction both genders inevitably share the peril and the beauty of this risky "adventure", but in *Lady Chatterley's Lover*, Connie is aware of the special nature of the groundkeeper's daring: "Don't you care about a' th' risk" (124)? For D.H. Lawrence the crucial "prompt" for risk-taking, and the related presence of real courage, remain instinctual rather than cerebral—an assertion reflected by him in that pithy and oxymoronic remark noted earlier: "The thought-adventure starts in the blood, not in the mind" ("On Being a Man" 214). Mailer builds on this synthesis of blood, courage, and adventure by directly engaging the issue of sexual performance as he formulates a useful definition that is relevant to any comparative discussion of Mellors and Lawrence: "A firm erection on a delicate fellow was the adventurous juncture of ego and courage" (*Prisoner of Sex* 44–5). One looks in vain for sustained commentary on Mellors that sufficiently stresses the delicate condition of his body and soul when he undertakes sex with Connie. Similarly, a dying Lawrence, a survivor of the oedipal scars from his young manhood who now must cope with the ravages of impotence, surely he would understand an essential notion that Mailer adapts from Hemingway as he writes about the arc of Lawrence's life-journey: "The phallus erect is nothing less than grace under pressure" (*Prisoner of Sex* 164). It is a form of secular grace related to two correlative and politically incorrect doctrines by Mailer that mesh with an implicit ethic in *Lady Chatterley's Lover*: "The sexual force of man was...his finest moral product" (*Prisoner of Sex* 45) and "a man can become more male and a woman more female by coming together in the full rigors of the fuck" (*Prisoner of Sex* 171). At bottom, Lawrence's self-image could only conceive the moral power of that force in heterosexual terms, and given the ambiguities and conflicts in his own sexual preferences, the "courage" of his creation of *Lady Chatterley's Lover* remains especially impressive. As the beleaguered and desperately ill writer nears the end of his life, his creation of Mellors's renewal must stand as an unusual species of artistic and personal transcendence.[13] Such is the superb and empathetic understanding by Mailer of the turbulent voyage of Lawrence's life.

It is not just Mellors who experiences a form of sexual revival, and not just Lawrence who dramatizes the conjoined issues of conflict, change, and courage. In an intriguing pattern of cultural synchrony and comparable authorial thematics, both *Lady Chatterley's Lover* and *The Deer Park* can be viewed as postwar depictions of male confrontations with and recoveries from impotence. In Mailer's novel, Sergius, Eitel, and Pelley all fitfully engage the residue of their past sexual trauma by searching for manipulative and ego-driven erotic relationships to repair their problematic libidos and enhance their career-confidence. While Pelley achieves a temporary solution through his unconventional liaison with Dorothea, the extended "tests" levied on the sexual performance of Sergius and Eitel comprise the emblematic themes in the novel. Both men initiate passionate and renewing affairs that at first bring them close to genuine love and enduring relationships. Their contrasting responses to the respective affairs serve as a valuable index to the province of risk and courage in erotic relations. Sergius discovers enough about himself to

---

13. Lawrence anticipates Mailer's insistence on the "moral" centrality of this phallic role of the male and its function in the transcendent power of marriage: "The phallus is a column of blood, that fills the valley of blood of a woman. The great river of male blood touches to its depth the great river of female blood...And it is one of the greatest mysteries: in fact, the greatest, as almost every apocalypse shows, showing the supreme achievement of the mystic marriage" (*Apropos* 324–5).

develop an independent strength and stability that he lacked at the start of the novel; his achievement of this reconstituted self is most evident when he ends his affair with Lulu on the realization that the relationship only provides him with food for his ego. In an interesting contrast, the real risk for Mellors consists in his decision to continue his intimacies with Connie on the future possibility of marriage. Sergius willingly takes the risk of declining the offer of fame and money when he lets Lulu go.

Predictably the once powerful Charles Eitel is again seduced by filmdom's offer of money and prestige to make bland but successful commercial movies. He decides to abandon a woman who potentially could help him achieve an uncompromised career as an artistic director as well as a secure and meaningful personal life. Thus Eitel's cowardice—in the stipulated doctrines of Lawrence and Mailer—emerges when he abandons his passionate union with Elena. When the affair inevitably demands more of his real and vulnerable self he will not, in Lawrence's terms, "take the risk". Similarly, in the words of Mailer's existential reading of Lawrencian ideology, Eitel remains unable to "win at love" because he is not "ready to lose everything he brings to it of ego, position, or identity", and thus he cowardly rejects that transcendent "delivery to the unknown" in favor of his old support system of celebrity and material comfort. On this notion of courage, it is also true that Elena can be partially blamed for the lost opportunity with Eitel: her progressive lack of self-confidence and her neurotic fear of failure move her from depression to a deep despair that understandably frightens and alienates him. It is a not uncommon vicious circle of deterioration for the lovers, but Mailer leaves little doubt that primary blame rests with Eitel. By the novel's conclusion, with neither able to commit to the other, they seem to embody those contemporary souls that Mailer describes in *Advertisements for Myself*, lovers who "cut a corner, tried to cheat the heart of life, tried not to face our uneasy sense that pleasure comes best to those who are brave" (23). Eitel's pattern of narcissistic deliberation and unmanly indecisiveness recalls Lawrence's admonition that obsessive thought exempts one from the instinctual motivations that must take priority: "In order to think, man must risk himself" ("On Being a Man" 213).

VI

Early in *The Deer Park*, Eitel confidently makes an assertion that integrates a seminal concept shared by Lawrence, Hemingway, and Mailer, and he packages it in a single sentence: "I've always thought that everything you learn is done by fighting your fear" (102). This statement by a once-shunned movie director reflects his optimism and adrenaline early in his affair with Elena, a sanguine perspective that is unsustainable once he sacrifices her for his career. The metaphors that Mailer uses to anticipate the delimited arc of their passion are recognizably Lawrencian. In "Apropos of *Lady Chatterley's Lover*", Lawrence writes caustically that "nearly all modern sex is a pure matter of nerves, cold and bloodless" (326). Even when the sex is intense between Eitel and Elena, it never moves them beyond routinized connection—never beyond the constraints of their dueling egos. Mailer's fundamental insight about the imperative need of lovers in Lawrence's fiction ("they have to deliver themselves over to the unknown") remains especially relevant in considering Eitel's inability to fulfill this mandate. In the following refracted passage of self-analysis by him, there is no "delivery" but only the meager satisfactions rooted in the easy lust of present time:

> It had happened before. He had had women who gave him their first honest pleasure, and he had taken all the bows for his vanity, but he had never met so royal a flow of taste. It was remarkable how they knew each other's nicety between love-making and extravagance. It had always been his outstanding gift, or so he felt, to be able to know a woman, and he had the certainty at little instants that he could discover every sympathetic nerve. "The onanist at heart," he had thought, and made love to a woman with care enough to have made love to himself. But Elena carried him to mark above mark (110).

It is a passionate rumination about new love and grand sex, but the praise is mired in the self-congratulation of performance and achievement. "Love to oneself"—Eitel embodies the onanist in heart, habit, and soul. All he aspires to is a love-project that functions as a way station to petty power and prestige, not unlike the manner in which Clifford Chatterley—pathetically buoyed by his dream of a Wragby heir and namesake—goes back to manage the mines with the conviction of a man who has discovered a lost paramour. Lawrence well knows how intrinsic vulnerability and insecurity in men lead them easily to onanistic temptations. The Lawrencian mandate for love requires a transcendent freedom from the security of self, and Mailer's touchstone passage about the delivery "to the unknown" is precisely confirmed by that comment in Lawrence's letter, in which he writes that "it is the hardest thing in life to get one's soul and body satisfied from a woman so that one is free from oneself" (*Letters II* 115). For Lawrence, the satisfaction remains elusive when the self-liberation is thwarted by the enclosures of pride and ego.

Even the predictable failure of the Eitel-Elena affair is conveyed by Mailer in exactly the metaphoric terms he will use fifteen years later in

The Prisoner of Sex in his discussion of Lawrencian doctrine: recall again the key portion of that lengthy trope as he aptly discusses Lawrence's antagonism to "taking a stance on the side of the bank, announcing one is in love, and then proceeding to fish in the waters of love with a breadbasket full of ego" (*Prisoner of Sex* 147). This image of the vain and persistent fisherman working his trade is painfully relevant to Mailer's imagery after Eitel contemplates his own unholy bargain with the treacherous Collie Munshin. At various stages in the weeks that follow the searing sex between Eitel and Elena at the start of their romance, there is ample opportunity for the lovers to build productively on their passion and to get beyond the petty games of easy lust stimulated by teacher-student fantasies. But when the high-profile director's job beckons, Mailer's fishing metaphor, inherited from Lawrence, becomes contorted and sadistic within the arc of Eitel's meditation:

> At the same time he did not want to end it immediately; that would be too disturbing to his work. The proper time was in a month, two months, whenever he was finished; and in the meantime, adroitly, like fighting big fish on slender tackle, he must slowly exhaust her love, depress her hope, and make the end as painless as the blow of the club on the fatigued fish brain. "My one-hundred-and-fourteen pound sailfish," Eitel would think, and what a match she gave him. He was as cool as any good fisherman, "I'm the coolest man I know," he would think, and with confidence, aloofness, and professional disinterest he maneuvered Elena, he brought her closer to the boat. There was always the danger she would slip the hook before he pulled her in, so the battle was wearying (203).

Thus Eitel now fishes with a Lawrencian metaphor that Mailer shrewdly reduces to its pointed essence; the ego itself is the primary lure—a grotesque form of hook and bait geared to bring Elena, alive and kicking, onto the bank, where the doomed affair eventually will suffocate as the necessary sacrifice on the altar of Eitel's career. Yes, a mixed metaphor, but Eitel's eclectic motivations encompass a pathetic mixture of sadism, narcissism, and indulgent fun-and-games.

The domain of water in Eitel's cruel imagery also makes sense in terms of the narcissistic, self-reflecting element that infuses his relationship with Elena. Both Eitel and Elena—for different reasons and at different periods—remain unwilling to undertake the *growth* that is intrinsic to the dialectic of erotic risk: that is, they prefer to settle for the same rhythms by repeating the petty rewards of reliable and static love. Throughout *The Deer Park* there are eloquent passages about risk and change that strikingly resemble the tone and meaning of Lawrence and Hemingway's aversion to any form of sentimentality. Perhaps the most evocative lines on this issue in Mailer's novel echo both Hemingway's sharp criticism of his bio-fictional father in "Fathers and Sons", and Lawrence's admiration for the young writer's understanding of the inevitable relation between stasis and deterioration. Here is Mailer's quasi-biblical formulation in *The Deer Park*: "There was that law of life so cruel and so just which demanded that one must grow or else pay more for remaining the same" (346). In Mailer's world there exists a divine economy imposed on successful sexual performance and on the emotional intensity of a love affair. This perspective insists that protecting the stability of present success through a conveniently static marriage or a routinized sex life reflects the sentimentalist's fundamental error that no payment comes due: "There were the laws of sex: borrow technique in place of desire, and sex life would demand the debt be paid just when one was getting too old to afford such a bill" (*The Deer Park* 204).

Eitel's stated reason "not to give her up" confirms a selfish fear in him that undercuts the motive for his anticipated wedding. Real growth, for him—once he has irreparably tired of Elena—would be to suffer his loneliness alone and without sentimentality. Eitel lacks the existential courage that would make his marriage to Elena meaningful in terms of Mailer's "law of life." He will merely borrow more technique and try to employ another affectation. The animus to stasis also informs Lawrence's life and writings, and often in acutely personal terms. In "Why the Novel Matters" Lawrence writes: "If the one I love remains unchanged and unchanging, I shall cease to love her. It is only because she changes and startles me into change and defies my inertia, and is herself staggered in her inertia by my changing, that I continue to love her" (*Hardy* 196–7).[14] The following lines from Lawrence's "The State of Funk" offer an even more incisive prediction of the state of Charles Eitel's mind and emotions at a key stage in his involvement with Elena. His comments also provide a salient summary of the temperament and actions of Clifford Chatterley when he returns from the war:

> If we fall into a state of funk, impotence, and persecution, then things may be very much worse than they are now. It is up to us. It is up to us to be men. When men are courageous and willing to change, nothing terribly bad can happen. But once men fall into a state of funk, with the inevitable accompaniment of bullying and repression, then only bad things can happen (220).

14. Mailer precisely echoes the same sentiment as he considers a major aspect of his relation to a woman, as he "can remain in love only so long as the love keeps changing" (Lennon 489).

VII

In *Lady Chatterley's Lover* it is, of course, Mellors and Connie who "explicitly"—in the double sense of the term appropriate for this novel—provide for Lawrence a dramatized standard of what is admirable erotic risk. John Worthen writes an incisive summary of the fundamental intent and effect of this work: "The novel acquired an exemplary tone: this is how to live and love, it says; it becomes a kind of testament" (*Life as an Outsider* 367). As I have described at length in *The Phallic Imagination* in relation to the coordinates and terminology of Lawrence's heat imagery, the sexual component of nurturant and normative warmth functions as the most valuable yet most elusive character-attribute in his fiction. Its crucial expression depends—in its frequent metaphoric embodiment—on an organic "forging" process that burns off the impurities of ego and will in the act of love. Connie's progressively receptive and stimulative response to Mellors, and his increasing confidence in his own sexual awakening and commitment to Connie—all this pervasive and courageous renewal of real "tenderness" (the novel's first tentative title) can be charted through the novel's integrated sex scenes by way of the images of flame and purgation that inform their responses.

But the characterization of Mellors is also a poignantly personal affair for the author. Lawrence's fictional achievement echoes even more impressively in the light of certain patterns and tendencies in his own life. One of the major contributions of Mailer's discussion of Lawrence in *The Prisoner of Sex* is his compelling account of why Lawrence's ability to engage in heterosexual sex was essential to him, and its consummation could not have been easy:

> But he had become a man by an act of will…he had lifted himself out of his natural destiny which was probably to have the sexual life of a woman, had diverted the virility of his brain down into some indispensable minimum of phallic force—no wonder he worshipped the phallus, he above all men knew what an achievement was its rise from the root, its assertion to stand proud on a delicate base. His mother had adored him. Since his first sense of himself as a male had been in the tender air of her total concern—now and always his strength would depend upon just such outsize admiration (*Prisoner of Sex* 154–5).

In this speculative context of family influence and psychosexual inclination—the gist of it confirmed by Lawrence's many biographers after Mailer's words in 1970—the dimensions of Lawrence's achievement in *Lady Chatterley's Love* carry a special poignancy. Mellors' return to health and potency is charted by an impotent and dying writer who now fully understands, and without bitterness, the long road he has traveled—in his books and in his life—to his current state of relative emotional stability in a mortally infected body. Who can know for sure how closely Mellors' sexual temptations in the war corresponded to Lawrence's repressed inclinations with several men with whom he established close friendships?

> He thought of his life abroad, as a soldier. India, Egypt, then India again: the blind, thoughtless life with the horses: the colonel who had loved him and whom he had loved: the several years he had been an officer, a lieutenant with a very fair chance of being a captain. Then the death of the colonel from pneumonia and his own narrow escape from death: his damaged health; his deep restlessness; his leaving the army and coming back to England to be a working man again. He was temporizing with life. He had thought he would be safe, at least for a time, in this wood (141).

"He was temporizing with life"—that is, even amid the flash memories of his painful past, Mellors instinctively knows that his isolation in the woods is a temporary stay against the confusions and lividities of his personal history; in effect, he understands that his disengaged life amounts to a convenient and intermittent form of evasion and escape. In Mailer's reading of Hemingway's ethic, and in Lawrence's review of Hemingway's *In Our Time*, respectively, it now doesn't "feel good" to him, and it is now time to be "through with sentimentality". In *The Deer Park*, Eitel has it exactly wrong, as the perspective for him becomes sadly reversed: he becomes convinced that the temporizing consists in his affair with Elena. His pathetic vision of transcendence amounts to the distorted view that in rising beyond the complications of intimacy and the demands of marriage, he has made life worth living. No renewal for him now—only the "freedom" to keep repeating the past.

VIII

Evidence of Lawrence's significant influence on Mailer receives an additional and unexpected embodiment. In a magazine piece eight years after *The Deer Park* that is later published in 1972 in his collection, *Existential Errands*, he quotes several of his favorite passages by other writers that he inscribed over many years in his writing notebook. He values the passages because they produce for him "a shift in [his] memory, a clarification of the past" (*Existential Errands* 266). One passage remains especially interesting in the context of the current essay, for it has obvious relevance to the ethical choices and doctrinal centers of both *Lady Chatterley's Lover* and *The Deer Park*:

> The essence of spirit, he thought to himself, was to choose the thing which did not better one's position, but made it more perilous. That was why the world he knew was poor, for it insisted morality and caution were identical. He was so completely of that world, and she was not. She would stay with him until he wanted her no longer, and the thought of what would happen afterward ground his flesh with pain as real as a wound (267).

Such sentiments might have been contemplated by Mellors early in his affair with Connie as he ponders the courage of her visits to the hut against the reality of her own anxiety and vulnerability. In much the same way, the words easily could describe the confidence Eitel feels at the start of his affair with Elena, before his cynicism and weakness undermine his strength and moral center.

This range of hypothesis seems correct, for Mailer designates the above passage—curiously without any citation of title—as "D.H. Lawrence" (267). Although I could not find the corresponding lines within Lawrence's prolific work, I am almost willing to take Mailer's word for its authorship, under the single assumption that I had not looked carefully enough to find it. But a more troubling issue remains, and one that suggests added complexities about my notion of Lawrence's dialectical influence on Mailer, and more specifically on *The Deer Park*. It is not surprising that the passage also recalls the context of the Eitel-Elena affair, for Mailer *includes it verbatim* in that novel at the crucial moment when Elena gradually gains Eitel's respect for refusing his transparent and pathetic offer of marriage. The marriage matrix for both writers—throughout the complete corpus of all their fictional and nonfictional prose—insists that such a marital proposal is only admirable and morally legitimate when it emerges from a position of existential strength reflected in the willingness to undertake that "delivery to the unknown". Eitel undercuts his authenticity with the sentimental baggage of ego and his immature reliance on stasis. Here is the passage from *The Deer Park*, misleadingly identified as "D.H. Lawrence", with the duplicated lines italicized by me:

> Finally, she had gained his respect, and he could never explain it to her. With numb fingers he touched her foot. The essence of spirit, he thought to himself, was to choose the thing which did not better one's position but made it more perilous. That was why the world he knew was poor, for it insisted morality and caution were identical. He was so completely of that world, and she was not. She would stay with him until he wanted her no longer, and the thought of what would happen afterward ground his flesh with pain as real as a wound. "I'm rotten," he said aloud, and with the desire to prove his despair, he began to cry, clutching her body to him, his

> fist against her back, while his chest shook from the unaccustomed effort to weep (257).

Who can explain the intriguing mystery of the passage's appearance in Mailer's novel in 1955, or its later *republication* in *Esquire* magazine in 1963, and *Existential Errands* in 1972? If it turns out that the passage is not from Lawrence's work at all, but is a quotation from another writer forgetfully inserted by Mailer under Lawrence's name in his notebook, *Esquire* article, and *Existential Errands*, and under his own name in *The Deer Park*, then Mailer's Lawrencian preoccupations must appear even more obsessive—to the odd extent of confirming a precise inheritance that remains untraceable. Mailer's notebooks were intended to produce a clarifying shift in his memory that might produce an engaged and active self-perspective so patently useful for a writer of fiction. Is the issue of Lawrence's profound influence on Mailer so entrenched that the contemporary writer cannot untangle his own language and vision from the enthusiasm of his acknowledged indebtedness? Have we finally uncovered a case of the amnesia of influence?

Happily, it turns out, Mailer himself explains the mystery, both in an earlier magazine piece and in a letter to me. No, it was neither forgetfulness, nor an inexplicable tangle in those notebooks—just a playful homage by Mailer to the considerable influence of Lawrence on his own work. For I quote below the relevant text of a letter I received from him, written on his birthday in 1989. My prompting letter to him, naturally enough, requested clarification of his inaccurate attribution in 1963 of the lines he used in *The Deer Park* in 1955. I have since confirmed the accuracy of this explanation. My reaction was both irritation that I failed to fully unravel Mailer's Nabokovian game, and pleasure that my essential point about the Lawrencian elements in his work receives even more resonant documentation. Further, that Mailer derived the masquerade—or better yet, developed this ventriloquistic skill—makes perfect sense to me. His novel remains, as all novels inevitably do, a pastiche of the writer's own craft and the lingering voices of a chosen few who preceded him. But one echo of influence rings loud and clear for Mailer, and my posthumous thanks to him for his confirmation:

> I have to tell you that the piece in which the "quote" from D.H. Lawrence occurs was a spoof. I was doing a column for Esquire back in the 60's, and at one point wrote the preface that you saw in *Existential Errands*, and then took quotes from six or seven of my books, ascribed other authors' names to them, put it in the piece, and waited to see how many people would spot the trick, which, as I recollect, was very few indeed, maybe one or two people. Then I came back to it in the following column and

gave the game away. It was a humbling experience; I realized that people do not read me all that closely. I must say, however, that the authors I chose had all been influences, and the effect of their influences can be proved by the fact that no one argues with the authenticity of the quotation, and although I did give clues, for instance, Hemingway offers, "Nobody could sleep." Those are the first words of *The Naked and the Dead*. At any rate, this ought to clear up your natural confusion twenty and more years later.[15]

15. Letter from Norman Mailer to Peter Balbert, January 31, 1989.

CHAPTER NINE

UNARTICULATED SYNERGY AND UNFASHIONABLE TRANSCENDENCE: TEACHING, RESEARCH, AND THE QUEST FOR SOMETHING[1]

> I measure my life in sentences pressed out, line by line, like the lustrous ooze on the underside of the snail, the snail's secret open seam, its wound, leaking attar.
>
> —Cynthia Ozick, "The Seam of the Snail"

> But there *is* a flame or a Life Everlasting wreathing through the cosmos forever, and giving us our renewal, once we get in touch with it.
>
> —D.H.Lawrence, "The Real Thing"

> Without transcendence, my friend, there's no great literature.
>
> —Norman Mailer

Dedicated To the Memory of James Gindin

I

During the fall semester in 1960 of my sophomore year at the University of Michigan, I took a superb introductory literature course from the late Jim Gindin: it was organized as a lower-level survey of various genres, and Jim's section emphasized modern and contemporary works from England, Ireland, and the United States. In my retrospect of almost six decades, it is evident that this course initiated a profound transformation in my life, a redirection that started an ongoing and conveniently *integrated* infatuation; indeed, since that course I have

[1] This is the transcript of a presentation at the Modern Language Association in Washington, D.C., in December, 1996.

remained fascinated both with literature and the indispensable skills involved in bringing a work "alive" within and beyond the imagination of students in the classroom, and in illuminating the work for interested readers through varieties of literary criticism. That inscrutable but strangely perceptible "beyond" was very important territory to the private and spiritual Jim Gindin, embodying, for him, an aura of indefinable mystery and beauty in the finest literature, a realm of beckoning Lawrencian "otherness" that finally remains resistant to any critic's too confident formulation of trendy theory, witty summary, or extant category. It is not surprising that the fiction of D.H. Lawrence provided a major inspiration for him. Put another way—if necessarily as vaguely—this unchartable area resembles an element of transcendent "livingness," a glow of subjective beauty and "différance" that will captivate the imagination of ideal close readers long before they set off to decipher objective correlatives and decode the hermeneutic context. Yes, I am aware that "captivating," in Robert Alter's mournful and accurate observation, "is not a word that has any status in current critical usage" (515).Yet a major premise of my remarks today will be an emphatic agreement with Alter that "for students as yet not born again to political correctness, and perhaps even for some already baptized in the new redeeming truths, the best argument is the work itself. Captivation strikes me as an entirely worthy aim of literary studies" (515). Similarly, the esteemed critic Frank Kermode takes Alter's wise prescription one step further by willingly using the currently shunned 'L' word—that evocative phrase so anathema to the academy's interpretive methodologies today: "University teachers of literature…can read what they like and deconstruct or neo-historicize what they like, but in the classroom they should be on their honour to make people know books well enough to understand what it is to love them" (Tudeau-Clayton 103).

I remember Jim's course as a tightly structured and gently visionary exercise in the subtle power of literature to move a reader beyond the confines of self. Whether the topic was the modernist inheritance of Joyce's short stories or Yeats's poetry, or the elliptical technique of Hemingway's fiction, or the contemporary innovations of Osborne's then recently published play, *Look Back in Anger*, Jim guided us—and our eminently receptive imaginations—to a series of luminous moments in the respective work where rhetorical devices intersected with verbal rhythms, and where psychological realism was enhanced evocatively by refracted narrative perspectives. The aesthetic patternings we discussed seemed infinite in their versatility, and the rapt attention from the class was consistent and impressive. I think of Jim's course as one of heightened sounds and enacted pictorial scenes, perhaps because Jim firmly believed that students and faculty must read appropriate lines aloud in class to catch a precise cadence or pause that figured significantly but subtly in the power and import of a respective passage in a work. Yet there was never any stipulated method to Jim's teaching or any closed-ended adamance to his conclusions. We were taken to the edges of mystery and meaning, and we were accompanied by a mere modicum of critical vocabulary and interpretive jargon; the work in question was never reducible, or even used to demonstrate, the viability and any political doctrine, social cause, or theoretic construct. It distinctly was the artistic craft of the respective writer that took center-stage in our discussion—not the fancy footwork of the critic or the clever conclusions of deconstruction. Fragments of the class return to me by way of small details that highlighted the special majesty of art. How distinctly I recall several students repeating Mrs. Sinico's name in a decrescendo of onamatopoesis as the train's pulsations in Joyce's "A Painful Case" receded in the rueful mind of James Duffy. S-i-n-i-c-o, S-i-n-i-c-o, S-i-n-i-c-o…

It would be inadequate to dismiss Jim's effective pedagogy as merely the product of young and bright readers in an introductory class interacting with an informed and gifted teacher. What Jim Gindin taught us was not only an awareness of those literary moments of aesthetic wholeness and beauty, but also a lifelong skill of engaged, respectful, and close reading that students rarely learn in the classroom today, and that faculty only occasionally display in their scholarship. William Cain described the imperatives of such teaching in the following way:

> You need to demonstrate for students the habit of asking questions, proceeding as William Empson frequently does, from the simple to the more complex. Why does the writer begin with this sentence? What are the key words and images in this paragraph? How is the paragraph organized from beginning to end? Local, specific questions need to be asked, followed by larger questions about the arrangement of scenes, the development of character, the modulations of tone in the narrative voice, the handling of central themes. This is the procedure through which students learn how a text is organized and structured. The focus should be on the language: all the questions, comments, and disagreements should keep returning to it for evidence and support (B4).

It is through such disciplined, neo-Socratic examination of the text that one may unearth the lode of gold, embodied in a quasi-religious discovery of crystalline moments in literature. My description here may sound hyperbolic only to those not initiated into the special dispensations offered by great art. The poet Robert Pack eloquently describes this classroom process of community decoding as something potentially holy, for the "sharing of art in the classroom is akin to worship, the sharing of faith" (42). Pack goes on to assert that "this sense of the holiness of art is missing in the academy today with its esoteric quibbles about interpretive methodology, its pinched specializations, and its eagerness to replace imaginative contemplation with social reform, conceived in partisan ideological terms" (42).

I am not sanguine about the state of literary studies today. The potential for synergism that once existed between teaching and scholarship, and that received its productive embodiment in lively, unideological, and engaged essays, as well as in classroom discussion filled with the zest and insights of close reading rather than preformulated advocacy—such reciprocal reenergizing stays unarticulated today for obvious reasons. The relation between teaching and research in the academy sadly has mutated in only a generation from synergy to symbiosis—that is, to a practical and indulgent partnership of professional responsibilities in which the classroom becomes the convenient vestibule of the disposable, recycled aspects of the teachers' doctrinaire scholarship, and often, sad to say, of their political ideology. The students, in effect, are fed digestible scraps of advocacy that easily sustain the course and often are substituted crassly for the vigor, respect, and nonpartisanship of careful reading and analysis. The critic is now deemed superior to the literature, and to focus too intensely on the aesthetic structure of the work is to fall into the error of logocentric bias. As my title today suggests, I believe that it is crucial for us to demonstrate how the microcosmic reading of a text, in the manner of Cain's prescription, offers large potential for a synergism throughout our academic duties that will enliven the study of literature while it also provides concrete public relations benefits that are indispensable in today's sound-bite culture in which the humanities remain increasingly unattractive to students.

In this unavoidable arena of public perception, it is sobering to realize that undergraduate students began to abandon the formal study of literature almost to the initiating date of our profession's progressive retreat from the norms and guidelines of close reading and text-centered discussion; Cleanth Brooks notes that "since 1970 the number of students enrolled in the humanities has dropped by half" (357). [The total number of humanities majors in 2016 remains approximately at 7%, a figure similar to the quoted percentage in my speech in 1996.] I highlight the role of the humanities not only because that area resides at the heart of the culture wars; the humanities also comprise a large portion of the knowledge that is at the core of a student's education, and their member disciplines carry a special vulnerability to the kind of radical reformulation that we witness today. It is in this regard that I quote from a trenchant summary by René Girard about his outlook on the current crisis:

> For a good book in the social sciences, the only chance of survival lies in its being adopted by the humanities…All the really good books ultimately belong to us and, as a result, students in the humanities are likely to read more good books than mediocre ones…a course in the humanities may be their only chance to read some really good books. That is why the humanities today are more necessary than ever to the education of our young people. The fact that the humanities are open to the best means, unfortunately, that, in times of crisis, they are open to the worst (62).

My own position—I must make this clear—is not that teachers should eliminate relevant discussion of literary theory or an appropriate range of fashionably critical notions in their classes. Again, as Cain states it with intelligent tolerance:

> For many upper-level undergraduates, theory is very rewarding. But it functions best for them when it is integrated with reading literary texts. Therefore, teachers should emphasize theorists and critics who exemplify some form of passionately engaged reading—Stanley Fish on seventeenth-century literature, for example, or Stephen Booth on Shakespeare's sonnets, Richard Poirier on Emerson, Cynthia Griffin Wolff on Edith Wharton, or Jane Tompkins on nineteenth-century American women novelists (B5).

II

Let me return to the impinging context of my own "conversion" to literature. From my early teenage years to the period of Jim Gindin's course, my world had centered on competitive tennis, and thus the 1957 national intercollegiate tennis champion, the University of Michigan, was my choice for the most challenging and prestigious sports arena in the late 1950s. While I enjoyed good books in high school, my routine of tennis tournaments, traveling, and private lessons left little time (or so I conveniently claimed) for the reading projects that were never quite completed. But I do remember that unseasonably warm Ann Arbor morning in October of 1960 when my affair with literature began, a burgeoning love that by the middle of my sophomore year would displace tennis as the major interest of my young life. It started in the trivial but magical manner that often provides hints of larger changes to come. In this case the moment combined some silly pride at a minor academic achievement with my amazement at the subtle distinctions a reader can perceive through close reading skills and an empathetic imagination.

The class was discussing Hemingway's early Nick Adams story, "The End of Something", and we arrived at the following lines in the tale:

> Nick said nothing. They rowed on out of sight of the mill, following the shore line. Then Nick cut across the bay.
>
> "They aren't striking," he said.
>
> "No," Marjorie said. She was intent on the rod all the time they trolled, even when she talked. She loved to fish. She loved to fish with Nick. (80)

On the issue of these lines, Jim recounted in class a little scenario that concluded with a question for us. The lesson comprised a relevant anecdote that—whether factually based or pedagogically embroidered—provides a perfect example of Jim's nurturant teaching talents. The story goes like this: A young Ernest Hemingway sends off an early draft of "The End of Something" to a man who later would become his meticulous editor at Scribners, Max Perkins. Perkins admires the story and accepts it immediately. As he later peruses the tale again during a second and more deliberate reading, he uses the proverbial blue pen to delete "She loved to fish," the line that precedes Hemingway's next sentence, "She loved to fish with Nick." Pleased with the logic of his editing correction, Max writes in the margin "del, red," (for delete, redundant), and he continues his reading of the story. But the catchy, intrusively repetitive rhythm of the lines in question reverberates in his mind; so he reads the passage again until he reaches a mini-shock of recognition that attentive readers reserve as their private reward. Perkins now knows that precocious Hemingway was right all along to dance with his prose along the edge of sing-song redundancy. With a touch of penance and approval, Max now crosses out his earlier comments and writes in the margin, "yes, yes, stet, retain." Jim's question to the class, after he completed telling this incident was simple, unadorned, and absolutely to the point of Hemingway's profoundly elliptical prose. I can hear Jim ask it as if yesterday, amid his cigarette cough and trailing clouds of smoke: why did Max Perkins make the correct decision to the let the lines stand in their emphatic flatness? Why, in short, did Perkins see their effect as other than a stylistic infelicity?

The too easy answer, of course, maintains that both lines are independently true and deserve a separate statement. But as an eighteen-year-old Balbert—at that time rarely a participant in class and never a silence-breaker—pondered the case of Nick and Marjorie as it develops in this delicate story, I volunteered my confident answer to the question.

With Jim's smile of approbation—perhaps more directed at my visible pleasure than at my answer—did he then sense that, unbeknownst to me, I was already embarked on a career? Yes, in the passage it is the second of the two sentences that offers the greater truth; it supplies the more poignant and overwhelming truth for Marjorie, echoed in a narrative line refracted from her own consciousness, as she modifies the first sentence with a more painfully honest appraisal of her attachment to Nick. The confessional bluntness of this second sentence lingers in our reading of it, just as the sound of Marjorie's boat will remain in Nick's ears after she hears his abrupt decision and gracefully, proudly departs from his presence. At the risk of an oxymoronic qualification, I must add that Hemingway has displayed a "little *tour de force*" of rhetorical artistry: his brilliant command of indirect narrative voice and the rites of adolescent dilemma emerges in the tone and adjusted progress of the two sentences. As his teaching style required, Jim asked me that day to recite the lines so as to fully catch the verbal music inherent in Hemingway's gift for poetry and mimicry. Not the neutral sound of "She loved to fish. She loved to fish with Nick"—but the rising tone, slowing pace, and gentle resolution of "She loved to fish. She loved to fish *with Nick*" (my emphasis).

On one of the few occasions I saw Jim Gindin after my graduation, I asked him if he remembered that Hemingway scene and the scenario he described about Perkins's response to the lines. He said that he did, and he only wondered why I seemed so palpably excited over my answer. Then Jim tellingly added, in reference to those very lines that he used to exemplify an aspect of close reading, "no one does much of that any more." This conversation took place at the MLA in San Francisco in 1987, and Jim's disappointment about the progressively changing fashions of criticism would be more acute today. The engagement with literature in the classroom or in professional journals rarely zeroes in for such sustained, nearly kinetic analysis of a frozen scene or isolated patch of dialogue. I am certain that Jim would have approved a recent assertion by Robert Pack that can easily apply to the resonant moment between Nick and Marjorie:

> Art enlarges our feelings by offering pleasure and by creating a sense of dignity, perhaps even "grace" through the power to understand the human condition and to endure inevitable sorrow…it enlarges our lives by inviting us to participate empathetically in the imagined lives of others. The role of the reader is to respond to and comprehend the intent of the work. This can be done only by willfully suspending one's own theological and political preferences. In this respect, the reading of a literary work derives from the wish to be enlarged, not merely confirmed or justified. To be a reader, then, is to affirm otherness (41).

Such "otherness" remains a distinct aspect of the power of literature to take us beyond the comfortable confines of self and our cherished preconceptions. It is the otherness also celebrated by the great writer D.H. Lawrence, as he often depicts his fictional characters struggling to embrace that concept within the intimate human relationships they establish. Yet the last several decades have generally moved away from a belief in the power of literature to accomplish Pack's special goal of affirmation, even to the revisionist extreme that such a usually tolerant critic as Andrew Delbanco describes most teachers of literature (and he includes himself) as "having given up…on the idea of transcendence" (541). Such a concession of crucial territory tends to confirm Gertrude Himmelfarb's complaint that "transcendent" has become "a pejorative term in the vocabulary of the new 'pluralists', who believe we can 'relate to,' as they say, only our particular conditions and situations" (361–2). This trendy belief, she further argues, "dominates the university, distorting the curriculum and demeaning all of us by suggesting that we cannot transcend the limitations of race, class, and gender" (362). John Searle places the current humanistic cynicism in even a larger frame of reference, and his words carry particular relevance for the study of literature. He explains that the move away from traditional education theory means devaluing the salutary notion that he calls "an invitation to transcendence" (697). Searle further insists that "one of the aims of a liberal education is to liberate our students from the contingencies of their backgrounds. We invite the students into the membership of a much larger intellectual community" (697). Today's self-styled "advocates" in the classroom, often brandishing the buzz words and polemical perspectives of phallocentrism, colonialism, Marxism, and feminism, do not so much liberate as further enclose in reductive categories that prevent the inimitable sense of belonging described by Searle and others.

What remains impressive about Jim Gindin's teaching centers on the consistency of incisive, respectful, and investigative involvement with the respective work and with the range of our exuberant responses to the renewing possibility of literature. For him this sense of "renewal" was more than metaphor. He believed in the enduring value of a solitary experience that sadly becomes increasingly uncommon for students amid the constant interruptions and sound-bites of computer screens, smartphones, and various electronic devices: the lonely and entranced reader, book in hand, learning to re-imagine the world and the self through the magical art of literature. Jim created his multi-genre course at Michigan with the emphatic belief that—in the related words of Robert Alter—"the construction of imaginative realities—narrative, lyric, and dramatic— through the evocative power of language, remains a central activity of human culture" (513). Such a fundamental view was accepted without much controversy in 1960, but as Alter articulately insists in the 1990's, we must now use every occasion to reiterate—during this unliterate "age of high technology and electronic distraction"—that "literature has to do above all with the *reading* of literary texts, not merely reading through them to a supposed network of discourses of power" (514). The real power, Jim insisted, was the care and concern we could bring to great art by close reading. Once again Alter is correct here to maintain that "the activity of reading remains urgently involving, and the willingness to abandon it is the real treason of the intellectuals—a betrayal of their vocation as teachers in our time" (514). As William Cain suggested, and as I reiterated earlier, the issue here is not absolute but one of degree, and by 1996 the pendulum has unmistakably tilted away from rewarding those who practice the basic skills of scrupulous reading. It is in this sense that although today's "ideologically driven trend in teaching and scholarship in sentiment is certainly intensely political", the reality of reward and recognition in academia suggests to Alter that "what really motivates it is the politics of profession" (510). While we now know what the 1950s may not have acknowledged—that literature is deeply and often subtly implicated in class, race, gender, and politics—in Alter's words it is defiantly "not reducible to any of these categories, as many campus ideologues have tended to argue" (514). By my own careful and depressing count, at least 70% of the sessions in this year's MLA program *are* reducible to these categories.

III

The commitment of the university to educate our students as careful and active readers, as impartial investigators of those conjoined realms of rhetoric and imagination, has been fractured by a too zealous and doctrinal overspecialization. As I indicated earlier, the traditional synergistic relation between the responsibilities of teaching and scholarship has eroded in many ways, but the prospect for the future looks even more bleak when we consider the directions undertaken by most of our graduate students. No doubt these apprentice professors have sterling minds: it is hard to deny, however, that their awareness of literature remains narrow and intensely focused; they appear to have insufficient knowledge of literary tradition and of the individual talents that nourished it. In fact, they tend to specialize so early in graduate school that their CVs usually list published essays and delivered presentations, as well as a completed dissertation. On these matters, I am forced to ask two rhetorical questions. First, is it unfair to call much of their work ideological, jargon-filled, and formulaic? Second, has no one noticed the proximate relation among such factors as the increasing amount of publication by graduate students, the increasing prominence of cultural and theoretical studies rather than traditional literary analysis, and the decreasing numbers of humanities majors over the last two decades? Certainly today's new PhDs are no smarter than their current and former colleagues from the 1940s, 50s, and 60s, yet look at the mass of credits they accumulate before the doctoral degree is finished. At least one of my colleagues has noticed the general dullness, predictability, and inflexibility in the research and teaching of newly-hired faculty, and William Cain's comments strike me as right on target in the context of my themes today:

> Part of the problem is that the graduate students who become our faculty members are not prepared to teach close reading. They have not learned the skills as undergraduates and, unfortunately, no one in graduate school has encouraged them to make up for their lack...—a compilation of graduate literature courses that are really courses in sociology, media, post-colonial politics, and the like. Courses on sexuality are everywhere. But I rarely detect courses on the literary subjects that graduate students might eventually teach in classes of their own (B4).

I want to say a related word about the broad subject area stipulated for this session, entitled "The Faculty and Its Publics: Explaining Our Work". On the latter half of such a heading, I have no difficulty in affirming our consensus understanding of meaning and intent here; surely any profession that declares its mission and implements its work without an informed awareness of "public" relations will find itself first misunderstood and later, no doubt, marginalized to the arcane periphery of modern life. But I also want to direct some attention to the assumption within the first half of this session's title, for those words bespeak a defensiveness about our invested role as teacher-scholars—indeed, they even reveal an unattractive and circular reasoning that tries to blame alleged misunderstandings and bad public relations on the multiple voting blocs that listen to our story. "Publics" must be considered a transparently political and dislocated phrase. It attempts to conceal ever more narrow appeals to interest groups by the academy behind a peculiar plural noun that was concocted to justify the primary cause of difficulty in literary studies: the fragmentation of the central mission of teaching and scholarship. True, more than ever, there now may be many "publics"—call them clamoring constituencies or vested enclaves—that the MLA often designates as oppositional, unreachable, or retrograde. Yet these groups will not listen to the academy, for in the range of their demands, excesses, frustrations, and legitimate concerns, they merely alert us to the sad absence of a single affirming voice from our discipline. We have lost the nerve, or belief, or commitment to speak proudly of the fundamental priorities of the study of literature—and that means to demonstrate the skills of close reading and the transforming properties of the unfettered imagination.

It was Ralph Waldo Emerson, in "The American Scholar", of course, who—in the pre-scientific United States of 1837—anticipated the danger, in society as well as in the university, of the increasing specialization of his fellow Americans' interests, self-definition, knowledge, and occupation—all part of a condition, he writes, "in which the members have suffered amputation from the trunk, and strut about as so many walking monsters—a good finger, a neck, an elbow, but never a man" (64). It was his well-publicized fear that vocational training, scientific primacy, and academic narrowness would adulterate the responsibility of the university to encourage universal understanding and spontaneous insight—an interconnected mandate in his view, and one that starts so famously for him from the scholarly apprehension of nature. For Emerson, "books are for nothing but to inspire" (67), and he maintains that such inspiration, when buoyed by that additional imperative of relevant experience and soul-searching, will offer the spiritual vision central to his transcendentalism. He began to lose the battle over specialization in the academy later in the industrialized decades of the nineteenth century, and fortunate for his ideal that he did not live to see the full flowering of the German-model research university. By the mid-twentieth century, it was left to rare educators, such as the powerful and unorthodox Robert Hutchins, who—speaking here in the receding tradition of men like William James, Lawrence Lowell, and Woodrow Wilson—articulates the following Emersonian lines. As I quote Hutchins's invigorating concepts, contemplate his likely perspective on the excessively technical language employed by so many humanists today, a jargon properly rejected as obfuscating by unconverted faculty and by a generally skeptical public:

> A university should be an intellectual community in which specialists, discoverers, and experimenters, in addition to their obligation to their specialties, recognize an obligation to talk with and understand one another. If they can restore the conditions of conversation among themselves, they can become a university, a corporate body of thinkers, that can exert intellectual leadership and hope to make some modest efforts to fashion the mind of its time (139).

Fear not Hutchins's use of "corporate" here, for he means it in its purest sense, meaning "combined as a whole, considered as one" (*Funk and W* 303), as he describes an organic model that Emerson might approve, one that reconnects the displaced and fragmented body that Emerson understandably ridiculed in the amputation trope from "The American Scholar". As Cain indicates, the narrow training received by graduate students and the careerist pressures for publication and conformity on young professors mentioned by Alter—all this distraction militates against the accessible dialogue desired by Hutchins. Cain's primary suggestion of close reading offers one helpful response, but perhaps more radical action is required, such as Jacques Barzun outlined:

> The newly-made PhD must no longer be forced to "produce" soon and abundantly so as to "get on the tenure track"...The side effects upon higher education are many and dire. The worst is the neglect of teaching—there is no time for both teaching and class preparation. This dilemma is also an obstacle to *scholarly teaching*; for it is clear that working on a little paper means a little subject, whereas the young teacher ought to be keeping up with the scholarship of the broad subject that he teaches (164).

IV

I shall conclude today with a few words on an unusually relevant poem by Robert Frost, a poet who in many ways employs a linguistic texture not unlike Hemingway's, with characteristic sharp images, elliptical compression, accessible phrasing, and acute attention to sense perception. "Take Something Like A Star" strikes me as a Frost poem that appropriately sums up—in its themes, metaphors, and visionary posture—many of the topics I briefly addressed in this presentation. This poem remains the quintessential homage to a version of the Emersonian transcendent, even as it offers an implicit anticipation of the very untranscendent habits of a world in the making. Also, in its gracious willingness to confirm a grand tradition of romantic art and its associated cult of nature, and in its witty but disheartened criticism of fact-centered humanity, the poem reads as a canny prediction of the deconstructionist excess and specialized zeal that will emerge several decades after this poem.

The poem presents Frost as the shrewd ventriloquist in the first fifteen lines, with the "we" cumulatively embodied as the plaintive voice of an indulgent, cocky, and fact-conditioned modern mind, an unattractive everyperson who has the effrontery to demand a revelation of precise statistics from this necessarily mysterious and magical star; the voice resonates as the whining sounds of pride from a twentieth-century Gradgrind who characteristically has been nourished by rote learning and technological dependency. Note how Frost also begins this lyrical but scathing poem with a witty, respectful glance at his talented forebears, conveyed to the reader through the hyperbolic Keatsian apostrophe to the star, but immediately qualified by a parenthetical superlative that charmingly lets the reader comprehend the rhetorical tactic. Thus the parenthesis functions as Frost's knowing wink to assure us of his own awareness of how anachronistic his romantic excess must sound in 1943—and yet, he suggests, play along with me and find meaning in my guise. The progressive sense of the egocentric speaker protected by imposed rules and accustomed habits emerges from that strangely childish and unequivocal "not allowed", anticipating the supremacy of factual knowledge that the speaker believes in and craves. The heavenly evidence of light refraction and energy combustion—proving that this proud and unreachable star "burns"—such fundamental scientific deduction remains insufficient for this spoiled modernist: he requires the star's exact temperature and chemical composition, yet all the star provides (or so the speaker thinks) is the unusable, "something" in the sky.

The power of this versatile poem to catch the sad spirit of future society is impressive to behold: within three decades of the poem's composition, and only a few years after his death, the presiding spirit of Frost might smile knowingly at the exponential developments in astrophysics and stellar spectroscopy—huge space-age advances that often bring approximate answers to the very questions about temperature and composition posed in the poem. But such breakthroughs, as Frost would predict and we can guarantee, do not assuage the century's growing aversion to chance, faith, or spiritual journeys that lack the forms of prescribed doctrine or the prescription of facts to guide them. In the poem's last ten lines, Frost immediately emerges in his own corrective voice to teach us *abstractly* about the beneficent potential of the natural "unknown". No, the star does not provide many factual answers in 1943, but with that lofty magnificence and inscrutability, it can put our own petty needs, dependencies, and certainties in some calming perspective. This real potential for a quiet strength and instinctive conviction from the transcendent—such affirmation exists only in those who can get beyond (i.e. be of "a certain height", which means be of necessary stature) ego restraints, the demands of the crowd, and the fashions of the day.

Frost paradoxically has fashioned a rare example of the pragmatism of spiritual otherness, and he has also crafted it partly out of his respect for Keats's vision of aesthetic stillness and sexual ecstasy: unlike the dying Romantic poet, Frost pitches his appeal through an empathy that goes beyond artistic stasis or eternal love. He creates the poem as an indictment of our own fears and self-protective systems; he frames it as a visionary call to travel by open-ended imagination into a realm that we cannot deconstruct and that we all need to embrace. How would Frost feel today about the student interpretation of "The Eve of St. Agnes" as a case study of date rape (Marcus 636), or of J. Hillis Miller's eminently politically correct and preposterous assertion that "nor do we any longer have recourse to some standard of intrinsic superiority allowing us to say that *Moby Dick* is a better work than *Uncle Tom's Cabin*, or vice versa, since that standard too is the result of ideological basis?" (31).

Frost's reiteration of "something" in the poem must also remind us of his similarly evocative yet inscrutable use of that term in two other early poems by him—"For Once, Then, Something," and "Mending Wall". In the former poem, such an abstract and teasingly imprecise term bespeaks a confidence in an unnamable transcendent reality beyond the power of formulaic theory or scientific fact to define: "Truth? A pebble of quartz? For once, then, something" (225). In the latter poem, it is an intense instinct in man that remains in touch with an urge beyond the self that objects to the presence of a barrier in a natural environment: "Something there is that doesn't love a wall" (33). Similarly, in D.H. Lawrence's multi-generational novel, *The Rainbow*, a powerful and currently unfashionable hymn to the province of "the unknown", recall Tom Brangwen's inebriated but heartfelt explanation of the numinous value of marriage and its connection to an undefinable reality he can extol but not explain: "There's very little on earth, but marriage. You can talk about making money, or saving souls. You can save your soul seven times over, and you may have a mint of money, but your soul goes gnawin', gnawin', gnawin', and it says there's something it must have" (128).

I close with some moving words of Albert Einstein, who also and inimitably lauds the terrain of "something":

> The most beautiful experience we can have is the mysterious. It is the fundamental emotion which stands at the cradle of true art and true science…It was the experience of mystery—even mixed with fear—that engendered religion. A knowledge of the existence of something we cannot penetrate, our perceptions of the profoundest reason and the most primitive forms are accessible to our minds (Einstein, *Ideas and Opinions*, quoted in Hook et. al. 127).

A Relevant Postscript

In a warm and generous letter to me on February 1, 1998 (subsequently published in *Selected Letters of Norman Mailer* 680–1) about my presentation at the MLA Conference, Norman Mailer artfully and incisively ruminates about his view of the depressing prospects for the future in the United States. His remarks presciently connect the rising tide of political correctness in the academy to impinging concerns about human nature, democracy, the province of courage, and the gradual erosion of invigorating standards in our culture. For him it is not so much the lure of an inscrutable "something" that remains the signal excitement and provocation for Lawrence, Frost, and Einstein; it is palpably more the need—both in personal and competitive terms—to energetically oppose the mediocrity in the world with his own standards of independent and prolific "art" that require productivity and passion difficult for any writer to maintain. Other projects and health issues intervened before he could return to *Harlot's Ghost*, but it remains intriguing to me that in this letter his often dyspeptic but always slashing and striving voice must call to mind the similar tone and subject material of D.H. Lawrence's letters and essays quoted in this book. We will miss Mailer's characteristic power and uncompromising vision.

Dear Peter,

Well, I can just begin to imagine the scene at the MLA when you read your paper on "unarticulated synergy and unfashionable transcendence." Brother, the air must have been scorching.

You know, among the things we share is a sense of cultural depression. I look back over my life, particularly after putting together that book of 50 years of writing, and I feel that nearly all the things I worked for and fought for are in decline. That what I used to see as the enemy, and with great optimism, as the enemy who would be overcome, has instead overcome us. And while I'm not about to feel sympathy ever for someone like John Foster Dulles, I can appreciate the fact that he put two powerful words together, and they are "agonizing reappraisal."

So the question that falls upon us both is where does the fault lie? Was it in us? By never doing enough, no matter how much we thought we did? Or is it in that abstraction, "human nature"? Did we fix our beliefs on a concept of men and women that was not adequate to the low facts?

And then sometimes I wonder whether this is just elitism of an unimagined sort on my part, and the real premise of democracy, that the unwashed must go through cheap soaps and deodorants and plastic clothing as one of the steps in mounting to a higher level, is actually what is going on now, or whether, as I fear, we are descending into a society of the ubiquitous mediocre man and woman governed by high mediocrities. For if that is true, then the ultimate answer can only be a techno-fascism that will be subtler and more pervasive and more married to plastic than anything the world has ever seen, and God knows when we'll get out of that.

So, old friend Peter, you see what your piece did to me, and plunged me right back into the gloom out of which I climb each morning. It's a rugged, bad world, isn't it? Yet, save this morning, I had the pleasure of reading you again. There is much to be said for the man who does not compromise and there you are with full integrity and your lack of fear of a full sentence.

Well, give my regards to your fine wife and your wonderful girls and know that my nine children are in reasonably good shape and are, for the most part, doing interesting things, and that I feel the stirrings, and I hope I'm not mistaken, of the beginning of a passion to write the second volume of *Harlot's Ghost*, for, Lord, I've been afraid of it these seven years since it came out. I hope it's not too late. I think I see a way to do it that will accomplish a little more than fulfilling my three-word promise at the end of Volume One, for, after all, keeping promises is an excellent way to live, but writing novels one does not really want to write is a sure way of advancing one's own termination. So, yes, I'm pleased that the novel is stirring. Let's see if I can keep from betraying it in the next few years.

Do give my regard[s] to Norman [Sherry] and tell him again how much I enjoyed his work on Graham Greene.

Cheers,

Norman

CHAPTER TEN

FROM REJECTION TO "RENUWEL" TO RENEWAL: CHAIRPERSON, FACULTY, AND THE RESEARCH IMPERATIVE[1]

Time is lost, which never will renew,
While we too far the pleasing Path Pursue.

—John Dryden, 1697

It is a question of renewal, of being renewed, vivified, made new and vividly alive and aware, instead of being exhausted and stale, as men are today.

—D.H. Lawrence, "The State of Funk", 1929

Prepare yourselves, then, my friends and comrades, for this renewal of your exertions.

—Winston Churchill, 1941

I

The cornerstone of this essay is that faculty renewal can be better understood and implemented when the resonant meanings of the term "renewal" are more fully appreciated. In essence, my approach integrates an etymological history of that word with several concrete programs that a chair and department can undertake to increase the production of high-quality research by colleagues. The shifting and multiple definitions of this richly-textured word since the time of Chaucer suggest its dynamic applicability today in any practical attempt to increase faculty productivity. I shall demonstrate that the phrase's lexiconic history of intriguing sub-meanings and suggestive connotations provides a useful

[1] This is the transcript of a presentation to the Society for College and University Planning (SCUP) in Atlanta, Georgia, in April, 1991.

index for notions about renewal that have immediate relevance to the research imperative that necessarily exists in the academy. Thus my wedded concerns are both with theoretical underpinnings of the theme of renewal *and* with substantive strategies that emerge from correlative discussion of faculty responsibility, cultural fashion, and the meaning of language.

My two working assumptions are also integrated in their awareness of theory and practice: one, there is a legitimate professional need for excellent research from all faculty in the university; two, despite the practical incentives usually offered for its achievement, the momentum for solid scholarship is occasionally stifled by such a familiar range of human maladies as ennui, lethargy, cynicism, depression, anxiety, ignorance, and self-doubt. In the spirit of recognizing those uncomfortable psychic realities that may intermittently bedevil the best of us, I shall employ linguistic analysis as well as case study outlines of representative faculty as a convenient way to offer several suggestions for healthy renewal in the area of research.

It is important, however, to first elaborate briefly on the fundamental notions that inform my emphasis in this essay—and in the department I chair—on published research by faculty. Although there are currently well-publicized differences in the academy on what constitutes legitimate areas of research for a given discipline,[2] there is, thankfully, not much disagreement on what I consider the confirming value of publication for those who teach in the university. I stress *confirming* in a relevant and always conjoined double-sense here: the resultant confirmation is for the individual faculty in terms of the acceptance and visibility of the work, and for his peers and his evaluators, who variously acknowledge its appearance, judge its contribution to the field, and evaluate it for yearly merit reviews. The ideal results of this continuing process of confirmation is that published research has a positive effect on a scholar's teaching outlook, increases the knowledge available in an area of study, and provides a reasonable arena for consideration of the colleague's expertise.

Publication is that privately undertaken and publicly submitted enterprise of an academic that in a major way further legitimizes the right to teach in front of a university classroom for the period of his tenure. By my qualification of "further", I of course recognize that the most crucial legitimacy for such a position rests on his effectiveness before students,

---

2. See especially the recent report by Ernest L. Boyer for the Carnegie Foundation for the Advancement of Teaching for an outline of the dimensions of controversy and for the revisions of traditional definitions of research that are under consideration.

and I grant that it is not impossible to find an excellent and informed teacher who survives for years without significant publication to his credit. But as a general rule such examples are not—and should not be—the model of the profession. In my view the species of "good teacher—no research" raises questions about that faculty member's real authority, engagement, and educational vision. Put simply, the research imperative is not an arbitrary or digressive obligation, but an integral, ongoing call for renewal that all faculty must consider part of their inheritance. It requires all teacher-scholars to willingly test a basic aspect of their competency not only before their generally accepting, supportive students, but also in the more competitive crucible presided over by their vigorously judgmental peers. The magic and the mandates of renewal are never finished in this context, just as the confirmation of one's professionalism is never complete. The vocation expects that faculty "renew" themselves at least until retirement, and it may be the rigor of that demand, as well as its fundamental nature, that justify the need for sustained discussion of renewal processes and the related desire for an understanding of the equivocal term in academia today that is often our topic and our totem.

The word is frequently spelled "renuwel" in Middle English, and its recognizably Latin roots, in "renovare", suggest the attendant meaning of "refashioning" that would predominate until the twentieth-century. Chaucer catches this spirit of complete "renovation", as he uses it most often with the related meaning of "to do over again, to revise." That seminal fourteenth-century sense of revision also emerges with a correlative definition celebrated by Chaucer and continued through Shakespeare—and even down to the central assumption of meaning that informs most renewal conferences for the last decade: "to make new, or as new, again; to restore to the same condition as when new, young, or fresh" (*OED* 446). This well-established link in the word's history—which I shall develop more fully later—between the rigors of applied revision and the rejuvenation of nearly apocalyptic renewal, provides a major clue for chairpersons about helpful program initiatives and persuasive techniques for the department. In short, through the disciplined and invariably arduous process of revision, we can "renuwe" (or remake) our product and ourselves. Thus, revision does more than merely improve the item, work, or standard of living: its successful completion renews the whole self involved in the difficult, organic demands of revising. The most meaningful analogy to this process for a scholar is the exhausting technique of essay-revision that moves through several drafts, and is followed by the completion of a final copy that palpably renews the spirit of the finally satisfied writer. One is renewed, in effect, by managing and surviving a sustained bout of revision. This Chaucerian penchant for a movement forward by repetition and refashioning—so evident in the celebrated linear structure and overt moral themes of *The Canterbury Tales*—is the intermediate stage of a more elusive final goal; in the Middle Ages it is a religious reaffirmation, and in the intellectually more liberal climate of the Renaissance, it is a zestful return to the vitality and freshness of a passionate youth. With Chaucer's varied cast of pilgrims, such "renuwel" carried profound spiritual implications, for these seekers of salvation could not be "renewed" (in the more final sense of *rejuvenated*) until they worked on their brand of faith ("reneuwed" it) with the diligence required for a revision of spirit.

The relevance of notions about renewed spirit to a university context is self-evident, and it suggests a related assumption that I shall require in my remarks: faculty renewal cannot occur without a willingness for individuals to acknowledge such a need and to search for ways to implement the emotional and professional logic of this desire. Thus faculty renewal, more precisely in relation to their research, must also first stress the crucial intermediate state of "renuwel", which for them requires an equally strenuous process of revision, perhaps involving not only the research project at hand, but also the goals and methodologies of scholarship and the associated "tactics" leading to publication. In this regard I shall presently describe in some detail the functions of a department research committee that I have instituted during my current five years of experience as a chair.[3] To make the potential responsibilities of this key committee more relevant to this essay's topic, I shall describe a series of four hypothetical instances of faculty who are in need of "renuwel" and "renewal"—that is, whose research has been unproductive because of its rejection by publishers, or its lack of intrinsic quality, or its incomplete state, or its faulty style and/or organization, or its misdirected channel for publication, or its over-ambitious scope. In each case I shall outline an individualized approach that the chair and the committee can employ to move these stalled colleagues from a status of "rejection" to one of Chaucerian "renuwel", and finally to that productive, full-person *renewal* that defines the holistic goals of relevant conferences on the subject. These faculty portraits are each related to the changing use and definition

3. I have written at length elsewhere on my firm conviction that an academic chair has significant potential to act as both effective model and persistent motivator for the production of quality teaching and research in a department, and on my related concern that a chair is often more interested in conducting annual evaluations than in stimulating his colleagues to the persistent *renewal* that must be central to their mission at the university. See *National Issues in Higher Education*.

through the literary ages of the word "renewal", and I pay particular attention to versions that term employed by Chaucer, Dickens, Jowett, Milton, Ruskin, Shakespeare, Shelley, Spenser, Tennyson, and Wyclif.

The four cases that I offer of various research maladies are hypothetical in terms of the precise details that illustrate each example. What is not hypothetical is the general profile of each category and the essential familiarity of the specific university archetype; while these instances may not occupy the collective unconscious of our disciplines, they certainly do bedevil the collective gatherings of any professoriate. I should add that any similarity in the details of these archetypes to people living or dead is purely coincidental and probably inevitable. I have chosen the exemplifying areas of scholarly expertise only for the purposes of convenient illustration, and I have no precise person in mind to serve as the model in all particulars. In each case my procedure will be to describe the archetype, hypothesize a more tangible description of the problem, and then further develop the issue of renewal to encompass relevant, variant uses and definitions of that term in literary history. Finally, perhaps, the momentum of common sense and imaginative license may produce results; our examples will combine with the magic of etymology and the passion of literature to suggest a few possible solutions for the research inadequacy discussed in each case.

II

The first archetype is likely the most woebegone, for he is afflicted with chronic rejection by publishers, editors, and proposal-referees. In his current depressed, rebuffed state, he is a long way from that intermediate, introspective stage of "renuwel" so common to the religiously-inspired pilgrims of medieval England. While he remains a capable teacher of Romantic literature, this colleague has been stalled at the Associate Professor level for nine years: his research on the relation of eighteenth-century European intellectual history to the visionary innovations of Blake's poetry and to the full flowering of British romanticism in the nineteenth-century, has not been published except for some marginal treatment by him in three book reviews, one short review-essay, and three presentations. This rejected scholar (RS) considers himself made of sturdy stuff and a stable demeanor, but after nearly a decade of editors' rejection (of four essays, one monograph, and one leave proposal) his confidence is waning, and even his manner in the classroom appears under some strain.

Let us return to the era of Chaucer for a possible clue about renewal for the RS and for a pragmatic way to approach his problem. As I noted earlier, the word in the Middle Ages, is "renuwel". It implies a spiritual remaking through an exhausting process of reading, writing, rereading, and rewriting—in effect, an intense process of revision, emotional stocktaking, and sustained study. It often involves a catechistic dialogue about goals, failures, and ultimate belief, and this serious line of questioning might be conducted with oneself or with one's peers. The emphasis in this undertaking is always on finding the precise *word* to describe spiritual malaise, with the implication that discovering an appropriate description will also carry the *insight* that leads to *renuwel* and later to what we would call *renewal*. Chaucer repeatedly captures this note of striving and self-inquiry in his ribald and incisive *Canterbury Tales*; as his pilgrims literally and narratively work their way down the road to that Oz-goal of religious renewal, Chaucer uses the fact and metaphor of this journey to explore their many motives for visiting this cathedral city; their stories are rife with the hypocrisies, evasions, and ironies that infiltrate their self-serving desires for spiritual purity. They seem less concerned with ethical or social responsibility than with precisely articulating their own moral and spiritual needs and idiosyncrasies. As the witty byplay within the tales and among the travelers suggests, they put much emphasis (and pride) on trying to find the right word for their predicament and the exact style and story to frame its articulation.

That journey to Canterbury offers an added dimension of meaning as it carries a useful brand of analogical significance for themes of renewal. I suspect that we would all agree that notions of "renewal" cannot be profitably discussed at conferences without a shared understanding of the virtue of renewal, and of the often elusive achievement of such virtue. Chaucer writes a wonderful poem in 1374—"To His Scribe Adam"—that uses the word "renuwe" in such a manner as to suggest its stubborn emphasis on the imperatives of revision and careful formulation that lead to a state of "renuwel". The poem lyrically expresses Chaucer's irritation that his personal secretary (or scribe/scrivener) does not accurately transcribe Chaucer's own words; thus the poet is forced to further correct the gratuitous mistakes made by his trusty employee. The implication in the poem is that the demanding Chaucer will not tolerate any careless interpretation of his use of language, and he will struggle and *revise* his own errors and those of his secretary until the words match the feelings: "So oft a daye I mot by werk renuwe, It to correct and eke to rubbe and scrape" (in *OED* 446). Thus not only will the great writer work diligently on his parchment to transcribe the exact word, but the discipline and revision that he "mot by werk renuwe" must emerge from a depth of self willing to struggle for the goal of a more comprehensive spiritual resurgence.

Similarly, the medieval theologian and writer, Wyclif, is a noted translator of the *Psalms*, and in one of his lyrical translations in 1382 he uses "renewe" to suggest its applicability to regeneration on a cosmic scale, as if the renewal of the spiritual force can become a contagion that might spread to rejuvenate the world: "Thou shalt renewe the face of the erthe" (*Psalm* ciii(i), 30, in *OED* 446). Finally, in the *Fabyan Chronicles* of 1494, the emphasis again is on complete transformation, as if repairing and revision ideally should be total and without caution or qualification: "He renewyrd and repayred al olde Temples thorough his Realme" (ii. Xxxviii. 27, in *OED* 446).

What possible relation is there between the use of the word and concept of renewal in Chaucer, the *Psalms*, and the *Fabyan Chronicles*, on the one hand, and the lingering malady of our RS, on the other? Most importantly, the dogmatic, universalizing use of that term both suggests the large dimension of change required in the professional outlook of the RS, and points to his need for a form of supportive, cathartic dialogue with the research committee. His first priority is to meet with the chair separately, and then with the chair and the rest of the research committee, to confirm his bedrock understanding that his research *can* and *must* improve; at the very least, he must openly agree that the pattern of rejection notices (and their explanatory comments), indicates unequivocally that his current strategies are not working. This initial step of confession is not nearly as obvious or as easy to implement as it sounds: there are many "rejected" faculty who do not accept their own responsibility for lack of publication, and they often look for convenient targets to assign blame. But the RS must understand that whether it is the inadequacy of the scholarship, or the poor judgment of the editors, or the vagaries of fashion, or any combination thereof, the work of the RS is not being published, and action and self-inquiry are now required. The RS does not even have a scrivener to blame. The renewal of his scholarship will not occur without the vigorous stock-taking toward "renuwel", and this intermediate stage must occur before any strategies by the research committee are implemented to address the practical problem of more publication.

What really might be accomplished for the RS, given the long-term condition of his failure, and his current lack of confidence in any future prospects? To begin, copies of all rejected work and rejection reports must be submitted to each member of the committee. Such members write individual letters that isolate common elements in the pattern of rejections, and they attach suggestions on improving each submission as well as a brief statement on a recommended, overall publishing strategy for the RS. This typed, two-page report by each committee member is sent to the RS as well as to colleagues on this committee, and topics covered in the reports may include observations on subject matter, methodology, authenticity of research material, style, and organization. Indeed, if any committee member feels that a topic or approach contained in rejected material is beyond revision, he states that sobering fact to the RS without equivocation and with sufficient explanation. When the RS receives all reports, and when each member has read the reports of colleagues on the committee, the committee and the RS meet again to openly discuss common lines of analysis and suggestions that are likely to emerge from the collective wisdom of the reports. There are often divisions of opinion expressed by members on the issues of revision, and this second meeting with the research committee attempts to arrive at a solid consensus for initial "renewal" strategies to be undertaken by the RS.

As a preliminary approach urged by the committee, such strategies may involve a willingness by the RS to offer a presentation, at the university or at a regional meeting of his professional organization, on romantic theory and influence. It should be noted that the RS, dispirited by constant rejection notices, has retreated during the last five years from any public reading of his research. In terms of future work from the RS to be submitted for publication, the committee will have met by itself between the first and second meetings with the RS, with the express purpose of deciding on a single article project they can urge him to pursue; perhaps they note that his discussion of continental influence is generally interesting but ignores its relevance to several contemporary issues of critical theory and canon debate. Yes, there is presumption in a committee urging a scholar to pursue a precise project, but is there a better preliminary strategy given the track record of the RS the last decade? When the draft for public presentation and/or article submission is completed, it is read carefully by the chair and one other member of the committee; after necessary revisions by the RS, he sends it to a journal that the research committee and the RS feels is most appropriate for the article. An alternate approach for this archetypal RS that may prove effective is to use the varied contacts and expertise of the committee members to help set up with an editor a lengthy review-essay assignment in a journal for the RS; the virtue of this tactic is that if fully implemented it prominently breaks the cycle of rejection for the RS and enables him to return to his own work with added vigor and confidence. I should also add that this framing process of two meetings by the committee with a colleague and a middle meeting only with the committee, remains the consultation pattern to be employed in *each* of the archetypes I describe. It is a system that works, and often very quickly; it has seemed to committee members that there is frequently a refreshing spirit of renewal achieved immediately in the process itself of enthusiastic, committed interaction between a variously unproductive colleague and an intra-department advisory group. A “rejected” scholar is often the last to acknowledge how desperately he would like guidance and exchange on the reasons for his cycle of failure.

III

The second archetype for discussion is the “long-range-project-scholar” (LRPS), and the acronym describes a professor long in potential and short in actual publication. She is a talented senior colleague who has virtually no published work of consequence since the award of tenure fifteen years earlier. In this regard, her “long-range project” is to be distinguished from that more pragmatic cousin, “work-in-progress”, as the latter is associated with periodic, published glimpses of a project, and the manuscript of our LRPS never surfaces in this useful way. She is gifted with a superb intelligence, possesses reams of notes on the LRP, emanates a teaching manner that is well informed and widely respected, attends conventions and regional meetings as an articulate observer, and graces university social and “service” situations with a charm and insight that comprise her signature style. But no section of her LRP appears in *any* formal fashion—not as a submitted article, or as a presentation at a regional meeting, or even as a lecture before colleagues in the university. The topic of her project is a comparison of the Trinitarian imagery in *Beowulf* and *Piers Plowman*, and it ambitiously encompasses an ongoing concern with the relation of religious doctrine to the development of artistic techniques in Old and Middle English literature. Her friends who have seen random pages of this research marvel at its insight and comprehensiveness, and the reputation of its brilliance is thus carried from year to year as an idiosyncratic, persistent tradition on campus.

From all outward appearances, the LRPS remains absolutely committed to her project. She is known to use the summer months for earnest study in Germany, England, and Italy, and often her weekends each academic year are spent in university libraries as far as a hundred miles from her village residence. There is currently little more than speculation by either the LRPS or her colleagues about when the project will be completed, or what is its exact title, or whether publishers have read it, or how much she has actually written. The LRPS does understand the community’s curiosity and frustration about her lack of supporting publication, but occasionally she does articulate a clear statement on its impinging concern: she regards it as each professor's accepted responsibility "to be engaged in meaningful research", and her argument, stated simply, is that she is more engaged in this activity than many colleagues who publish periodically in a handful of journals. The LRPS takes umbrage at the suggestions by faculty that the LRP does not really exist, and at their more intense conviction that unpublished research cannot be considered as meaningful scholarship. When colleagues respond that her position on this issue of ongoing research is too extreme, and that an LRP can quietly develop with greater dignity and legitimacy only if aspects of it are presented occasionally in some formal fashion, she remains silent and clearly offended by the suggestion that she break her cycle of mysterious work.

The committee must deal with the engrained habits of many years by the LRPS. How can its members help her to bridge that enormous gap between engaged research and actual publication? How can this Freudian case study of over-retentiveness, this Jungian archetype of a downward spiral toward quiescence, be encouraged to share some of the bounty of her long-accumulated research with her colleagues and related organizations? How can we convince her to convince the community that this empress does, in fact, have suitable scholarly clothes? As a start, it would appear that the first meeting between the committee and the LRPS must be to urge her to accept the fundamental notion that periodic feedback on her developing research is likely to be invigorating to her large project: the stimulus of outside reactions to her scholarship may enable her to achieve more focus and expeditious publication. This preliminary discussion with the committee might stress the excellence of her topic, the confirmed respect in the university for her teaching ability, and the related, understandable defensiveness of her friends and admirers on the heretofore invisible quality of her research. It is not inappropriate at this meeting to admit a practical, correlative point that the LRPS no doubt has perceived the last decade: merit pay cannot be awarded to her on the basis of her private diligence. The academy considers the *public* steps leading to (and including) publication as the necessary rituals of faculty professionalism, as they ideally provide standards for peer judgments as well as increased knowledge in the respective discipline.

Clearly, what this ceaselessly "promising" colleague needs is a new outlook—a rebirth, if you will, not so much of incentive as of vision and tactic. She must unambiguously acknowledge that her predicament requires a fresh perspective on her research ambitions, a new approach that will do justice to her scholarship *and* provide tangible evidence of her own commitment and dedication. Perhaps in this sense the fire of her resolution can be stoked if she conveniently sees this university "community" as her skeptical antagonist: in this fashion, her responsibility will be to finally take up arms against this legion of doubters by applying a strategy of selective but effective engagement. These heightened metaphors of confrontation, of course, are all from Elizabethan culture, and not surprisingly, the most frequent meaning for "renewal" during the English Renaissance is pertinent here. From about 1550 to 1650 the word is most commonly used with an attendant sense of rebirthing, of "beginning a fresh attack" (*OED* 446) on a strong enemy who needs to be defeated, persuaded, and/or silenced. In his 1606 play, *Trolius and Cressida*, Shakespeare supplies a vivid illustration of this combative use of the term, when he forcefully writes: "Renew, renew, renew, the fierce Poldamas hath beate downe Menon" (V.v.6, in *OED* 446). Similarly, in his earlier *Henry V* (1599), the call to active response is ever more intense, as he memorably commands: "Awake remembrance of those valiant dead, And with your puissant Arme renew their Feats" (1. ii,116, in *OED* 446).

This seventeenth-century concept of embattled renewal reflects the celebrated Elizabethan zest for victory, for conquest, and for achievement amid tribulation and struggle. "The Elizabethans called it 'the aspiring mind'. The great projector of this mood is Christopher Marlowe, who has his heroes fling themselves into the pursuit of power…or into the lust for gold…or into the search for knowledge" (Norton 492):

> All things that move between the quiet poles
> Shall be at my command; emperors and kings
> Are but obeyed in their several provinces,
> Nor can they raise the wind or rend the clouds;
> But his dominion that excels in this
> Stretcheth as far as doth the mind of man" (*Norton* 492).

It is the latter quest for "knowledge" that has most relevance for our LRPS: she must be convinced by the committee that the "province" of knowledge discovered but hidden from scrutiny is of empty value to the "dominion" of scholars. A neighborhood of skeptics provides an opportunity for the LRPS to "rend the clouds" in the interest of her own reputation and professional authority. In the end, there is nothing complex about the substance of the fresh attack that she must renew to retain her "command". She must first give a well-publicized lecture in the university on aspects of her research, in which the department acts as the enthusiastic sponsor by offering supporting posters and an appropriate reception after her public remarks. This presentation by the LRPS should provide the nucleus and momentum for future periodic offering of her scholarship at local and national conferences; this gradual rebirth should coincide with her developing work on a related specific article that is directly adopted (in conjunction with advice from the research committee) from the best of what we can now happily call her "work-in-progress". In summary, it is not magic that offers the solution to the conundrum of the LRPS archetype. The prognosis depends on her interrelated understandings of the support machinery that can help her, of the wasteful indulgence of her current non-strategy, and of the exciting prospects that will follow her emergence from a perverse hibernation.

IV

The third archetype is a version of the preceding case study, but it offers sufficiently different problems as to require a separate category. It describes the colleague who has significant scholarly achievement early in his career, and who oddly has published little since that considerable initial success. I shall call him the ECBS, for "early-career-breakthrough-scholar", and he is currently in his second decade of an early-awarded full professorship. Although he is clearly alive and well on campus, his unusual "aura" emanates from the nostalgia of a celebrity long past; he is best remembered for a brilliant study of the child-motif in nineteenth-century British fiction—an important, innovative work that emerged from an illuminating but less comprehensive doctoral dissertation more than two decades ago. While there have been a few scattered articles, an edited book, and regional presentations (all on diverse subjects) since the publication of that renowned work the year before his tenure decision, he still has not recaptured the confident style and visionary intensity of that first book. There is currently no extended work-in-progress that he can develop, and he appears neither content nor concerned about the less than scintillating progress of his career the past fifteen years. But his equanimity amid such stasis may be deceiving, for in physical appearance he is aging before his time; he emits a quiet sense of fatigue and purposelessness that his occasional publication and his committee service at the university do not really camouflage. A reasonably effective teacher, his classroom techniques are to be faulted only in their unvarying approach and unaltered syllabus from year to year. His choice of elective courses to teach has not departed much from the two or three he imported to the university as a fresh PhD graduate.

What is at issue here is not his intelligence or critical acumen, as that early study (still used today) is justly regarded as a model of socio-literary criticism and meticulous research. The understandable concern is whether the ECBS will ever repeat his early achievement, or whether he will continue to suggest, through his paltry productivity, that the first book was the precocious contribution that sadly broke the back of his future scholarship and career ambitions. In his current decade of "ungrowth", the ECBS is a sad example of a living Tithonus, enduring a cruel immortality that recalls the Trojan prince. This mythological reference brings to mind the most memorable poem about Tithonus, the paradoxes of growing old, and the heavy price we can pay for inappropriate bargains or compromises that imply a lack of adjustment to this mortal process. Tennyson's figure of Tithonus, and the themes in his allusive poem about him, also suggest the Victorian penchant for depicting a warm and effective nostalgia about past achievement and harmony. Such preoccupations are evident in the common mid-nineteenth-century definition of "renewal" as "a recovery of one's original strength" (*OED* 446), as when—in Tennyson's painfully nympholeptic "Tithonus"—"thou wilt renew thy beauty morn by morn" (4, in *OED* 446). Similarly, in Jowett's famous 1875 translation of Plato, there is more about the fascination with recapturing the past, as we also anticipate Wilde's Dorian Gray: "In age we may renew our youth, and forget our sorrows" (ed. 2, V. 236, in *OED* 446). Ruskin moves the mythology from Tithonus to the Phoenix, but the focus is still on the magical need to restore some state of lost youth and vanished beauty: "To dip themselves for an instant in the font of death, and to rise renewed of plumage" (*Wild Olive*, pref. 29, in *OED* 446).

The Victorian themes heighten our own awareness of how the ECBS has brought upon himself a fate not unlike that of Tithonus. This colleague has been granted a worldly form of immortality with his tenure, but that state appears to have sapped his strength and his lust for renewal; he is awkwardly content to pass his long professional life without the diligence and dedication so apparent early in his career. Is there now any way for him to rise from the ashes of his own history, to break his resemblance to a modern Tithonus who acts as if a permanent job was an easy gift instead of an earnest vow? The best opportunity for his resurgence is first to use that stipulated triptych of meetings by the colleague, chair, and research committee to emphatically remind the ECBS that the impressive ability he displayed in his famous study is an accurate reflection of his best talent, and not an accident of fate or lucky effect of casual circumstance. The critical reception of that study spoke of the organic integrity of mind behind the project. The ECBS must be made to understand that the right new project combined with his former passionate purpose *can* duplicate the success of his youth—indeed, can actually provide a link with his notable past that will be analogous to that familiar sense of renewal described by Dickens in 1880: "Your handwriting came like the renewal of some old friendship" (*Letters* I, 11, in *OED* 446–7).

His early book, and the essays that have appeared the last decade, must be read with *great care* by each member of the committee; one of their primary objectives will be to suggest how the essential methodology of that first work may be applicable to interests by the ECBS that are on the edge of his more recently published work. Without excessively exploring the psychology of this archetype, it would appear that the ECBS does not want to commit to any large design in a research project for fear it will not measure up to the impact and continuing relevance of his breakthrough achievement. Yet with diplomatic patience and care by the committee, it should not be difficult to find that new topic, and to gradually restore the confidence of this colleague. Happily, his confidence in the committee probably is already renewed, as he no doubt expressed his own gratitude for their impressive grasp of his own previous work: members have also pledged to read diligently all developing sections of his new work-in-progress. The ECBS should also be encouraged by the chair to teach an elective course for *selected* upper class students that will be related more directly to his new line of research than to the subject of his famous study. In addition, it should be further explained to him how a series of articles can easily be translated today into a persuasive book proposal; with that still resonating first book as his effective marketing chip, the contract for a new study should be possible for him to obtain. It also may be advisable to suggest to him how his two articles in the last decade have begun to form a larger argument, and how those articles, when revised, can combine with two more projected articles in the next two years to create a stimulating and practical plan for his research renewal.

V

The final archetype consists of a salient quality that is implicit, in differing degrees, in the other case studies, but it is now the defining characteristic of a colleague's relation to the research imperative. The quality is lethargy, and it is manifested primarily in a marginal interest in scholarship, minimal productivity in publication, and a generalized listlessness that seems related to a lack of committed engagement in her discipline. The colleague has a good critical mind, is an average teacher, periodically speaks on unmemorable topics at conferences, and occasionally competently reviews in second-tier journals the work of her peers. It has been noted by many in the community that the LS (lethargic scholar) was not always so remote and uninvolved in her work, and those who know her best date the onset of her lassitude to the period a decade earlier of a difficult divorce and the tragic illness of one of her children. It is also common knowledge that recently both in her classroom and at social gatherings, the LS has openly questioned the value of faculty scholarship and publication—a cynical stance very different from the optimistic and engaged perspective that she brought to the university as an idealistic teacher in the late 1960s.

A scholar of Renaissance and Restoration England, with an emphasis on Jacobean playwrights, it is apparent that the LS needs a dose of sixteenth and seventeenth century medicine—a tonic of revivification that capitalizes on the frequent use in that era of the word "renewal" as meaning "to take up again or afresh" (*OED* 446). The question is how to achieve such a new outlook, one that will break the cycle of cynicism and depression by infusing the LS both with the moral vision in her research that she once possessed, and with the accompanying desire to narrate the "tale" of scholarship in a manner that is both relevant and meaningful. And what of literary history and its fickle use of "renewal"? Are there writers in that period from 1550 to 1700 who might suggest a possible cure for her disaffection? I would argue that John Milton and Edmund Spenser may be of great help here, and for the different reasons of theme and structure, respectively. Milton's prolific history of achievement illustrates the galvanizing effect on his writing of his assaults against the political establishment; the moral passions of his literary creations would often assuage the well-document personal despairs of his blindness, uneven career, difficult married life, and untenable political isolation. The conjoining lines of his life and literature unmistakably dramatize an unwillingness to give in to his demons, or to cease striving against all odds. A memorable line in *Paradise Regained* is convenient here, as it becomes a metaphor encompassing both natural renewal *and* a self-willed renewal of indomitable spirit: "As surging waves against a solid rock, Though all to shivers clash't the assault renew" (IV, 19, in *OED* 446). There is a firm sense in these lines (and throughout Milton's best poetry) of the mandate to combine moral conviction with personal energy, as if the major sin is a lassitude in purpose or a cowardly retreat from an honorable and legitimate belief. The crusading words from *Paradise Regained* are consistent with the heightened passions of that great work, which is an epic poem in four books that describes Christ's temptation in the wilderness. Milton's ambition in his more famous and companion epic poem, *Paradise Lost*, is even more grandiose, for it is nothing less than to "justify the ways of God to man".

We must be reasonable here, as Milton is a hard model on any level for our best scholars, much less for the aloof LS. But obviously I ask for no epic work from her, only her own seminal realization that her "renewal" in literary criticism cannot occur without the force of her moral purpose behind it. She can be a Satan, Christ, Adam, or Eve, but let us feel the force of her convictions in writing and not in the pretenses of detachment. She must emerge from her wilderness of professional doubt to a belief in her vocation—that is, in her Arnoldian commitment in research and teaching to clarify "the best that is known and thought in the world". The crusading Miltonic example may not be sufficient antidote for this scholar's full-blown lethargy. To be sure, she claims to be uninspired not only by the disengaged themes of her research, as she also reflects a limited understanding of the flexible, amenable formats of literary criticism that are available to her. To our unimaginative LS, academic publication is merely an opportunity to recycle the dry conclusions of critics in the tedious, discursive style of academic essays. Here Spenser and the Renaissance might provide inspiration and reeducation for the LS, as he perfectly illustrates his era's proud emphasis on the power (and imperative) of all good literature to teach by its evident *delight* in the telling of a story. This double mandate of informing *and* engaging is not only applicable to celebrated poems and plays of the period, but also to a variety of long and short prose narratives, by writers such as Lyly and Bacon. Spenser's great allegorical poem, *The Faerie Queen*, is a fine example of a literary work's need to "delight" its audience, and the sixteenth-century gloss on "renewal" as meaning "to go over again" (*OED* 446) is also pertinent to our concerns. The Elizabethan writer "goes over" not merely to renew old connections, but to renew his audiences sense of the thing or concept described, so that the reader sees it in a new light. In this regard, the "telling" of known events or familiar concepts is made meaningful by the new perspectives conveyed by unusual, individualized narrative techniques. As Spenser himself writes in his brilliantly, insistently repetitive *The Faerie Queen*, "then gan he all this storie to renew, And tell the course of his captivitie" (IV, viii, 64, in *OED* 446). Note the provocative litany of terms—"renew", "tell", "storie"—for that poem is not just a spiritual allegory about known events: it also "delightfully" frames a struggle for salvation in the form of a slowly developing story. His heroes emerge from periods of wandering and lethargy to gradually comprehend their own true commitment and salvation.

There are, of course, countless stories for the LS to tell in the myriad of subjects that can nourish her literary criticism; there are also endless ways for her to tell them so that they will please her readers with the force of her convictions and the power of her insights. But that potential is now lost upon her. She may need to broaden the scope of her reading to reacquire the zest for literature that she once possessed. In this way, she may begin to confound her lethargy with the excitement that comes when a professor reads great books without feelings of guilt for not writing about them. The committee's emphasis to the LS must be on the resurgence of moral commitment in her research, on the intriguing potential in her exposition to tell a story as part of the province of criticism, and on the ability of such engaged work to mount a struggle against the depression that now afflicts her. In terms of initial practical solutions for her lack of productivity (other than the three meetings with her, and the related discussion of her published research), the committee will likely look more to her classroom interests than to her unstimulating publications. Whatever pride she feels about her vocation is only occasionally evident in her teaching, and my guess is that clues can be discovered in that arena about the literature and themes that are most meaningful to her. There is a well-established system of constructive "buddy evaluation" of teaching that I have instituted in my department among its tenured members, and this system—based on a yearly and arbitrary grouping of two faculty for mutual observations—is a likely place to begin the search for encouraging topics that may lead to an effective renewal in her research.

A final comment of unfashionable optimism. An implicit belief throughout my presentation is that there is unlikely to be terminably dead wood in any department, but (it is unfortunately true) there may be crusty, dried, and overloaded parchment that is eminently suitable for revision and renewal. It is with such tired "palimpsestic scholars"—upon whom new signatures of life can still be engrained and deciphered—that the formats and suggestions I describe may prove helpful and energizing. To change established habits of non-productivity and dissatisfaction is never an easy chore. Henry David Thoreau, as he so often does, expresses the mandate of such renewal with some timely lines on the imperative of change: "It seemed to me that I had several more lives to lead, and could not spare any more time for that one. It is remarkable how easily and insensibly we fall into a particular route, and make a beaten track for ourselves" (213).

Let me close my remarks today in Atlanta where I began, with a reference to two of the writers who provide epigraphs for our theme today. For the poet and the dramatist John Dryden at the end of the seventeenth century, "renewal" still carries the implication of gathering more knowledge to increase the *power* of the mind—a species of embattled metaphor that I earlier connected to issues of conquest and kingdom so prevalent in the literature and politics of the late Renaissance. D.H.

Lawrence conveys a vitalistic vision of the whole self and a related mandate to embrace opportunities for personal development and *re-creation* of the soul. His essay, "The State of Funk", carries acute relevance for a condition shared by the academic professionals described in my presentation today:

> We've got to change. And in our power to change, in our capacity to make new intelligent adaptations to new conditions, in our readiness to admit and fulfil new needs, to give expression to new desires and feelings, lies our hope and our health. Courage is the great word. Funk spells sheer disaster" (220).

Exactly a quarter-century ago, Norman Mailer displayed an impressive grasp of Lawrence's life and art in his lyrical and ruminative discussion of that writer in *The Prisoner of Sex*. But fifteen years before that nonfictional work, Mailer's novel *The Deer Park* contained evocative lines that recalled Lawrence's words from "The State of Funk", and their resonance provides the most essential advice about the imperative of renewal:

> There was that law of life so cruel and so just which demanded that one must grow or else pay more for remaining the same (346).

Bibliography

Abrams, M.H. *The Fourth Dimension of a Poem*. New York: Norton, 2012.

Allen, Walter. *The Short Story in English*. Oxford: Clarendon Press, 1981.

Alter, Robert, "The Persistence of Reading." *Partisan Review* 4 (1993): 510–516.

Asquith, Lady Cynthia. *Diaries 1915–1918*. New York: Alfred A. Knopf, 1969.

Balbert, Peter. *D.H. Lawrence and the Phallic Imagination: Essays on Sexual Identity and Feminist Misreading*. New York: St. Martin's, 1989.

—. *D.H. Lawrence and the Psychology of Rhythm*. The Hague: Mouton, 1974.

—. "From Hemingway to Lawrence to Mailer: Survival and Sexual Identity in *A Farewell to Arms*." *The Hemingway Review* 3 (1983): 30–43.

—. "Ten Men and a Sacred Prostitute: The Psychology of Sex in the Cambridge Edition of *The Lost Girl*." *Twentieth Century Literature* 36 (1990): 381–402.

—. The Chairperson as Model and Motivator: Department Scholarship and Teaching. *National Issues in Higher Education* 34 (1990): 39–47.

Balbert, Peter and Marcus, Phillip, Ed. *D.H. Lawrence: A Centenary Consideration*. Ithaca: Cornell UP, 1985.

Barzun, Jacques. *Begin Here: The Forgotten Conditions of Teaching and Learning*. Chicago: U of Chicago P, 1991.

Beauman, Nicola. *Cynthia Asquith*. London: Hamish Hamilton, 1987.

Bergler, Edmund. "D.H. Lawrence's 'The Fox' and the Psychoanalytic Theory on Lesbianism." In *A D.H. Lawrence Miscellany*, edited by Harry T. Moore, cited below.

Bloom, Allan. *The Closing of the American Mind: How Higher Education Has Failed Democracy and Impoverished the Souls of Today's Students*. New York: Simon and Schuster, 1987.

Bogdan, Georgieann and David S. Weaver. "Pre-Columbian Treponematois in Coastal North Carolina." *Disease and Demography in the Americas*. Ed. John W. Verano and Douglas H. Ubelaker. Washington, D.C.: Smithsonian Institution Press, 1992. 155–163.

Boyer, Ernest L. *Scholarship Reconsidered: Priorities of the Professoriate*. Princeton: Princeton UP, 1990.

Brayfield, Peggy L. "Lawrence's 'Male and Female' Principles and the Symbolism of 'The Fox'" *Mosaic* 4 (1971): 41–52.

Brooks, Cleanth. "The Remaking of the Canon." *Partisan Review* 2 (1991): 350–360.

Cain, William E. "A Literary Approach to Literature: Why English Departments Should Focus on Close Reading, Not Culture Studies." *The Chronicle of Higher Education*. December 13, 1996.

Chester, Robert and G. A. Kooy. *Divorce in Europe*. Leiden: Martinus Nijhoff. Social Sciences, 1977.

Cowan, James C.*D. H. Lawrence's American Journey: A Study in Literature and Myth*. Cleveland: The Press of Case Western Reserve U, 1970.

—. "D. H. Lawrence's Dualism: Apollonian and Dionysian Polarity and *The Ladybird*."*Forms of Modern British Fiction*. Ed. Allan Warren Friedman. Austin: U of Texas P, 1975. 75–99.

—. "Lawrence, Freud, and Masturbation." *Mosaic: A Journal for the Interdisciplinary Study of Literature* 28 (1995): 69–98.

—. "The Fall of John Thomas."*Literature and Medicine II* (1992): 266–93.

Cushman, Keith. "The Virgin and the Gipsy and the Lady and the Game Keeper," in *D.H. Lawrence's Lady: A New Look at Lady Chatterley's Lover*. Ed. Michael Squires and Dennis Jackson. Athens: University of Georgia Press, 1985. 154–69.

Daalder, Joost. "Background and Significance of D. H. Lawrence's *The Ladybird*."*The D. H. Lawrence Review* 15 (1982): 107–28.

Daleski, H. M. "The Encoding of *The Lost Girl*." *D.H. Lawrence Review 30* (2001): 15–26.

—. *The Forked Flame: A Study of D.H. Lawrence*. Madison: U of Wisconsin P, rev. ed. 1987.

Darroch, Sandra Jobson. "Katherine Mansfield: D. H. Lawrence's "'Lost Girl.'"*Rananim* 17 (2010). www.dhlawrencesocietyaustralia.com.au p.6.

Davis, Patricia C. "Chicken Queen's Delight: D.H. Lawrence's 'The Fox'." *Modern Fiction Studies* 19 (1973–74): 565–71.

Delaney, Paul. *D.H. Lawrence's Nightmare*. New York: Basic Books, 1978.

Delbanco, Andrew. "The Politics of Separatism." *Partisan Review* 4 (1993): 534–42.

Doherty, Gerald."A 'Very Funny Story': Figural Play in D.H. Lawrence's *The Captain's Doll*." *D.H. Lawrence Review* 18 (1985–86): 5–17.
—. "Connie and the Chakras: Yogic Patterns in D.H. Lawrence's *Lady Chatterley's Lover*." *D.H. Lawrence Review* 13 (1980): 70–92.
Draper, R.P. "The Defeat of Feminism: D.H. Lawrence's 'The Fox' and 'The Women Who Rode Away'." *Studies in Short Fiction* 3 (1965–66): 186–98.
Dyer, Geoff. *Out of Sheer Rage: Wrestling with D.H. Lawrence*. New York: Farrar, Strauss, and Giroux, Picador Edition, 1997.
Einstein, Albert. *Ideas and Opinions*. New York: Crown, 1954.
Ellis, David. *D.H. Lawrence: Dying Game, 1922–1930*. Cambridge: Cambridge UP, 1998.
—. *Death and the Author: How D.H. Lawrence Died, and Was Remembered*. New York: Oxford UP, 2008.
Ellis, John M. *Literature Lost: Social Agendas and the Corruption of the Humanities*. New Haven: Yale UP, 1997.
Emerson, Ralph Waldo. "The American Scholar." *Selections from Ralph Waldo Emerson*. Ed. Stephen E. Whicher. Boston: Houghton Mifflin, Riverside Edition, 1960. 63–80.
Feinstein, Elaine. *Lawrence and the Women: The Intimate Life of D. H. Lawrence*. New York: Harper Collins, 1993.
Fitzgerald, F. Scott. *The Great Gatsby*. New York: Scribner's, 1953.
Fleishman, Avrom. "He Do the Polis in Different Voices: Lawrence's Later Style." *D. H. Lawrence: A Centenary Consideration*. Ed. Balbert and Marcus. 162–79.
Ford, George. *Double Measure: A Study of the Novels and Stories of D.H. Lawrence*. New York: Holt, Rinehart, and Winston, 1965.
Franks, Jill. "Myth and Biography in *Where Angels Fear to Tread* and *The Lost Girl.*" *D. H. Lawrence Review* 30(2001): 27–42.
Frazer, James. *The Golden Bough*. New York: Macmillan, 1963.
Freud, Anna. *The Ego and the Mechanisms of Defence*. New York: International UP, 1946.
Freud, Sigmund. *A General History of Psychoanalysis*. New York: Washington Square Press, 1960.
—. *An Outline of Psycho-Analysis*. New York: Norton, 1949.
—. *Leonardo da Vinci and a Memory of His Childhood*. Trans. Alan Tyson. New York: Norton, 1964.
—. "Mourning and Melancholia." *The Freud Reader*. Ed. Peter Gay. New York: Norton, 1989. 584–88.
—. *New Introductory Lectures on Psychoanalysis*. New York: Norton, 1965.

—. "On the Universal Tendency to Debasement in the Sphere of Love (Contributions to the Psychology of Love II)."*The Freud Reader*. Ed. Peter Gay. New York: Norton, 1989. 394–400.
—. "On Narcissism: An Introduction."*The Freud Reader*. Ed. Peter Gay. 545–62.
—. *The Ego and Id*. New York: Avon, 1962.
—. *The Interpretation of Dreams*. New York: Avon, 1965.
—. *Three Essays on the Theory of Sexuality*. New York: Avon, 1962.
Frost, Robert. *The Poetry of Robert Frost*. Ed. Edward Connery Lathem. New York: Henry Holt and Company, 1979.
Fulmer, O. Bryan."The Significance of the Death of the Fox in D.H. Lawrence's 'The Fox'."*Studies in Short Fiction* 5 (1967–68): 275–82.
Funk and Wagnalls Standard College Dictionary. New York: Harcourt, Brace, and World, 1963.
Gay, Peter. *Freud:A Life for Our Time*. New York: Norton, 1988.
Gilbert, Sandra. "Potent Griselda: *The Ladybird* and the Great Mother." *D.H. Lawrence: A Centenary Consideration*. Ed. Balbert and Marcus. 130–61.
Girard, René. "The Humanities: A Treasury for All the Disciplines." *Academic Questions* Winter (1994–95).
Granofsky, Ronald. *D.H. Lawrence and Survival: Darwinism in the Fiction of the Transitional Period*. Montreal:McGill–Queens UP, 2003.
—. "Illness and Wellness in D. H. Lawrence's *The Ladybird*." *Orbis Litterum* 51 (1996): 99–117.
Gregor, Ian. "'The Fox': A Caveat." *Essays in Criticism* 9 (1959): 10–21.
Gurko, Leo. "D.H. Lawrence's Greatest Collection of Short Stories: What Holds It Together." *Modern Fiction Studies* 18 (1972–73): 173–82.
Harris, Janice Hubbard. *The Short Fiction of D.H. Lawrence*. New Brunswick: Rutgers UP, 1984.
Hemingway, Ernest. "Big Two-Hearted River, Part I." *The Complete Short Stories of Ernest Hemingway. The Finca Vigía Edition*. New York: Scribner's Sons, 1987. 163–69.
—. "Fathers and Sons." *The Complete Short Stories of Ernest Hemingway*. The Finca Vigia Edition. New York: Scribner's Sons, 1987. 369–77.
—. "Indian Camp." *The Complete Short Stories of Ernest Hemingway*. 67–70.
—. "Soldier's Home."*The Complete Short Stories of Ernest Hemingway*. 111–16.
—. "The End of Something." *The Complete Short Stories of Ernest Hemingway*. 163–69.

Himmelfarb, Gertrude. "The Remaking of the Canon." *Partisan Review* 2 (1991): 360–64.

Hook, Sidney, Paul Kurtz, and Miro Tudorovich, Ed. *The Idea of the Modern University*. Buffalo: Prometheus, 1974.

Hough, Graham. *The Dark Sun: A Study of D.H. Lawrence*. New York: Capricorn, 1956.

Humma, John. B. *Metaphor and Meaning in D. H. Lawrence's Later Novels*. Columbia: U of Missouri P, 1990.

Hunter, George. "The History of Style as a Style of History." *Addressing Frank Kermode: Essays in Criticism and Interpretation.* Ed. Margaret Tudeau-Clayton and Martin Warner. Urbana: U of Illinois P, 1991. 74–88.

Hutchins, Robert M."The University and the Mind of the Age."*Measure* 2 (1950).

Jenkins, Lee M. *The American Lawrence*. Gainesville: UP of Florida, 2015.

Jones, Ernest. *The Life and Work of Sigmund Freud: Vol. II, Years of Maturity*, 1901–1914. New York: Basic Books, 1955.

Jones, Lawrence. "Physiognomy and the Sensual Will in *The Ladybird* and *The Fox*." *The D. H. Lawrence Review*13 (1980): 1–29.

Joyce, James. "The Dead." *Dubliners*. New York: Viking, 1961.

Kermode, Frank."The Men on the Dump: A Response." *Addressing Frank Kermode: Essays in Criticism and Interpretation*. Ed. Margaret Tudeau-Clayton and Martin Warner. London: Macmillan, 1991.

Kinkead-Weekes, Mark. *D. H. Lawrence: Triumph to Exile, 1912–1922*. Cambridge: Cambridge UP, 1996.

Lawrence, D. H. *Apocalypse and the Writings on Revelation*. Ed. Mara Kalnins. Cambridge: Cambridge UP, 1980.

—. "Apropos of *Lady Chatterley's Lover*." *Lady Chatterley's Lover*. Ed. Michael Squires. New York: Cambridge UP, 1993. 303–35.

—. "Art and Morality." *Study of Thomas Hardy and Other Essays*. Ed. Bruce Steele. Cambridge: Cambridge UP, 1985. 163–68.

—. "The Bad Side of Books." *Introductions and Reviews*. Ed. N.H. Reeve and John Worthen. Cambridge: Cambridge UP, 2005. 73–78.

—. "Blessed are the Powerful." *Reflections on the Death of a Porcupine and Other Essays*. Ed. Michael Herbert. Cambridge: Cambridge UP, 1988. 319–28.

—. "The Crown." *Reflections on the Death of a Porcupine and Other Essays*. 251–306.

—. "Dance of the Sprouting Corn." *Mornings in Mexico and Other Essays*, Ed. Virginia Crosswhite Hyde. Cambridge: Cambridge UP, 2009. 71–76.

—. "Democracy." *Reflections on the Death of a Porcupine and Other Essays*. 61–83.

—. "Education of the People." *Reflections on the Death of a Porcupine.* 85–166.

—. Foreword to *Women in Love*. Ed. David Farmer, Lindeth Vasey and John Worthen. Cambridge: Cambridge UP, 1987. 485–86.

—. *The Fox* (first version). In *A D.H. Lawrence Miscellany*, 28–48, Ed. Harry T. Moore. Cited below.

—. *The Fox, The Captain's Doll, The Ladybird.* Ed. Dieter Mehl. Cambridge: Cambridge UP, 1992.

—. "The Hopi Snake Dance." *Mornings in Mexico and Other Essays*. 79–94.

—. "Indians and Entertainment." *Mornings in Mexico and Other Essays.* 59–68.

—. "Introduction to These Paintings." *Late Essays and Articles*. Ed. James T. Boulton. Cambridge: Cambridge UP, 2004. 182–217.

—. *Introductions and Reviews*. Eds. N.H. Reeve and John Worthen. Cambridge: Cambridge UP, 2005.

—. *Late Essays and Articles*. Cited above.

—. *The Letters of D.H. Lawrence, I, 1901–13*. Ed. James. T. Boulton. Cambridge: Cambridge UP, 1979.

—. *The Letters of D. H. Lawrence, II, 1913–16*. Ed. George J. Zytaruk and James T. Boulton. Cambridge: Cambridge UP, 1981.

—. *The Letters of D.H. Lawrence, III, 1916–21*. Ed. James T. Boulton and Andrew Robertson. Cambridge: Cambridge UP, 1984.

—. *The Letters of D. H. Lawrence, IV, 1921–24*. Ed. Warren Roberts, James T. Boulton, and Elizabeth Mansfield. Cambridge: Cambridge UP, 1987.

—. *The Letters of D. H. Lawrence, V, 1924–27*. Ed. James T. Boulton and Lindeth Vasey. Cambridge: Cambridge UP, 1989.

—. *The Letters of D.H. Lawrence, VI, 1927–28*. Ed. James T. Boulton and Margaret H. Boulton with Gerald M. Lacy. Cambridge: Cambridge UP, 1991.

—. *The Letters of D.H. Lawrence, VII, 1928–1930*. Ed. Keith Sagar and James T. Boulton. Cambridge: Cambridge UP. 1993.

—. *The Lost Girl*. Ed. John Worthen. Cambridge: Cambridge UP, 1981.

—. "Love was Once a Little Boy." *Reflections on the Death of a Porcupine and Other Essays*. 329–46.

—. "Memoir of Maurice Magnus."*Introductions and Reviews*. 11–72.
—. "Morality in the Novel." *Study of Thomas Hardy and Other Essays*. Ed. Bruce Steele. Cambridge: Cambridge UP. 171–76.
—. *Movements in European History*. Ed. Philip Crumpton. Cambridge: Cambridge UP, 1989.
—. "The Novel." *Study of Thomas Hardy*. 177–90.
—. "The Novel and the Feelings." *Study of Thomas Hardy*. 199–205.
—. "On Being a Man." *Reflections on the Death of a Porcupine and Other Essays*. 211–22.
—. "Pan in America," *Mornings in Mexico and Other Essays*. 155–64.
—. "Pornography and Obsenity." *Late Essays and Articles*. 233–53.
—. "The Princess" *St. Mawr and Other Stories*. Ed. Brian Finney. Cambridge: Cambridge UP, 1983. 157–96.
—. *Psychoanalysis and the Unconscious* and *Fantasia of the Unconscious*. Ed. Bruce Steele. Cambridge: Cambridge UP, 2004.
—. *The Rainbow*. Ed. Mark Kinkead-Weekes. Cambridge: Cambridge UP, 1989.
—. "The Real Thing." *Late Essays and Articles*. 304–10.
—. "Review of *In Our Time* by Ernest Hemingway." *Introductions and Reviews*.311–12.
—. *St. Mawr and Other Stores*. Ed. Brian Finney. Cambridge: Cambridge UP, 1983.
—. "The State of Funk." *Late Essays and Articles*. 218–24
—. *Studies in Classic American Literature*. Ed. Ezra Greenspan, Lindeth Vasey, and John Worthen. Cambridge: Cambridge UP, 2003.
—. *The Virgin and the Gipsy and other Stories*. Ed. Michael Herbert, Bethan Jones and Lindeth Vasey. Cambridge: Cambridge UP, 2005.
—. "Why the Novel Matters." *Study of Thomas Hardy*. 191–98.
—. *Women In Love*. Ed. David Farmer, Lindeth Vasey, and John Worthen. Cited above in Foreword.
Lawrence, Frieda. *Not I, But the Wind*. New York: Viking P, 1934.
Leavis, F.R.*D.H. Lawrence: Novelist*. New York: Simon and Schuster, Clarion Book, 1969.
—. *Thought, Words and Creativity: Art and Thought in Lawrence*. New York: Oxford UP, 1976.
Lennon, J. Michael. *Norman Mailer: A Double Life*. New York: Simon and Schuster, 2013.
Lessing, Doris. "Foreword."In *The Fox* by D.H. Lawrence. London: Hesperus Press, 2002.
—. *The Golden Notebook*. New York: Ballantine, 1962.

MacDonald, Robert H. "Images of Negative Union: The Symbolic World of D.H. Lawrence's 'The Princess.'" *Studies in Short Fiction* 16 (1979): 289–93.
Mailer, Norman. *Advertisements for Myself.* New York: G.P. Putnam's Sons, 1959.
—. *Armies of the Night*. New York: The New American Library, 1968.
—. *Cannibals and Christians*. New York: The Dial Press, 1966.
—. *The Deer Park*. New York: G.P. Putnam's Sons, 1955.
—. *Existential Errands*. Boston: Little Brown, 1972.
—. *Marilyn: A Biography*. New York: Grosset and Dunlap, 1973.
—. "Norman Mailer: Interview, The Art of Fiction, No. 193." *The Paris Review* 181 (2007): 44–80.
—. *Of a Fire on the Moon*. Boston: Little Brown, 1970.
—. *The Prisoner of Sex*. Boston: Little Brown, 1971.
—. *Selected Letters of Norman Mailer*. Ed. J. Michael Lennon. New York: Random House, 2014.
—. "The White Negro."*Advertisements for Myself.* 337–58.
Mansfield, Katherine. *Journal*. Ed. J. Middleton Murry. New York: Knopf, 1946.
—. *The Scrapbook of Katherine Mansfield*. Ed. J. Middleton Murry. New York: Knopf, 1939.
Marcus, Steven. "Soft Totalitarianism." *Partisan Review* 4 (1993): 630–38.
Martin, W.R. "Hannele's 'Surrender': A Misreading of *The Captain's Doll*." *D.H. Lawrence Review* 18 (1985–86): 19–24.
McDowell, Frederick P.W. "'The Individual in His Pure Singleness': Theme and Symbol in *The Captain's Doll*."*The Challenge of D.H. Lawrence*. Ed. Michael Squires and Keith Cushman. Madison: U of Wisconsin P, 1990. 143–48.
Mellown, Elgin. "*The Captain's Doll*: Its Origins and Literary Allusions." *D.H. Lawrence Review* 9 (1976): 26–35.
Merivale, Patricia. *Pan the Goat-God: His Myth in Modern Times*. Cambridge: Harvard UP, 1969.
Meyers, Jeffrey. *D.H. Lawrence: A Biography*. New York: Cooper Square, 2002.
Miles, Thomas H. "Birkin's Electro-Mystical Body of Reality: D. H. Lawrence's Use of Kundalini."*D. H. Lawrence Review* 9 (1976): 194–212.
Miller, J. Hillis. "Literary Study in the University Without Idea." *ADE Bulletin* 113 (Spring 1993).
Millett, Kate. *Sexual Politics*. Garden City: Doubleday, 1970.

Moore, Harry T. Ed. *A D.H. Lawrence Miscellany*. Carbondale: Southern Illinois UP, 1959.

—. "D.H. Lawrence and the 'Censor-Morons.'" *D.H. Lawrence: Sex, Literature, and Censorship*. New York: Viking, 1959.

—. *The Priest of Love*. New York: Farrar, Straus and Giroux, 1974.

Moynahan, Julian. *The Deed of Life: The Novels and Tales of D. H. Lawrence*. Princeton: Princeton UP, 1963.

Murry, J. Middleton. *Athenaeum* 17 Dec. 1920: 836.

Online Slang Dictionary (American, English, and Urban Slang) http://onlineslangdictionary.com.

Ortner, Donald J. "Skeletal Paleopathology: Probabilities, Possibilities, and Impossibilities." *Disease and Demography in the Americas*, Ed. Verano and Ubelaker, cited above under Bogdan.

Ouspensky, Peter A. *Tertium Organum: A Key to the Enigmas of the Universe*. 1911. Trans. Nicholas Bessaradoff and Claude Bragdon. New York: Random House, 1970.

Pack, Robert. "God Keep Me a Damned Fool." *Academic Questions* 8 (Summer 1995).

Preston, Peter. *A D.H. Lawrence Chronology*. New York: St. Martin's, 1994.

Pryse, James M. *The Apocalypse Unsealed*. New York: James M. Pryse, 1910.

Rieff, Philip. "Introduction." In *Psychoanalysis and the Unconscious* and *Fantasia of the Unconscious* by D.H. Lawrence. New York: Viking, 1960. vii–xxiii.

Ross, Michael L. "Losing the Old National Hat: Lawrence's *The Lost Girl*."*D. H. Lawrence Review* 30 (2001): 5–14.

Rossi, Patrizio. "Lawrence's Two Foxes: A Comparison of Texts." *Essays in Criticism* 22 (1972): 265–78.

Rossman, Charles. "'You Are the Call and I Am the Answer': D. H. Lawrence and Women." *D.H. Lawrence Review* 8 (1975): 225–328.

Ruderman, Judith. *D.H. Lawrence and the Devouring Mother: The Search for a Patriarchal Ideal of Leadership*.Durham, Duke UP, 1984.

—. "Lawrence's 'The Fox' and Verga's 'The She Wolf': Variations on the Theme of the 'Devouring Mother'." *Modern Language Notes* 94 (1979): 153–65.

—. "Tracking Lawrence's *Fox*: An Account of its Composition, Evolution, and Publication." *Studies in Bibliography* 33 (1980): 207–21.

—. *Race and Identity in D.H. Lawrence: Indians, Gypsies, and Jews*. New York: Palgrave Macmillan, 2014.

Sagar, Keith. *D. H. Lawrence: Life In to Art*. Athens: U of Georgia P, 1990.

Sandler, Joseph, with Anna Freud. *The Analysis of Defense: The Ego and the Mechanisms of Defense Revisited*. New York: International Universities Press, 1985.

Schneider, Daniel. *The Consciousness of D. H. Lawrence: An Intellectual Biography*. Lawrence: UP of Kansas, 1986.

Scott, James F. "D. H. Lawrence's Germania: Ethnic Psychology and Cultural Crisis in the Shorter Fiction."*The D. H. Lawrence Review* 10 (1977): 142–64.

Searle, John R. "Is There a Crisis in American Higher Education?" *Partisan Review* 4 (1993): 693–709.

Siegel, Carol. *Lawrence Among the Women: Wavering Boundaries in Women's Literary Traditions*. Charlottesville: UP of Virginia, 1991.

Simpson, Hilary. *D.H Lawrence and Feminism*. DeKalb: Northern Illinois UP. 1982.

Spilka, Mark. *Renewing the Normative D. H. Lawrence: A Personal Progress*. Columbia: U of Missouri P, 1992.

—. *The Love Ethic of D.H. Lawrence*. Bloomington: Indiana UP, 1955.

Squires, Michael and Keith Cushman, Ed. *The Challenge of D.H. Lawrence*.

Squires, Michael, and Lynne K. Talbot. *Living at the Edge: A Biography of D. H. Lawrence and Frieda von Richthofen*. Madison: U of Wisconsin P, 2002.

Stevens, Wallace. "Thirteen Ways of Looking at a Blackbird." *Wallace Stevens: Collected Poetry and Prose*. Ed. Joan Richardson and Frank Kermode. New York: Library of America, 1997. 74.

Tedlock, E.W. *D.H. Lawrence: Artist and Rebel*. Albuquerque: U of New Mexico P, 1963.

The Compact Edition of the Oxford English Dictionary. New York: Oxford UP, 1974.

The Norton Anthology of English Literature Ed. M.H. Abrams et al. New York: Norton, 1974.

Thoreau, Henry David. *Walden and Civil Disobedience*. Ed. Owen Thomas. New York: Norton, 1966.

—. *Walden and Other Writings*. New York: The Modern Library, 1950.

Thornycroft, Rosalind [Baynes].*Time Which Spaces Us Apart*. Completed by Chloë Baynes. Batcombe: Private Publication, 1991.

Turner, John. "Purity and Danger in D.H. Lawrence's *The Virgin and the Gipsy*." *D.H. Lawrence's Centenary Essays*. Ed. Mara Kalnins. Bristol: Bristol Classical, 1986. 211–28.

Verano, John W. and Douglas H. Ubelaker, Eds. "Health and Disease in the Pre-Columbian World." *Seeds of Change: A Quincentennial Commemoration*. Ed. Herman J. Viola and Carolyn Margolis. Washington D.C.: Smithsonian Institution Press, 1991. 217–21.

Vickery, John B. *The Literary Impact* of *The Golden Bough*. Princeton: Princeton UP, 1973.

Vivas, Eliseo. *D.H. Lawrence: The Failure and the Triumph of Art*. Bloomington: Indiana UP, Midland Book, 1964.

Webster's Collegiate Dictionary. Tenth Edition. Springfield: Merriam Webster, 1993.

Webster's New World College Dictionary. New York: Macmillan, 1997. Third Edition.

Weiner, S. Ronald."Irony and Symbolism in 'The Princess.'" *A D.H. Lawrence Miscellany*. 221–38.

Widmer, Kingsley.*Defiant Desire: Some Dialectical Legacies of D. H. Lawrence*. Carbondale: Southern Illinois UP, 1992.

—. *The Art of Perversity: D. H. Lawrence's Shorter Fictions*. Seattle: U of Washington P, 1962.

Wilde, Alan. "The Illusion of *St. Mawr*: Technique and Vision in D. H. Lawrence's Later Novels."*PMLA* 79 (1964): 164–70.

Wolkenfeld, Suzanne. "The Sleeping Beauty Retold: D.H. Lawrence's 'The Fox'." *Studies in Short Fiction* 14 (1977): 345–52.

Worthen, John. *D.H. Lawrence: The Early Years, 1885–1912*.Cambridge: Cambridge UP, 1991.

—. *D. H. Lawrence: The Life of an Outsider*. New York: Counterpoint, 2005.

Young, Richard O. "Where Even the Trees Come and Go: D.H. Lawrence and the Fourth Dimension." *D.H. Lawrence Review* 13 (1980): 30–44.

INDEX

Note: page numbers in italics refer to figures.

Aaron's Rod (Lawrence), 16
Abrams, M. H., 235–36n17
Academic Questions (periodical), 8
Advertisements for Myself (Mailer), 265
Alter, Robert, 275, 281–82, 285
An American Dream (Mailer), 254
"The American Scholar" (Emerson), 284–85
anal sex. *See also* coccygeal continuum; *The Lost Girl* (Lawrence)
  chakra theory in Lawrence and, 18–19, 18–19n4, 36n9
  instinctual desire in Lawrence and, 15
  in *Lady Chatterley's Lover*, 19n4, 35–36
  limited critical attention to, 36n9
  psychological meaning of for Lawrence, 23–24
  in *The Rainbow*, 24, 35–36
  in *Women in Love*, 24
appleyness (animate vitality)
  in Cezanne, 183–85
  Dollie's lack of in "The Princess," 192
  and intuitive perception, 195
  Lawrence on, 183–85, 195
  in Lawrence's paintings, 184–85, 195–96
  as link to transcendent unknown, 184
  O'Keeffe's "The Lawrence Tree, 1929" and, 191
  and Pan-power, 191–92
  in "The Princess," 196–98, 203
"Apropos of *Lady Chatterley's Lover*" (Lawrence), 249, 266
The Armies of the Night (Mailer), 252, 258
"Art and Morality" (Lawrence)
  on act of seeing in age of camera, 191–92
  on art and fluidity, 198
  on fourth-dimensional prose, 224, 225
  Lawrence on writing of, 214
  on self-conception based in appearance, 202
  writing of, 209
art criticism of Lawrence
  desire to "review a book plainly," 214, 215
  and illness of 1925, 192
Asquith, Cynthia
  accomplishments of, 123
  affair with Blackwood, 129
  diary of, 123
  family's awareness of Lawrence's obsession with, 149
  friendship with Lawrence, 149
  lack of sexual interest in husband, 141, 144
  Lawrence characters based on, 125n4, 129, 130, 130n10
  Lawrence on character of, 150
  Lawrence's correspondence with, 20, 101–2, 106, 149–50
  Lawrence's "Dance Sketch" and, 231
  Lawrence's obsession with, 123, 148–49

Lawrence's suppression of feelings for, 152
marriage of, 123
as model for Daphne in *The Ladybird*, 123, 129, 140, 141
naming of, 134
penchant for flirtation short of adultery, 125n4, 129, 135
as subject of Lawrence's "North Sea," 150, *151*
troubled relationship with Lawrence, 127
Asquith, Herbert "Beb," 124, 127, 129, 143
Athenaeum (periodical), 16, 17, 20, 25

"The Bad Side of Books" (Lawrence), 37, 177, 178–79
Balder, Norse myth of in *The Captain's Doll*, 76–82, 85n16, 87
Baynes, Rosalind Thornycroft
Lawrence's affair with, 17, 20, 52, 116, 257–58
Lawrence's correspondence with, 19–20
memoirs of, 17, 17n3
Beauman, Nicola, 129, 134, 141, 143, 149, 150
Blackwood, Basil, 129, 142
"Blessed are the Powerful" (Lawrence), 221
blood-consciousness. *See also* instinctual primacy
animal metaphors for, 215
of Hepburn in *Captain's Doll*, 82–84
Lawrence on, 90–91n4, 247–48
in Lawrence's novels, 253–54
in Mailer, 250n4, 253
in *The Rainbow*, 251–52, 253
Bloom, Allan, 9–10
"The Borderline" (Lawrence), 155
border-line people
Hepburn as in *The Captain's Doll*, 80–82
in *The Ladybird*, 146
Lawrence's fascination with, 81
Lawrence's self-perception as, 81, 82
Borrow, George, 211n4
Boulton, James, 211
The Boy in the Bush (Lawrence), 154
Brett, Dorothy, 173, 212, 262
Brewster, Earl, 86
Brooks, Cleanth, 277

Cain, William, 276, 278, 282, 283, 285
Cannibals and Christians (Mailer), 249
The Canterbury Tales (Chaucer), 293, 295
The Captain's Doll (Lawrence)
as comedy, 58–59, 58–59n5
critics on, 55–60, 57n3, 58–59nn4–5, 58n2, 60n6
ending of as issue for Lawrence, 86–87
excursion to Karlinger Glacier, 74–87
fourth level added to, 83–86
Hannele's taunting of Hepburn during, 78, 79
as Hepburn's battle for male primacy, 74, 75–76, 78, 79, 81, 85–86
Hepburn's climb onto glacier, 83–86
Hepburn's fear of heights and, 74, 82
Hepburn's poor conditioning and, 74–75, 76, 78, 79
Hepburns' proposal during, 85
Hepburn's triumph over fear in, 83–86
image of doll carried in, 74, 80, 87
Lawrence's style in, 84, 84–85n15

and Norse myth of Balder, 76–82, 85n16, 87
three levels of, 74, 78–79, 80, 81–82
topographic anthropomorphism in, 74, 75–76, 82
and Frazer's influence on Lawrence, 76–77
Hannele
attraction to Hepburn's emotional distance, 62, 68–69, 80–81
confidence of, 61
éducation sentimentale of, as theme, 56
engagement to von Poldi, 73–74
Hepburn's separation from after wife's death, 71–72
infatuation with Hepburn, 62–63
parallels to Frieda Lawrence, 81
as trapped within ego's defenses, 63, 64, 66
as war casualty, 64
Hannele-Hepburn marriage
critics on, 56–58
parallels to Lawrence's marriage, 56, 56n2, 59, 86–87
as recognition of her deepest need, 56
Hepburn
depression of, 67, 70
emotional distance of, 62, 66, 80–81
god-like indifference of, 65, 67
Hannele's power to heal, 68
indecisiveness of, 62, 64–65, 66
instinctual primacy in, 253
on life, heartache in, 70
on marriage as imprisonment, 69–70
and need to achieve transcendent unknown, 66, 83
parallels to Hemingway's Krebs, 70–71
parallels to Lawrence, 59, 81, 86–87
as part mythical figure, 65–66, 67, 69, 76–82, 85n16, 87
as person on border-line, 80–82
process of ego reconstruction in, 60
recovery of, through narcissistic libido, 72–73
renewal of, 5, 68, 72, 77, 79, 85n16
retreat from society following wife's death, 69–72
return to Hannele, 72–73
struggle for primacy, 59–60, 73, 75–76, 78, 79, 81, 85–87
war-damaged psyche of, 62, 65
integration of theme and technique in, 60
Leavis on theme of, 55–56, 59
manikin/doll of Hepburn
and ego as doll-like, 63
Hannele's abuse of, 61, 64
Hannele's relinquishment of, 87
Hepburn's anger at, 73, 74, 80, 85–86, 87
Hepburn's return to Hannele and, 72–73
reappearance in other forms, 63
spell cast by, 72–73

totemic power of, 87
as type of betrayal, 77, 85–86, 87
as type of revenge, 61
marriage matrix as theme in, 5
"The Mortal Coil" and, 60n6
Mrs. Hepburn
belittling of Hepburn in front of Hannele, 67–68
death of as murder, critics on, 58, 58n4, 69–70
discovery of Hepburn's affair, 64
on Hepburn as war-damaged psyche, 68
Hepburns' efforts to repair breach with, 64–65, 66–67
ignorance of husband's needs, 68
mistaking of Mitchka for mistress, 67, 68
and mythical component to Lawrence's characters, 65
opening scene of, 60–67
patriarchal ethic of, 58, 59
political incorrectness of, 59
telescope as metaphor in, 64
on war's damage to men's psyches, 61–62, 62n7, 70–71
Carco, Francisco, 53–54
Carswell, Catherine, 153, 180
censorship of Lawrence's works, 126, 182, 245
Cezanne, Paul, "appleyness" in, 183–85, 195, 196
chakra theory
and anal sex in Lawrence, 18–19, 18–19n4, 36n9
and Lawrence's conception of malehood, 18–19
in *Psychoanalysis and the Unconscious*, 21, 22–23
change
anal sex and, in *The Lost Girl*, 38, 53
imperative of
and faculty research, 306–7
instinct and, 22
Lawrence on, 249, 268, 307
Mailer on, 307
Chaucer, 292, 293, 294–95, 296
Christianity and English art, Lawrence on, 182, 183
coccygeal continuum. *See also* anal sex; *The Lost Girl*, coccygeal continuum in
and anal sex, 18–19, 18–19n4
as antidote to oedipal complex, 22, 23, 24–25
association with darkness, 18–19, 22–23
chakra theory and, 18–19
drive of toward transcendent unknown, 24, 48–50, 53, 54
and existential self-definition, 24
in Lawrence's Whitman essays, 19
as most secret center of being, 25
in *Psychoanalysis and the Unconscious*, 22–23
repression of by logical faculties, 23, 24
as source of instinctive knowledge, 19
conscious being
expanded boundaries of as goal in Lawrence's writing, 15
as goal of Lawrence's characters, 1
as goal of life, 22, 39–40
unconscious mind as drive toward, 24
courage
and embrace of change, 249
and embrace of transcendent unknown, 262
and erotic risk

Lawrence on, 246–47, 249, 251, 255, 261, 262–63
Mailer on, 246–47, 249, 250–51, 264–68, 270, 271–72, 280
instinctual primacy and, 113, 247
and male primacy, 22, 52, 59, 83
Cowan, James, 123n2, 147n19, 157n6, 157n7, 158n8, 163n13, 181n1
critical reception, Lawrence's concerns about, 126
"The Crown" (Lawrence), 213
Cushman, Keith, 207n1, 220n11, 229n13, 241n19

Daleski, H. M., 18n4, 99n10, 208
"Dance Sketch" (Lawrence), 231–32, *232*, 233
darkness in Lawrence. *See also* coccygeal continuum
association with coccygeal continuum, 18–19, 22–23
of Ciccio in *The Lost Girl*, 28, 29–32, 33, 35–37, 44–45
Fantasia of the Unconscious on, 139
of fox in *The Fox*, 95–96, 97–98
as freedom from rational caution, 30
and Pan-power, *in St. Mawr*, 163
of Psanek in *The Ladybird*, 131, 132, 140–41, 143–44, 144–45, 146
The Deer Park (Mailer)
censorship of, 6
demeaning notions of sex in, 260–61
ego-based sexual posturing in, 255, 260–61
and erotic risk, 250–51, 264–65, 265–68, 270, 271–72
existentialism in, 248
failed search for genuine love in, 264–65, 266–68, 271–72
on imperative of change, 307
influence of Lawrence on, 222–23, 271–72
O'Shaugnhessy's seduction of Lulu in, 250–51, 251n5
parallels to *Lady Chatterley's Lover*, 259–61
on sex without love, 259
as story of recovery from impotence, 264–65
"Democracy" (Lawrence), 13, 22
devouring mother syndrome. *See also* Oedipal complex
coccygeal continuum as source of healing for, 23
Lawrence on Frieda and, 13, 16
Lawrence on his susceptibility to, 12
Ruderman on, 25–26n6
sexual debasement as antidote for in *The Lost Girl*, 29, 32, 36–38
D.H. Lawrence and the Phallic Imagination (Balbert), 6, 269
Dodge, Mabel, 82, 117
dreams, interpretation of, 100–101

"Education of the People" (Lawrence), 14, 14n1
ego-dominated poses in Lawrence's fiction, 254–55, 260–61
Einstein, Albert, 287
Ellis, David
on Frazer's influence on Lawrence, 159n9, 189n7
on Frieda's guilt about children, 154
on Frieda's sex life, 212
on Lawrence's "Dance Sketch," 231
on Lawrence's final years, 155, 220
on Lawrence's love for Frieda, 257n10
on Lawrence's tuberculosis, 177
on *St. Mawr*, 157n6
Ellis, John, 3, 4, 10, 125n4

Emerson, Ralph W., 246–47n2, 284–85
"The End of Something" (Hemingway), 279–80
English art and sexual repression, Lawrence on, 181–83
erotic risk
Lawrence on, 249, 255, 261, 262–63, 266
Mailer on, 246–47, 249, 250–51, 264–68, 270, 271–72, 280
essays of 1925, 209, 213–14, 218, 225
Existential Errands (Mailer), 270–71, 272

Fabyan Chronicles, 296
faculty research
as call for renewal, 292
factors stifling, 291
importance of, 291–92
faculty research, strategies for renewal of
in case of later-career lapse into unproductivity, 300–303
in case of lethargic scholar, 303–6
in case of rejected scholar, 294–98
in case of scholar with long-range project, 298–301
department chair and, 293n3
essay revision as analog of, 292–93, 295–96
imperative of change and, 306–7
necessity of individual's cooperation in, 293
The Faerie Queen (Spenser), 305
Fantasia of the Unconscious (Lawrence)
attack on Freud in, 90
on balance of upper and lower *chakras*, 47
on blackness of creative depths, 92
on body-self relationship, 112
critique of Freud in, 21, 91
on dark inner truth *vs.* white surface, 139
on dreams, interpretation of, 100
on dreams of wild animals, 97n9
Foreword to, 117
on Frazer's *Golden Bough*, 91
and Frazer's influence on Lawrence, 76–77, 77n10
on human senses, 106
on magic and ritual, 93
on male "deep purpose," 115
on male primacy, 113, 114, 117
on modern modes of vision, 96
on pause before whole soul speaks, 112
on sanctity of life, 67
struggle between emotion and intellect as central theme in, 90
on vibratory rapport of man and surroundings, 102
on wholeness of soul, as human goal, 55
writing of, 117
"Fathers and Sons" (Hemingway), 248–49, 268
Fitzgerald, F. Scott, 113–14
flame, and forging of ego
in *The Captain's Doll*, 80
in *The Fox*, 99, 99n10, 104
in *The Ladybird*, 139, 142
and Pan-power, in *St. Mawr*, 158, 159, 167, 169–70
in *The Virgin and the Gipsy*, 216, 218–19, 222–23, 230, 237
"For Once, Then, Something" (Frost), 287
fourth dimension, Lawrence's theory of, 218. *See also* transcendent unknown; *The Virgin and the Gipsy* (Lawrence), fourth dimension experience in
as anticipation of film theory, 224
"Dance Sketch" and, 231–32
development of, 217–18
and instinctual primacy, 218, 222, 226
Ouspensky and, 217–18, 221, 222

on primal energies underlying existence, 224
as space for recognition of design, 198, 224
transcendent unknown and, 216, 218–19, 221, 224
fourth dimensional prose
in *The Ladybird*, 253
Lawrence on, 184, 195, 224, 225
M. H. Abrams on, 235–36n17
in *The Rainbow*, 252
as representation of relation between man and circumambient universe, 224
and simultaneous revelation of stasis and motion, 224–25
The Fox (Lawrence)
Banford
as force of reason opposed to dark attraction of fox/Henry, 95–96, 103, 104
invitation to Henry to remain on farm, 102
ridicule of Henry's marriage plans, 104, 108
struggle against loss of March, 108, 110
criticism on, limitations of, 88–90, 91
draft of 1918, 116–17
fire as force of renewal in, 99, 104
fox
as call of attractive dark instinct, 95–96, 97–98
as corn-spirit, 94, 96–97, 99
as demon and serpent, 93, 94
Henry's killing of, 105–6
killing of as release of March's repressed sexuality, 103, 106
March's identification of with Henry, 94, 96–97, 97–98, 102, 103–6
as phallus, 94–95, 99–100, 99n10
as witch impairing fertility, 93, 106
Frazer's influence on, 76–77, 91, 91n5, 93, 94, 96–97, 98, 113
Freudian theory in, 91
and fox as phallus, 94–95
March's dreams and, 97, 99–100, 103–4, 106–7
and March's identification of fox and Henry, 97–98, 103–4
and March's repression of Henry's sexual threat, 98
Henry
acute sensory perception in, 106
awareness of March's otherness, 109
Banford's view of as inconsequential boy, 96, 101–2
as call of dark instinct, 98
connection of to farmland, 102
departure from England with March, 114
fear of phallic testing with March, 110–11, 118
hesitant response to call of transcendent unknown, 110–11
killing of Banford, 112–13
killing of fox, 105–6
lack of realistic understanding of marriage matrix, 98, 103

lack of sexual force necessary to conquer March, 14–15, 111, 114–15, 118n19
March and Banford's early underestimation of, 101–2
March's identification of with fox, 94, 96–97, 97–98, 102, 103–6
marriage proposals by, 103
marriage to March, 113
maturity of, as short-lived, 112–13
maturity stemming from relationship with March, 106, 109–10, 112–13
motive in decision to marry March, 102–3
quasi-incestuous interest in older women, 15
and release of March's repressed sexuality, 103–4
sexual desire for March, 108–9
skills of observation in, 97–98, 101–2
stronger sexual force of in 1918 draft, 116–17
wartime experience of, 118n19
Lawrence's changing doctrine and, 89
Lawrence's restructuring of, 14
male primacy as issue in, 14–15, 113–14, 117, 254
March
attraction to Henry as call of transcendent unknown, 110
attraction to phallic fox, 95
blackness of creativity underlying, 92
dream of repressed sexual desire, 99–101
experience of Henry's otherness, 107, 110
Henry's release of repressed sexuality in, 103–4
hesitant response to call of transcendent unknown, 110, 111
identification of Henry with fox, 94, 96–97, 97–98, 102, 103–6
lack of understanding of marriage matrix, 98
lesbianism of, as unlikely, 107–8, 111n15
letter rejecting Henry, 112
masculinity of, 92
phallic projections onto fox, 94
refusal to accept male primacy, 113–14
rejection of Henry's otherness, 112
renewed influence of Banford after Henry's return to his regiment, 111–12
repression of sexual threat of Henry, 98
second dream, 106–7, 110
typological associations with fox, 94
March-Banford relationship
ending of, 106–7
obsessional bond between, 93–94, 104
as unnatural and decreative, 92
marriage matrix in, 5
characters' lack of understanding about, 98, 103
and issues of maturity and experience, 110

Lawrence's marriage as context for, 89–90, 91, 115–20
as palimpsestic fiction, 91–92, 97
renewal in, 5, 99, 104, 113, 118n19
tentative conclusion of, 115
thematic patterns in, critics' disregard of, 89
uncertain conclusion of, 15, 117–19
writing of, 116, 117
Frazer, James. *See The Golden Bough* (Frazer)
Freud, Anna, 175
Freud, Sigmund
on dreams, 97, 97n9, 100, 201
on Frazer's *Golden Bough*, 97
Lawrence's critiques of, 21–22, 90, 91
on melancholia in mourning, 72
on postwar psychical impotence, 212
on rarity of correct fusion of affection and sensuality, 37–38
on sexual debasement as antidote for Oedipal complex, 36–38, 51
on sublimation and art, 174–75, 175–76
"From Rejection to "Renuwel" to Renewal" (Balbert), 290–307. *See also* faculty research
Frost, Robert, 43–44n10, 285–87

Gilbert, Sandra, 58n5, 128, 132, 134
Gindin, Jim, 274–76, 278–80, 281–82
The Golden Bough (Frazer)
on Apollo/fire link to fertility, 169–70
on Biblical song, 146
on cats, ritual sacrifice of, 162n12
on crocodile terrorizing land of Thoth, 135
on curative power of royal touch, 188–90
on foxes as witches impairing fertility, 93
Freud on, 97
on horses as spirits of germination, 160
influence on Lawrence, 38, 65, 69, 76–77, 77n10, 82, 87, 87nn18–19, 90–91, 90–91n4, 147n19, 158, 159n9, 172n18, 189n7 (*See also specific works*)
critics' inadequate appreciation of, 91, 91n5
on intercourse as ritual for ensuring fruitfulness of earth, 38–39
on link between manliness and hair, 162
on magical power of shorn hair, 134
on myth of Balder, 76–77, 82, 87
and "Pan in America," 190
on pine trees, worship of, 174
on soul as shadow, 137
on sympathetic magic, 132, 137, 167–68, 202
on trees, souls of, 113
on trees, spiritual link between people and, 167–68
The Golden Notebook (Lessing), 147
Granofsky, Ronald, 60n6, 85n15, 147n19
Gray, Cecil, 115–16
The Great Gatsby (Fitzgerald), 113–14
Grenzen der Seele (Lucka), 81
growth, in Lawrence
marriage and, 45
need for social contact for, 40
organic conception of, 22
as struggle into conscious being, 22, 39–40
Gurko, Leo, 60n6

Harlot's Ghost (Mailer), 254, 288, 289
Harris, Janice H., 122n1, 199
Hemingway, Ernest
influence on Mailer, 248
and instinctual primacy, 250
Lawrence on honesty of, 248
Lawrence's affinities with, 249
on sentimentality, destructiveness of, 248–49, 267–68
on war's destruction of men's psyches, 70–71
Himmelfarb, Gertrude, 281
Hocking, William Henry, 115, 118–19
"The Horse Dealer's Daughter" (Lawrence), 208, 239
Hough, Graham, 121–22n1, 157n6, 165n15, 208
humanities
importance to education, 277–78
student flight from, 277, 283
Humma, John B., 126n5, 207, 207n2
Hutchins, Robert, 284–85

impotence of Lawrence after illness of 1925, 212
as context for *The Virgin and the Gipsy*, 209–13, 219, 221, 234, 241
critical commentary on, 212–13n6
turn to healing power of art, 212–13
Innovative Higher Education (periodical), 8
In Our Time (Hemingway), 70–71, 78, 248, 269–70
instinct
Lawrence on primacy of, 90, 90–91n4
as source of growth and creativity, 22
as source of risktaking, 247–48, 263
instinctual desire, portrayal of as goal in Lawrence's fiction, 15
instinctual primacy. *See also* blood-consciousness
of Ciccio in *The Lost Girl*, 253–54
coccygeal continuum and, 19
of Dollie in "The Princess," 253
fourth dimension experience and, 218, 222, 226
in *The Fox*, 95–96, 97–98, 254
of Hepburn in *The Captain's Doll*, 253
in Lawrence, Hemingway and Mailer, 249–50
in Lawrence's doctrine, 215, 262
Lawrence's fourth dimension and, 218, 222, 226
and logic of the soul, 9, 84, 251–54
of Lou in *St. Mawr*, 254
in Mailer, 254
multiple forms taken by in Lawrence, 253–54
sentimentalism and, 249
in *The Virgin and the Gipsy*, 227–28, 253
The Insurrection of Miss Houghton (Lawrence), 24, 25
"Introduction to These Paintings" (Lawrence)
on animate vitality ("appleyness") in painting, 183–85, 195
on Cezanne, 183–84, 185
on desexualized body, 181
on English painting, 181–83
on instinctive-intuitive awareness, 247
on landscape as escape from human body, 173, 183
Lawrence's synthesis of arts in, 182
on Pan-power, 191
polemical thrust of, 182
"The Princess" and, 181
on still lifes, 192
intuitive perception, and appleyness, 195
Italy, Lawrence in (1919), 19–21

"Jimmy and the Desperate Woman" (Lawrence), 155
"John Thomas" (Lawrence), 14
Jung, Carl, 91

Kermode, Frank, 18n4, 208, 275
Kinkead-Weekes, Mark
 on anal sex in Lawrence, 25
 on *The Captain's Doll*, 59, 59n5, 62n7
 on *The Fox*, 116–17
 on *The Ladybird*, 126
 on Lawrence's homosexual tendencies, 119
 on Lawrence's marriage, 14, 15–16
 on *The Lost Girl*, 35, 36n9
 success in integrating Lawrence's life and work, 90n3
 on Whitman essays, 19
"The Kiowa Ranch" (Lawrence), 173–74
Kundalini, 18

The Ladybird (Lawrence)
 balance of metaphor and reality in, 125–26n5
 Basil
  Daphne's dissatisfaction with sexual practice of, 140, 141
  fascination with Psanek, 145
  Herbert Asquith as model for, 124, 127
  immature sexuality of, 147n19
  name of, 129
  Psanek's demeaning of sexual force of, 124, 127–28, 130, 135
  and Psanek's move to Voynich Hall, 145
 critical responses to, 121–22, 121–23nn1–2, 124–26, 124–26nn4–5
 Daphne
  acceptance of Psanek's dark love/white love dichotomy, 140–41, 145–46, 147
  attraction to darkness inside Psanek, 131, 132, 140–41, 143–44, 144–45, 146
  Cynthia Asquith as model for, 123, 129, 140, 141
  dark knowledge absorbed by, 123n2
  decimation of her self-definition as Psanek's goal, 128
  dissatisfaction with husband's sexual practice, 140, 141, 143–44, 145, 147
  instinctual primacy in, 253
  as Persephone descending to lower world, 145
  reliance of on beauty, 130
  sexual capitulation to Psanek, 144
 Daphne's visits to Psanek
  in hospital, 128, 130–38
  Psanek's escalation of aggressiveness in, 132–34, 134–36
  Psanek's frank discussion of orgasm and g-spots, 142, 142n16
  Psanek's introduction to Basil, 144–45
  Psanek's strategies of manipulation in, 134
  at Voynich Hall, 137–41
 doctrinal adamance of, 127
 dualistic metaphors in, 125, 139, 140–41, 145–46, 147
 ego-dominated posturing in, 255
 feminist readings of, 128

Frazer's influence on, 132, 134, 135, 137, 145–46
incremental repetition in plot of, 125
Lawrence's anger and anxiety underlying, 122n1, 126, 127
and Lawrence's contempt for passionless marriages, 124, 125, 128–29
Lawrence's desire for Cynthia Asquith as theme of, 125n4, 127, 142, 148–52
marriage matrix as theme in, 5, 123
parallels to *Lady Chatterley's Lover*, 145–46
Psanek
on attraction of otherness, 136
on Daphne as wild cat, 138, 139
on Daphne's compulsion to obey him, 145
on dark inner truth *vs.* white surface, 139–40
as Dionys-Osiris, 132, 145
establishment of secret bond with Daphne, 137–38
hammer metaphor used by, 141–42
hold on Daphne's imagination, 137–38
inside-out metaphor used by, 124, 130, 131, 139–40, 143
Lawrence as model for, 124, 126, 137
link between recovery and seduction of Daphne, 131
melancholia of, 131
metaphors used by, 122n1, 133
physical resemblance to Asquith's lover Blackwood, 142–43
recovery of as regaining of patriarchal voice, 132
seduction of Daphne as goal of, 128, 131
shadow separating him from others, 137
Psanek's seduction of Daphne, 145, 146
as assault on her superficial infatuations, 141
Daphne's attraction to darkness inside Psanek, 131, 132, 140–41, 143–44, 144–45, 146
as descent into darkness, 146
as entry into transcendent unknown, 146
escalation of aggressiveness, 132–34, 134–36
as initiated by Daphne, 148–49
larger significance of, 124
as refashioning of earlier draft, 127
renewal in, 5, 131, 132
as *roman à clef*, 123, 149
and thimble as type of sympathetic magic, 137
on vaginal *vs.* clitoral orgasms, 124, 140–41, 143–44, 147–48
writing of, 126
Lady Chatterley's Lover (Lawrence)
anal sex in, 19n4, 35–36
censorship of, 6
and *chakra* theory, 18–19n4
Clifford's paralysis as reflection of moral inadequacy, 261
demeaning notions of sex in, 260–61

ego-dominated posturing in, 254, 260–61
and erotic risk, 261–62, 269–70
imagery of purifying flame in, 269
influence on Mailer, 259
and instinct as source of risktaking, 263
Lawrence's failing health as context for, 261–62, 263–64, 269–70
marriage matrix as theme in, 6
Mellors
concerns about impotence, 261
courage of, 261, 262–63
delicate bodily condition of, 263
sexual renewal of, and Lawrence, 6, 264, 269–70
on novel as Lawrence's preferred genre, 245–46
parallels to *The Ladybird*, 145–46
parallels to Mailer's *Deer Park*, 259–61
and sex with love as supreme human experience, 256
societies' obsession with money and success in, 260
as story of recovery from impotence, 264
The Virgin and the Gipsy as anticipation of, 207–8
landscape painting, Lawrence on, 173–74
animate vitality ("appleyness") in, 183–85, 195
British tradition of, 183
"The Last Laugh" (Lawrence), 155
Lawrence, Arthur (father)
death of, 178, 204
views on Lawrence's work, 177–78
Lawrence, D. H.
affinities with Hemingway, 249
anger at Frieda's divided loyalties, 153–54
on art, moral system underlying, 246
and courage in erotic risk, 249, 261, 262–63
and devouring mother syndrome, 12, 13, 16
efforts to forget Frieda in America, 154
on ego-based sexual posturing, 261
espionage charges against, 115
gap between sexual doctrine and behavior, 257–58
homosexual tendencies in, 118–20
illness of 1925, 209
diminished condition after, 210–11
essays written after, 209
literary doctrine and style after, 214
novels written after, 214–15
slow recovery after, 210–11, 214
terminal diagnosis in, 210, 211, 219
turn to healing power of art after, 212–13
The Virgin and the Gipsy as first fiction after, 210, 213–14
impotence following illness of 1925, 212
as context for *The Virgin and the Gipsy*, 209–13, 219, 221, 234, 241
critical commentary on, 212–13n6
turn to healing power of art, 212–13
integration of biography and art in work of, 12

Mailer on frail male sexuality of, 269–70
merging of autobiography and fiction in, 211n4
mother's dominance over father and, 178
on narcissism of loveless sex, 255
Oedipal complex of, 13, 17, 17n2, 37, 51–52
organic unity of work by, 2
on physical toll of writing fiction, 210
relationship with father, 178, 204
return to England (1923), 154
sexual inadequacies of, and *The Fox*, 118–19
on shedding of one's sickness in books, 177
tuberculosis of
"Murry Stories" and, 155
and writing of *St. Mawr*, 177
unselfconsciousness of letters by, 2, 12, 21
views on mother's dominance, 204

Lawrence, Frieda (wife). *See also* marriage of Lawrence
affairs by, 115–16, 117, 126, 154–55, 212, 219, 257n10
denial of male primacy to Lawrence, 13–14, 23, 37, 51–52, 116, 126
emotional instability of, 115, 116
in Italy (1919), 20–21
on Lawrence after illness of 1925, 210, 211–12
Lawrence on intransigence of, 13
and Lawrence's "Kiowa Ranch" painting, 173
Lawrence's sexual connection to, 23
Lost Girl's Alvina as embodiment of, 52
marriage to Ravagli, 219
openness about affairs, 116
postwar marital problems, 116
resemblances to Lawrence's mother, 51, 211n4
return alone to England (1923), 153–54
seduction of Lawrence, 51
separations from, 14, 18

Lawrence, Lydia (mother)
domination of family by, 178, 204, 211n4
Lawrence's connection to, 1
and Lawrence's devouring mother syndrome, 12
and Lawrence's Oedipal complex, 13, 17, 17n2, 37, 51–52

"The Lawrence Tree, 1929" (O'Keefe), 170, *171*, 191

Leavis, F. R., 55–56, 59, 60n6, 124n3, 125–26n5, 156n5, 206

Lennon, J. Michael, 247n2, 251n5, 252n6, 252n7, 257, 257n9

Lessing, Doris, 108n14, 111n15, 147

liberal education, goals of, 8

literary studies, modern
as doctrinaire political ideology, 277, 282
Dyer critique of, 4
graduate students' narrow, ideological education, 282–83
and jargon, 284–85
overspecialization, and loss of larger mission, 282–85
race-gender-class program in, 3, 281, 282
rare use of close reading in, 277, 280, 282
and role of theory, 278
and student flight from humanities, 277, 283
and transcendence above self, abandonment of, 281

literature
author's initial engagement with, 274–76, 278–80
and construction of imaginative realities, 281–82

and receptivity to otherness, 10, 280–81
literature, close reading analysis of
abandonment of in literary studies, 277, 280, 282
academy's hostility toward, 2, 7
current graduate students' inability to teach, 283
as fundamental priority of literary studies, 284
inscrutable "beyond" revealed in, 275
as method of this study, 2–4
value of, 274–78, 281–82
logic of the soul, and instinctual primacy, 9, 84, 251–54
Look! (Lawrence), 16
The Lost Girl (Lawrence)
Alvina
attraction to darkness, 33, 35
awareness of instinctual force unlocked by Ciccio, 43–46, 47–50
cancellation of marriage plans, 42
cracking open of ego of, 35–36
decision to marry Ciccio, 44–45
deepening of sexual bond with Ciccio, 46
descent into darkness of coccygeal continuum, 29–32, 33, 35–37, 44–45
early inability to escape from conventional mind, 39–42, 43
as embodiment of Frieda, 52
encounter with transcendent unknown, 47–50
engagement to Dr. Mitchell, 42–43
knees, protective function of, 31, 32, 34, 40–41
leeriness of male insecurity, 26–27
on love, 30–31
Madame's post-coital gift of flowers to, 38–39
as midwife, 42–44
parting from Ciccio after first encounters, 42–43
postmarital growth of, 47–50
pregnancy of, 49–50, 51
renewal of, 5, 30, 31, 161
romantic history of, 26–27, 30
sources of interest in Ciccio, 28–29
strength developed by, 51, 52
as threat to Madame, 27–28
Alvina and Ciccio's lack of knowledge about each other, 42, 45–46
anal sex in, 18–19n4, 34, 35–36
emotional changes resulting from, 38, 53
limited critical attention to, 38
as move toward existential growth, 38–40
as attempt to resolve issues of sexual maturity, 38
chakra theory and, 18–19n4
Ciccio
and Alvina as escape from devouring mother figure, 29, 32, 36–37, 39, 40–41
and Alvina's descent into darkness, 29–32, 33, 35–37, 44–45
announcement of betrothal to Alvina, 33
association with darkness, 28, 29–32, 33, 35–37, 44–45

brutal first sexual experience with Alvina, 35–36
as fantasy synthesis of male equanimity, 28
imbalance of upper and lower *chakra* centers in, 47
instinctual primacy in, 253–54
Lawrence's empathy with, 50–51, 52
Madame's threat to manhood of, 26
and male primacy, assertion of, 29, 36, 40–41, 49, 51, 52
and murdering of Alvina's conventional consciousness, 35–36
and murdering of Alvina's virginity, 32
Oedipal complex of, 25–26, 27, 51
postmarital unfolding of, 45–46
seduction of Alvina, 29–30, 34
stalled development in, 42, 47, 48, 52
stereotypical characteristics of, 28
coccygeal continuum in, 26–27n7, 38
Alvina's descent into, 29–32, 33, 35–37, 44–45
descent into as ascent into conscious being, 30, 31
and drive toward greater intimacy, 49–50
Mansfield's reaction to, 53
as pathway to transcendental unknown, 48–50, 53, 54
Lawrence's expansion of psychosexual boundaries in, 15
Lawrence's marriage as context for, 25, 52
on love as concept of conventional mind, 39
Madame
Alvina as threat to control of, 27–28
as bad mother figure, 26n6
crass characterizations of Alvina, 34
as devouring mother figure, 29, 32, 36–37, 39, 40–41
efforts to control Alvina, 33–34
efforts to control Ciccio, 26, 26n6, 35
response to announced betrothal of Ciccio, 33
marriage matrix as theme in, 5
reversal of male primacy in, 24, 51, 52
on rise from coccygeal darkness to transcendence, 24
and sexual debasement as antidote for Oedipal complex, 29, 32, 36–38
and transformative potential of sex, 41–42
travel to Ciccio's village, 46–47
writing of, 52
"Love Was Once A Little Boy" (Lawrence), 62, 63

Mailer, Norman. *See also The Deer Park* (Mailer); *The Prisoner of Sex* (Mailer); *other works*
on art, purpose of, 246
on author's address to MLA, 287–89
on blood-consciousness, 243, 250n4

consonance with Lawrence's doctrines, 245
defense of Lawrence, 244
on ego-dominated sexual posturing, 255
environment of novels *vs.* Lawrence's, 245
on erections and courage, 263, 264
on erotic risk, 246–47, 249, 250–51, 264–68, 270, 271–72, 280
existentialism of, 248
gap between sexual doctrine and behavior, 257, 257n9
influence of Hemingway on, 248
influence of Lawrence on, 6, 222–23, 237, 244–48, 251, 252n6, 255, 259–60, 270–73
on influences on his generation, 248
and instinctual primacy, 246, 249–50, 254
on "law of life," 268, 307
on Lawrence, 16, 179, 223
and Lawrence's transcendent unknown, 246–47
on love and change, 268n14
on man's sexual force as moral product, 264
and marriage as institution, 252, 252nn6–7, 253, 256–57, 271
on moon power, 253n8
on necessity of growth, 268
on novel as art form, 245, 246
on rise of US techno-fascism, 288–89
on risk and open-endedness, 253, 256
on sex as last frontier of fiction, 246
sexual aesthetic of, 246
on sexual honesty in fiction as lesson learned from Lawrence, 249
on sexual identity, 264
on sexual insecurity, 251
on sex with love as central tenet of Lawrence's ideology, 255–56
shared subject matter with Lawrence, 245
on subtle logic of love, 249–51
synergistic interrelation of instinctual primacy, negative capability, and experience in, 247n2
on synthesis of existential and transcendent in Lawrence, 246
male-female equilibrium in Lawrence's early novels, 16
male primacy
in *The Captain's Doll*, Hepburn's battle for, 74, 75–76, 78, 79, 81, 85–86
"Democracy" on, 22
as essential to marital happiness, 13
Fantasia of the Unconscious on, 113, 114, 117
in *The Fox*, 14–15, 113–14, 117, 254
Frieda's denial of to Lawrence, 23, 37, 51–52, 116, 126
Lawrence on, 81
in *The Lost Girl*, Ciccio's assertion of, 29, 36, 40–41, 49, 51, 52
struggle for as focus of Lawrence's life, 12–13, 16–17, 36
struggle for in Lawrence's novels, 13
manhood, Lawrence's conception of, 18–19
Mansfield, Katherine
affair with Carco, 53–54

Lawrence's correspondence with, 12–14, 15, 16, 20, 21, 22, 23, 25, 86, 113–14, 115, 119
Lawrence's relationship with, 12, 17
on *The Lost Girt*, 19, 52–53, 54
marriage of, Lawrence on, 13, 14
and Murry, 53–54
Marlowe, Christopher, 300
marriage
acceleration of male maturity in, 23
as adventure, 4
conflict and renewal in, 1
ebb-and-flow in, Lawrence on, 23
Lawrence's support for, 256–57
Lawrence's views on seriousness of, 162
link to transcendent unknown as goal of, 1, 2, 4, 9
as concept alien to modern readers, 8–10
in Lawrence, 258, 271
Lawrence's own marriage and, 257n10
in Mailer, 258–59, 271
necessity of for experiencing transcendent other, 45, 252, 252n7
as source of healing for Oedipal complex, 23–24, 29
as thematic center of Lawrence's works, 1
unstable, emotional deficiencies of partners and, 1
marriage matrix
in The Fox, 5, 89–90, 91, 98, 103, 110, 115–20
gestational resonance of, 1
in *The Ladybird*, 5, 123
in *Lady Chatterley's Lover*, 6
in *The Lost Girl*, 5
as organic theme in Lawrence's works, 4–5
in "The Princess" (Lawrence), 5, 181, 192–93, 204
in *St. Mawr*, 5, 168–69
transitional periods as focus of, 1
in *The Virgin and the Gipsy*, 5, 227–28, 237
marriage of Lawrence
affairs by Frieda, 115–16, 117, 126, 154–55, 212, 219, 257n10
affairs by Lawrence, 17, 20, 52, 116, 212, 257–58, 262
conflict and renewal as preoccupation in, 1
Lawrence on stabilizing effect of, 23
Lawrence's commitment to despite Frieda's infidelities, 257, 257n10
Lawrence's inability to assert male primacy in, 13–14, 23, 37, 51–52, 116, 126
Mailer on, 255
parallels with Alvina marriage in *The Lost Girl*, 46n11
parallels with relationship to mother, 13, 16
and refocusing of Lawrence's art, 15–16
separate bedrooms, 17–18
as source of healing for Oedipal complex, 23
volatility of, 16, 17–18
McDonald, Edward, 177, 213
Mellown, Elgin, 58n5, 60n6, 82n12
Memoirs of the Foreign Legion (Magnus), Lawrence introduction to, 150
"Mending Wall" (Frost), 287
Merivale, Patricia, 160n10, 165n14, 191n8
methodology of this study, 2–4
Milton, John, 304–5
Modern Language Association, author's address to (1996), 6, 274–89

Moore, Harry T., 149, 208, 212n6
"Morality and the Novel" (Lawrence), 209, 214, 220, 224
Morrell, Ottoline, 20, 150
"Mourning and Melancholia" (Freud), 72
Movements in European History (Lawrence), 76, 82, 83
Moynahan, Julian, 26n6, 36n9, 122n1, 207
Murry, J. Middleton
  affair with Frieda Lawrence, 154–55
  as *Athenaeum* editor, 16, 17
  Lawrence dream about, 119–20
  Lawrence's correspondence with, 154
  Lawrence's relationship with, 12, 16, 17, 25
  on *The Lost Girt*, 52–53, 54
  sexual immaturity of, 54
"Murry Stories" (Lawrence), 155, 175

New Mexican landscape
  appleyness of, 196–98, 203
  Pan-power in, 169–70, 191, 194–95
"North Sea" (Lawrence), 150, *151*
novel, as Lawrence's preferred genre, 245–46
"The Novel" (Lawrence), 209, 213, 240
"The Novel and the Feelings" (Lawrence), 201, 209, 215, 241

Oedipal complex. *See also* devouring mother syndrome
  of Ciccio in *The Lost Girl*, 25–26, 27, 51
  coccygeal continuum as antidote for, 22, 23, 24–25
  Lawrence's coming to terms with, 37
  Lawrence's conscious awareness of, 37, 51–52
  Lawrence's susceptibility to, 13, 17, 17n2
  marriage as source of healing for, 23–24, 29
  as preoccupation in Lawrence's early fiction, 25
  sexual debasement as antidote for in Freudian theory, 36–38, 51
O'Keeffe, Georgia, 170, *171*, 191
"On Being a Man" (Lawrence), 263
"On the Universal Tendency to Debasement in the Sphere of Love" (Freud), 36–38, 51
orgasms
  as issue in *The Lost Girl*, 18n4, 19n4, 31–32, 39, 42, 46
  Lawrence's marriage and, 21
  vaginal *vs.* clitoral, in *The Ladybird*, 124, 140–41, 143–44, 147–48
Ouspensky, Peter D., 217, 221, 222
Out of Sheer Rage (Dyer), 4

Pack, Robert, 276–77, 280
painter, Lawrence as
  and illness of 1925, 214
  influence on his fiction, 3
  simplicity of style after 1925, 214
paintings by Lawrence
  "Dance Sketch," 231–32, *232*, 233
  "The Kiowa Ranch," 173–74
  "North Sea," 150, *151*
  "Red Willow Trees," 195, *196*
  "Two Apples," 184–85, *185*
  "Villa Mirenda," 195–96, *197*
"Pan in America" (Lawrence)
  on American Indians and Pan-power, 190–91
  on civilization's shift from intuitive consciousness, 190, 191
  on danger of sentimental pantheism, 170
  on desexualized body, 181

Frazer's influence on, 190
on Frazer's skepticism about Pan-power, 168
on Pan-energy, 159, 163, 164–65, 174, 190
on pine trees as locus of Pan-power, 170, 171, 194–95, 203
on primitive sex roles, 200
"The Princess" and, 181
on rationalist world, 166
Pan-power. *See also St. Mawr* (Lawrence), Pan-power in
and appleyness (animate vitality), 191–92
combination of resistance and assertion in, 191, 193
development of in response to sexual dysfunction, 155, 169–70, 175
"Murry Stories" and, 155, 175
remnant of in modern world, 190, 193–94
tenets of, 155–56
trees as central image in, 191
Partisan Review, 7–8
phallophobia
in "Murry Stories," 155
in *St. Mawr*, 156–59, 160, 168–69, 170–71, 172
photography and painting, Lawrence on, 184, 191–92
The Plumed Serpent (Lawrence), 210, 212, 214
political correctness, critics of, 7–8
"Pornography and Obscenity" (Lawrence), 246
power, Lawrence on, 221
"The Princess" (Lawrence)
on civilizations' loss of Pan-power, 204
Colin Urquhart
dread of procreative body in, 187–88
on family's royal blood, 188
syphilis and, 187–90, 188n6
criticism on, 180–81, 180–81n1
death of Lawrence's father as context for, 204
Dollie
attraction to Romero, 193
belief in royal blood, 188
as dead to intuitive awareness, 192, 199
dread of procreative body in, 189n7, 192–93, 198, 200
dream in shack, 201–2
eternal pre-pubescence of, 188, 192
inadequate reaction to Pan-power of mountains, 189n7
Indian poachers encountered by, 194
instinctual primacy in, 253
lack of appleyness in, 192, 202, 204–5
lack of creative flux in, 198–99, 200
later marriage to elderly man, 204
obsessive interest in clothes, 202
sex with Romero as mechanical act, 199–202
sex with Romero as reaching out to other, 201–2
syphilis and, 188n6
view of marriage, 193
Dollie and Romero's mountain journey, 195, 196, 198–99, 201
failure of renewal in, 5, 193
Frazer's influence on, 188–90, 202
"Introduction to These Paintings" and, 181
Lawrence's style and Pan mythology in, 180, 196–98

Lawrence's view of parents and, 204
marriage matrix as theme in, 5, 181, 192–93, 204
and New Mexican landscape
appleyness of, 196–98, 203
Pan-power in, 194–95
"Pan in America" and, 181
Romero
alienation shared with Dollie, 193
death of as de facto suicide, 203
efforts to reach through to Dollie, 202
as embodiment of Pan-power remnant, 193–94, 203
lack of creative flux in, 198
loss of Pan-power, 200–201, 203, 204
tossing of Dollie's clothes in pond, 202
vindictive rape of Dollie, 203
The Prisoner of Sex (Mailer)
on changes since Lawrence's death, 245
controversy surrounding, 244
on courage and erotic risk, 249, 266–67
defense of Lawrence in, 244
on importance of heterosexual sex to Lawrence, 269
on Lawrence's ideal of love in marriage, 255
on Lawrence's oedipal complex, 17n2
Lawrence's "On Being a Man" and, 263
Mailer's deep understanding of Lawrence and, 6, 307
on *Women in Love*, 256
propriety, Lawrence's different version of, 246
Pryse, J. M., 18–19, 18–19n4, 21, 34n8
Psychoanalysis and the Unconscious (Lawrence)
chakra theory and, 21, 22–23, 47
on Oedipal complex, 23, 25, 51
revisions of, 21, 25
on sexual development, 13, 39, 40

The Rainbow (Lawrence)
anal sex in, 24, 35–36
and blood-consciousness in Tom Brangwen, 9, 84, 251–52, 253
and experience of transcendence as goal of marriage, 4, 9, 258
fourth dimensional prose in, 252
Mailer on, 252n6
on otherness of Lydia, 251–52
Tom Brangwen on marriage in, 9, 45–46n11, 287
unfolding of Tom Brangwen after marriage, 45
on value of marriage, 252n7
Ravagli, Angelo, 212, 219
"The Real Thing" (Lawrence), 66
"Red Willow Trees" (Lawrence), 195, *196*
"Reflections on the Death of a Porcupine" (Lawrence), 209
religious/visionary component of human beings, Lawrence on, 90
renewal, in Lawrence, 5, 6. *See also* flame, and forging of ego
achievement of through art, 212–13
in *The Captain's Doll*, 5, 68, 72, 77, 79, 85n16
failure of in *The Princess*, 5, 193
in *The Fox*, 5 104, 99, 113, 118n19
instinctual primacy as path to, 247
in *The Ladybird*, 5, 131, 132
in *Lady Chatterley's Lover*, 6, 264, 269–70
in *The Lost Girl*, 5, 30, 31, 161

need for social contact for, 71
as preoccupation, 1
in *St. Mawr*, 5, 161, 172, 176–77
transcendent unknown as source of, 1
in *The Virgin and the Gipsy*, 5, 219–20, 239
renewal of faculty. *See* faculty research, strategies for renewal of; "From Rejection to 'Renuwel' to Renewal" (Balbert)
risktaking. *See also* erotic risk
and coccygeal continuum, 24
instinct as source of, 247–48, 263
Ruderman, Judith
on devouring mother motif, 25–26n6
on *The Fox*, 91n5
on *The Ladybird*, 124–25n4
on *The Lost Girl*, 26n6, 46n11
on "The Princess," 203n10
on *The Virgin and the Gipsy*, 206–7, 229n13, 236n18, 241n19
Ruskin, John, 302

St. Mawr (Lawrence)
Cartwright as spokesman for Pan-power in, 163–64, 163n13
critical response to, 157–58nn6–7
ego-dominated posturing in, 255
events surrounding completion of, 177–79
Frazer's influence on, 158, 162, 162n12, 167–68, 169–70, 174
Lawrence's damaged sexuality and marriage as context for, 153–55, 160, 161, 162–63, 165, 169, 173, 176–77, 178
Lewis
Mrs. Witt's symbolic emasculation of, 161–62
on Panophilia, 165–68
rejection of Mrs. Witt's marriage proposal, 161–62
sensitivity to Pan-energy, 160–61
on transcendent unknown, 167
on trees, animistic properties of, 167–68
Lou
as anticipation of Mellors, 176
attraction to Pan-power, 161, 163–64, 169–70
attraction to St. Mawr's otherness, 158
as cross-gendered authorial projection, 176–77
dismissal of interest in Phoenix, 161, 168–69
eschewing of sex and marriage, 161, 162–63, 164, 169, 176–77
instinctual primacy in, 254
letters to mother from, 168
yearning for transcendent unknown, 169
Lou's ranch
history of, 170
Lawrence's "The Kiowa Ranch" painting and, 173–74
Lou's commitment to engage Pan-power of, 172, 174
Pan-power of, 170, 171, 172
marriage matrix in, 5, 156, 168–69
Mrs. Witt

character of, 157
paradoxical views on men, 156–57, 161, 162
skepticism about Pan-power, 168
symbolic emasculation of Lewis, 161–62
Pan-power in, 159
Cartwright as spokesman for, 163–64, 163n13
dangerous aspects of, 164–65, 172, 174
Lewis's description of, 165–68
links to darkness, 163
Lou's attraction to, 161, 163–64, 169–70
Lou's commitment to engage, 172, 174
as portal to transcendent unknown, 172–73, 174
as pre-sexual world, 172
ranch as source of, 170, 171, 172
phallophobia in, 156–59, 160, 168–69
on rationalist world, 166
renewal of Lou in, 5, 161, 172, 176–77
Rico
ego-dominated posturing in, 254–55
lack of manly force in, 156
St. Mawr
and dangerous aspects of Pan-power, 164–65, 172
as force of Pan-energy, 157–58nn7–8, 157–59, 160, 163–64
limited mention of after move to America, 157–58n7
Lou's gifting of to Rico, 159
phallophobic description of, 160
renewed sexuality of in America, 158n7
trees in
Pan-power in, 166–67, 170–72
and phallophobia, 160, 170–71, 172
and writing as way to "shed one's sickness," 177
Schacht, Lore, 175
Searle, John, 8, 281
Seltzer, Adele, 154
senses, Lawrence on primacy of, 90, 90–91n4
sentimentality, Lawrence on, 249, 267–68, 270
sex. *See also* anal sex; impotence of Lawrence after illness of 1925
as avenue to transcendent unknown
in ideology of Lawrence, 255, 258, 266
in ideology of Mailer, 258–59
postwar replacement by Panophilia in Lawrence, 169–70
with love
and achievement of freedom-through-transcendence, 255, 266
as central tenet in Lawrence's ideology, 255–56
erotic risk involved in, 255
modern, as cold and bloodless, 266
as primary self-definition, destructiveness of, 47
sexual energy, cycles of time and nature in, 255

sexual satisfaction, Lawrence's struggle for, 12–13, 21, 23
as union of male and female rivers of blood, 264n13
without love
Lawrence on, 255, 256–58
Mailer on, 256–59
Siegel, Carol, 206, 207n2, 208, 220–21n11, 241n19
Society for College and University Planning (SCUP), author's address to, 8, 290–307
"Soldier's Home" (Hemingway), 70–71
Sons and Lovers (Lawrence), 25, 37
soul. *See also* logic of the soul
central importance in Lawrence's ideology, 1–2
Lawrence's conception of, 9
time as current of, in *The Virgin and the Gipsy*, 222–23, 228, 237
wholeness of soul, as human goal, 55
Spilka, Mark
on anal sex in Lawrence, 18n4
on *The Captain's Doll*, 57, 58
on fourth dimension in Lawrence, 218n8
on *The Ladybird*, 142n16
on *Lady Chatterley's Lover*, 261
on Lawrence's impotence after 1925, 212–13n6
on orgasm in Lawrence, 147, 148n20
on soul in Lawrence's ideology, 1–2
and *The Virgin and the Gipsy*, 208
"The State of Funk" (Lawrence), 268, 307
Studies in Classical American Literature (Lawrence), 21, 60, 247n2
Study of Thomas Hardy (Lawrence), 213
sublimation
and art, Freud on, 174–75, 175–76
and ego development, Anna Freud on, 175
Lawrence's damaged sexuality and, 175
The Sun Also Rises (Hemingway), 248
syphilis
Colin Urquhart in "The Princess" and, 187–90, 188n6
debilitating effect on imagination, 187
as Europe epidemic
and British sexual repression, 182–83, 184–87
modern research on, 186–87n5

"Take Something Like a Star" (Frost), 285–87
Tennyson, Alfred, Lord, 302
Tertium Organum (Ouspensky), 217
Thoreau, Henry D., 246–47n2
"The Time of Her Time" (Mailer), 258
Time Which Spaces Us Apart (Baynes), 17n3
"Tithonus" (Tennyson), 302
"To His Scribe Adam" (Chaucer), 295
Tough Guys Don't Dance (Mailer), 254
transcendent unknown. *See also* fourth dimension; Pan-power
academy's entrenched aversion to, 6, 9
appleyness (animate vitality) in representation as link to, 184
in *The Captain's Doll,* Hepburn's urge toward, 66
coccygeal continuum's drive toward, 24, 48–50, 53, 54
as concept alien to modern readers, 8–10
courage to embrace, Lawrence on, 262

- Cynthia's link to in *The Virgin and the Gipsy*, 216
- experience of as goal of marriage
  - as concept alien to modern readers, 8–10
  - in Lawrence, 1, 2, 4, 9, 258, 271
  - Lawrence's marriage and, 257n10
  - in Mailer, 258–59, 271
- and fourth dimension, 216, 218–19, 221, 224
- as goal of liberal education, 8
- impact of realization on character's perception, 9
- and logic of the soul, 254
- in *The Lost Girl*, Alvina's encounter with, 47–50
- Mailer and, 246–47
- modern loss of faith in, 285–87
- necessity of marriage for experiencing, 45, 252, 252n7
- in *St. Mawr*, 167, 169, 172–73, 174
- sex as avenue to
  - in ideology of Lawrence, 255, 258, 266
  - in ideology of Mailer, 258–59
  - postwar replacement by Panophilia in Lawrence, 169–70
- and transformative power of self, 247

Turner, John, 206, 207n2, 211n4, 229n13, 235n16, 236n18, 241n19

"Two Apples" (Lawrence), 184–85, *185*

Uhlfelder, Dr., 210, 211, 211n4, 219

"Unarticulated Synergy and Unfashionable Transcendence" (Balbert) [MLA, 1996], 6, 274–89

unconscious mind
- as drive toward conscious being, 24
- Lawrence on nature of, 21–22, 24

universities, overspecialization in, and loss of larger mission, 282–85

Vickery, John
- on *The Fox*, 91n5
- on Frazer's influence on Lawrence, 65, 69, 72, 76, 87n18, 147n19, 167n16, 172n18, 189n7
- on Norse myth of Balder, 85n16

"Villa Mirenda" (Lawrence), 195–96, *197*

The Virgin and the Gipsy (Lawrence)
- animal metaphors in, 215–16
- as anticipation of *Lady Chatterley's Lover*, 207–8
- characterization as minor work, 206, 207–8
- clarity of doctrine in, 208–9, 214
- couples in as inadequate models for marriage, 227
- critical responses to, 206–8, 209
- critique of bourgeois morality in, 225–26
- Cynthia
  - and lack of models for successful relationships, 227
  - link to flame and transcendent unknown, 216
  - narrator's sympathy for, 225–26
  - as outside time and space, 216
  - selfishness of, as only means of salvation, 216
- ego-dominated posturing in, 255
- essays of 1925 and, 213–14, 225

film version of (1970), 235n16
as first fiction after illness of 1925, 210, 213–14
fourth dimension experience in, 218–19
conventional characters' inability to access, 236–37
and distortion of time and space, 221–23, 226, 229–35, 235n16, 239–40
fortune-telling scene and, 219, 230–33
links to flame and molten ego imagery, 218–19, 222–23, 230, 237
and normal time perception as trap, 225–26
Yvette's move toward, 219, 220–22, 226, 228, 229–35, 237–40
gipsy
connection to fourth dimension, 220, 226, 233, 237, 240
critics on, 220–21n11
as flame to forge Yvette's ego, 219
as key to Lawrence's own renewal, 219–20
protection of Yvette by, 235
rescue of Yvette from flood, 239
Yvette's bond with, 237–38
and Yvette's move toward fourth dimension, 220–21, 226, 229–35, 237–40
importance in Lawrence canon, 208
on industrial rape of land, 229
influence on Mailer, 222–23
Lawrence's ill health as context for, 209–13, 219, 221, 234, 241
marriage matrix in, 5, 227
characters' lack of understanding about, 227
and instinctual primacy as only source of true marriage, 227–28
Yvette's musings on, 237
Mater
animal metaphors used to describe, 215
death of, 240–41
detachment of from vital force of reality, 240–41
as locked within conventional time, 228
static rule over Saywell family, 217
renewal in, 5, 219–20, 239
Saywell family
as locked within conventional time, 216, 225–26, 228
as repressed and contained, 217
structural simplicity of, 208–9, 215
synthesis of innocence and power in, 234
time, conventional, undermining of, 209
on time as current of soul in flow, 222–23, 228, 237
Yvette
attraction to Eastwoods, 236, 238
bond established with gipsy, 237–38
as cross-gendered authorial projection, 219–20, 221

embrace of
fourth-dimensional
experience, 226,
236–37, 238–40
final embrace of gipsy, 239,
241, 241n19
first meeting with gipsy,
229–33
gipsy's rescue of from flood,
239
Leo's marriage proposal to,
227
move toward
fourth-dimensional
experience, 219,
220–22, 226, 228,
229–35, 237–40
organic virginity of, 227,
234
repression of yearning in,
217
and sexual consummation,
unfulfilled, 238
suitors, lack of maturity in,
216–17, 227
turn to instinctual primacy
in, 228, 253
yearning for lover with
power to violate her
innocence, 221, 227
yearning for sexual
otherness, 217

The Wedding Ring (Lawrence), 4
Weiner, Ronald, 180–81n1, 203n10
"The White Negro" (Mailer), 248
Whitman Essays (Lawrence)
on coccygeal continuum, 19, 24,
25, 31, 34n8
focus on selfhood and
independence in, 19
on love as concept of
conventional mind, 39
"Why the Novel Matters" (Lawrence)
on ego as facade, 217, 227
on love and change, 268
on novel as Lawrence's preferred
genre, 245
writing of, 209
Widmer, Kingsley, 18–19n4, 46n11,
241n19
Women in Love (Lawrence)
anal sex in, 24
chakra theory and, 18, 18n4, 19
Foreword to, 18, 22, 177
male-female equilibrium in, 16
revisions of, 18, 19
Worthen, John, 53n13, 56n2, 204, 269

Young, Richard, 217–18, 221